The Gravity Model in International Trade

T0298784

How do borders affect trade? Are cultural and institutional differences important for trade? Is environmental policy relevant to trade? How does one's income or wage relate to the fact that trade partners are nearby or far away?

These are just some of the important questions that can be answered using the gravity model of international trade. This model predicts and explains bilateral trade flows in terms of the economic size and distance between trading partners (e.g. states, regions, countries, trading blocs). In recent years, there has been a surge of interest in this model and it is now one of the most widely applied tools in applied international economics. This book traces the history of the gravity model and takes stock of recent methodological and theoretical advances, including new approximations for multilateral trade resistance, insightful analyses of the measurement of economic distance, and analyses of foreign direct investment.

PETER A. G. VAN BERGEIJK is Professor of International Economics and Macroeconomics at the Institute of Social Studies, the Hague. He is also Deputy Director of CERES, the coordinating body for development economics research in the Netherlands. His most recent book is *Economic Diplomacy and the Geography of International Trade* (2009).

STEVEN BRAKMAN is Professor of International Economics at the University of Groningen, the Netherlands. His most recent book is the *The New Introduction to Geographical Economics* (Cambridge University Press, 2009), coauthored with Harry Garretsen and Charles van Marrewijk.

The Gravity Model in International Trade

Advances and Applications

Edited by

Peter A. G. van Bergeijk

Institute of Social Studies/Erasmus University Rotterdam and CERES, Utrecht

and

Steven Brakman

University of Groningen

CAMBRIDGE
UNIVERSITY PRESS

CAMBRIDGE UNIVERSITY PRESS
Cambridge, New York, Melbourne, Madrid, Cape Town,
Singapore, São Paulo, Delhi, Tokyo, Mexico City

Cambridge University Press
The Edinburgh Building, Cambridge CB2 8RU, UK

Published in the United States of America by Cambridge University Press, New York

www.cambridge.org
Information on this title: www.cambridge.org/9780521196154

© Cambridge University Press 2010

First published 2010

A catalogue record for this publication is available from the British Library

ISBN 978-0-521-119615-4 Hardback

Contents

Figures

Tables

Contributors

EMIEL R. AFMAN, Ministry of Finance, the Netherlands

JAMES E. ANDERSON, Boston College and NBER, USA

SCOTT L. BAIER, Clemson University and Federal Reserve Bank of Atlanta, USA

PETER A. G. VAN BERGEIJK, International Institute of Social Studies of Erasmus University, the Hague and CERES, Utrecht, the Netherlands

JEFFREY H. BERGSTRAND, University of Notre Dame, USA

JACOB A. BIKKER, De Nederlandsche Bank and Utrecht School of Economics, the Netherlands

E. MAARTEN BOSKER, University of Groningen, the Netherlands

HERVÉ BOULHOL, OECD, Paris, France

STEVEN BRAKMAN, University of Groningen, the Netherlands

SJEF EDERVEEN, Ministry of Economic Affairs, the Netherlands

PETER EGGER, University of Munich and Ifo Institute, Germany

GUS GARITA, Erasmus University Rotterdam, the Netherlands

HARRY J. GARRETSEN, University of Groningen, the Netherlands

HENRI L. F. DE GROOT, Department of Spatial Economics, VU University Amsterdam, Tinbergen Institute, and CPB Netherlands Bureau of Economic Policy Analysis, the Hague, the Netherlands

KEITH HEAD, University of British Columbia, Canada

GERT-JAN M. LINDERS, Department of Spatial Economics, VU University Amsterdam, the Netherlands

CHARLES VAN MARREWIJK, University of Utrecht, the Netherlands

MATHILDE MAUREL, Centre d'Economie de la Sorbonne, CNRS, University of Paris 1, France

THIERRY MAYER, CERAS, CEPII, CEPR, University de Paris 1, France

L. JAN MÖHLMANN, Department of Spatial Economics, VU University Amsterdam, and CPB Netherlands Bureau of Economic Policy Analysis, the Netherlands

ANDREW K. ROSE, University of California, USA

ALAIN DE SERRES, OECD, Paris, France

MARK M. SPIEGEL, Federal Reserve Bank of San Francisco, USA

1 Introduction

The comeback of the gravity model

P. A. G. van Bergeijk and S. Brakman

1.1 Introduction

The gravity model describes one of the most stable relationships in economics: interaction between large economic clusters is stronger than between smaller ones, and nearby clusters attract each other more than far-off ones. This formulation of the model admittedly is vague. What is meant by large economic clusters, or "far-off"? In fact, this ambiguity reflects the success of the gravity model in economics. Although the model is probably best known in the context of international trade and capital flows between countries, it has also been successfully applied to describe how consumers flow between different shopping malls, patients between hospitals and much more. Also "distance" is a very broad concept. It might reflect actual distances in miles, as an approximation of transportation costs, but over the years more subtle elements of distance-related factors have been considered. Economic factors such as tariffs and non-tariff barriers have been included in applications of the gravity model, but also "non-economic" factors have been included, such as cultural differences, differences in religion, language (dis)similarities, the presence or absence of former colonial ties, institutional differences, differences in technological development, and so on.

The list of applications is long and, most remarkably, empirical tests show that this simple idea is very successful from an empirical point of view and is able to show that many economic phenomena between different locations can empirically be described by a gravity equation.

The papers in this volume were presented in October 2007 at a conference at the Faculty of Economics, University of Groningen, the Netherlands and coorganized with the Ministry of Economic Affairs, Directorate-General for International Economic Relations (DG-BEB). We would like to thank Harry Garretsen, conference participants, and the referees – selected by Cambridge University Press – for their comments and suggestions on earlier versions of the papers and this chapter in particular. We would also like to thank Chris Harrison and his team for editorial support and the Ministry of Economic Affairs, Directorate-General for International Economic Relations (DG-BEB) and the Faculty of Economics of the University of Groningen for financial support for the conference.

2 vanvan Bergeijk and Brakman

Remarkably and in contrast to popular belief, recent estimates of the gravity equation show that distance-related variables have become *more* instead of *less* important. A recent special issue of the *Cambridge Journal of Regions, Economy and Society* (2008), for example, was titled "The World is not Flat," in order to indicate that distance is still one of the most salient characteristics to describe economic interaction in the world economy.[1]

Table 1.1 summarizes (most of) the contributions in this book. The table shows the versatility of the model and provides a good impression of the many questions that can be studied with a gravity model. Why do borders matter (and by how much)? Are cultural and institutional differences important for trade? What is the contribution of an ambassador to bilateral trade? Is environmental policy relevant for trade? How does one's income or wage relate to the fact that trade partners are nearby or far away? These are just a small sample of all the questions that can be answered by the gravity equation. The collection of papers in this book also provides a rich sample of different empirical approaches with regard to the gravity model. Indeed, many chapters contain comparisons and tests of the different modeling strategies including – extended versions – of Tinbergen's straightforward OLS, the method proposed by Anderson and van Wincoop, and more practical variants thereof. One finding stands out – as Table 1.1 testifies: although the magnitude of the distance effect on trade may differ, its sign and significance endure the hardship of scientific scrutiny.

Since the gravity equation was introduced by Tinbergen in 1962 in his *Shaping the World Economy* (where it actually was developed in one of the appendices), the gravity model has always been around in policy circles, because of its robustness and as a versatile tool to analyze all kinds of (trade) policy issues. The academic popularity of the gravity analysis, however, waned in the 1970s and 1980s, especially since the gravity equation could be derived from almost any international trade model, thus offering no scope to test between theories. The lack of a convincing and unambiguous micro-economic foundation gave the gravity model a somewhat ambivalent reputation: perhaps useful as an empirical tool, but unsatisfactory from a theoretical point of view. In the last twenty years the model has again become fashionable due to seminal contributions by Anderson and Bergstrand. The chapters in this book vividly reflect this renewed interest.

[1] In Chapter 2 Bergstrand and Egger attack another myth related to the assumed flatness of the world, namely the idea that increased exports and direct investments from developing countries dominate international trade and investment flows.

Table 1.1. *Overview of gravity analyses in this book*

Chapter	Subject	Period	Sample	Range of the distance parameters	Significant positive regional trade agreements
2 Bergstrand, Egger	GE theory bilateral FDI, final goods and intermediate goods	1990–2000	160 countries	−0.58[a] / −0.83[b]	−1.08[a] / 0.31[b]	n.a.
4 Baier, Bergstrand	Replication Anderson and van Wincoop (2003) and application of GE approximation	1993	10 Canadian and 20 US states	−0.79	−1.26	n.a.
5 Bikker	Trade creation *versus* trade diversion	2005	178 countries	−1.30	−1.70	Yes, not for EU
6 Head, Mayer	Interpretation of border effects in relation to measurement of distance	1997 / 1993–95	US states / European countries	−0.47 / −0.74	−0.73 / −1.20	n.a.
7 Bosker, Garretsen	Market access	1996	97 countries	−0.72	−0.0	n.a.
8 Möhlmann, Ederveen, de Groot, Linders	Cultural and institutional distance by product group	2000	55 countries (27 OECD)	−0.53	−1.42	Yes
9 Rose, Spiegel	Trade impact of international environmental arrangements	2001–03	68 source and 221 host countries	−0.49	−1.07	Yes
10 Afman, Maurel	Diplomacy and trade in the context of East–West Trade	1995, 2000, 2005	56 countries (26 OECD)	−1.13	−1.44	Yes
11 Brakman, Garita, Garretsen, van Marrewijk	Cross-border mergers and acquisitions	1986–2005	211 countries	−0.26[b]	−0.36[b]	n.a.

[a] Final goods and intermediate goods.
[b] FDI.

This introductory chapter is organized as follows. First we give a brief historical account of developments surrounding the gravity model. Next we turn to the empirical applications and highlight some of the problems that arise when estimating the model. The main aim of this introduction is to place the contributions of this volume into perspective, rather than providing a full-fledged survey.[2] The final section formulates some of the challenges that lie ahead.

1.2   The gravity model

1.2.1   The history of gravity

The gravity model has a long history as many authors have noted the relationship between, on the one hand, flows between different locations and on the other hand, the "weight" of these locations and the inverse of distance. An early cogent formulation of the gravity narrative is Ravenstein (1885, pp. 198–99) who explains how "currents" of migration are driven by the "absorption of centers of commerce and industry" but "grow less with the distance proportionately." Noteworthy is also the discontent with the classic trade model's neglect that was voiced in the first half of the twentieth century by Ohlin and in the German trade and location school that comprises Weber, Furlan, Engländer, Predöhl, and Lösch. Building on these theories and motivated by a desire to bring multilateral trade and distance into the trade economist's common toolkit, Isard and Peck (1954) empirically demonstrate the negative impact of distance for different modes of both domestic and international transport.[3] Isard (1954), in fact, comes close to formulating a gravity equation, but he uses a somewhat different metaphor from physics than Newton's gravity (electric potential rather than gravity). Still, Isard had already envisioned many of the issues that engage researchers of the gravity model today as he stresses the importance of measurement issues, the composition of trade, cultural factors, and politics for empirical research into the determinants of bilateral trade flows that takes distance seriously. Although the gravity narrative thus has many fathers, the first mathematical formulation and empirical application of the gravity model is due to a group of Dutch economists headed by Tinbergen who were the first to actually publish a gravity model and an empirical application (Tinbergen 1962,

---

[2] The reader may wish to consult Anderson and van Wincoop (2004), or Combes *et al.* (2008).

[3] Interestingly the same desire to integrate gravity into the much wider class of general equilibrium trade models is still a strong motivation. See, for example, Chapter 3 by Anderson.

Appendix VI).[4] Tinbergen supervised the Ph.D. thesis of Linnemann (1966) that has become the standard reference to the early version of the gravity equation.

These early contributions started the first wave of applications in the early 1960s (see for critical discussions of this early literature, Taplin 1967, and Leamer and Stern 1970, chapter 6). Although the model itself can be applied to many phenomena, most applications involved bilateral trade flows and in our discussion we will thus concentrate on trade. The basic form of the gravity equation is as follows:

$$T_{ij} = \frac{GDP_i^\alpha \, GDP_j^\beta}{D_{ij}^\theta}, \tag{1.1}$$

where: T_{ij} indicates bilateral trade between country i, and j; GDP_i indicates the economic size of i, measured by GDP; and D_{ij} indicates the bilateral distance between the two countries. The parameters α, β, and θ are often estimated in a log-linear reformulation of the model. This equation explains bilateral trade using economic size and distance: the larger the two trading partners, the larger the trade flows; the larger the distance between the two countries, the smaller bilateral trade. Usually the model explains 70–80 per cent of the variance in bilateral trade flows.

What was missing during the early days of the gravity equation, despite its popularity, was a convincing micro-economic foundation. Tinbergen (1962 p. 263) actually introduced his trade flow equation in a straightforward manner as "a turnover relationship in which prices are not specified," providing only a common sense rationale for this quasi-postulated reduced form equation: trade is determined by supply potential (exporter GDP), market demand potential (importer GDP), and transportation costs (distance). Linnemann (1966) provided some theoretical arguments to justify the formulation of the trade flow equation, deriving it in the context of a quasi-Walrasian model.[5] Neither his attempt nor those of Pöyhönen (1963) and Pullianen (1963) provided a solid

---

[4] Other members of the group at the Nederlands Economisch Instituut that developed the model were R. Rijken van Olst, F. Hartog, H. Linnemann, and A. van Oven. It is noteworthy that a group of Finnish economists at the same time worked along the same lines, but their scientific publications appeared a year later (Pöyhönen 1963 and Pullianen 1963).

[5] Leamer and Stern (1970, p. 158) who were probably the first to explicitly refer to these models in a standard textbook as "gravity models" mention two other non-economic rationales for the model, simply referring to Newton and pointing out that bilateral trade is the expected value of trade between two partners based on the probability that they meet on the world market.

micro-foundation. Leamer and Stern (1970, p. 169) for example conclude: "The significance of such research must be found in the context of seeking a broader understanding of the empirical base of the pure theory of international trade. This is something a number of studies cited have failed to make clear."

The lack of a sound theoretical foundation gave the gravity model a somewhat dubious reputation among academics although its empirical strength was recognized as it was able to "identify extreme cases of artificial barriers to trade, the role of distance and the effects of membership in various customs union and trade preference groups" (Taplin 1967, p. 442). According to the survey of Leamer and Levinsohn (1995, p. 1387) this state of affairs was still present in the early 1990s: "The gravity models are strictly descriptive. They lack a theoretical underpinning so that once the facts are out, it is not clear what to make of them." They further note that the model is not linked with any issue or raises only further problems (p. 1397): ". . . the basic proposition that free trade is beneficial doesn't seem obviously at risk if distance is added to the model, so why bother? . . . once we admit distance between countries into our theories, it begs the question: what about the role of distance within them?" Leamer and Levinsohn (1995) were clearly not impressed by the gravity model, but also noted that the fact that distance is found to be important creates a tension "that needs to be remedied by a much closer association of the descriptive gravity models with the theory . . . of international economics."[6] Deardorff (1998), taking a serious look at the micro-foundations of the gravity model at the same time as Leamer and Levinsohn (1995), is also critical with respect to the theories behind it, but ironically not because of a lack of micro-economic foundations, but of too many. He shows that the model is consistent with a large class of trade models. This implies that the use of the gravity model as a tool to distinguish between theories becomes problematic.[7]

Paradoxically the fact that the gravity model could be derived from Heckscher-Ohlin, as well as increasing returns to scale, Ricardian models,

[6] Somewhat ironically they note that (p. 1387) ". . . a theoretical foundation by Anderson (1979) is formally fruitful but seems too complex to be part of the everyday toolkit." At the time of the publication of the Handbook of International Economics (Grossman and Rogoff 1995), the gravity model was again gaining ground, and the work of Anderson was pivotal for the revitalization of the gravity model.

[7] See also Evenett and Keller (1998). Feenstra et al. (2001, p. 446) agree with Deardorff (1998), but take the discussion a step further: ". . . the theoretical foundations for the gravity equation are actually quite general, but the empirical performance is quite specific . . . different theories lead to measurable different home market effects . . ." These differences in parameter values can be used as guides in empirical tests.

and so on, was offering great confidence to policy makers. Advice based on the gravity analysis did not seem to depend on a particular vision of the economic process, that is: policy makers argued that the gravity equation was robust with respect to economic theories. Actually, in the early and mid 1990s the model was very fashionable in policy institutions especially for analyzing the big changes in the world trade system when the Iron Curtain fell and a substantial empirical literature developed on this policy-relevant question.[8] These studies predicted substantial improvements of the world trade potential and important shifts in global trade patterns. Havrylyshyn and Pritchett (1991), for example, predicted that the geographic pattern of trade by the mid-European countries would change dramatically. In the 1950s to 1980s 60–80 per cent of their activities focused on the other communist countries and only about 20–30 per cent on Northern and Western Europe, but their calculations showed that the natural "undistorted" trading pattern would be exactly the reverse. The gravity predictions regarding this major systemic shock were spot on, as is illustrated by the discussion of the trade transition in European East–West trade in Chapter 10 by Afman and Maurel.[9] The case of East–West trade is an example that fits in a number of more general-oriented evaluations of the predictive power of the gravity model, such as the analysis of predictive out of sample performance by Ward and Hoff (2005).[10]

All in all, the general consensus in the literature was that the ambiguous or "lack of theoretical underpinnings significantly weakens the credibility of a model, as it introduces a certain degree of subjectivity in the interpretation of the estimated coefficients" (Piermartini and Teh 2005, p. 37). The empirical performance of the model in itself could not convince theorists and also on this account the search for a sound micro-foundation for the model continued.

1.2.2   The micro-foundation of gravity

The discussion above illustrates that starting from the earliest applications of the gravity equation, and stimulated by the empirical success of the model, the search for its micro-foundations were always high on the research agenda.

---

[8] Examples are: van Bergeijk and Oldersma (1990), Havrylyshyn and Pritchett (1991), Wang and Winters (1991), Döhrn and Milton (1992), Ezran *et al.* (1992), and Hamilton and Winters (1992).

[9] The development of post-1989 trade between East and West continues to inspire evaluations with the gravity model, see for example Bussière *et al.* (2005).

[10] Ward and Hoff (2005) also find that a substantial and persistent amount of trade variation is attributable to country-specific importer and exporter effects.

Anderson (1979) provided a sound micro-economic foundation, but his achievement initially did not get the attention that it deserved (see note 7). Using standard economic techniques, he showed how the gravity model fits into an optimizing framework and inter alia shows some of its limitations. He assumes a (weakly) separable social utility function with respect to traded and non-traded goods. Each region produces both types. In the first round of utility maximization, the share of j's income which is spent on traded goods, a_j, can vary among different regions, and depends on income, and population size in j. In the second round region j maximizes a homothetic (Cobb–Douglas) utility function which is identical across all regions. This implies that, ignoring price discrimination, the share that country j spends on the exports of tradeable goods from i, s_i, is equal for all j (i.e. s_i varies only with i). Country j's imports from country i can be expressed as:

$$T_{ij} = s_i a_j GDP_j \qquad (1.2)$$

Equilibrium on the traded goods market implies: $a_i GDP_i = s_i \sum_j a_j \times GDP_j$. Solving for r_i and substituting in the bilateral trade equation gives:

$$T_{ij} = a_i GDP_i a_j GDP_j \bigg/ \sum_i \sum_j T_{ij}$$

$$\text{note that } \sum_i \sum_j T_{ij} = \sum_j a_j GDP_j \qquad (1.3)$$

This is already a simple variant of the gravity model in which economic masses determine the trade flows. The applicability to real world problems, however, is limited to years with balanced trade. Furthermore, countries must have similar demand structures. It is relatively easy to extend the model with population variables and, most importantly, trade barriers. Bergstrand (1985, 1989) is the second author to provide a theoretical foundation for the model, in which he highlights (complicated) price terms, which are absent in the derivation above.[11] Bergstrand (1985, 1989, 1990) develops a relationship between trade theory and bilateral trade, and includes the supply side of the economy explicitly. The income of destination countries enters the equation because of demand;

---

[11] The appendix in Anderson (1979) is interesting, as all modern variants of the gravity equation are based on the derivation in this appendix – it anticipates the famous multilateral resistance terms introduced explicitly in Anderson and van Wincoop (2003). These are also acknowledged in Bergstrand (1989, 1990).

income of the exporting countries because it reflects the supply capacity of the exporting country; and distance because it reflects transportation costs which are passed on to the consumers in the destination countries (cif/fob difference between prices in countries of destination and countries of origin). With the benefit of hindsight the contributions of Anderson and Bergstrand initiated a renewed interest in the gravity model, culminating in Anderson and van Wincoop (2003) that extends Anderson (1979), but also introduces a method to deal with the complicated price (index) terms (which are already present in the appendix of Anderson 1979 and in Bergstrand 1985, 1989, 1990).[12]

Anderson and van Wincoop (2003) has become the main reference for subsequent work on the gravity equation. This is why we give a simplified derivation of the model, in six steps, that is based on Baldwin and Taglioni (2006):

Step 1: The first step is a supply equals demand equation. The expenditure share identity, that includes the relevant prices, says that the *value* of trade flow from country i to j, $p_{ij}x_{ij}$, should equal the share country i has in expenditure of j.

$$p_{ij}x_{ij} = s_{ij}E_j, \text{ where } p_{ij} = \text{import price, from } i \text{ to } j,$$

$$s_{ij} = \text{share of } i \text{ in } j\text{'s expenditure, } E_j. \tag{1.4}$$

Step 2: Next s_{ij} follows from a familiar CES demand structure and it is easy to derive an explicit expression for the imported goods share in E_j. Assuming that all goods are traded this share depends on the bilateral prices relative to a price index.

$$s_{ij} = \left(\frac{p_{ij}}{P_j}\right)^{1-\sigma} \quad \text{where } P_j = \left(\sum_{i=1...N} n_i \left(p_{ij}\right)^{1-\sigma}\right)^{1/(1-\sigma)} \tag{1.5}$$

is the exact price index associated with the CES demand structure; $\sigma > 1$ is the elasticity of substitution between "varieties"; N is the number of nations; n_i is the number of varieties supplied by nation i. Note that varieties are defined symmetrically, which allows us to ignore a variety index.

Step 3: Adding trade costs. A crucial element in all gravity equations is the presence of trade costs. These are easily introduced. If t_{ij} indicates

---

[12] Bergstrand (1989, 1990) is the first to give explicit attention to the price index terms, but in the empirical applications he uses existing price indices. This is also the approach taken in Baier and Bergstrand (2001).

bilateral trade costs, the price in market j equals:

$$p_{ij} = p_i t_{ij},$$ (1.6)

where p_i is the mill price of a variety in country i (note again the absence of an index for varieties; varieties are defined symmetrically). After transportation the price in market j becomes p_{ij}.

Step 4: The gravity equation describes total trade between two countries; this implies that we have to aggregate across varieties

$$T_{ij} = n_i s_{ij} E_j = n_i \left(p_i t_{ij} \right)^{1-\sigma} \frac{E_j}{P_j^{1-\sigma}},$$ (1.7)

where the second equality follows from combining equations (1.5) and (1.6) in the bilateral trade equation (1.7).

Step 5: All goods are traded, so the budget constraint says that total output of country i, Y_i, equals total sales to all destination countries j (including country i itself).

$$Y_i = \sum_j T_{ij} = n_i p_i^{1-\sigma} \sum_j \left(t_{ij}^{1-\sigma} \frac{E_j}{P_j^{1-\sigma}} \right),$$ (1.8)

where the second equality follows from combining equation (1.7) with (1.8). We can rewrite equation (1.8) as:

$$n_i p_i^{1-\sigma} = \frac{Y_i}{\Pi_i^{(1-\sigma)}}, \quad \text{where } \Pi_i = \left(\sum_j \left(t_{ij}^{1-\sigma} \frac{E_j}{P_j^{1-\sigma}} \right) \right)^{1/(1-\sigma)}$$ (1.9)

Step 6: A gravity equation can now be derived from inserting equation (1.9) into equation (1.7) which gives:

$$T_{ij} = Y_i E_j \left(\frac{t_{ij}}{\Pi_i P_j} \right)^{1-\sigma}$$ (1.10)

Equation (1.10) is identical to equation (9) in Anderson and van Wincoop (2003).[13] Note that the main difference between equation (1.1)

---

[13] Note that Anderson and van Wincoop (2003) use income shares. To see that the two expressions are identical, multiply and divide equation (1.10) and Π_i by world income, y^W.

and equation (1.10) consists of the price indices P and Π, which are the so-called multilateral resistance terms.[14] These are intuitively easy to understand. Bilateral trade between two countries does not only depend on bilateral variables related to these two countries alone, but also on their position relative to the world economy. Consider for example the ranking of OECD countries by Boulhol and de Serres in Chapter 12 by different measures of centrality. They empirically distinguish remote countries, such as Australia and New Zealand, peripheral countries, such as Korea and North America, and centrally located and dense economies such as Belgium and the Netherlands. In the context of multilateral trade resistance a pair of countries in the EU, for example, faces tougher competition from nearby trading partners than a similar pair of countries that are more isolated from the world economy. So trade between two countries in the EU is, ceteris paribus, smaller than trade between the two similar countries that are more isolated (and for which P and Π are higher).[15] Equation (1.10), and variants thereof, has become the standard formulation in recent applications of the gravity equation (see also Anderson and van Wincoop 2004).

1.2.3   *Empirical applications of the gravity equation: empirical strategies*

Recent empirical research discusses four main topics that have to be dealt with in applications of the gravity equations: how to deal with the multilateral resistance terms, how to deal with the large number of zeroes in trade statistics, how to measure distance and what is the appropriate level of (dis)aggregation for the gravity analysis.

1.2.3.1 Multilateral resistance Although equation (1.10) looks simple it is also difficult to estimate. In essence this is caused by the fact that the multilateral resistance terms depend on trade costs and the multilateral resistance terms themselves, which are part of the estimation. This causes a circular dependence in the estimation of equation (1.10). This complication is a drawback of empirical applications of equation (1.10). Anderson and van Wincoop solve this by making the additional assumption of symmetrical trade costs, $t_{ij} = t_{ji}$, and a custom programmed system of (non-linear) equations.

---

[14] Anderson and van Wincoop (2003) introduce a further simplification: symmetry of trade costs, $t_{ij} = t_{ji}$ that allows a further simplification.

[15] See for an extensive discussion of the multilateral resistance terms, Anderson and Neary (2005, Chapter 10) and Chapter 3 by Anderson in this volume.

Three alternatives have been proposed in the literature to deal with this problem: including fixed effects as an approximation of the multilateral resistance terms, a linearization, and an analytical solution.

First, the multilateral resistance terms are unobserved, but can be estimated using fixed effects. This is a method used by, for example, Rose and van Wincoop (2001) or Redding and Venables (2004). For this purpose equation (1.10) can be rewritten as (where the income terms are used as correction factors for the bilateral trade flows):

$$\ln(T_{ij}/Y_i E_j) = (1 - \sigma)t_{ij} + \alpha_1^i D^i + \alpha_2^j D^j + \alpha_3 \varepsilon_{ij}, \tag{1.11}$$

where D^i is a dummy that is unity when i is the exporter and zero otherwise, and D^j a dummy that is unity when j is the importer and zero otherwise, and ε_{ij} is the error term. The coefficients measure the multilateral resistance terms: $\alpha_1^i = \ln(\Pi_i)^{\sigma-1}, \alpha_2^j = \ln(P_j)^{\sigma-1}$. Feenstra (2004) expresses a preference for this method as it is easy to implement and gives consistent estimates of the average effects. A disadvantage of the fixed effects method, however, is that the estimates cannot be used in order to calculate comparative-static effects involving changes in trade costs, for which the gravity equation is often used (the multilateral resistance terms, in principle, have to be recalculated for each exercise as transport costs are an element of the multilateral resistance terms).

Second, the solution proposed by Straathof (2008) shows that, using the same assumptions as Anderson and van Wincoop (2003) the non-linear problem that results from them can be linearized and solved analytically. The advantage of this method is that no approximations are necessary, and that standard econometric estimates can be used in order to derive identical results as in Anderson and van Wincoop (2003). However, as Straathof observes, his method results in an endogeneity problem.

Third, Baier and Bergstrand (2009) recently proposed an elegant method that addresses both the issue of the estimation of the multilateral resistance terms as well as the applicability in comparative-static exercises and does not suffer from Straathof's endogeneity problem. Using the same assumptions as Anderson and van Wincoop (2003) they first apply first-order Taylor-series expansion to the multilateral resistance terms (that depend on – weighted – trade costs), and substitute these in (a variant of) equation (1.10). Baier and Bergstrand further develop this theory for the case of symmetric trading costs in Chapter 4 in this book.

All these methods illustrate the relevance of the contribution of Anderson and van Wincoop (2003), and since this seminal publication, applications of the gravity model have to deal with the multilateral resistance terms, one way or another, in order to be taken seriously.[16]

1.2.3.2 Zero trade flows Another important problem with the analysis of trade flows is the occurrence of zero bilateral trade flows. Helpman *et al.* (2008, p. 443) indicate that 50 per cent of the 158 countries in their sample do not trade with one another. If the gravity equation is applied to FDI flows this number increases to more than 80 per cent. This can be caused by rounding errors, missing observations or truly zero trade flows. The standard procedure (following Linnemann 1966) in empirical studies is simply to drop the zero flows from the sample (Chapter 10 by Afman and Maurel is an example), or add a small constant to all trade flows in order to be able to estimate a log-linear equation (Chapter 11 by Rose and Spiegel is an example); both these procedures – among additional alternatives – have been used in, for example, Santos Silva and Tenreyro (2006).

These approaches are correct as long as the zero values are randomly distributed; however, if they are not random, as is most often the case, it introduces selection biases. Until recently, this problem has been ignored in gravity studies, but it can be handled by means of sample selection correction.[17] In this light, Helpman *et al.* (2008) propose a theoretical model rationalizing the zero trade flows and propose estimating the gravity equation with a correction for the probability of countries to trade. In order to estimate their model, they apply a two-step estimation technique (similar to sample selection models commonly used in labor economics). To implement the new estimator, one needs to find an appropriate exclusion restriction for identification of the second-stage equation, which can be quite difficult. Indeed, zero flows need to be taken more seriously. For one thing the problem occurs more often when a great many developing

---

[16] Although the multilateral resistance terms received a lot of attention in the literature it is not the only empirical problem with the gravity equation. Baldwin and Taglioni (2006), for example, stress three problems. First, they show that the multilateral resistance terms change over time, which implies that the gravity equation developed by Anderson and van Wincoop (2003) can only be estimated in cross-section studies. Second, they point out that if the gravity equation is applied to trade between country pairs one should take the average of the logs instead of the log of the average. In the case that trade between countries is balanced the error is small; however with unbalanced trade the error is large. Third, trade data are often deflated by a price index that is the same for all bilateral trade flows (often the US aggregate price index). This can create spurious correlation if there are global inflationary trends in the data that affect both the left-hand side of the equation as well as the right-hand side.

[17] The fact that zero flows contained potentially useful and relevant information was also recognized by Bikker (1982, pp. 399–411) in an early application of the Tobit model to international trade.

countries are included from different continents (see Chapter 7 by Bosker and Garretsen), when lower levels of aggregation are used, for example in the analysis of trade at the level of individual product groups (see Chapter 8 by Möhlmann *et al.*) and in FDI (see Chapter 11 by Brakman *et al.*). These chapters provide examples of econometrical solutions to the zero-observation problems.

1.2.3.3 Measurement of distance Finally, without much exaggeration one can claim that the most important contribution of the gravity equation is that it points out the relevance of trade costs. The measurement of these costs is often crude as researchers rely – in addition to actual distance – on the use of dummies to indicate borders, language similarities, cultural differences, colonial ties, membership of Preferential Trading Areas, etc. Only a few studies use actual data on shipping costs, such as Limao and Venables (2001) or Combes and Lafourcade (2005). These studies show that distance might be an inadequate proxy for transport costs. Direct measurement is difficult and differs between commodities. Anderson and van Wincoop (2004) show that on average trade costs are about 170 per cent of the mill price of manufactured goods and consist of 55 per cent of internal costs, 21 per cent transportation costs, and 44 per cent related to border effects ($2.7 = 1.55 * 1.21 * 1.44$). Studies like these confirm that the world is still far from being "flat."

To be more specific it is instructive to look at Figure 1.1, which is based on data underlying the Disdier and Head (2008) study. They performed a so-called meta-analysis of gravity-equation estimates, based on 1,467 estimated distance effects (indicated by θ in their study) in 103 publications using the gravity equation. Their findings can be effectively summarized with the help of Figure 1.1.[18] The higher the estimated parameter θ, the stronger the negative effect of distance on the size of trade flows, and therefore the more important distance and location is for determining these trade flows. The mean effect of distance on trade for the period as a whole is around 0.9 (with 90 per cent of all estimates between 0.28 and 1.55).[19] This implies that a 10 per cent increase in distance leads to a 9 per cent reduction of international trade flows. The estimates in Figure 1.1 suggest that the distance effect became less important between 1890 and 1940. Most striking, however, is the *increased* (not decreased) estimated distance effect in the second half of the twentieth century (also

[18] We are grateful to Anne-Célia Disdier and Keith Head for providing us with the data for this figure. The dates indicate the mid points in a sample.
[19] This can be compared to the estimates in this book that are in the range of 0.47 to 1.70; see Table 1.1.

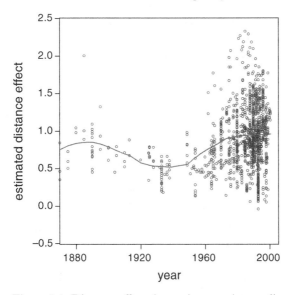

Figure 1.1. Distance effects in gravity-equation studies
Data source: Disdier and Head (2008). Our kernel fit is based on
Epanechnikov (h = 19.575).

with some increased variance). In sharp contrast to the opinion of the
death-of-distance group, distance is therefore becoming *more* (not less)
important for determining international trade flows. See Berthelon and
Freund (2008) and Disdier and Head (2008) for further discussion.

1.2.3.4 Micro-data and product groups For a long time, gravity has hardly
been studied at disaggregated levels. This may have been due to its
originally macro-economic formulation, the importance of country characteristics, limited availability of data or the still limited computational
capacity during the early phases of gravity modeling. Whatever the reason may have been, at the turn of the century it was still "surprising how
little work has been done on examining disaggregated gravity equations"
(Harrigan 2002). Since then a lot of progress has been made mainly
in the slipstream of theories about the international activities of essentially heterogeneous firms (Melitz 2003, see also Chaney 2008 for an
overview). Krautheim (2007), for example, models a reduction of fixed
export costs through information networks that enables firms to share
and spread the available knowledge about foreign markets. Krautheim
(2007) thus suggests a solution to the distance puzzle since in this setup
the fixed costs of exporting are endogenously increasing in trade.

An important issue in the empirical debate is the channel through which gravity works. Does distance influence the extensive margin (the number of firms, the number of products, the number of international trade and/or investment relations) or the intensive margin (value per product, per firm, per bilateral trade and/or investment relationship)? Typically micro-data studies find a strong negative relationship between distance and the numbers of exporting firms, products, and bilateral trade and investment relations (see for example Buch *et al.* 2003 or Hillberry and Hummels 2008). Empirical application of theories that recognize the importance of firm heterogeneity in the context of the gravity model presently often still use macro-data (Bernard *et al.* 2007; Helpman *et al.* 2008), but we assume that with the greater availability of micro-datasets for more countries (see for example International Study Group on Exports and Productivity 2007) more broader empirical testing of theories of characteristics and behavior of heterogeneous firms will become the standard.

A more disaggregated analysis is not only warranted by a better understanding of the actual behavior of the firm; it is also driven by measurement issues related to distance. Border effects, for example, appear to be to a large extent driven by the extent of transportability of goods, as shown by Head and Mayer (Chapter 6). Möhlmann *et al.* (Chapter 8) report significant differences in the distance parameter for different product categories. Both chapters show that an analysis by product type generates both new insights and research questions. The need for further analysis is illustrated by the fact that the findings in these two chapters sometimes agree – for example, that the markets for refined petroleum products are local – but sometimes disagree. Head and Mayer classify tobacco and beverages as products which are difficult to transport whereas Möhlmann *et al.* characterize the markets of these goods as international.[20]

1.3   About this book

The renewed interest in and further development of the gravity equation contrasted with actual policy discussion that assumed whether the world has become "flat." Actually the period following the publication of Friedman's *The World is Flat* in 2005 was a somewhat strange time for the gravity equation, as distance (which is the key feature of gravity) was

[20] One possible explanation is that Möhlmann *et al.* also deal with the trade between continents, while Head and Mayer provide an analysis for a national market (USA) c.q. the internal EU market.

increasingly being ignored in policy circles, while at the same time much progress was made on the theoretical and empirical side in academia.[21] This contrast and the wish to take stock of recent advancements provided the reasons to organize the conference "The Gravity Equation or: Why the World is not Flat" in Groningen in October 2007. We have organized the contributions in this book in three coherent parts: methodology, measurement of distance, and applications.

1.3.1 Methodology

In the first contribution Bergstrand and Egger (Chapter 2) develop a general equilibrium model that endogenizes the decision to import, export or to invest abroad. In this model goods can be produced in any country and can potentially be composed of intermediates from all other countries. Flows in goods are further distinguished from FDI. The general equilibrium model is calibrated using a newly created dataset that decomposes the world trade matrix into final and intermediate goods. This tool enables them to theoretically distinguish three gravity specifications for trade in intermediate and final goods and FDI, respectively. This method is a novel approach to arrive at testable unambiguous theoretical rationales regarding the gravity equation: all three types of bilateral flows should be positively related to both the size and similarity of GDP and all own-price effects should be negative, and cross-price effects indicate that barriers to FDI increase flows of final goods (and vice versa: barriers to trade in final goods increase FDI). These hypotheses are confirmed by empirical testing.

Anderson (Chaper 3) extends the applicability of the by now famous multilateral resistance terms that were introduced in Anderson and van Wincoop (2003). Anderson shows that by applying simplifying assumptions a more straightforward derivation is possible by assuming that shipments are to a basket of commodities and demand also comes from this basket; the incidence of trade costs is then divided between supply and demand. This extension of Anderson and van Wincoop (2003) has the potential to get a wider application of the gravity model, in particular in trade and investment theories that so far have not considered distance as an explanatory variable.

Baier and Bergstrand (Chapter 4) take up the issue of how comparative-static analyses that are key to policy makers can be reconciled with the estimation of the multilateral resistance terms. Building on Baier and

---

[21] See also the review of Friedman by Leamer (2007).

Bergstrand (2009), and extending the analysis for the case of symmetric trade costs, extensive Monte Carlo simulations illustrate that this new method gives almost identical estimates to the method proposed by Anderson and van Wincoop or the fixed effects method. The additional advantage of this method, however, is that the multilateral resistance terms can be retrieved and used in comparative static exercises, as their application to the NAFTA and the European Economic Area illustrate. This solution to the difficulties involved in estimating and simulating along the lines of Anderson and van Wincoop (2003) will be of interest to many applied trade policy analysts.

Bikker (Chapter 5) uses quite a different technology that, however, provides the same sort of result as Anderson and van Wincoop (2003). One of the limitations of the gravity model is that it focuses on bilateral trade, and in fact can only explain an increase or decrease in a bilateral trade flow. Still, the model is applied to issues of trade integration, where trade creations and diversions are key concepts. However, by assumption the model cannot explain substitutions between flows. Bikker extends the standard formulation of the gravity model in such a way that also substitutions between flows can be analyzed by constructing measurement of trade totals in the bilateral trade matrix. Substitution can thus be distinguished from creation.

1.3.2   Distance in the gravity model

The concept of bilateral distance is the main determining characteristic of the gravity model and thus measurement issues related to distance are key to the validity of any empirical application, but also to the interpretation of the results of the econometric findings. Economics is no physics. In the natural sciences distance is well defined and its measurement can be exact and unambiguous. Economic distance, however, is a multifaceted concept, and measurement and interpretation accordingly are subject to continuous debate. Originally distance entered the model because it could be used as an approximation of transportation costs and transport time. Also, distance was used as a measure for the "mental" distance of exporters and importers that increases with distance. New and challenging measures of intangible distances related to different legal and economic institutions, different cultures, and different technologies have recently been added to the gravity model (Martínez-Zarzoso and Márquez-Ramos 2005; Dekker et al. 2006). The three chapters in this part provide a perspective on distance in all its manifestations, its importance in describing bilateral economic relations between countries, and the need to address measurement issues.

Head and Mayer (Chapter 6) start from the intuitive notion that border effects are too large to be explained on the basis of the trade barriers that are typically being considered in the literature. This is especially true because large border effects also occur in situations where one would expect that trade barriers are negligible (for example on the European internal market). They show that distances, as they appear in the literature, are mismeasured and lead to a systematic overestimation of the border effect and consequently they develop a new measure of "effective" distance that is used as a benchmark against other measures of distances. Typically the extent of overestimation of distance effects is stronger for countries that are located near each other.[22] They apply this method to the case of the US states and EU member countries, where formal barriers to trade are absent. Although the border effect shrinks for these cases, it remains present.

Bosker and Garretsen (Chapter 7) follow a completely different approach, focusing on different functional forms that so far have been used in the trade literature to describe the relation between distance and costs. They test different specifications for trade costs. Bosker and Garretsen apply the concepts of market access and supplier access in the context of the "New Economic Geography" (NEG) wage equation and show that the specification of trade costs can be very important. Market access is insignificant in four out of six specifications and estimated elasticities may differ up to a factor of six. By way of illustration this chapter also provides numerical insights into the impact of the trade cost specification into the transmission of income shocks, a topic that may gain in relevance due to the financial crisis that may provide a natural experiment to test competing theories.

Chapter 8 by Möhlmann et al. includes a measure of cultural and institutional distance into a traditional gravity model thus offering an empirical perspective on the non-economic component of border effects. Building on the seminal work by Rauch (1999) they focus on different product categories. The effect of cultural and institutional distances appears to be small at the level of aggregate trade flows, but significant at the level of individual product groups. Möhlmann et al. suggest that the tradeoff between FDI and trade – that is also studied in Chapter 2 by Bergstrand and Egger and Chapter 11 by Brakman et al. – can explain this result.

---

[22] This may actually offer an explanation of an anomaly in Bikker's finding in Chapter 5 of a negative coefficient for EU membership because most EU members typically are located near to each other.

1.3.3   Specific applications

One of the great benefits of the gravity model is that its central notion – economic interaction depends positively on masses corrected for distance – can be applied to many different situations and applications. The contributions in this part both indicate the versatility of the gravity model and put its usefulness into perspective.

A first promising branch of extensions is the inclusion of political and diplomatic interaction that may offer a bridge for the cultural and institutional distances studied by Möhlmann *et al.* in Chapter 8. The importance of these international political non-economic factors is an issue that was investigated (but only for broad classes of political and diplomatic conflict and cooperation) in the late 1980s and early 1990s. Pollins (1989) and van Bergeijk (1992) combined bilateral political events data and trade data in gravity models covering the impact of such events on trade flows in the 1960s to the 1980s inclusive. In recent years, following Rose's (2007) seminal paper, specific aspects of political and diplomatic interaction between countries have become the subject of ongoing research, of which Chapters 9 and 10 provide examples.[23]

Rose and Spiegel (Chapter 9) investigate how bilateral and multilateral spillovers from international treaties can help to build a nation's reputation and how this may exert an impact on economic interaction through the trade credit channel. Their contribution broadens the literature of the 1980s and 1990s that dealt with bilateral impacts only. Rose and Spiegel specifically investigate whether participation in international environmental arrangements (IEAs) is beneficial for economic relations, but argue that the basic logic of the argument can be extended to other facets of international relations such as security. Their model indicates that being part of a political network also benefits economic relations. The other side of the coin is that withdrawing from such a network can have (negative) economic implications as well. A gravity model for cross-border asset holdings uncovers statistically significant and small, but economically meaningful, coefficients both for involvement in bilateral and multilateral treaties.

Afman and Maurel (Chapter 10) investigate the impact of embassies and other diplomatic activity on the trade with Eastern Europe in the post Cold War period. This period provides a unique "natural experiment" in which new diplomatic relationships are established (so the number

---

[23] Rose (2004) provides a challenging perspective on the impact of multilateral economic diplomacy. This gravity analysis of GATT/WTO membership opened another line of research that is discussed by Piermartini and Teh (2005, pp. 47–49). Van Bergeijk (2009, pp. 5–9, 35–41, and 83–86) discusses gravity studies on the trade impact of bilateral political and diplomatic conflict and cooperation.

of embassies actually shows a lot of variation). Their contribution is to provide both the dynamic counterpart to Rose (2007) and the first application of the Anderson and van Wincoop (2004) model to the question of the impact of political and diplomatic factors on bilateral trade. The paper thus provides an interesting basis for comparison between the methodologies that have been used. Importantly, diplomacy can have beneficial effects on trading relations, as illustrated by their findings that the opening of an embassy is equivalent to a 2–12 per cent reduction of ad valorem tariffs and an increase of bilateral trade by 25 per cent.

The application of Brakman *et al.* (Chapter 11) is different in the sense that the gravity model is applied to mergers and acquisitions, a subset of FDI for which Bergstrand and Egger in Chapter 2 develop a general equilibrium model and provide empirical tests for 1990–2000. Distinguishing empirically between the active group of countries that invest abroad and the non-active group of "zero" investors, Brakman *et al.* show that the phenomenon of a stronger influence of distance over time is not limited to trade flows, but also occurs in mergers and acquisitions over the years 1986–2005. Chapter 11 investigates different hypotheses related to the question of whether FDI acts as a substitute for exports in the context of trade barriers, an issue also raised but now answered by Möhlmann *et al.* in Chapter 8, and furthermore addresses an empirical puzzle, see for instance Neary (2008): why do we see more horizontal M&As while at the same time countries become more and more integrated (where the standard theory predicts a negative relation)? The gravity approach uncovers evidence against the export platform motive and in favor of economic integration as a source of reductions in takeover costs.

Boulhol and de Serres (Chapter 12) offer yet another application in which distance and in particular the proximity to areas of dense economic activity feature prominently. Their approach in a sense fits into the two-stage estimation of the wage equation in the NEG literature that is discussed by Bosker and Garretsen in Chapter 7 and who use per capita GDP as a proxy for wage levels. Boulhol and de Serres develop a framework that directly relates per capita GDP to market and supplier access measures derived from gravity equations as they test these measures in augmented Solow models. Their inclusion of physical and human capital offers a more concrete treatment in a well-known theoretical framework than the exogenous technology parameter that most of the literature is using.[24] Like Bosker and Garretsen they consistently find a significant impact of five measures of proximity to markets on GDP per capita which inter alia suggests the need for testing causality in gravity equations that

---

[24] Bosker and Garretsen, for example, assume that technological differences can be captured by a simple i.d.d. error term that is uncorrelated with the other regressors.

are estimated using panel data over a longer time horizon.[25] Boulhol and de Serres use the same analytical framework also to investigate the impact of transportation and communication costs. These findings generally are quantitatively smaller than the measures derived from gravity equations, offering additional evidence from an alternative methodology that multi-lateral resistance is an important addition to transportation costs that are a significant element of bilateral trade resistance.

1.4   The road ahead

All in all, this book shows that the gravity approach recovered from its apparent midlife crisis in the 1970s and 1980s. The model has survived almost half a century of economic scrutiny. This is not because it fits the data so nicely, but because it has been part and parcel of a construc-tive methodological development that provided theoretical answers to the intriguing questions that emerged during and due to its application to real world problems. We expect a bright future for the gravity model.

In particular we see four challenges that will help it to stay alive and kicking. A first challenge is the further analysis of disaggregated trade flows both at the level of product groups (sector data) and at the firm level (micro-data). A stimulus of this line of research could be expected when data at the micro-level become more readily available for increasing numbers of countries. A second challenge consists of a detailed analysis of the absence of trade (or in the words of Harrigan 2002, "instances where gravity fails"). A more detailed analysis of zero trade/FDI flows is necessary when the analysis takes place at increasingly lower levels of aggregation. In addition we expect that the collapse of trade and FDI in 2008–09 will stimulate investigations on different developments in bilat-eral trade and investment flows during the financial crisis. An interesting topic will be whether the reduction of trade and investment volumes occurs at the extensive or the intensive margin. This is a question that can only be answered by estimations using micro-data. A third challenge is the further investigation into intangible barriers to trade and invest-ment, such as the political co-determinants of trade and new modes of distance. This is also relevant for our fourth challenge, which is identi-fying and understanding the substantial heterogeneity that exists under the veil of the averages and estimated coefficients. Typically, country experiences diverge, and institutions, economic policies, culture, and even religion have been suggested as an explanation for heterogeneity.

---

[25] Boulhol and de Serres take endogeneity of trade openness into account in their analysis and use instrument variables in the growth Solow regressions.

Indeed, many questions lie on the road ahead and we expect that gravity will continue to offer a tool to build new knowledge about international interactions.

REFERENCES

Anderson, J. E. (1979). "A Theoretical Foundation for the Gravity Equation," *American Economic Review* **69**: 106–16.

Anderson, J. E. and J. P. Neary (2005). *Measuring the Restrictiveness of International Trade Policy*, Cambridge, MT: The MIT Press.

Anderson, J. E. and E. van Wincoop (2003). "Gravity with Gravitas: A Solution to the Border Puzzle," *American Economic Review* **93**: 170–92.

(2004). "Trade Costs," *Journal of Economic Literature* **42**(3): 691–751.

Baier, S. L. and J. H. Bergstrand (2001). "The Growth of World Trade: Tariffs, Transport Costs, and Income Similarity," *Journal of International Economics* **53**: 1–27.

(2009). "Bonus Vetus OLS: A Simple Method for Approximating International Trade-Costs Effects Using the Gravity Equation," *Journal of International Economics* **77**: 77–85.

Baldwin, R. and D. Taglioni (2006). "Gravity for Dummies and Dummies for Gravity Equations," NBER working paper no. 12516, National Bureau of Economic Research, Inc.

Bergeijk, P. A. G. van (1992). "Diplomatic Barriers to Trade," *De Economist* **140**: 44–63.

(2009). *Economic Diplomacy and the Geography of International Trade*, Cheltenham, UK: Edward Elgar.

Bergeijk, P. A. G. van and H. Oldersma (1990). "Détente, Market-Oriented Reform and German Unification. Potential Consequences for the World Trade System," *Kyklos* **43**(4): 599–609.

Bergstrand, J. H. (1985). "The Gravity Equation in International Trade, Some Microeconomic Foundations and Empirical Evidence," *Review of Economics and Statistics* **67**: 474–81.

(1989). "The Generalized Gravity Equation, Monopolistic Competition, and Empirical Evidence," *Review of Economics and Statistics* **71**: 143–53.

(1990). "The Heckscher-Ohlin-Samuelson Model, the Linder Hypothesis and the Determinants of Bilateral Intra-Industry Trade," *Economic Journal* **100**: 1216–29.

Bernard, A. B., J. B. Jensen, S. Redding and P. K. Schott (2007). "Firms in International Trade," CEP discussion paper no. 795, London: LSE.

Berthelon, M. and C. Freund (2008). "On the Conservation of Distance in International Trade," *Journal of International Economics* **75**: 310–20.

Bikker, J. A. (1982). *Vraag-aanbodmodellen voor stelsels van geografisch gespreide markten toegepast op internationale handel en ziekenhuis-opnames in Noord-Nederland* (Demand and Supply Models of Geographically Delineated Markets with Applications to International Trade and Hospitalisations in the Northern Part of the Netherlands; in Dutch), Ph.D. thesis, Amsterdam: Free University.

24   van Bergeijk and Brakman

Buch, C. J. Kleinert and F. Toubal (2003). "Determinants of German FDI: New Evidence from Micro-Data," discussion paper no. 09/03, Frankfurt: Bundesbank.
Bussière, M., J. Fidrmuc and B. Schnatz (2005). "Trade Integration of Central and Eastern European Countries: Lessons from a Gravity Model," ECB working paper no. 545, Frankfurt: ECB.
Cambridge Journal of Regions (2008). *Economy and Society* 1(3): Special Issue "The World is not Flat: Putting Globalization in its Place." Oxford University Press.
Chaney, T. (2008). "Distorted Gravity: The Intensive and Extensive Margins of International Trade," *American Economic Review* 98: 1707–21.
Combes, P.-P. and M. Lafourcade (2005). "Transport Costs: Measures, Determinants, and Regional Policy; Implications for France," *Journal of Economic Geography* 5: 319–49.
Combes, P.-P, T. Mayer and J.-F. Thisse (2008). *Economic Geography; The Integration of Regions and Nations,* Princeton University Press.
Deardorff, A. (1998). "Determinants of Bilateral Trade: Does Gravity Work in a Neoclassical World?" in J. Frankel (ed.), *The Regionalization of the World Economy,* University of Chicago Press.
Dekker, P., S. Ederveen, H. de Groot, A. van der Horst, A. Lejour, B. Straathof, H. Vinken and C. Wenneker (2006). "Divers Europe," *European Outlook 4,* The Hague: SDU.
Disdier, A.-C. and K. Head (2008). "The Puzzling Persistence of the Distance Effect on Bilateral Trade," *The Review of Economics and Statistics* 90: 37–48.
Döhrn, R. and A. R. Milton (1992)."Zur künftigen Einbindung der osteuropäischen Reformländer in der Weltwirtschaft" (On the Integration into the World Economy of the Reforming Countries in Eastern Europe; in German), *RWI-Mitteilungen* 43: 19–40.
Evenett, S. J. and W. Keller (1998). "On Theories Explaining the Success of the Gravity Model," NBER working paper no. 6529, Cambridge, MA.
Ezran, R., C. Holmes and R. Safadi (1992). "How Changes in the CMEA Area May Affect International Trade in Manufactures," World Bank PRIT working paper series 972, Washington DC: World Bank.
Feenstra, R. C. (2004). *Advanced International Trade,* Princeton University Press.
Feenstra, R. C., J. R. Markusen and A. K. Rose (2001). "Using the Gravity Equation to Differentiate Among Alternative Theories of Trade," *Canadian Journal of Economics* 34: 430–47.
Friedman, T. L. (2005). *The World is Flat,* London: Penguin.
Grossman, G. M. and K. Rogoff (1995) (eds.) *Handbook of International Economics* III, Amsterdam: North-Holland.
Hamilton, C. B. and L. A. Winters (1992). "Opening Up International Trade with Eastern Europe," *Economic Policy* 14: 77–116.
Harrigan, J. (2002). "Specialization and the Volume of Trade: Do the Data Obey the Laws?" in E. Kwan Choi and J. Harrigan (eds.), *Handbook of International Trade,* Blackwell, pp. 85–118.
Havrylyshyn, O. and L. Pritchett (1991). "European Trade Patterns After the Transition," World Bank PRE working paper series 748, Washington DC: World Bank.

Helpman, E., M. Melitz and Y. Rubenstein (2008). "Estimating Trade Flows: Trading Partners and Trading Volumes," *Quarterly Journal of Economics* **123**: 441–87.

Hillberry, R. and D. Hummels (2008). "Trade Responses to Geographic Frictions: A Decomposition Using Micro-Data," *European Economic Review* **52**: 527–50.

International Study Group on Exports and Productivity (2007). "Exports and Productivity: Comparable Evidence for 14 Countries," research paper no. 2007/41, Leverhulme Centre for Research on Globalisation and Economic Policy: Nottingham.

Isard, W. (1954). "Location Theory and Trade Theory: Short-run Analysis," *Quarterly Journal of Economics* **68**: 305–20.

Isard, W. and M. J. Peck (1954). "Location Theory and International and Regional Trade Theory," *Quarterly Journal of Economics* **68**(1): 97–114.

Krautheim, S. (2007). "Gravity and Information: Heterogeneous Firms, Exporter Networks and the 'Distance Puzzle'," mimeo, Florence: European University Institute.

Leamer, E. E. (2007). "A Flat World, a Level Playing Field, a Small World After All, or None of the Above? A Review of Thomas L. Friedman's 'The World is Flat'," *Journal of Economic Literature* **45**: 83–126.

Leamer, E. E. and J. Levinsohn (1995). "International Trade Theory: The Evidence," in G. M. Grossman and K. Rogoff, *Handbook of International Economics* 3, Amsterdam: North-Holland.

Leamer, E. E. and R. M. Stern (1970). *Quantitative International Economics*, Chicago: Aldine Publishing Company.

Limao, N. and A. J. Venables (2001). "Infrastructure, Geographical Disadvantage and Transport Costs," *The World Bank Economic Review* **15**: 451–79.

Linnemann, H. (1966). *An Econometric Study of International Trade Flows*, Amsterdam: North-Holland.

Martínez-Zarzoso, I. and L. Márquez-Ramos (2005). "International Trade, Technological Innovation and Income: A Gravity Model Approach," IVIE working paper no. 2005–15, Catellón: IVIE.

Melitz, M. (2003). "The Impact of Trade on Intra-industry Reallocations and Aggregate Industry Productivity," *Econometrica* **71**: 1695–1725.

Neary, P. (2008). "Trade Cost and Foreign Direct Investment," in S. Brakman and H. Garretsen (eds.), *Foreign Direct Investment and Multinational Enterprise*, Cambridge, MA: MIT Press, pp. 13–39.

Piermartini, R. and R. Teh (2005). "Demystifying Modelling Methods for Trade Policy," WIT discussion paper no. 10, Geneva: WTO.

Pollins, B. M. (1989). "Conflict, Cooperation and Commerce," *American Journal of Political Science* **33**: 737–61.

Pöyhönen, P. (1963). "A Tentative Model for the Volume of Trade Between Countries," *Weltwirtschaftliches Archiv* **90**: 93–99.

Pullianen, K. A. (1963). "World Trade Study: An Econometric Model of the Patterns of the Commodity Flows in International Trade 1948–1960," *Ekonomiska Samfundets Tidskrift* **2**: 78–91.

26   van Bergeijk and Brakman

Rauch, J. E. (1999). "Networks versus Markets in International Trade," *Journal of International Economics* **48**: 7–35.

Ravenstein, E. G. (1885). "The Laws of Migration," *Journal of the Royal Statistical Society* **48**: 167–227.

Redding, S. and A. J. Venables (2004). "Economic Geography and International Inequality," *Journal of International Economics* **62**: 53–82.

Rose, A. K (2004). "Do We Really Know that the WTO Increases Trade?" *American Economic Review* **94**: 98–114.

——— (2007). "The Foreign Service and Foreign Trade: Embassies as Export Promotion," *The World Economy* **30**: 22–38.

Rose, A. K. and E. van Wincoop (2001). "National Money as a Barrier to International Trade: The Real Case for Currency Union," *American Economic Review* **91**: 386–90.

Santos Silva, J. and Tenreyro, S. (2006). "The Log of Gravity," *The Review of Economics and Statistics* **88**(4): 641–58.

Straathof, B. (2008). "Gravity with Gravitas: Comment," CPB discussion paper no. 111, The Haag.

Taplin, G. B. (1967). "Models of World Trade," IMF staff papers no. 14: 433–55.

Tinbergen, J. (1962). *Shaping the World Economy: Suggestions for an International Economic Policy*, New York: Twentieth Century Fund.

Wang, Z. K. and L. A. Winters (1991). "The Trading Potential of Eastern Europe," CEPR discussion paper no. 610, London: CEPR.

Ward, M. D. and P. D. Hoff (2005). "Persistent Patterns of International Commerce," Center for Statistics and the Social Science, working paper no. 45, University of Washington.

Part I

Methodology

2 A general equilibrium theory for estimating gravity equations of bilateral FDI, final goods trade, and intermediate trade flows

J. H. Bergstrand and P. Egger

> I think that we have spent way too much time on differentiated final goods, and neglected trade in intermediates . . . intermediates-inputs approach seems empirically very relevant, and formal econometric work would be very welcome.
> (James Markusen, interview in Leamer 2001, p. 382)

1 Introduction

Contrary to popular hype, the vast bulk of intermediates trade – that is, outsourcing – is *among* developed countries, not between developed and developing countries. This is consistent with Jabbour (2007), who showed in an extensive empirical analysis of 4,305 French firms (using survey data) that the vast bulk import their intermediate inputs from *other developed economies* through *arm's-length transactions*. Consequently, most intermediates trade is intra-industry (and likely "Ethier-type" intermediates trade). Because of the previous absence of a comprehensive dataset on intermediates and final goods trade flows, econometric analysis of the *determinants* of intermediates trade volumes/values is virtually non-existent, as our quote from Markusen (2001) suggests.[1] Egger and Egger (2005) provide one of only two empirical (gravity) analyses of a narrow aspect of outsourcing trade flows – bilateral "processing" trade among twelve European Union economies by national and multinational enterprises. The other empirical study is Baldone *et al.* (2002).[2] Aside

---

[1] Most of the empirical analyses of the consequences of outsourcing have had to focus instead on *multilateral* issues, such as relative price effects (that is, the effects on the "wage skill premium"), and for only a few specific countries.

[2] "Processing trade" refers to intermediates goods imports (exports) of countries that are "processed" (or value is added) in a special economic "zone" without tariffs imposed,

29

from these two empirical analyses, the absence of systematic intermediates versus final goods trade data has confined many researchers of
outsourcing to employing numerical simulations to study final and intermediates trade volumes (see Baier and Bergstrand 2000 and Yi 2003).
Moreover, the absence of bilateral trade data decomposed by final versus
intermediate goods has resulted in no motivation for developing a theoretical foundation for (separate) gravity equations for final goods bilateral
trade versus intermediates bilateral trade – much less one that accounts
for multinational enterprises, FDI, and potential consequences of outsourcing for these factors. As Markusen's quote suggests, it is now time to
pursue "formal econometric work" on the determinants of intermediates
trade flows – with Ethier-type intermediates trade in mind.

Consequently, in the spirit of the "Knowledge-Capital" model in
Markusen (2002) and the "Knowledge-and-Physical-Capital" model in
Bergstrand and Egger (2007), we develop a three-factor, three-country,
three-good general equilibrium model of multinational and national firms
with intermediates. A numerical version of the general equilibrium (GE)
model motivates a theoretical rationale for estimating gravity equations
of bilateral intermediate goods trade – and in a manner consistent with
estimating gravity equations of bilateral final goods trade and FDI flows.
Interestingly, the theoretical gravity equations for all three types of flows
are *not exactly the same*, and we use the GE model to explain the slightly
different theoretically motivated gravity specifications.[3] We find that economic size-related Ethier-type trade explains empirically the *vast bulk* of
the variation in bilateral intermediates international trade flows. Moreover, we provide empirical evidence that bilateral final goods trade flows,
intermediates trade flows, and FDI flows are all driven by a "common
process." This conclusion is important because it implies that previous
gravity equations of bilateral trade (FDI) flows including on the RHS
bilateral FDI (trade) flows are seriously mis-specified, likely suffering
from endogeneity bias.

The remainder of the paper is as follows. Section 2 motivates the analysis and discusses the construction of our new dataset of annual bilateral
final goods and intermediate goods trade flows among 160 countries for
the period 1990–2000. Section 3 presents the theoretical framework.

---

and then are re-exported to the original country with tariff exemption again. This is economically a very small portion of these countries' intermediates trade. Another empirical
analysis (non-gravity equation) of processing trade is Görg (2000).

[3] The introduction of intermediate goods introduces a complexity not present in Bergstrand
and Egger (2007), which did not distinguish between final and intermediates goods.
Markusen (2002, chapter 9) introduced a traded intermediate input; however, he
assumed (for some "exogenous reason") it could be produced in only one country (which
precluded two-way trade).

Section 4 summarizes the calibration of our theoretical model. Section 5 provides numerical results using our model suggesting a theoretical rationale for estimating gravity equations for bilateral final goods trade, intermediate goods trade, and FDI flows. Section 6 provides the empirical gravity equation results. Section 7 concludes.

2   Decomposing aggregate bilateral trade flows into final and intermediate goods trade flows

Recent books in the popular press such as Thomas Friedman's *The World is Flat* (2005) and associated newspaper articles on international "outsourcing" (also known as "fragmentation" or "slicing up the value chain") of intermediate stages of production suggest that the bulk of outsourcing is due to differences between countries in the cost of labor (relative wage rates). The stories suggest that increased international imports of developed economies from developing economies or increased outward FDI of developing countries to developed countries dominate international trade and FDI flows, respectively, in the past several years. However, it is useful first to look at the data – which suggest a *much different* story.

Table 2.1a presents a decomposition of international trade and FDI flows between and among developed and developing economies between 1990 and 2000. The first panel in the upper left corner of Table 2.1a provides data on the share of world trade flows (where, for empirical purposes, our "world" consists of 160 countries) among two groupings of economies, developed and developing. For empirical purposes, we consider the original 24 members of the Organization for Economic Cooperation and Development (OECD) as the "developed" economies and another 136 economies as the "developing" (or non-OECD) economies; in 1990 (our sample's beginning year) the OECD had only 24 members. As this panel shows, more than half of world trade flows are among the 24 richest (highest per capita income) economies in the world, which comprise only one-sixth of the number of countries in our sample. Moreover, only 15 per cent of OECD imports come from the developing economies – which contrasts sharply with the suggestions of *The World is Flat* and similar newspaper articles.

The panel in the upper right of Table 2.1a shows that (outward) FDI flows are also concentrated among the developed economies, in similar proportions to trade flows. 58 per cent of all outward FDI was among the 24 richest countries in the world. Thus, if multinational firms of OECD economies are investing abroad, the *vast bulk* of their FDI is with similar high per capita income economies, not with the developing world. Only 20 per cent of world outward FDI flows are from developed to developing economies. Therefore, as has been established in such

Table 2.1a. *Distribution of goods export flows and stocks of outward FDI among 24 OECD and 136 non-OECD countries (1990–2000)*

| | Total goods exports | | | Outward FDI stocks | |
	Importers			Hosts	
Exporters	OECD	Non-OECD	Parents	OECD	Non-OECD
OECD	55.56	19.89	OECD	57.58	20.32
Non-OECD	14.69	9.86	Non-OECD	16.50	5.60
	Final goods exports			Intermediate goods exports	
	Importers			Importers	
Exporters	OECD	Non-OECD	Exporters	OECD	Non-OECD
OECD	56.12	18.37	OECD	54.89	21.71
Non-OECD	16.72	8.79	Non-OECD	12.26	11.14

Table 2.1b. *Average annual growth of goods export flows and stocks of outward FDI among 24 OECD and 136 non-OECD countries (1990–2000)*

| | Total goods exports | | | Outward FDI stocks | |
	Importers			Hosts	
Exporters	OECD	Non-OECD	Parents	OECD	Non-OECD
OECD	4.21	7.70	OECD	13.15	10.12
Non-OECD	15.22	19.25	Non-OECD	18.92	9.40
	Final goods exports			Intermediate goods exports	
	Importers			Importers	
Exporters	OECD	Non-OECD	Exporters	OECD	Non-OECD
OECD	4.41	6.98	OECD	3.96	8.38
Non-OECD	14.57	18.46	Non-OECD	16.27	19.97

Notes: There are 24 OECD and 136 non-OECD countries in the data. Intermediate goods exports account for about 46 per cent of total exports in the data (for old OECD definition see the Appendix). FDI figures are based on data from the OECD (*Foreign Direct Investment Statistics Yearbook 2006*) and UNCTAD (Major FDI Indicators; *World Investment Report 2007*).

sources as Markusen (2002) and Barba Navaretti and Venables (2004, *Fact 2*), the bulk of international trade *and* FDI is among a small number of similar, developed economies; Markusen (2002) and others term this "horizontal" FDI.

Yet, data such as those presented in the upper panels of Table 2.1a are quite well known and are readily obtainable. *Much less known* is the information in the bottom two panels of Table 2.1a. These two panels decompose world trade flows into final goods trade flows and intermediate goods trade flows, using the new dataset that we constructed. Before explaining these data, we provide some background. As discussed briefly in the introduction, there has been limited systematic empirical analysis of international outsourcing of intermediates production owing to a dearth of comprehensive data decomposing trade into final and intermediate products.[4] As Feenstra (1994) notes, there have been only a few selected empirical treatments of outsourcing, which he cites. For instance, even though input-output tables exist for the United States and a few other industrialized economies, the US Input-Output (I-O) tables do not decompose intermediate inputs into imported and domestically produced intermediates (Feenstra 1994, p. 38). However, Feenstra and Hanson (1999) combine US industry data with US economy-wide I-O tables to calculate the increased share of imported intermediates in production in the United States. Campa and Goldberg (1997) perform similar calculations for Canada, Japan, the United Kingdom, and the United States and show similar trends, except for Japan. Hummels, Rapaport, and Yi (1998); Hummels, Ishii, and Yi (2001); and Yi (2003) do like computations for ten OECD economies to demonstrate increased outsourcing or – in their framework – increased "vertical specialization."

However, none of these studies or others has made an attempt to build a comprehensive dataset of bilateral trade flows for final and intermediates trade flows, starting with highly disaggregated bilateral trade flow data. Using the United Nations' (UN's) COMTRADE database, we aggregated five-digit Standard International Trade Classification (SITC) bilateral trade flows into (aggregate) bilateral final goods trade flows and bilateral intermediate goods trade flows according to the UN's *Classification by Broad Economic Categories* (2003), which distinguishes intermediates from final (consumer and capital) goods. The final goods trade flows aggregate 1,561 five-digit SITC categories and the intermediate goods trade flows aggregate 1,560 different five-digit SITC categories. Table 2.2 shows a decomposition into final and intermediates of the 3,121 economic categories used to create the two aggregates.

---

[4] A more typical decomposition of aggregate trade has been by industry classification rather than by final versus intermediates classification. Also, we note now that our intermediates (or final goods) data includes "intra-firm" intermediates trade, that is, intermediates trade between an MNE and an affiliate abroad; such trade is more accurately termed "offshoring" rather than outsourcing (since the latter is an arm's-length transaction). As we will address later, the share of intra-firm trade in total trade has been quite constant over time (especially within our sample).

Table 2.2. *Classification of Broad Economic Categories (BEC), revision 3, in terms of standard international trade classification five-digit lines*

Broad Economic Categories, revision 3, code	Number of SITC five-digit lines covered	Of which classified as intermediates
1 – Food and beverages	372	113
11 – Primary	140	44
111 – Mainly for industry	44	44
112 – Mainly for household consumption	96	0
12 – Processed	232	69
121 – Mainly for industry	69	69
122 – Mainly for household consumption	163	0
2 – Industrial supplies not elsewhere specified	1,526	1,107
21 – Primary	228	228
22 – Processed	1,298	879
3 – Fuels and lubricants	32	9
31 – Primary	9	9
32 – Processed	23	0
321 – Motor spirit	1	0
322 – Other	22	0
4 – Capital goods (except transport equipment), and parts and accessories thereof	637	273
41 – Capital goods (except transport equipment)	435	71
42 – Parts and accessories	202	202
5 – Transport equipment and parts and accessories thereof	112	58
51 – Passenger motor cars	1	0
52 – Other	53	0
53 – Parts and accessories	58	58
6 – Consumer goods not elsewhere specified	428	0
61 – Durable	96	0
62 – Semi-durable	208	0
63 – Non-durable	124	0
7 – Goods not elsewhere specified	14	0
Total	3,121	1,560

Notes: Source is the United Nations' Statistics Division. The total number of headings classified as intermediate goods is 1,560. The remaining categories are final goods.

The bottom two panels of Table 2.1a show the shares of world final goods and intermediate goods trade flows between and among OECD and non-OECD countries. The most notable conclusion is the striking similarity of the pattern of trade flows in final and intermediate goods. For *both* types of goods, approximately 55–56 per cent of world trade flows are among the OECD countries. Moreover, the remaining shares are also nearly identical to those for aggregate goods exports. Furthermore, the share of intermediate goods imports of OECD countries from non-OECD countries is only 12 per cent, even smaller than the 17 per cent for final goods imports. Thus, final goods – not intermediate goods – dominate developed countries' imports from the developing world.

Such data suggest that much – if not the majority – of world intermediates trade flows are *intra-industry* trade flows among similar, high per capita income economies – as is the case for the well-documented intra-industry trade in final goods that has been the subject of theoretical and empirical study for the last thirty years, see Grubel and Lloyd (1975). This conjecture regarding data is behind Markusen's quote above suggesting Ethier's (1982) "intermediates-input approach" as a motivation for much of world trade and "formal econometric work (of intermediates trade) would be very welcome." To put it simply, just as the bulk of international trade flows are intra-industry in nature and were explained by Helpman and Krugman (1985) using a model of intra-industry trade in final goods – and Markusen (2002) and Barba Navaretti and Venables (2004) showed that the bulk of FDI flows are intra-industry (horizontal) in nature – we show here that the bulk of intermediates outsourcing is intra-industry (Ethier-type) trade in nature. This is consistent with the results in Jabbour (2007) using an empirical analysis of survey data for 4,305 French firms.

Another interesting stylized fact from our dataset is that intermediates trade growth among OECD countries (3.96 per cent annually) has been slightly less than that of final goods trade growth (4.41 per cent annually) from 1990 to 2000. These growth rates are consistent with the data discussed in Hummels, Ishii, and Yi (2001) using the same *Classification by Broad Economic Categories*. However, we note that intermediates trade growth has exceeded final goods trade growth for trade between developed and developing countries and among developing countries between 1990 and 2000, in contrast to their conclusion of a "steadily declining since 1970" intermediates trade share.

In the remainder of this paper, we provide a theoretical and empirical model to address these stylized facts. The framework will address the main economic determinants of intermediate goods trade – in a manner consistent with explaining *final* goods trade *and* FDI flows.

3   **The theoretical model**

In this section, we develop a theoretical model to motivate estimating gravity equations of bilateral final goods trade, intermediate goods trade, and FDI flows (simultaneously) and to explain the growth of FDI (multinational firms) relative to trade (national firms). In the spirit of Ethier (1982), a key consideration is international trade in intermediate goods among similar developed economies. Since the vast amount of outsourcing and FDI is among developed economies with similar relative factor endowments and consequently similar relative real wage rates, then one could argue that "outsourcing" in general will not have the impact upon the convergence of relative wage rates internationally that the popular press suggests.[5]

To address these issues, we need a model that explains first the relationships between multinational enterprises that invest capital directly in foreign countries, national firms that trade either final or intermediate goods, FDI flows, final goods trade flows, and intermediate goods trade flows. To address bilateral flows in a multilateral world, we need three countries. The model we develop is a three-country, three-factor, three-good model of MNEs and national enterprises with internationally immobile skilled and unskilled labor, internationally mobile physical capital, and final and intermediate goods, in the spirit of Markusen's "Knowledge-Capital" model. In fact, the "Knowledge-and-Physical-Capital" model developed in Bergstrand and Egger (2007), which is an extension of the "Knowledge-Capital" model of Markusen (2002), is a special case (with no intermediates production) of our model here.

As background, the Knowledge-and-Physical-Capital model in Bergstrand and Egger (2007) is a three-factor, three-country, two-good extension of Markusen's $2 \times 2 \times 2$ Knowledge-Capital model with national enterprises (NEs), horizontal multinational enterprises (HMNEs), and vertical multinational enterprises (VMNEs). The demand side in the Knowledge-and-Physical-Capital model is analogous to that in the Knowledge-Capital model. However, the former extends the latter in two significant ways. The first distinction is to use *three* primary factors of production: unskilled labor, skilled labor (or human/knowledge capital), and physical capital. We assume unskilled and skilled labor are immobile

---

[5] We do not argue that vertical FDI and inter-industry trade between developed and developing countries with differing relative factor endowments (such as the United States and China) has not grown; it has (as our Table 2.1b suggests) and has likely contributed to the rise in income inequality in developed economies. Rather, our goal *here* is to highlight, and confirm empirically, the overlooked argument that the *bulk* of outsourcing is more likely due to horizontal (intra-industry) considerations.

internationally, but physical capital is mobile in the sense that MNEs will endogenously choose the optimal allocation of domestic physical capital between home and foreign locations to maximize profits, consistent with the BEA definition of foreign "direct investment positions" using domestic and foreign-affiliate shares of real fixed investment.[6] Thus, unlike the Knowledge-Capital model, we actually have *FDI* (as well as foreign affiliate sales).[7] The introduction of a third factor – combined with an assumption that headquarters' fixed setups require home skilled labor (to represent, say, research and development [R&D] costs) while the setup of a plant in any country requires the home country's physical capital (to represent, say, equipment) – can explain "coexistence" of HMNEs and NEs for two identically sized developed countries for a wide range of parameter values (which is precluded in the Knowledge-Capital model).[8]

The second distinction of the Knowledge-and-Physical-Capital model is to introduce a "third country." The presence of the third country helps explain the "complementarity" of bilateral foreign affiliate sales (FAS) and trade with respect to a country pair's economic size and similarity and that bilateral FDI empirically tends to be maximized when the home country's GDP is larger than the host country's. Hence, the three-factor, three-country, two-good model in Bergstrand and Egger (2007) provides a theoretical foundation for estimating "gravity equations" of bilateral

[6] In the typical 2 × 2 × 2 model, headquarters use home skilled labor exclusively for setups; home (foreign) plants use home (foreign) skilled labor for setups (see Markusen 2002, p. 80). With only immobile skilled and unskilled labor, the two-factor models preclude home physical capital being utilized to set up foreign plants. We often refer to the transfer of physical capital by MNEs as capital "mobility." Consistent with Markusen (2002) and the modern MNE literature, the model is "real"; there are no paper assets. In this regard, we follow the more traditional (pre-1960) literature defining capital mobility in terms of movement of physical capital, see Mundell (1957, pp. 321–23), Jones (1967), and Helpman and Razin (1983). Moreover, while physical capital can be "utilized" in different countries, "ownership" of any country's endowment of such capital is immobile; again, we follow Mundell (1957) in this regard: "Capital is here considered a physical, homogeneous factor . . . It is further assumed that capitalists qua consuming units do not move with their capital, so national taste patterns are unaltered." In reality, of course, the presence of (paper) "claims" to physical capital allows much easier "transfer" of resources and is *one* way of measuring FDI. However, the "current-cost" method of measuring FDI is related to the shares of an MNE's *real* fixed investment in plant and equipment that is allocated to the home country relative to foreign affiliate(s); this effectively measures physical capital mobility, see Borga and Yorgason (2002, p. 27). Also, (bilateral) FDI stocks are the accumulation of (bilateral) FDI flows over several periods. Since our model is static, FDI flows and stocks are necessarily identical in the model.

[7] Markusen (2002, p. 8) notes clearly that the models in his book "are addressed more closely to affiliate output and sales than to investments stocks."

[8] As in Markusen (2002), internationally immobile skilled labor still creates firm-specific intangible assets that are costlessly shared internationally by MNEs with their plants. This aspect is maintained.

FDI and aggregate trade flows *simultaneously*. However, the model in Bergstrand and Egger (2007) does not differentiate between final goods trade and intermediate goods trade.

The model in this chapter is a more general version of the model in Bergstrand and Egger (2007) by introducing a third good (intermediates) – more accurately, a *second production stage* – to distinguish final from intermediate goods. Here, we separate national firms that produce and export final goods for consumers from national firms that produce and export intermediate goods that can be purchased by other national firms that produce final goods *or* horizontal MNEs with headquarters and a plant in one country but additional plants in either one or two other countries to serve local markets *or* vertical MNEs with headquarters in one country but a plant in another country due to different relative factor endowments between the two countries. Hence, a representative intermediates firm in some country *i* can sell its output to final goods-producing NEs, HMNEs or VMNEs based in its own country, in another country *j*, or in the rest of the world (*ROW*). All intermediate goods purchases are "arm's-length" transactions between legally distinct entities; hence, they conform to the conventional definition of "outsourcing." Introducing domestic and international outsourcing of intermediates to the model of Bergstrand and Egger (2007) enhances dramatically the complexity of the model.[9]

3.1   Consumers

The demand side of this model (described in this section) is identical to that in Bergstrand and Egger (2007). Consumers are assumed to have a Cobb–Douglas utility function between final differentiated goods (*X*) and homogeneous goods (*Y*). Consumers' tastes for final differentiated products (e.g. manufactures) are assumed to be of the Dixit–Stiglitz constant elasticity of substitution (CES) type, as typical in trade. We let V_i denote the utility of the representative consumer in country *i*. Let η be the Cobb–Douglas parameter reflecting the relative importance of manufactures in utility and ε be the parameter determining the constant elasticity of substitution, σ, among these manufactured products ($\sigma \equiv 1 - \varepsilon$, $\varepsilon < 0$). Manufactures can be produced by three different firm types: national firms (n), horizontal multinational firms (h), and vertical multinational

---

[9] Moreover, introducing MNE intra-firm trade in intermediates introduces yet another level of complexity far beyond the scope of this paper. However, we will document later that data used in other studies suggest that the share of intra-firm trade in all intermediates trade has been *constant* (or declining) over the 1990s, the period examined in our study.

firms (v). In equilibrium, some of these firms may not exist (depending upon absolute and relative factor endowments and parameter values). These will be reflected in three sets of components in the first of two RHS bracketed terms in equation (2.1) below:

$$
V_i = \left[\begin{array}{c} \sum_{j=1}^{3} n_j \left(\dfrac{x_{ji}^{n}}{1 + \tau_{Xji}} \right)^{\frac{\varepsilon}{\varepsilon-1}} \\[2ex] + \left(\sum_{j=1}^{3} h_{3,j} (x_{ii}^{h3})^{\frac{\varepsilon}{\varepsilon-1}} \right. \\[2ex] + \sum_{j \neq i} h_{2,ij} (x_{ii}^{h2})^{\frac{\varepsilon}{\varepsilon-1}} \\[2ex] \left. + \sum_{j \neq i} h_{2,ji} (x_{ii}^{h2})^{\frac{\varepsilon}{\varepsilon-1}} \right) \\[2ex] + \sum_{k \neq j} \sum_{j=1}^{3} v_{kj} \left(\dfrac{x_{ji}^{v}}{1 + \tau_{Xji}} \right)^{\frac{\varepsilon}{\varepsilon-1}} \end{array} \right]^{\frac{\varepsilon-1}{\varepsilon}\eta} \left[\sum_{j=1}^{3} Y_{ji} \right]^{1-\eta}
$$

(2.1)

The first component reflects *national* (non-MNE) firms, or NEs, that can produce final differentiated goods for the home market or export to foreign markets from a single plant in the country with their headquarters, where: x_{ji}^{n} denotes the (endogenous) output of country j's representative national firm in industry X sold to country i; n_j is the (endogenous) number of these national firms in j; and τ_{Xji} is the gross (shipment) trade cost of exporting X from j to i.

The second set of components reflects *horizontal* multinational firms, or HMNEs, that may have plants in either two or three countries to be "proximate" to markets to avoid trade costs; HMNEs cannot export goods. Every HMNE has a plant in its headquarters country. Let x_{ii} denote the output of a horizontal multinational firm producing in i and selling in i; $h_{3,j}$ denote the (endogenous) number of multinationals that produce in all three countries and are headquartered in j ($j = 1, 2, 3$); $h_{2,ij}$ denote the number of two-country multinationals headquartered in i with a plant also in j; and $h_{2,ji}$ denote the number of two-country multinationals headquartered in j with a plant also in i. Hence, x_{ii}^{h3} is output produced in country i (and consumed in i) of the representative three-country HMNE headquartered in country j and x_{ii}^{h2} is the output produced in country i (and consumed in i) of the representative two-country multinational firm either headquartered in i with a plant also in j or headquartered in j with a plant also in i. Note that h_2 plants arise when market size in one of the three countries is insufficient to warrant a local plant, and is more efficiently served (given transport and investment costs) by its own national firms and imports from foreign firms.

The third component reflects *vertical* multinational firms or VMNEs. VMNEs have headquarters in one country and a plant in one of the other countries, just not in the headquarters country. The primary motivation for a vertical MNE is "cost differences"; different relative factor intensities and relative factor abundances motivate separating headquarters from production into different countries. Let v_{kj} denote the number of vertical multinational firms with headquarters in k, a plant in j, and output can be sold to any country (including k). Let x_{ji}^v denote the output of the representative VMNE with production in j and consumption in i.[10]

In the second bracketed RHS term, let Y_{ji} denote the output of the homogenous good (e.g. agriculture) produced in country j under constant returns to scale using unskilled labor and consumed in i. Let t_{Xji} (t_{Yji}) denote the gross trade cost for shipping final differentiated (homogeneous) good X (Y) from j to i; let t_{Zji} be defined for intermediates similarly.[11] Let $t_{Xji} = 1$ for $i = j$, and analogously for t_{Yji} and t_{Zji}. It will be useful to define gross trade costs as follows:

$$t_{Xji} = (1 + b_{Xji})(1 + \tau_{Xji})$$
$$t_{Yji} = (1 + b_{Yji})(1 + \tau_{Yji})$$
$$t_{Zji} = (1 + b_{Zji})(1 + \tau_{Zji})$$

where τ denotes a "natural" trade cost of physical shipment (cif/fob $-$ 1) of the "iceberg" type, while b represents a "policy" trade cost (i.e. tariff rate) which generates potential revenue. For instance, b_{Xji} denotes the tariff rate (e.g. $0.05 = 5$ per cent) on imports from j to i in differentiated final good X.

[10] Recently, some researchers have considered hybrid MNEs, see Grossman *et al.* (2003), Yeaple (2003), and Ekholm *et al.* (2007). The focus of these papers is much different than ours; they demonstrate conditions when an MNE pursues both horizontal and vertical integration. Research there has been directed towards understanding more clearly how multinational firms endogenously become "hybrids" in the presence of intermediate goods production and a third country. The goal of their research is to examine theoretically the sectoral factors, such as transport costs, investment costs, and headquarters setup relative to plant setup costs, driving the "optimal" structure of a multinational firm, in terms of location of plants and headquarters. Our model here could be enriched by allowing hybrid MNEs, but at a high cost of introducing a complexity that would obscure the main issues of this paper. We leave this for future research.

[11] For modeling convenience, we define Y_{ji} net of trade costs; trade costs t_{Yji} surface explicitly in the factor-endowment constraints in the Appendix.

The budget constraint of the representative consumer in country i is assumed to be:

$$\sum_{j=i}^{3} n_j p_{Xj}^n x_{ji}^n + \sum_{j=i}^{3} h_{3,j} p_{Xi}^{h3} x_{ii}^{h3} + \sum_{j\neq i} h_{2,ij} p_{Xi}^{h2} x_{ii}^{h2} + \sum_{j\neq i} h_{2,ji} p_{Xi}^{h2} x_{ii}^{h2}$$

$$+ \sum_{k\neq j} \sum_{j\neq i} v_{kj} p_{Xj}^v x_{ji}^v + \sum_{j=i}^{3} p_{Yj} Y_{ji}$$

$$= r_i K_i + w_{Si} S_i + w_{Ui} U_i + \sum_{j\neq i} n_j b_{Xji} p_{Xj}^n x_{ji}^n$$

$$+ \sum_{k\neq j} \sum_{j\neq i} v_{kj} b_{Xji} p_{Xj}^v x_{ji}^v + \sum_{j\neq i} b_{Yji} p_{Yj} Y_{ji} + \sum_{j\neq i} o_j b_{Zji} p_{Zj} z_{ji}$$

$$(2.2)$$

where p_{Xi}^{h3} (p_{Xi}^{h2}) denotes the price charged by the representative three-country (two-country) horizontal MNE with a plant in i. Let p_{Xj}^n, p_{Xj}^v, p_{Yj}, and p_{Zj} denote the prices charged by producers in j for goods X (national firms and vertical MNEs, respectively), Y, and Z, respectively. The first three RHS terms denote factor income; the last four denote tariff revenue redistributed lump-sum by the government in i back to the representative consumer. Let r_i denote the rental rate for capital in i, K_i is the capital stock in i, w_{Si} (w_{Ui}) is the wage rate for skilled (unskilled) workers in i, and S_i (U_i) is the stock of skilled (unskilled) workers in i. Let o_j denote the number of intermediate good producers in country j.

Maximizing (2.1) subject to (2.2) yields the domestic demand functions:

$$x_{ii}^\ell \geq \left(p_{Xi}^\ell\right)^{\varepsilon-1} P_{Xi}^{-\varepsilon} \eta E_i; \quad \ell = \{n, h_3, h_2, v\} \qquad (2.3)$$

where E_i is the income (and expenditure) of the representative consumer in country i from equation (2.2), and

$$P_{Xi} = \left[\sum_{j=1}^{3} n_j \left(t_{Xji} p_{Xj}^n\right)^\varepsilon + \sum_{j=1}^{3} h_{3,j} \left(p_{Xi}^{h3}\right)^\varepsilon + \sum_{j\neq i} h_{2,ij} \left(p_{Xi}^{h2}\right)^\varepsilon \right.$$

$$\left. + \sum_{j\neq i} h_{2,ji} \left(p_{Xi}^{h2}\right)^\varepsilon + \sum_{k\neq j} \sum_{j=1}^{3} v_{kj} \left(t_{Xji} p_{Xj}^v\right)^\varepsilon \right]^{\frac{1}{\varepsilon}} \qquad (2.4)$$

is the corresponding CES price index. Following the literature, we assume that all firms producing in the same country face the same technology and marginal costs and we assume complementary-slackness conditions (see Markusen 2002). Hence, the mill (or ex-manufacturer) prices of all varieties in a specific country are equal in equilibrium. Then, the relationship between differentiated final goods produced in j and at home is:

$$\frac{x_{ji}}{x_{ii}} = \left(\frac{p_{Xj}}{p_{Xi}}\right)^{\varepsilon-1} t_{Xji}^{\varepsilon}(1 + b_{Xji})^{-1} \tag{2.5}$$

Hence, from now on we can omit superscripts for both prices and quantities of differentiated products for the ease of presentation. It follows that homogeneous goods demand is:

$$\sum_{j=1}^{3} Y_{ji} \geq \frac{1-\eta}{p_{Yi}} E_i \quad \perp \quad p_{Yi} \geq 0 \tag{2.6}$$

where Y_{ji} denotes output of the agriculture good of county j demanded in country i.

Beginning with the next section, the model generalizes that in Bergstrand and Egger (2007) by addressing final *and intermediates* production issues.

3.2   Final differentiated good producers

We assume that final goods can be produced in all three countries, composed potentially of intermediates from all three countries and three primary factors: skilled labor, unskilled labor, and physical capital. Each country is assumed to be endowed with exogenous amounts of skilled labor and unskilled labor, which are internationally immobile. We assume an exogenous world endowment of physical capital which is mobile internationally; physical capital moves endogenously across countries to maximize MNEs' profits. Thus, we model explicitly the endogenous determination of bilateral FDI flows. Final differentiated goods producers operate in monopolistically competitive markets, similar to Markusen (2002, chapter 6); intermediates will be discussed later in Section 2.4.

An important distinction of our model from the $2 \times 2 \times 2$ Knowledge-Capital model is that we introduce the third factor, physical capital. As summarized in Markusen (2002), the $2 \times 2 \times 2$ model has tended to use skilled labor and unskilled labor as its two internationally immobile factors. Other papers in this literature have used labor and capital, but

with the latter usually assumed internationally immobile. Yet, all formal
models in this class have had only two factors. Three critical assumptions
for our theoretical results that follow are the existence of a third, internationally mobile factor – physical capital – and that any headquarter's
setup (fixed cost) requires home skilled labor – to represent the notion of
R&D – and any plant's setup in any country requires the home country's
physical capital – to represent the resources needed for a domestic or
foreign direct investment.[12]
    Assume the production of differentiated final good X is given by the
nested Cobb–Douglas–CES technology:

$$F_{Xi} = B(K_{Xi}^\chi + S_{Xi}^\chi)^{\frac{\alpha}{\chi}} (U_{Xi}^\delta + Z_{Xi}^\delta)^{\frac{1-\alpha}{\delta}} \qquad (2.7)$$

where F_{Xi} denotes production of final goods for both the domestic and
foreign markets; we assume MNEs and national enterprises (NEs) have
access to the same technology. K_{Xi}, S_{Xi}, U_{Xi}, and Z_{Xi} denote the quantities used of physical capital, skilled labor (or human capital), unskilled
labor, and intermediates, respectively, in country i to produce X. The
specific form of the production function is motivated by three literatures.
First, the Cobb–Douglas function is useful in characterizing analytically
and empirically the relatively constant production shares of capital and
labor. Second, early work by Griliches (1969) indicates that physical capital and human capital tend to be complements, rather than substitutes,
in technology; recent evidence for this in the MNE literature is found
in Slaughter (2000). This suggests nesting a CES production function
within the Cobb–Douglas function to allow for the potential complementarity or substitutability of physical and human capital. Third, recent
work on outsourcing suggests that intermediate goods are substitutes for
unskilled labor; the second CES sub-production function allows the elasticity of substitution between intermediates and unskilled labor to exceed
unity. As the latter two issues are less known to trade economists, we
address them in more depth in Section 4 when we describe the calibration
of the numerical general equilibrium (GE) model.
    National firms and MNEs differ in fixed costs. Each NE incurs only
one firm setup and one plant setup; each MNE incurs one firm setup
(the cost of which is assumed larger than that of an NE, as in Markusen

---

[12] Note that, while physical capital can be "utilized" in different countries, the "ownership"
of any country's endowment of such capital is immobile. In the typical $2 \times 2 \times 2$ model,
headquarters use home skilled labor exclusively for setups; home (foreign) plants use
home (foreign) labor for setups (see Markusen 2002, p. 80). With only immobile skilled
and unskilled labor, these models naturally preclude home physical capital being utilized
to set up foreign plants.

2002) and a plant setup for its home market and for each foreign market it endogenously enters. A horizontal MNE has a headquarters at home and plants potentially in either two or three markets to serve them; it has no exports. A vertical MNE has a headquarters at home and one plant abroad, which can export to any market.

Let Z_{Xi} denote the CES aggregate of intermediate inputs:

$$Z_{Xi} = \left[\sum_{j=1}^{3} o_j \left(\frac{z_{ji}}{t_{Zji}} \right)^{\frac{\theta}{\theta-1}} \right]^{\frac{\theta-1}{\theta}} \tag{2.8}$$

where z_{ji} denotes the output of the representative firm in country j supplying intermediates goods to country i and $\theta < 0$. The corresponding CES price index for Z_{Xi} is:

$$P_{Zi} = \left[\sum_{j=1}^{3} o_j \left(t_{Zji} p_{Zj} \right)^{\theta} \right]^{\frac{1}{\theta}} \tag{2.9}$$

Maximizing profits subject to the above technology yields the following conditional factor demands (denoted with $*$) and input coefficients:

$$K_{Xi}^* = F_{Xi} \underbrace{\frac{1}{B} \left(\frac{w_{Ui}}{r_i} \frac{\alpha}{1-\alpha} \right)^{1-\alpha} T_{1i}^{\frac{\alpha(\chi-1)-\chi}{\chi}} T_{2i}^{\frac{(1-\alpha)(\delta-1)}{\delta}}}_{a_{KXi}}$$

$$S_{Xi}^* = F_{Xi} \underbrace{\frac{1}{B} \left(\frac{w_{Ui}}{w_{Si}} \frac{\alpha}{1-\alpha} \right)^{1-\alpha} T_{2i}^{\frac{(\alpha-1)(1-\delta)}{\delta}} T_{3i}^{\frac{\alpha(\chi-1)-\chi}{\chi}}}_{a_{SXi}}$$

$$U_{Xi}^* = F_{Xi} \underbrace{\frac{1}{B} \left(\frac{r_i}{w_{Ui}} \frac{1-\alpha}{\alpha} \right)^{\alpha} T_{1i}^{\frac{\alpha(\chi-1)}{\chi}} T_{2i}^{\frac{\alpha(1-\delta)-1}{\delta}}}_{a_{UXi}}$$

$$Z_{Xi}^* = F_{Xi} \underbrace{\frac{1}{B} \left(\frac{r_i}{P_{Zi}} \frac{1-\alpha}{\alpha} \right)^{\alpha} T_{1i}^{\frac{\alpha(\chi-1)}{\chi}} T_{4i}^{\frac{\alpha(1-\delta)-1}{\delta}}}_{a_{ZXi}}$$

$$\text{(2.10a–2.10d)}$$

where B is a constant and we introduce definitions:

$$T_{1i} = 1 + \left(\frac{r_i}{w_{Si}}\right)^{\frac{\chi}{1-\chi}} ; \qquad T_{2i} = 1 + \left(\frac{P_{Zi}}{w_{Ui}}\right)^{\frac{\delta}{1-\delta}} ;$$

$$T_{3i} = 1 + \left(\frac{w_{Si}}{r_i}\right)^{\frac{\chi}{1-\chi}} ; \qquad T_{4i} = 1 + \left(\frac{w_{Ui}}{P_{Zi}}\right)^{\frac{\delta}{1-\delta}} \qquad (2.11a\text{-}2.11d)$$

3.3   Final homogeneous goods producers

We assume that the homogeneous good (Y) is produced under constant returns to scale in perfectly competitive markets using only unskilled labor; assume the technology $Y_i = U_i \, (i = 1, 2, 3)$. In the presence of positive trade costs, we assume country 1 is the numeraire; hence, $p_{Y1} = w_{U1} = 1$.

3.4   Intermediate differentiated goods producers

Our model is a more general version of the three-factor, three-country, two-good model in Bergstrand and Egger (2007) to include outsourcing of intermediate goods. Outsourcing, by definition, is a trade between unaffiliated firms. Feenstra (1994) cites several empirical studies suggesting that trade in intermediates is growing faster than trade in final goods, reflecting the outsourcing issue. With much of this paper focused on MNE behavior, one might assume that our model will introduce *intra-firm* (MNE) trade in intermediates, or "intermediates offshoring." By contrast, we will assume that intermediates are produced by *national* firms (not MNE affiliates); thus, arm's-length intermediate imports generate "outsourcing," using the conventional definition.[13] However, our model allows final goods offshoring by vertical MNEs.

Importantly, the vast bulk of intermediates trade is between *unaffiliated* firms. We note several studies supporting this claim. First, data on intra-firm trade is scarce, with only the Japanese, Swedish, and US governments as possible sources. Grimwade (1989) presents data from the US Tariff Commission that indicates, in 1977, only 36 (64) per cent of total US exports were intra-firm (between unaffiliated firms); however, this data is admittedly dated. Second, Markusen (2002, chapter 1) presents US BEA data on parent-affiliate trade as a proportion of total affiliate sales with major trading partners for 1987 and 1997. Regardless

---

[13] Of course, in the context of the model, there is costless intra-firm exchange of intangible assets of MNEs.

46   Bergstrand and Egger

of year, exports vs. imports, or outward vs. inward data, parent-affiliates trade was *never more than 15 per cent* of total affiliate sales. Third, Filipe *et al.* (2002) report annual data from the US BEA specifically on intrafirm trade as a share of total US trade (by exports, imports or both) from 1989 to 1998. Interestingly, averaging imports and exports, intra-firm US trade by MNEs was at a maximum of 44 per cent in 1989–90 and actually *declined* to only 38 per cent in 1997–98, even though intermediates trade was growing as a share of final and intermediates trade in the 1990s, see Hummels, Ishii, and Yi (2001) and Yi (2003). Fourth, this is consistent with Jabbour (2007) using French firm data showing that intra-firm MNE trade is no more than 30 per cent of international offshoring. Finally, Bernard *et al.* (2005) provide data for the United States for 1993 and 2000 and show that intra-firm trade as a share of MNEs' trade was virtually constant from 1993 to 2000, precluding an increased intra-firm trade share as a possible source of increased FDI to final goods trade. These studies confirm the importance of intermediates trade among *unaffiliated* firms. To be consistent with these observations (while also limiting the model's complexity and scope), we model intermediates trade as among unaffiliated firms, even though we still allow vertical MNEs to export *final* goods from a foreign plant to a home country's consumer.[14]

We assume that differentiated intermediate products for the (national) representative (type o) firm in country i are produced in monopolistically competitive markets given a Cobb–Douglas technology:

$$z_i = AS_{Zi}^{\beta}U_{Zi}^{1-\beta} \tag{2.12}$$

where z_i denotes production of intermediate goods for both the domestic and foreign markets. Local intermediate goods supply from a single intermediate goods producer in market i for local demand is referred to as z_{ii}, whereas supply to (and, in equilibrium, demand gross of transport costs in) a foreign market j is denoted by z_{ij}. As for national final goods exporters, any (national) intermediate firm incurs one headquarters setup and one plant setup.[15] The above technology yields the

[14] In the future, one could also allow intra-firm trade in intermediates, as in Markusen (2002, chapter 9). However, at this time, this would introduce yet another level of complexity well beyond the scope of this already fairly intricate model.
[15] One might argue that – since we are precluding multinational firms in producing intermediates – there might be no reason to distinguish headquarters fixed costs from plant fixed costs, as is done for national firms producing final goods. However, as will be apparent shortly in equations (2.16a)–(2.16e), the input requirements are general enough simply to allow different relative factor requirements of human and physical capital in

following conditional factor demands and input coefficients:

$$S_{Zi}^* = z_i \underbrace{\frac{1}{A}\left(\frac{w_{Ui}}{w_{Si}}\frac{\beta}{1-\beta}\right)^{1-\beta}}_{a_{SZi}}$$

$$(2.13a-2.13b)$$

$$U_{Zi}^* = z_i \underbrace{\frac{1}{A}\left(\frac{w_{Si}}{w_{Ui}}\frac{1-\beta}{\beta}\right)^{\beta}}_{a_{UZi}}$$

An intermediate goods producer in the intermediate goods market equilibrium is faced with local (domestic) demand:

$$z_{ii} \geq \left(\frac{P_{Zi}}{p_{Zi}}\right)^{1-\theta} a_{ZXi}\left[n_i \sum_{j=1}^{3} x_{ij} + x_{ii}\left(\sum_{j=1}^{3} h_{3,j} + \sum_{j\neq i} h_{2,ji} + \sum_{j\neq i} h_{2,ij}\right)\right.$$

$$\left. + \sum_{j\neq i} v_{ji}\left(\sum_{j=1}^{3} x_{ij}\right)\right] \qquad (2.14)$$

and the relationship between foreign and domestically sourced intermediates is:

$$\frac{z_{ji}}{z_{ii}} = \left(\frac{p_{Zi}}{p_{Zj}}\right)^{1-\theta} t_{Zji}^{\theta}\left(1+b_{Zji}\right)^{-1} \qquad (2.15)$$

3.5   Profit functions and pricing equations

All firms are assumed to maximize profits given the technologies assumed and the demand curves suggested above. The profit functions are:

$$\pi_{oi} = (p_{Zi} - c_{Zi})\sum_{j=1}^{3} z_{ij} - a_{Soi}w_{Si} - a_{Koi}r_i$$

$$\pi_{ni} = (p_{Xi} - c_{Xi})\sum_{j=1}^{3} x_{ij} - a_{Sni}w_{Si} - a_{Kni}r_i$$

the setups of headquarters and plants for national final good and national intermediate good producers. For now, we allow each intermediates producer to "set up" a headquarters (to research, advertise, or distribute its product) and a plant.

$$\pi_{h3,i} = \sum_{j=1}^{3} (p_{Xj} - c_{Xj})x_{jj} - a_{Smi}w_{Si} - a_{Kmi}\left[3 + \sum_{j \neq i} \gamma_{ij}\right]r_i$$

$$\pi_{h2,ij} = (p_{Xi} - c_{Xi})x_{ii} + (p_{Xj} - c_{Xj})x_{jj} - a_{Smi}w_{Si} - a_{Kmi}[2 + \gamma_{ij}]r_i$$

$$\pi_{v,ij} = (p_{Xj} - c_{Xj})\sum_{k=1}^{3} x_{jk} - a_{Smi}w_{Si} - a_{Kmi}[1 + \gamma_{ij}]r_i$$

$$(2.16a\text{--}2.16e)$$

Equation (2.16a) is the profit function for an intermediate goods producer in country i. Let c_{Zi} denote marginal costs of intermediate goods production in i and the latter two RHS terms represent fixed (domestic) skilled labor and physical capital costs for the intermediate goods producer to set up a headquarters and a plant. Equation (2.16b) is the profit function for each national final goods enterprise (NE) in i. Let c_{Xi} denote marginal production costs of differentiated final good X in country i and the latter two RHS terms represent fixed human and physical capital costs for the national enterprise final goods producer. Equation (2.16c) is the profit function for each horizontal final-good-producing multinational firm in country i with three operations (one in the parent country and one in each of two foreign markets). The last two terms in (2.16c) represent fixed costs of each three-country horizontal MNE. As with previous firms, the MNE incurs a single fixed cost of home skilled labor to set up a firm. However, each three-country MNE incurs a fixed cost of home physical capital for each plant. Moreover, each foreign investment incurs a potential investment cost γ (say, policy or natural FDI barrier). Equation (2.16d) is the profit function for each horizontal final-good-producing multinational firm in country i with two operations (one at home). Finally, equation (2.16e) is the profit function for a vertical MNE with a headquarters in i and a plant in j.

A key element of our model is that – in each country – the numbers of national intermediates producers (type o), national final goods enterprises (type n), three-country horizontal MNEs (type h_3), two-country horizontal MNEs (type h_2), and vertical MNEs (type v) are *endogenous* to the model. Two conditions characterize models in this class. First, profit maximization ensures markup pricing equations:

$$p_{Zi} \leq \frac{c_{Zi}(\theta - 1)}{\theta} \qquad p_{Xi} \leq \frac{c_{Xi}(\varepsilon - 1)}{\varepsilon} \qquad (2.17)$$

Second, free entry and exit ensures:

$$a_{Soi}w_{Si} + a_{Koi}r_i \geq \frac{c_{Zi}(\theta - 1)}{\theta} \sum_{j=1}^{3} z_{ij}$$

$$a_{Sni}w_{Si} + a_{Kni}r_i \geq \frac{c_{Xi}(\varepsilon - 1)}{\varepsilon} \sum_{j=1}^{3} x_{ij}$$

$$a_{Smi}w_{Si} + a_{Kmi}\left[3 + \sum_{i \neq j} \gamma_{ij}\right] r_i \geq \sum_{j=1}^{3} \frac{c_{Xj}(\varepsilon - 1)}{\varepsilon} x_{jj}$$

$$a_{Smi}w_{Si} + a_{Kmi}[2 + \gamma_{ij}]r_i \geq \frac{c_{Xi}(\varepsilon - 1)}{\varepsilon} x_{ii} + \frac{c_{Xj}(\varepsilon - 1)}{\varepsilon} x_{jj}$$

$$a_{Smi}w_{Si} + a_{Kmi}[1 + \gamma_{ij}]r_i \geq \frac{c_{Xj}(\varepsilon - 1)}{\varepsilon} \sum_{k=1}^{3} x_{jk}$$

$$(2.18a)-(2.18e)$$

3.6   Factor-endowment and current-account-balance constraints

We assume that, in equilibrium, all factors are fully employed and that every country maintains multilateral (though not bilateral) current account balance; endogenous bilateral current account imbalances allow for endogenous bilateral FDI of physical capital. Following the established literature, this is a static model. The formal factor-endowment and multilateral current-account-balance constraints are provided in the Appendix.

4   Calibration of the model

The complexity of the model, including the complementary-slackness conditions shown, introduces a high degree of non-linearity, and it cannot be solved analytically. Consequently, we provide numerical solutions to the model, as in Markusen (2002) and related studies. In order to address interesting issues, we can potentially employ our three-country model to distinguish among four different scenarios: (i) bilateral trade and FDI flows between two developed economies, or intra-DC flows (with a less developed third country or LDC); (ii) bilateral flows from a DC to an LDC (with a developed third country); (iii) bilateral flows from an LDC to a DC (with a developed third country); and (iv) bilateral flows from an LDC to another LDC, or intra-LDC flows (with a developed third country). A key consideration is that – due to the non-linearities of the model – the *marginal* effects of bilateral economic sizes, relative factor endowment differences, and transaction costs on bilateral trade and investment flows will differ depending upon the economic characteristics of the ROW. As the stylized facts in Section 2 suggest though, we focus on intra-DC (or OECD) flows, reserving analysis of DC-LDC flows and intra-LDC flows for future work. We use GAMS for our numerical analysis.

4.1   Exogenous variables

Our intent is to keep as close to the spirit of modern GE models of multinational firms as possible. In this regard, we note the following assumptions made about the exogenous variables in our model.[16]

For analytical purposes, the relative size of endowments among the three countries matters. We assume a world endowment of capital (K) of 240 units, skilled labor (S) of 90 units, and unskilled labor (U) of 100 units. In our case studying intra-DC trade, ROW represents the developing world. Since our focus will be on estimating gravity equations using primarily OECD data, it makes sense to treat the ROW as the developing world. Initially, we set country i's (j's) relative shares of the world endowments of physical capital and skilled labor at 1/3 (1/3) and ROW's at 1/3 (as in Bergstrand and Egger 2007), and country i's (j's) share of unskilled labor at 1/4 (1/4) and ROW's at 1/2 (to make ROW a developing country). Hence, both DCs are capital- and skilled-labor abundant relative to ROW. While initially i and j have the same GDPs as ROW, our simulations will show that our theoretical relationships hold for a wide choice of relative economic sizes (that match the distribution of GDPs for OECD countries), so that the choice of initial endowments is not limiting.

We appealed to actual trade data to choose initial values for transport costs (rather than choosing values arbitrarily as in the literature). Using the United Nations' (UN's) COMTRADE data, we aggregated bilateral five-digit Standard International Trade Classification (SITC) trade flows into aggregate bilateral *intermediate goods* and aggregate bilateral *final goods* trade flows, according to the UN's *Classification by Broad Economic Categories* (2003). Using the bilateral trade data for weights, we calculated the mean final goods and intermediate goods bilateral transport cost factors [(cif − fob)/fob] for intra-DC trade, intra-LDC trade, and trade between DCs and LDCs. For final goods (differentiated or homogeneous), the transport cost factor was 7.6 per cent for intra-DC trade, 19.2 per cent for intra-LDC trade, 20.2 per cent for trade flows

---

[16] It is common in the GE literature to denote trade costs, investment costs, and factor endowments as "parameters." We term these "exogenous variables" here.

from DCs to LDCs, and 20.2 per cent for flows from LDCs to DCs. For intermediate goods, the transport cost factor was 9.8 per cent for intra-DC trade, 21.2 per cent for intra-LDC trade, 20.0 per cent for trade flows from DCs to LDCs, and 20.1 per cent for flows from LDCs to DCs. We constructed initial values for tariff rates using Jon Haveman's TRAINS data for the 1990s. Tariff rates are available at the Harmonized System eight-digit level. Using the UN's *Classification by Broad Economic Categories* again, we classified tariff rates by final and intermediate goods five-digit SITC categories. We then weighted each country's five-digit SITC tariff to generate average tariffs at the country level for each year 1990–2000. Tariff rates were then weighted by aggregate bilateral final goods or intermediate goods imports to obtain mean regional tariff rates, accounting for free trade agreements and customs unions. For final goods, the tariff rate was 1.1 per cent for intra-DC trade, 9.3 per cent for intra-LDC trade, 9.7 per cent for trade from DCs to LDCs, and 4.0 per cent for trade from LDCs to DCs. For intermediate goods, the tariff rate was 0.2 per cent for intra-DC trade, 6.2 per cent for intra-LDC trade, 6.1 per cent for trade from DCs to LDCs, and 0.6 per cent for trade from LDCs to DCs.

Data on bilateral costs of investment (say, informational costs) and on policy barriers to FDI are not available. Carr *et al.* (2001) used a country "rating" score from the World Economic Forum's *World Competitiveness Report* that ranges from 0 to 100. However, ad valorem equivalent measures are not available across countries, much less over time. Consequently, we assumed values to represent informational costs and policy barriers to FDI between countries. We assumed initially a tax-rate equivalent (for γ) of 90 per cent for intra-DC FDI, 120 per cent for FDI flows from LDCs to DCs, and 140 per cent for FDI flows from DCs to LDCs, but results are robust to alternative values. While these choices are somewhat arbitrary, they seem feasible in the context of recent estimates of analogous "trade costs" in Anderson and van Wincoop (2004) of 170 per cent.

4.2   Other parameter values

We now discuss other parameter values assigned initially. Consider first the utility function. In equation (2.1), the only two parameters are the Cobb–Douglas share of income spent on final differentiated products from various producers (η) and the CES parameter (ε) influencing the elasticity of substitution between final differentiated products ($\sigma \equiv 1 - \varepsilon$). Initially, we use 0.71 for the value of η. This is based upon an estimated share of manufactures trade in overall world trade averaged between

1990 and 2000 using five-digit SITC data from the UN's COMTRADE dataset; this is a plausible estimate of the importance of differentiated products in overall utility of developed countries. The initial value of ε is set at -5, implying an elasticity of substitution of 6 among differentiated final goods. This value is consistent with a wide range of recent cross-sectional empirical studies estimating this elasticity between 2 and 10, see Feenstra (1994); Baier and Bergstrand (2001); Head and Ries (2001); Eaton and Kortum (2002); and Hanson (2005).

Consider next production function (2.7) for final differentiated goods. Labor *and* intermediates share of final differentiated goods gross output is assumed to be 0.8, which is conventional; the Cobb–Douglas formulation implies the elasticity of substitution between capital and labor is unity. In one of a series of papers, Griliches (1969) proposed – in a three-factor world with unskilled labor, skilled labor, and physical capital – that skills (or human/knowledge capital) were more complementary with physical capital than with unskilled labor.[17] Griliches found convincing econometric evidence that physical capital and skilled labor were relatively more complementary in production than physical capital and unskilled labor. Most evidence to date suggests that skills and physical capital are relatively complementary in production. In (to our knowledge) the only empirical study of MNE behavior considering this issue, Slaughter (2000) finds statistically significant evidence in favor of capital-skill complementarity. Initially, we assume $\chi = -0.25$, implying an elasticity of substitution of 0.8 and complementarity between physical and human capital.

Regarding unskilled labor and intermediates, the national debate on outsourcing among industrialized economies is basically concerned with the substitution of intermediate goods produced in relatively unskilled-labor-abundant economies (with some final processing at home) for immobile unskilled labor at home. To capture this substitutability, we allow $0 < \delta < 1$; specifically, we assume an elasticity of substitution of 1.2 ($\delta = 0.167$).

We assume initially that intermediate products are better substitutes for each other in production than final goods are substitutes in consumption and choose an intermediates elasticity of substitution of 8 ($\theta = -7$) in equation (2.8). Results are robust to alternative values.

Production of intermediates uses skilled and unskilled labor. We assume this production is Cobb–Douglas, and that the cost share of skilled labor in production (β) is 0.1 in equation (2.8).[18]

---

[17] In fact, human and physical capital may even be absolute complements, rather than just more complementary.

[18] The choice of 0.1 was somewhat arbitrary. Empirical evidence suggests that human capital's share of final goods production is approximately one-third. We know less about

As in the $2 \times 2 \times 2$ Knowledge-Capital model in Carr *et al.* (2001), a firm (or headquarters) setup uses only skilled labor. For national intermediates and final goods producers, we assume the headquarters setup requires a unit of skilled labor per unit of output ($a_{So1} = a_{So2} = a_{So3} = a_{Sn1} = a_{Sn2} = a_{Sn3} = 1$). As in the Knowledge-Capital model, we assume "jointness" for multinational firms; that is, services of knowledge-based assets are joint inputs into multiple plants. Markusen suggests that the ratio of fixed headquarters setup requirements for a (two-plant) horizontal or (one-plant) vertical multinational relative to a domestic firm ranges from one to two. We assume initially a ratio of 1.01 ($a_{Sh1} = a_{Sh2} = a_{Sh3} = a_{Sv1} = a_{Sv2} = a_{Sv3} = 1.01$). Hence, to bias the theoretical results initially *in favor of multinational activity* (that is, in favor of MNEs completely displacing trade), we assume the additional firm setup cost of an MNE over a national firm is quite small. We assume that every plant (national or MNE) requires one unit of home physical capital ($a_K = 1$). However, an MNE setting up a plant abroad can face an additional fixed investment cost (γ), values of which were specified earlier.

5   A theoretical rationale for gravity equations of FDI, final goods trade, and intermediates trade

We use our numerical general equilibrium model to motivate a theoretical rationale for identifying the main economic determinants of bilateral intermediate goods trade – in a manner consistent with identifying the main economic determinants of bilateral FDI and bilateral final goods trade – using gravity equations. The two critical factors in the gravity equation explaining flows are GDPs and "frictions." We address each in turn.

5.1   *Economic size and similarity*

We discuss first the expected relationships between exporter (home) and importer (host) GDPs and the three types of flows suggested by our theory. However, we must first show two key features of the gravity equation. First, in a simple theoretical world of N (>2) countries, one final differentiated good, no trade costs, but internationally immobile factors (e.g. labor and/or capital), we know from the international trade gravity-equation literature that the trade flow from country i to country j in year

intermediates. However, we conjecture that skills are even less important in intermediates production. The results in the remainder of the paper are robust to changing this value.

t ($Flow_{ijt}$) will be determined by:

$$Flow_{ijt} = GDP_{it} GDP_{jt} / GDP_t^W \qquad (2.19)$$

where GDP^W is world GDP, or in log-linear form:

$$\ln Flow_{ijt} = -\ln(GDP_t^W) + \ln(GDP_{it}) + \ln(GDP_{jt}) \qquad (2.20)$$

However, the standard frictionless trade gravity equation can be altered algebraically to separate influences of economic size ($GDP_i + GDP_j$) and similarity ($s_i s_j$), where $s_i = GDP_i / (GDP_i + GDP_j)$ and analogously for j:

$$Flow_{ijt} = GDP_{it} GDP_{jt} / GDP_t^W$$
$$= (GDP_{it} + GDP_{jt})^2 (s_{it} s_{jt}) / GDP_t^W \qquad (2.21)$$

When countries i and j are identical in economic size ($s_i = s_j = 1/2$), $s_i s_j$ is at a maximum. In log-linear form, (2.21) is:

$$\ln Flow_{ij} = -\ln(GDP^W) + 2\ln(GDP_i + GDP_j) + \ln(s_i s_j) \qquad (2.22)$$

Second, while the gravity equation is familiar in algebraic form, it will be useful to *visualize* the frictionless "gravity" relationship. Figure 2.1a illustrates the gravity-equation relationship between bilateral trade flows, GDP size, and GDP similarity summarized in equation (2.21) for an arbitrary hypothetical set of country GDPs ($N > 2$). First, we explain the figure's axes and labeling. The lines on the y axis in the bottom plane range from 1 to 2.2. The y axis indexes the joint economic size of countries i and j; line 1 denotes the smallest combination of GDPs and line 2.2 denotes the largest combination. The GDP values are scaled to this index with the range tied to our *World Development Indicators* dataset on GDPs. The x axis is indexed from 0 to 1. Each line represents i's share of both countries' GDPs; the *center line* represents 50 per cent, or *identical GDP shares for i and j*. The z axis measures the "flow" from i to j as determined by equation (2.21), which is a simple algebraic transformation of typical (frictionless) gravity equation (2.19). Figure 2.1a illustrates the relationships between country economic size (measured by sum of GDPs of i and j) on the y axis, GDP similarity on the x axis, and the "flow" from i to j as determined by simple frictionless gravity equation (2.21).

Common to Knowledge-Capital-type theoretical GE models, analytic solutions are unobtainable and we rely on numerical solutions to the GE model to obtain "theoretical" relationships, using figures generated by the

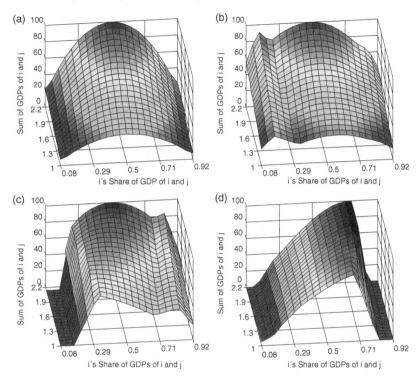

Figure 2.1. Theoretical flows of final goods and intermediate goods nominal exports and nominal outward FDI; (a) Gravity-equation flow from i to j; (b) Final goods nominal exports from i to j; (c) Intermediate goods nominal exports from i to j; (d) Nominal FDI from i to j.

numerical GE version of our model, as in Markusen (2002), Braconier *et al.* (2005), and Bergstrand and Egger (2007). We can now focus on the bilateral relationships between two economies with identical bilateral relative factor endowments and transaction cost levels. That is, we can examine using the numerical model the relationships between economic size (sum of GDPs of i and j) and GDP similarity with bilateral final goods exports from i to j (X_{ij}), bilateral intermediate goods exports from i to j (Z_{ij}), and the bilateral foreign direct investment flow from i to j (FDI_{ij}), shown in Figures 2.1b, 2.1c, and 2.1d, respectively.[19]

---

[19] Gross bilateral FDI from i to j is for HMNEs in industry X, since relative factor endowments are equal between i and j and unchanged.

5.1.1   Proposition 1 First, we note in Figures 2.1b–2.1d that (gross) bilateral final goods trade, intermediate goods trade, and FDI from i to j, respectively, are all positive monotonic functions of the *size* of the two countries' GDPs, as the gravity equation suggests for a given GDP$_{ROW}$ (see Figure 2.1a). For any given share of i in i's and j's total GDP, an increase in the absolute endowments of both countries increases their bilateral final goods trade, bilateral intermediate goods trade, and FDI flow. The numbers of NEs and HMNEs increase monotonically with a larger joint economic size (sum of GDPs of i and j); figures are omitted for brevity, but are available on request. More resources cover more setup costs of final and intermediate goods NEs and of HMNEs; economies of scale and love of variety for consumers and intermediates specialization for producers expand the number of total varieties produced for all three countries by both types of firms in i. This is testable *Proposition 1*.

5.1.2   Proposition 2 Second, we note that final goods, intermediate goods, and FDI flows from i to j are all positively related to the *similarity* of economic sizes. This is testable *Proposition 2*. With the exception of FDI, final goods and intermediate goods trade flows from i to j are maximized when countries i and j are identically sized; this is a traditional feature of the gravity equation. In the case of FDI, the flow from i to j is maximized when i is slightly larger than j; this subtle feature of FDI will be addressed shortly below. Thus, the surfaces suggest that (using aggregate bilateral final goods, intermediates, and FDI flows) the flows are all *complements*, even though final goods trade and FDI are inherently substitutes. What explains this?

The intuition can be seen by starting at the far right-hand side (RHS) of Figures 2.1b–2.1d, when j's GDP is small relative to i's. When j's GDP share becomes positive (via an exogenous reallocation of initial factor endowments from i to j), j's relatively small (final) consumer market is most profitably served by exports from national final goods firms in i and some domestic production in j. In contrast to Bergstrand and Egger (2007) which had no intermediates, intermediates trade from i to j also increases as domestic production in j uses differentiated intermediates from home and foreign producers. As i's (j's) share of their combined GDPs gets smaller (larger), the number of exporters and varieties in i and overall demand in j expand (figures not shown), such that exports from i to j of final and intermediate goods increase.

At some point (around 0.75 on the x axis), as i's (j's) GDP share gets even smaller (larger), it becomes more profitable for i to serve j's market using HMNEs based in i; hence, FDI from i to j increases. Since the number of HMNEs increases, the demand for intermediates increases. While in the Markusen $2 \times 2 \times 2$ KC model, the increase in HMNEs would eventually *completely displace* national final goods exporters in i, the increase in multi-plant HMNEs in our model leads to a fall in the relative demand and price of skilled labor and a rise in the relative demand and price of physical capital in i; figures are not shown for brevity, but are available on request. These relative factor price changes in i curb the creation of HMNEs in i as i's GDP share gets smaller and curb the displacement of final goods national exporting firms in i, such that national final goods exports in i, national intermediate goods exports, and HMNEs based in i with production in j can all coexist as the GDPs of countries i and j become identical.[20]

5.1.3   Proposition 3 Overall, Figures 2.1b–2.1d suggest a theoretical rationale for explaining gross bilateral final goods trade, intermediates trade, and FDI flows from i to j in terms of the product of GDPs of i and j (or size and similarity). However, a third *subtler* issue is that the gross FDI flow from i to j is *not* maximized when i and j are identically sized. Rather, the theoretical model suggests that FDI from i to j should be maximized when i's share is larger than j's. This is consistent intuitively with the notion that profit-maximizing firms in i will want to serve the relatively small market j using HMNEs rather than exports, once j crosses a minimum market-size threshold. This is testable *Proposition 3*.

5.2   Trade and investment costs

While gravity equations typically include bilateral distance and several dummy variables to reflect trade and investment frictions, our theoretical

---

[20] The small temporary dip in intermediates exports from i to j as j's GDP share increases toward $1/2$ in Figure 2.1c is easily explained, and demonstrates the richness of the model's interactions. First, we note that intermediate goods exports *from j to i* (not shown for brevity) is the mirror image of Figure 2.1c, where consequently the "wrinkle" would occur at i's GDP share of 0.16–0.24, as in Figure 2.1b for final goods exports from i to j. Start initially when i's GDP share is small. When i's share of the two countries' endowments increases beyond 0.16 (0.16–0.24, or third column of the x axis), the relative economic size of i crosses the threshold where a large number of *vertical* MNEs based in i with plants in (relatively unskilled-labor-abundant) *ROW* surface (beyond the less dramatic increase in HMNEs of i in j and *ROW*). This causes a physical capital outflow from i to *ROW*, reducing capital available for national final goods exporters in i to exist profitably (and hence, the "wrinkle" at i's GDP share of 0.16–0.24 in Figure 2.1b for final goods exports from i to j). Consequently, with fewer final goods exports from i to j, demand for intermediate goods exports from j to i falls; this explains the "wrinkle" for intermediate goods exports from j to i at i's GDP share of 0.16–0.24 (not shown), and analogously the (mirror) "wrinkle" for intermediate goods exports from i to j at i's GDP share of 0.76–0.84 (shown in Figure 2.1c). In a robustness analysis, this "wrinkle" dissipates as *ROW*'s share of unskilled labor converges to those of countries i and j.

58   Bergstrand and Egger

model includes bilateral iceberg-type final goods trade costs, intermediate goods trade costs, and investment costs (FDI barriers). Moreover, as discussed earlier, we have time-varying empirical measures of all three variables, allowing some testable propositions.

5.2.1 *Proposition 4* For all types of flows, the own-price effect should be negative. Final goods trade from i to j should be a negative function of natural (such as transport) final goods trade costs between i and j. Intermediate goods trade from i to j should be a negative function of intermediate goods trade costs between i and j. FDI from i to j should be a negative function of FDI barriers between i and j. These effects are straightforward and figures (omitted for brevity) confirm these conjectures. These three predictions form testable *Proposition 4*.

5.2.2 *Proposition 5* Regarding cross-price effects, in most cases economically conflicting effects are potentially at play; however, there is one unambiguous prediction. An increase in the barrier to FDI (final goods trade cost) from i to j should be positively related to final goods exports (FDI) from i to j. These relationships are expected since horizontal FDI and final goods trade are gross substitutes (with respect to prices).[21] This forms testable *Proposition 5*.

The remaining cross-price effects are ambiguous. Consider for instance the effect of intermediate goods trade costs on final goods. An increase in intermediate goods trade costs from i to j will tend to increase the cost and price of final good exports, tending to reduce final goods exports from i to j. However, in general equilibrium a rise in intermediate trade costs, by reducing demand for intermediate goods and factors of production, makes production of final goods more competitive, potentially increasing final goods exports from i to j.

Consider next the cross-price effects of final goods trade costs on intermediate goods trade from i to j. An increase in final goods trade costs between i to j should reduce demand for final goods exports from i to j and j to i, reducing demand for intermediate products from j to i and i to j; intermediates trade from i to j could decline. However, the change in relative prices could make intermediate goods production more competitive, potentially increasing intermediates trade from i to j.

Similar ambiguities arise for the cross-price effects on FDI from i to j. However, for brevity, discussion of these effects is omitted. Finally, the

---

[21] Regarding vertical trade, an increase in this FDI barrier would tend to reduce final goods exports from j to i, but not i to j.

model was calibrated for a wide range of alternative values of parameters; the theoretical surfaces were qualitatively the same for a wide choice of values.

6   Estimation of gravity equations for final goods, intermediate goods, and FDI flows

In this section, we evaluate empirically the five "testable" propositions identified in Section 5. In Section 6.1, we describe the dataset we used to estimate the relationships and the other RHS variables we included to avoid specification error. Note, of course, that the theoretical figures generated by our numerical CGE model in Section 5 implicitly *hold constant* all other factors influencing trade and FDI, notably the usual costs of trade and investment associated with frictions such as distance and language. In Section 6.2, we provide the empirical results and evaluate the testable propositions. Section 6.3 provides a summary of an analysis for robustness of the results.

6.1   Specifications and data

To evaluate these five testable propositions, we run typical log-linear gravity equations using pooled cross-section time series data for the period 1990–2000. We specify traditional gravity equations for the log of the gross flow from i to j for either final goods trade, intermediate goods trade, or FDI on the LHS. The RHS variables can be decomposed into three groups. The first group is the log of the exporter GDP and log of the importer GDP. The second group includes explicit time-varying measures of logs of final goods trade costs (bilateral cif-fob factors for final goods trade), intermediate goods trade costs (bilateral cif-fob factors for intermediate goods trade), and a measure of the costs of FDI (to be described below). The third group includes traditional bilateral "friction" variables (controls): log of bilateral distance between economic centers, a dummy variable for adjacency (sharing a common land border), and a dummy for sharing a common language.

We now summarize the data used. The trade flow data were described earlier in Section 2. The outward FDI (stock) data were constructed from UNCTAD data (country profiles). GDP data are from the World Bank's *World Development Indicators*. Bilateral distances are from the CEPII database in France. The adjacency and language dummies were compiled using the CIA *World Factbook*. Time-varying final goods and intermediate goods bilateral cif-fob factors were computed using import and export data from our trade flow dataset. The time-varying investment cost index is that used in Carr *et al.* (2001), Markusen (2002), and Markusen and Maskus (2001, 2002), and was kindly provided by Keith Maskus.

It is important to emphasize that the theoretical surfaces describing the relationships between trade and FDI flows from i to j are based upon the results of a numerical model where countries i and j are initially *identical* in all respects (and ROW is a developing economy, representing a group of developing economies). Consequently, the three theoretical propositions relating flows from i to j to the two countries' economic sizes and economic similarities are based upon two developed countries' GDPs, *assuming* the two countries' relative factor endowments are identical and unchanging. Consequently, while we computed final and intermediates trade flows among 160 countries, we would only expect the testable propositions to hold for a group of *similar, advanced economies*, such as members of the OECD. Consequently, in our basic results we examine only trade and FID flows among all twenty-four member countries of the OECD (in 1990, there were only twenty-four members). We will, however, provide some results in the sensitivity analysis for trade and FDI flows with and among non-OECD countries, noting that we have no prior expectations for such flows (the analysis of which is beyond the scope of this already lengthy chapter and the subject of future research).

6.2   Empirical results

Table 2.3 reports the gravity-equation estimates for the three types of flows among OECD countries. We discuss the results for this table in the order above for *Propositions 1–5*.

First, we report the GDP elasticities for the exporter (home) and importer (host) countries. The coefficient estimates for GDPs are positively signed and are statistically significant. These elasticity estimates confirm *Proposition 1* that bilateral final goods trade, intermediate goods trade, and FDI flows are positively related to the economic size of the two countries.

Second, in light of the discussion at the beginning of Section 5, the similarly sized GDP coefficient estimates for exporter and importer countries tend to confirm the second proposition as well; final goods and intermediate goods trade flows are increasing in similarity of economic size. However, for the two trade flows in Table 2.3, the coefficient estimate for exporter GDP is slightly larger than that for importer GDP. Yet theoretical Figures 2.1b and 2.1c suggested that the gross trade (FDI) flows should be maximized when the two countries are identically sized (when i is larger than j). To provide further confirmation of *Proposition 2*, we illustrate in Figure 2.2 the predicted values from all three regressions reported

Table 2.3. *Bilateral flows of final and intermediate goods exports and bilateral stocks of outward FDI within the OECD (1990–2000)*

	Dependent variable is log of:					
	Final goods exports$_{ijt}$		Intermediate goods exports$_{ijt}$		Outward FDI stocks$_{ijt}$	
Log GDP$_{it}$	0.835	0.025[b]	0.952	0.031[b]	1.164	0.044[b]
Log GDP$_{jt}$	0.794	0.027[b]	0.799	0.031[b]	0.809	0.062[b]
Log final goods trade costs$_{ijt}$	−0.785	0.148[b]	−0.196	0.119	−0.237	0.254
Log intermediate goods trade costs$_{ijt}$	−0.124	0.089	−0.849	0.104[b]	−0.425	0.179[a]
Log investment costs$_{jt}$	0.025	0.111	−0.021	0.137	−0.621	0.261[a]
Other control variables:						
Log distance$_{ij}$	−0.719	0.037[b]	−0.958	0.044[b]	−0.826	0.084[b]
Adjacency$_{ij}$	0.166	0.141	−0.056	0.150	−0.665	0.314[a]
Language$_{ij}$	0.510	0.122[b]	0.789	0.120[b]	1.955	0.232[b]
Time dummies	yes		yes		yes	
Number of observations	5,328		5,328		2,731	
R^2	0.850		0.815		0.660	
Root MSE	0.799		1.040		1.630	

Notes: Reported coefficients and standard errors are pooled OLS estimates. Standard errors are robust to heteroskedasticity and clustering at the country-pair level. Superscripts a and b refer to significance levels of 5% and 1%, respectively.

in Table 2.3. In particular, Figures 2.2a and 2.2b provide the *predicted* empirical final goods and intermediate goods trade flows, respectively, based upon the regression equations. Figures 2.2a and 2.2b are strikingly similar to the corresponding predicted *theoretical* trade flows generated by the numerical version of our general equilibrium model, where the data for GDP size and similarity are based upon our empirical distributions using actual GDP data (Figures 2.1b and 2.1c). In Figures 2.2a and 2.2b (predicted empirical) final goods and intermediate goods trade flows are indeed maximized when the two countries are identically sized.

Third, Table 2.3 reveals that the *difference* in the home and host countries' GDP coefficient estimates for FDI from i to j is the largest of the three regressions. A larger elasticity estimate for the home country's GDP compared to that of the host country's GDP implies that the FDI flow should be maximized when i's share of the two countries' GDP is larger. Figure 2.2c confirms using the predicted empirical values of FDI flows based upon the regression equation that FDI from i to j is indeed

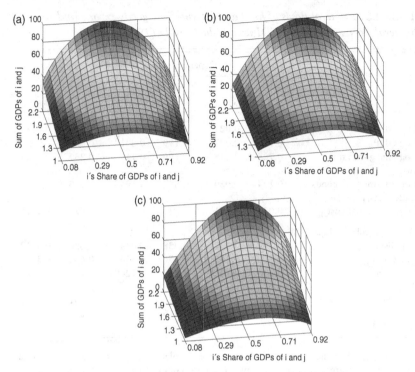

Figure 2.2. Empirical (intra-OECD) flows of final goods and intermediate goods nominal exports and nominal outward FDI; (a) Intra-OECD final goods nominal exports from i to j; (b) Intra-OECD intermediate goods nominal exports from i to j; (c) Intra-OECD FDI from i to j.

maximized when i's GDP share is *larger* than j's share. This confirms *Proposition 3*, and is consistent with Figure 2.1d in the theory that FDI is maximized when i's share is larger.

Fourth, the third, fourth and fifth rows of Table 2.3 provide the coefficient estimates for the *own-price* effects of bilateral final goods trade costs, bilateral intermediate goods trade costs, and (multilateral) investment costs, respectively (no measure of *bilateral* investment costs is available). *Proposition 4* stated that the own price effects should all be negative. The results for the own-price effects in Table 2.3 confirm this proposition robustly. For final goods exports, final goods trade costs have an economically and statistically significant negative effect on such trade. Intermediate goods trade costs from i to j have an economically and statistically significant negative effect on intermediate goods exports from

i to j as expected. Also, the investment cost index has an economically and statistically significant negative effect on outward FDI from i to j. *Proposition 4* is confirmed with strong statistical support.

Fifth, the only testable proposition for *cross-price* effects was an expected positive coefficient estimate for the effect of investment (final goods trade) costs on final goods trade (FDI). *Proposition 5* is confirmed only for investment costs' effect on final goods trade, and that coefficient estimate is neither economically nor statistically significant.

Finally, we note that the coefficient estimates for standard control variables for trade and investment "frictions" – bilateral distance, adjacency dummy, and language dummy – generally accord with earlier studies, even though our theoretical model is agnostic on these variables (as in Markusen 2002), and the R^2 values are in line with these studies. The negative coefficient estimates for bilateral distance are in line with previous estimates and are statistically significant. The coefficient estimate for the adjacency dummy has the typical sign for final goods, but is statistically insignificant. Since no previous studies have used the gravity model for intermediate goods trade flows, there is no expectation for this regression; the coefficient estimate is negative, but economically and statistically insignificant. The negative and statistically significant coefficient estimate for adjacency for FDI is plausible because adjacent markets are more likely to be served by trade rather than horizontal FDI. Finally, the coefficient estimates for the language dummy in each regression have plausible signs and are economically and statistically significant.

6.3   Robustness analysis

We have conducted numerous robustness analyses. For brevity, we report only three to confirm that our results are robust. First, because outward FDI stocks often are zero, the results provided in Table 2.3 for FDI exclude zeroes. Santos Silva and Tenreyro (2006) showed that a Poisson quasi-maximum likelihood (PQML) estimator may avoid the bias associated with heteroskedasticity associated with Jensen's inequality. Moreover, the technique also allows a natural way for including zeroes on the LHS, a problem for the FDI variable as noted. Table 2.4 provides the results from re-estimating all three models in Table 2.3 using the PQML estimator instead; note that the inclusion of zeroes has enlarged the FDI sample. The results for all the variables' coefficient estimates are robust to this alternative estimation procedure, with adjacency now having a statistically significant effect on intermediates.

Second, the bilateral trade- and investment-cost variables included may not represent all such potential costs. Gravity-equation analyses have

Table 2.4. *Sensitivity analysis I: Poisson quasi-maximum likelihood estimation of bilateral flows of final and intermediate goods exports and bilateral stocks of outward FDI within the OECD (1990–2000)*

	Dependent variable is log of:					
	Final goods exports$_{ijt}$		Intermediate goods exports$_{ijt}$		Outward FDI stocks$_{ijt}$	
Log GDP$_{it}$	0.783	0.038^c	0.801	0.033^c	0.870	0.052^c
Log GDP$_{jt}$	0.803	0.046^c	0.786	0.042^c	0.750	0.042^c
Log final goods trade costs$_{ijt}$	−0.707	0.165^c	−0.359	0.159^b	−0.243	0.356
Log intermediate goods trade costs$_{ijt}$	−0.211	0.146	−0.638	0.111^c	−0.798	0.231^c
Log investment costs$_{jt}$	−0.063	0.133	0.092	0.135	−0.510	0.196^c
Other control variables:						
Log distance$_{ij}$	−0.578	0.049^c	−0.627	0.049^c	−0.535	0.079^c
Adjacency$_{ij}$	0.244	0.113^b	0.292	0.112^c	−0.989	0.213^c
Language$_{ij}$	0.336	0.101^c	0.461	0.092^c	1.318	0.132^c
Time dummies	yes		yes		yes	
Number of observations	5,328		5,328		3,439	
Log pseudo-likelihood	−1786.68		−1432.95		−6091.52	

Notes: Reported coefficients and standard errors are pooled Poisson QMLE estimates. Standard errors are robust to heteroskedasticity and clustering at the country-pair level. Superscripts a, b, and c refer to significance levels of 10%, 5%, and 1%, respectively.

often replaced specific bilateral variables with country-pair fixed effects. Table 2.5 presents the results of applying country-pair-specific (ij) fixed effects, which eliminates the "Other control variables" in Table 2.3. We note that once again our coefficient estimates are robust to using country-pair fixed effects, with the exception that FDI's coefficient estimate for investment costs becomes statistically insignificant.

Third, we were curious to see how well the gravity equation for intermediates trade (as well as for final goods trade and FDI) held up for a sample of countries *outside* the OECD. One might expect that the gravity equation (and Ethier-type intermediates trade) would not explain the variation in developing countries' intermediates trade that well. Interestingly, the gravity equation works well also for the sample of non-OECD countries; see Table 2.6. Not surprisingly, the R^2 values are all lower than those for the OECD countries in Table 2.3. For intermediates trade, the R^2 is only 11 per cent less than for the OECD countries. Also, the coefficient estimates are similar. And where they differ, it can be explained

Table 2.5. *Sensitivity analysis II: fixed country-pair effect estimates of bilateral flows of final and intermediate goods exports and bilateral stocks of outward FDI within the OECD (1990–2000)*

	Final goods exports$_{ijt}$		Intermediate goods exports$_{ijt}$		Outward FDI stocks$_{ijt}$	
	Dependent variable is log of:					
Log GDP$_{it}$	0.125	0.042	0.170	0.096	0.307	0.171
Log GDP$_{jt}$	0.809	0.043	0.571	0.096	0.609	0.146
Log final goods trade costs$_{ijt}$	−0.474	0.018	0.034	0.041	−0.107	0.070
Log intermediate goods trade costs$_{ijt}$	0.013	0.014	−0.732	0.031	−0.171	0.059
Log investment costs$_{jt}$	0.004	0.036	−0.085	0.080	−0.088	0.116
Other control variables:						
Time dummies	yes		yes		yes	
Number of observations	5,328		5,328		2,731	
Within R^2	0.460		0.201		0.307	
Root MSE	0.258		0.583		0.566	

Notes: Reported coefficients and standard errors are pooled OLS estimates. Standard errors are robust to heteroskedasticity and clustering at the country-pair level. Superscripts a, b, and c refer to significance levels of 10%, 5%, and 1%, respectively.

readily. For instance, in Table 2.3 the coefficient estimate for adjacency was negative (positive) and statistically significant (insignificant) for outward FDI (final goods trade). These signs are consistent with HMNEs and final goods trade for developed countries; adjacent countries should trade final goods more and have less horizontal FDI, because relative trade costs are low. However, for developing countries, if MNEs are vertical, then adjacency's positive and statistically significant coefficient estimate in the FDI equation is theoretically justified in Table 2.6, as adjacency lowers relative trade costs which are important for national firms *and* VMNEs (which export final goods).

7 Conclusions

We note three potential contributions of our study. First, we have constructed from five-digit SITC bilateral trade flows among 160 countries the most comprehensive bilateral trade flow dataset decomposed into *final* goods and *intermediate* goods trade flows. Second, developing a Knowledge-and-Physical-Capital model of multinationals including a

Table 2.6. *Sensitivity analysis III: bilateral flows of final and intermediate goods exports and bilateral stocks of outward FDI outside the OECD (1990–2000)*

	Dependent variable is log of:					
	Final goods exports$_{ijt}$		Intermediate goods exports$_{ijt}$		Outward FDI stocks$_{ijt}$	
Log GDP$_{it}$	1.143	0.015	1.392	0.016	1.403	0.083
Log GDP$_{jt}$	0.984	0.022	0.855	0.025	0.384	0.125
Log final goods trade costs$_{ijt}$	−0.650	0.018	−0.116	0.019	0.342	0.203
Log intermediate goods trade costs$_{ijt}$	−0.040	0.015	−0.699	0.017	0.644	0.206
Log investment costs$_{jt}$	−0.735	0.074	−0.072	0.084	−0.714	0.304
Other control variables:						
Log distance$_{ij}$	−0.831	0.033	−1.083	0.037	0.311	0.181
Adjacency$_{ij}$	0.937	0.179	0.784	0.183	1.156	0.421
Language$_{ij}$	0.931	0.077	1.031	0.094	1.081	0.403
Time dummies	yes		yes		yes	
Number of observations	22,103		22,103		1,686	
R^2	0.678		0.708		0.513	
Root MSE	1,649		1,810		1,898	

Notes: Reported coefficients and standard errors are pooled OLS estimates. Standard errors are robust to heteroskedasticity and clustering at the country-pair level. Superscripts a, b, and c refer to significance levels of 10%, 5%, and 1%, respectively.

second production stage (intermediates) and calibrating it numerically, we formulated a theoretical rationale for estimating (simultaneously) *gravity equations* for bilateral final goods trade flows, bilateral intermediate goods trade flows, and bilateral outward FDI flows. Third, we showed that the predicted theoretical final goods trade, intermediate goods trade, and FDI flows from i to j from the model explained very well empirical final goods trade, intermediate goods trade, and FDI flows from i to j. As Markusen's introductory quote suggests, Ethier's (1982) intermediate-inputs approach is empirically "very relevant" and goes a long way to explain the actual pattern of bilateral intermediates *outsourcing* flows.

REFERENCES

Anderson, J. E. and E. van Wincoop (2004). "Trade Costs," *Journal of Economic Literature* 42(3): 691–751.

Baier, S. L. and J. H. Bergstrand (2000). "The Growth of World Trade and Outsourcing," working paper, University of Notre Dame.

(2001). "The Growth of World Trade: Tariffs, Transport Costs, and Income Similarity," *Journal of International Economics* **53**(1): 1–27.

Baldone, S., F. Sdogati and L. Tajoli (2002). "Patterns and Determinants of International Fragmentation of Production: Evidence from Outward Processing Trade between the EU and Central-Eastern European Countries," in S. Baldone, F. Sdogati and L. Tajoli (eds.), *EU Enlargement to the CEECs: Trade Competition, Delocalisation of Production, and Effects on the Economies of the Union*. Milan: FrancoAngeli, pp. 73–100.

Barba Navaretti, G. and A. J. Venables (2004). *Multinational Firms in the World Economy*, Princeton University Press.

Bergstrand, J. H. and P. Egger (2007). "A Knowledge-and-Physical-Capital Model of International Trade Flows, Foreign Direct Investment, and Multinational Enterprises," *Journal of International Economics* **73**(2): 278–308.

Bernard, A. B., J. B. Jensen and P. K. Schott (2005). "Importers, Exporters, and Multinationals: A Portrait of Firms in the US that Trade Goods," NBER working paper no. 11404, National Bureau of Economic Research, Inc.

Borga, M. and D. R. Yorgason (2002). "Direct Investment Positions for 2001: Country and Industry Detail," *Survey of Current Business*, July, 25–35.

Braconier, H., P.-J. Norbäck and D. Urban (2005). "Reconciling the Evidence on the Knowledge-Capital Model," *Review of International Economics* **13**(4): 770–86.

Campa, J. and L. S. Goldberg (1997). "The Evolving External Orientation of Manufacturing Industries: Evidence from Four Countries," NBER working paper no. 5919, National Bureau of Economic Research, Inc.

Carr, D., J. R. Markusen and K. E. Maskus (2001). "Estimating the Knowledge-Capital Model of the Multinational Enterprise," *American Economic Review* **91**(3): 693–708.

Eaton, J. and S. Kortum (2002). "Technology, Geography, and Trade," *Econometrica* **70**(5): 1741–79.

Egger, H. and P. Egger (2005). "The Determinants of EU Processing Trade," *World Economy* **28**(2): 147–68.

Ekholm, K., R. Forslid and J. R. Markusen (2007). "Export-Platform Foreign Direct Investment," *Journal of the European Economic Association* **5**(4): 776–95.

Ethier, W. (1982). "National and International Returns to Scale in the Modern Theory of International Trade," *American Economic Review* **72**(3): 389–405.

Feenstra, R. C. (1994). "New Product Varieties and the Measurement of International Prices," *American Economic Review* **84**(1): 157–77.

Feenstra, R. C. and G. Hanson (1999). "The Impact of Outsourcing and High-Technology Capital on Wages: Estimates for the US, 1979–1990," *Quarterly Journal of Economics* **114**: 907–40.

Filipe, J. P., M. P. Fontoura and P. Saucier (2002). "US Intrafirm Trade: Sectoral, Country, and Location Determinants in the 90s," working paper, CEDIN/ISEG/Technical University of Lisbon, July.

Friedman, T. (2005). *The World is Flat*. New York: Farrar, Strauss, and Giroux.

Görg, H. (2000). "Fragmentation and Trade: US Inward Processing Trade in the EU," *Weltwirtschaftliches Archiv* 136(3): 403–22.

Griliches, Z. (1969). "Capital-Skill Complementarity," *Review of Economics and Statistics* 51(4): 465–68.

Grimwade, N. (1989). *International Trade*. London: Routledge.

Grossman, G. M., E. Helpman and A. Szeidl (2003). "Optimal Integration Strategies for the Multinational Firm," *Journal of International Economics* 70(1): 216–38.

Grubel, H. G. and P. Lloyd (1975). *Intra-Industry Trade: The Theory and Measurement of International Trade in Differentiated Products*. London: Macmillan.

Hanson, G. (2005). "Market Potential, Increasing Returns, and Geographic Concentration," *Journal of International Economics* 67(1): 1–24.

Head, K. and J. Ries (2001). "Increasing Returns Versus National Product Differentiation as an Explanation for the Pattern of US-Canada Trade," *American Economic Review* 91(4): 858–76.

Helpman, E. and P. Krugman (1985). *Market Structure and Foreign Trade*. Cambridge, MA: MIT Press.

Helpman, E. and A. Razin (1983). "Increasing Returns, Monopolistic Competition, and Factor Movements," *Journal of International Economics* 14: 263–76.

Hummels, D., J. Ishii and K.-M. Yi (2001). "The Nature and Growth of Vertical Specialization in World Trade," *Journal of International Economics* 54: 75–96.

Hummels, D., D. Rapaport and K.-M. Yi (1998). "Vertical Specialization and the Changing Nature of World Trade," The Federal Reserve Bank of New York *Economic Policy Review* 4(2): 79–99.

Jabbour, L. (2007). "'Slicing the Value Chain' Internationally: Empirical Evidence on the Offshoring Strategy by French Firms," working paper, GEP, University of Nottingham.

Jones, R. W.(1967). "International Capital Movements and the Theory of Tariffs and Trade," *Quarterly Journal of Economics* 81(1): 1–38.

Markusen, J. R. (2001). "Editor's Queries," in E. E. Leamer (ed.), *International Economics*, New York: Worth.

    (2002). *Multinational Firms and the Theory of International Trade*. Cambridge, MA: MIT Press.

Markusen, J. R. and K. E. Maskus (2001). "Multinational Firms: Reconciling Theory and Evidence," in M. Blomstrom and L. S. Goldberg (eds.), *Topics in Empirical International Economics: A Festschrift in Honor of Robert E. Lipsey*, University of Chicago Press, pp. 71–95.

    (2002). "Discriminating Among Alternative Theories of the Multinational Enterprise," *Review of International Economics* 10(4): 694–707.

Mundell, R. (1957). "International Trade and Factor Mobility," *American Economic Review* 47(3): 321–35.

Santos Silva, J. and S. Tenreyro (2006). "The Log of Gravity," *Review of Economics and Statistics* 88(4): 641–58.

Slaughter, M. J. (2000). "Production Transfer within Multinational Enterprises and American Wages," *Journal of International Economics* 50(2): 449–72.

United Nations (2003). *Classification by Broad Economic Categories*. Revision 3. New York: United Nations.

Yeaple, S. R. (2003). "The Role of Skill Endowments in the Structure of US Outward Foreign Direct Investment," *Review of Economics and Statistics* **85**(3): 726–34.

Yi, K.-M. (2003). "Can Vertical Specialization Explain the Growth of World Trade?" *Journal of Political Economy* **111**: 52–102.

APPENDIX

We assume that, in equilibrium, all factors are fully employed for each country i ($i = 1, 2, 3$), so that:

$$K_i \geq a_{KXi} \left[n_i \sum_{j=1}^{3} x_{ij} + x_{ii} \left(\sum_{j=1}^{3} h_{3,j} + \sum_{j \neq i} h_{2,ji} + \sum_{j \neq i} h_{2,ij} \right) \right.$$

$$\left. + \sum_{j \neq i} v_{ji} \left(\sum_{j=1}^{3} x_{ij} \right) \right] + a_{Koi} o_i + a_{Kni} n_i + a_{Kmi}$$

$$\times \left\{ \left[3 + \sum_{j \neq i} \gamma_{ij} \right] h_{3 \cdot i} + [2 + \gamma_{ij}] h_{2 \cdot ij} + [1 + \gamma_{ij}] v_{ij} \right\}$$

$$S_i \geq a_{SXi} \left[n_i \sum_{j=1}^{3} x_{ij} + x_{ii} \left(\sum_{j=1}^{3} h_{3,j} + \sum_{j \neq i} h_{2,ji} + \sum_{j \neq i} h_{2,ij} \right) \right.$$

$$\left. + \sum_{j \neq i} v_{ji} \left(\sum_{j=1}^{3} x_{ij} \right) \right] + a_{SZi} o_i \sum_{j=1}^{3} z_{ij} + a_{Soi} o_i + a_{Sni} n_i$$

$$+ a_{Smi} \left(h_{3,i} + \sum_{j \neq i} (h_{2,ij} + v_{ij}) \right)$$

$$U_i \geq a_{UXi} \left[n_i \sum_{j=1}^{3} x_{ij} + x_{ii} \left(\sum_{j=1}^{3} h_{3,j} + \sum_{j \neq i} h_{2,ji} + \sum_{j \neq i} h_{2,ij} \right) \right.$$

$$\left. + \sum_{j \neq i} v_{ji} \left(\sum_{j=1}^{3} x_{ij} \right) \right] + a_{UYi} \sum_{j=1}^{3} t_{Yij} Y_{ij} + a_{UZi} o_i \sum_{j=1}^{3} z_{ij} \qquad (2.A.1)$$

Multilateral current account balance for each country i ($i = 1, 2, 3$) requires the following to hold:

$$o_i p_{Zi}(z_{ij} + z_{ir}) + (n_i + v_{ji} + v_{ri})p_{Xi}(x_{ij} + x_{ir}) + p_{Yj}Y_{ij} + p_{Yr}Y_{ir}$$

$$+ \frac{1}{1-\varepsilon}([h_{2,ij} + h_{3,i}]p_{Xj}x_{ij} + [h_{2,ir} + h_{3,i}]p_{Xr}x_{rr})$$

$$+ \frac{1}{1-\varepsilon}(v_{ij}p_{Xj}[x_{ij} + x_{ji} + x_{jr}] + v_{ir}p_{Xr}[x_{rr} + x_{ri} + x_{rj}])$$

$$= o_j p_{Zj}z_{ji} + o_r p_{Zr}z_{ri} + (n_j + v_{ij} + v_{rj})p_{Xj}x_{ji}$$

$$+ (n_r + v_{ir} + v_{jr})p_{Xr}x_{ri} + p_{Yi}(Y_{ji} + Y_{ri})$$

$$+ \frac{1}{1-\varepsilon}(h_{2,ji} + h_{3,j} + h_{2,ri} + h_{3,r})p_{Xi}x_{ii}$$

$$+ \frac{1}{1-\varepsilon}(v_{ji} + v_{ri})p_{Xi}(x_{ii} + x_{ij} + x_{ir}) \qquad (2.A.2)$$

The first line in equation (2.A.2) represents the exports of intermediate and final goods of country i. The second and third lines represent income earned on capital invested by country i in horizontal and vertical affiliates, respectively, in country's j and r (denoting the *ROW*). The fourth line represents country i's imports of goods from j and r. The fifth and sixth lines represent i's repatriation of income on capital of countries' j and r invested in country i in horizontal and vertical affiliates, respectively.

3   The incidence of gravity

J. E. Anderson

The gravity model is one of the great success stories of economics. The success of the model is its great explanatory power: the equations fit well statistically and give quite similar answers across many different datasets – inferred bilateral trade costs are big, varying with distance and border crossings.

Despite this success, the inferred trade costs have had little impact on the broader concerns of economics until very recently. The costs have been hard to integrate with other models used to understand trade.[1] There are two difficulties. First, national buyer and seller responses to bilateral trade costs depend on their *incidence* instead of the full cost. Second, the high dimensionality of bilateral trade costs requires aggregation, both for elementary comprehension of magnitude and for use in the wide class of trade models that focus on resource and expenditure allocation as sectoral aggregates.

This paper discusses a solution to both problems. Measures of aggregate incidence described here provide intuitive guides to the consequences of geography, illustrated with results drawn from a study of Canada's changing economic geography (Anderson and Yotov 2008). The paper goes on to show how the aggregated incidence measures can be used in a standard class of applied general equilibrium trade models. This opens the way to richer applied work, both in simulation and in econometric inference.

The solution to incidence and aggregation problems exploits the properties of the structural gravity model. Gravity was initially developed by analogy with the physical gravity model, using only its "two-body" representation. Anderson (1979) derived an economic theory of gravity from

I am grateful to Adrian Wood for helpful comments.

[1] Eaton and Kortum (2002) develop a Ricardian many country, many goods trade model with bilateral trade costs. The methods used in this paper apply to their model as well, but the promise of the methods lies in integrating gravity with the much wider class of general equilibrium trade models in the common toolkit.

demand structure, at the same time providing the economic analogy to a solution for the physical N-body problem. See also Anderson and van Wincoop (2003, 2004), who coin the term "multilateral resistance" for the key solution concept that captures the N-body properties of the trade system.

Inward and outward multilateral resistance are, respectively, the demand and supply side aggregate incidence of trade costs. For each product, it is as if each country shipped its output to a single "world" market and shipped home its purchases from the single world market. Each country's multilateral resistances depend on all bilateral trade costs in the world system, not just the bilateral cost between country i and country j and not just i's costs with all its partners and j's costs with all its partners. Multilateral resistance thus embeds the effect of trade costs between third and fourth parties, meeting an objection to the earlier gravity model raised by Bikker in Chapter 5.[2] For example, via its impact on multilateral resistances around the world, the implementation of the NAFTA agreement should theoretically have an effect on the trade of its members with EU countries through multilateral resistance, and moreover it also has an effect on the trade of the EU countries with Japan and China.

The integration of aggregated incidence measures with standard general equilibrium models builds on the structure sketched in Anderson and van Wincoop (2004). Allocation between sectors is separated from allocation within sectors by the simplifying assumption of "trade separability." Production for sale in all destinations depends only on the "average" sellers' incidence of trade costs while purchases from all origins depend only on the "average" buyers' incidence. Within sectors the global bilateral distribution of shipments is conditioned on each region's aggregate expenditure and production allocations to the sector. This paper develops the implications of the structure further.

1   Trade frictions and incidence

Some impediments to trade are due to the sellers' side of the market (like export taxes or export infrastructure user costs), some are due to the buyers' side of the market (like import taxes or import infrastructure user

---

[2] Bikker claims, misleadingly, that previous gravity models do not account for substitution between trade flows. This is wrong, because the class of theoretical models following Anderson (1979) are based on CES demand structure. But the empirical literature until very recently did not act on Anderson's original point that ordinary gravity models were biased estimators because they omitted the influence of what now are called multilateral resistances. Bikker additionally proposes an Extended Gravity Model with a demand structure less restricted than the CES, a procedure that has both advantages and disadvantages.

costs) while still others are difficult to identify with either side (such as transport costs, information costs or costs due to institutional insecurity). Whatever their origin, however, all trade impediments will have economic incidence that is shared between buyer and seller. Economic incidence differs from naive incidence based on who initially pays the bill: the seller typically may pay for transport cost and insurance, but the seller's price to the buyer includes a portion of these costs with the portion being economically determined.

The gravity model is used first to predict a benchmark of what bilateral trade flows would look like in a frictionless world. Then the deviations of actual from benchmark flows are econometrically related to a set of proxies for trade costs. The results are used to infer unobservable trade costs associated with such frictions as distance and trade policy barriers, discriminatory regulatory barriers, and other variables related to national borders – different languages or legal systems, differential information about opportunities, extortionist actions at border bottlenecks – all have been found to impede trade very significantly. Chapters 6 by Head and Mayer and 7 by Bosker and Garretsen pursue some of the many important issues of specification of the proxies themselves and the way in which they enter the trade cost relationship.

Each producing nation in each product class provides a variety[3] to the world market. The total value of outward and inward shipments is given. Each consuming nation buys available varieties from the world market.

The gravity model makes the enormously useful simplifying assumption that tastes (and for intermediate products, technology) are the same everywhere in the world. In a truly frictionless world, this would mean that the shares of expenditure falling on the varieties of products from every origin would be the same in every destination. That is, destination h would spend the same share of its total expenditure on goods class k as would destination $i \neq h$, and within goods class k would spend the same share on goods from origin j as would destination $i \neq h$.

Bilateral trade costs shift the pattern of bilateral shipments from the frictionless benchmark. Below, the expenditure shares are assumed to derive from constant elasticity of substitution (CES) preferences. Different expenditure shares are explained by different bilateral trade costs in a tightly specified fashion.

It is analytically convenient to develop the gravity model logic by focusing on shipments from "the factory gate" to a world market that includes local distribution. This differs from many standard treatments of costly

---

[3] For purposes not germane here, free entry monopolistic competition can endogenize the number of firms that together provide each nation's varieties. See Bergstrand (1985) and his subsequent work.

trade, so it is important to keep in mind that "shipments to the world market" in this paper include shipments that end up being sold at home and "purchases from the world market" include products produced at home. Local distribution costs are ordinarily less than distribution costs to the rest of the world, but are in fact substantial (as discussed in Anderson and van Wincoop 2004).

Arbitrage ties together prices in different locations. For shipment from j to h in goods class k, the zero-profit arbitrage condition implies that $p_k^{jh} = \tilde{p}_k^j t_k^{jh}$ where: p_k^{jh} denotes the buyers' price in h for goods in class k purchased from source j; $\tilde{p}_k^j$ denotes the cost of good k at j's 'factory gate'; and $t_k^{jh} > 1$ is the trade cost markup factor.

The average (across all destinations h) incidence of trade frictions on the supply side – the average impact on the sellers' price of the set of t_k^{jh}'s that contains all destinations h – is represented by an index $\prod_k^j$ for each product category k in each country j. The index is derived from the simple notion that the complex actual shipment pattern is equivalent in its impact on sellers to a hypothetical world economy that behaves as if there was a "world" destination price for goods k delivered from j, $p_k^j = \tilde{p}_k^j \prod_k^j$.

Figure 3.1 illustrates the hypothetical equilibrium for the case of two markets, suppressing the goods class index k for clarity. Market 1 to the right may be thought of as the home market with market 2 to the left being the export market. Distribution costs are lower in the home market than in the export market. The equilibrium factory gate price $\tilde{p}^j$ is preserved by maintaining the total quantity shipped while replacing the non-uniform trade costs with the uniform trade cost $\prod^j$.

The incidence of bilateral trade costs on the buyers' side of the market is given by $t_k^{jh} / \prod_k^j$, taking away the sellers' incidence. The average buyers' incidence of all bilateral costs to h from the various origins j is given by the buyers' price index P_k^h. The balance of the effects of all bilateral trade costs on the trade flow in goods class k from origin j in destination h, X_k^{jh}, is given by $t_k^{jh} / \prod_k^j P_k^h$. This relative trade cost incidence form is intuitive, but strictly valid only for the special CES form of demand structure, detailed in the next section.

The usage of "incidence" here to describe the indexes $\prod_k^j$ and P_k^h is derived from the familiar partial equilibrium incidence analysis of the first course in economics. $\prod_k^j$ and P_k^h will be given an exact formal description below that reveals how they can be calculated in practice and how they indeed capture incidence in conditional general equilibrium (i.e. preserve the same factory gate prices, conditional on observed aggregate shipments and expenditures).

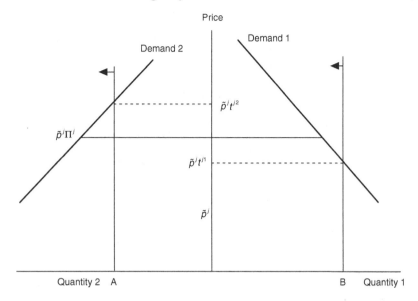

Price

Demand 1

Demand 2

$\bar{p}^j t^{j2}$

$\bar{p}^j \Pi^j$

$\bar{p}^j t^{j1}$

$\bar{p}^j$

Quantity 2   A   B   Quantity 1

Total shipments AB are preserved by moving the goalposts left
such that a uniform markup is applied to each shipment.

Figure 3.1. Quantity-preserving aggregation.

Figure 3.2 illustrates the division of a single trade cost into its incidence
on the buyers' and sellers' prices. The demand and supply schedules of
the first course in economics are converted here into value functions,
the revenue from sales for sellers and the expenditure for buyers. This
conversion aids connection later on with the gravity model. For simplicity
the goods class subscript k is again dropped. The actual trade flow is
given by the value at F, which is conveniently chosen to be equal to the
frictionless value of trade. F represents an average effect on bilateral trade
(including local trade) from the system of trade costs. This is because
the value of shipments Y^j is fixed and the bilateral costs simply shift
the pattern around in such a way that the effects of bilateral trade costs
average out.

   A hypothetical partial equilibrium bilateral trade flow is given by point
A projected down from the "demand" schedule labeled $X^{jh}\left(\tilde{p}^j t^{jh}/1\right)$,
the expenditure associated with the buyers' price p^{jh} when the index
$P^h = 1$, the frictionless value of the price index. The "demand" schedule
expresses the dependence of demand on the sellers' price $\tilde{p}^j$, holding constant the price index P, which in reality is possible only when h spends
a very small share on goods from j. It is downward sloping because the

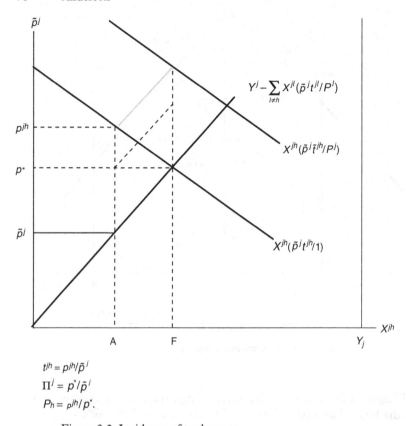

$$t^{jh} = p^{jh}/\tilde{p}^j$$
$$\Pi^j = p^*/\tilde{p}^j$$
$$P_h = p^{jh}/p^*.$$

Figure 3.2. Incidence of trade costs.

elasticity of demand is assumed to be greater than 1 (an assumption that is empirically sound based on the extensive gravity literature). The "supply" schedule is a residual from supply to all other destinations for j's good: $Y^j - \sum_{l \neq h} X^{jl} \left(\tilde{p}^j t^{jl}/P^l \right)$. It is upward sloping in $\tilde{p}^j$ because all the bilateral "demand" schedules are downward sloping. The "supply" schedule expresses dependence on the sellers' price while holding constant a combination of all the price indexes, a constancy which is possible only in a very special case.

The elementary analysis of incidence decomposes t^{jh} into the sellers' incidence Π^j and the buyers' incidence t^{jh}/Π^j based on the frictionless equilibrium price p^* generated by the intersection of demand and supply with no frictions. The vertical line segment between the demand and supply schedules at trade level A divides into the sellers' incidence

$p^*/p^j = \Pi j$ and the buyers' incidence p^{jh}/p^*. Incidence depends on the relationship between demand and supply elasticities. For large supply elasticities, as might be expected in the context of bilateral trade where supply is diverted from many other large markets, the sellers' incidence falls toward its limit of 1 and all incidence is borne by buyers.

The gravity model incorporates the effect of all bilateral trade frictions on Πj, as will be detailed below; and on the demand for goods from j through their effect on average prices of substitute goods from all sources acting through the price index P^h. Replacing the actual system of trade costs with the hypothetical system $\tilde{t}^{jh} = \prod^j P^h$ results in the frictionless quantity demanded on the vertical line erected from point F in Figure 3.2. For the very special case chosen to simplify the presentation of principles, the effect of the switch to hypothetical trade costs on the supply schedule to market h is nil. More importantly, the special case assumes that the actual trade cost is equal to the hypothetical trade cost: $t^{jh} = \tilde{t}^{jh}$. The dashed lines parallel to the supply schedule project the standard textbook incidence decomposition northeast to the line segment between the two demand schedules on the vertical line from frictionless sales point F. Thus the sellers' incidence is Πj and the buyers' incidence is P^h.

It is tempting to think that incidence is determined by the same ratio of demand to supply elasticities as in the textbook case, and indeed for the case drawn intuition is aided by exactly this analogy derived from projecting backward and forward between the line segment above A and the line segment above F.[4] Unfortunately, the general equilibrium relationship between markets is far too complex for the relative elasticity intuition of the diagram to be illuminating.

Thinking about the sales pattern of supplier j in terms of Figure 3.2, but for cases where the bilateral flow is not equal to the frictionless flow, some actual trade flows will be above average (to the right of the frictionless level on Figure 3.1). This is certainly true for the local shipments from j to itself, the well-known phenomenon of home bias in sales patterns.

Most trade flows, likely all but local ones, will be to the left of the frictionless level in Figure 3.2. In an average sense, across markets the trade flow shifts from the frictionless level cancel out because the volume of goods shipped from j must add up to the given amount Y^j. (This is true in conditional general equilibrium: the effect of actually changing trade costs would result in reallocations of resources such that the amounts produced would change in full general equilibrium.)

---

[4] Using a linear approximation, the standard algebra of incidence implies that $P = t(\beta + \delta)/(\beta t + \delta)$ and $\Pi = (\beta t + \delta)/(\beta + \delta)$, where $-\beta$ is the demand slope and δ is the supply slope.

The sellers' incidence Π is conceptually identical to a productivity penalty in distribution. j's factors of production must be paid less in proportion to $\prod$ in order to get their goods to market. For intermediate goods demand, P is a productivity penalty reflecting the distribution cost incidence that falls on users of intermediate goods. This link to productivity is exploited by Anderson and Yotov (2008) to convert their incidence results into total factor productivity (TFP) measures.

2   Determination of incidence

The incidence of trade costs within each sector is determined in a conditional general equilibrium that distributes bilateral shipments across origin-destination pairs for given bilateral trade costs and given total shipments and total expenditures. See the next section for a defense of this separation and the validity of conditioning on total shipments and expenditures.

Impose CES preferences on the (sub-)expenditure functions for each goods class k, where σ_k is the elasticity of substitution parameter for goods class k and $(\beta_k^j)^{1-\sigma_k}$ is a quality parameter for goods from j in class k. (For intermediate products demand impose the analogous CES structure for the cost functions.) Then the bilateral trade flow from j to h in goods class k, valued at destination prices, is given by

$$X_k^{jk} = \left(\frac{\beta_k^j \tilde{p}_k^j t_k^{jh}}{P_k^h} \right)^{1-\sigma_k} E_k^h \qquad (3.1)$$

where: $\tilde{p}_k^j$ is the cost of production of good k in the variety produced by j; $t_k^{jh} > 1$ is the trade cost markup parameter in class k from j to h; E_k^h is the expenditure on goods class k in destination h; and P_k^h is the true cost of living index for goods class k in location h. P_k^h is defined by

$$P_k^h \equiv \sum_j \left[\left(\beta_k^j \tilde{p}_k^j t_k^{jh} \right)^{1-\sigma_k} \right]^{1/(1-\sigma_k)}$$

Let the value of shipments at *delivered* prices from origin h in product class k be denoted by Y_k^j. Market clearance requires:

$$Y_k^j = \sum_h \left(\frac{\beta_k^j \tilde{p}_k^j t_k^{jh}}{P_k^h} \right)^{1-\sigma_k} E_k^h \qquad (3.2)$$

Now solve (3.2) for the quality adjusted efficiency unit costs $\left\{ \beta_k^j \tilde{p}_k^j \right\}$

$$\left(\beta_k^j \tilde{p}_k^j \right)^{1-\sigma_k} = \frac{Y_k^j}{\sum_h \left(t_k^{jh} / P_k^h \right)^{1-\sigma_k} E_k^h} \tag{3.3}$$

Based on the denominator in (3.3), define

$$\left(\Pi_k^j \right)^{1-\sigma_k} \equiv \sum_h \left(\frac{t_k^{jh}}{P_k^h} \right)^{1-\sigma_k} \frac{E_k^h}{\sum_h E_k^h}, $$

where $\sum_h E_k^h$ replaces $\sum_j Y_k^j$.

The outward multilateral resistance term Π_k^j gives the supply side incidence of bilateral trade costs to origin j. It is as if j ships to a single world market at cost factor Π_k^j. To see this crucial property, divide numerator and denominator of the right-hand side of (3.3) by total shipments of k and use the definition of Π, yielding:

$$\left(\beta_k^j \tilde{p}_k^j \Pi_k^j \right)^{1-\sigma_k} = Y_k^j / \sum_j Y_k^j \tag{3.4}$$

The right-hand side is the world's expenditure share for class k goods from country j. The left-hand side is a "global behavioral expenditure share," understanding that the CES price index is equal to 1 due to the normalization implied by summing (3.4):

$$\sum_j \left(\beta_k^j \tilde{p}_k^j \Pi_k^j \right)^{1-\sigma_k} = 1 \tag{3.5}$$

The global share is generated by the common CES preferences over varieties in the face of globally uniform quality adjusted efficiency unit costs $\beta_k^j \tilde{p}_k^j \Pi_k^j$.

Outward and inward multilateral resistances can readily be computed once the empirical gravity model has been estimated and the implied trade costs t_k^{jh} have been constructed from its results. Substitute for quality adjusted efficiency unit costs from (3.3) in the definition of the true cost of living index, using the definition of the Π's:

$$\left(P_k^h \right)^{1-\sigma_k} = \sum_j \left\{ \frac{t_k^{jh}}{\Pi_k^j} \right\}^{1-\sigma_k} \frac{Y_k^j}{\sum_j Y_k^j} \tag{3.6}$$

Collect this with the definition of the Π's:

$$\left(\Pi_k^j\right)^{1-\sigma_k} = \sum_h \left\{\frac{t_k^{jh}}{P_k^h}\right\}^{1-\sigma_k} \frac{E_k^h}{\sum_h E_k^h}. \tag{3.7}$$

These two sets of equations jointly determine the inward multilateral resistances, the P's and the outward multilateral resistances, the Π's, given the expenditure and supply shares and the bilateral trade costs, subject to a normalization. A normalization of the Π's is needed to determine the P's and Π's because (3.6)–(3.7) determine them only up to a scalar.[5]

Notice that the Π's and the P's generally differ, even if bilateral trade costs are symmetric: $t_k^{hj} = t_k^{jh}$.

Anderson and van Wincoop (2004) show that the multilateral resistance indexes are ideal indexes of trade frictions in the following sense. Replace all the bilateral trade frictions with the hypothetical frictions $\tilde{t}_k^{jh} = \Pi_k^j P_k^h$. The budget constraint (3.6) and market clearance (3.7) equations continue to hold at the same prices, even though individual bilateral trade volumes change.

Thus for each good k in each country j, from the point of view of the factory gate, it is as if a single shipment was made to the "world market" at the average cost. On the demand side, similarly, inward multilateral resistance consistently aggregates the demand side incidence of inward trade and production frictions. From the point of view of the "household door" it is as if a single shipment was made from the "world market" at the average markup. This discussion is the formal counterpart to the intuitive claim that Figure 3.2 represents an "average" good in a partial equilibrium representation of the incidence decomposition.

The CES specification of within-class expenditure shares, after substitution from (3.3), implies the gravity equation

$$X_k^{jk} = \left\{\frac{t_k^{jh}}{\Pi_k^j P_k^h}\right\}^{1-\sigma_k} \frac{Y_k^j}{\sum_j Y_k^j} \tag{3.8}$$

For a "representative" trade flow with $t_k^{ij} = \Pi_k^j P_k^h$, the gravity equation implies that the flow is equal to the frictionless flow, conditional on $Y_k^j E_k^h$.

---

[5] If $\left\{P_k^0, \Pi_k^0\right\}$ is a solution to (3.6)–(3.7), then so is $\left\{\lambda P_k^0, \Pi_k^0/\lambda\right\}$ for any positive scalar λ, where P_k denotes the vector of P's and the superscript 0 denotes a particular value of this vector, and similarly for Π_k.

The normalization (3.5) in combination with a frictionless equilibrium normalization $\sum_j \left(\beta_k^j \tilde{p}_k^{j*}\right)^{1-\sigma_k} = 1$ completes the extension of the partial equilibrium theory of incidence to conditional general equilibrium.[6]

3 Incidence in practice

Computing the multilateral resistances is readily operational, given estimates of gravity models that yield the inferred t's and given the global shares $\left\{E_k^h/\sum_h E_k^h, Y_k^j/\sum_j Y_k^j\right\}$. The multilateral resistance indexes permit calculation of Constructed Home Bias $\left(t_k^{hh}/\prod_k^h P_k^h\right)^{1-\sigma_k}$ indexes. These are equal to the ratio of predicted trade to frictionless trade in the home market.

Multilateral resistance is equivalent to a TFP penalty. The Π's push below the world price the "factory gate" price $\tilde{p}$ that sellers receive, which determines what they can pay their factors of production. Similarly, the P's raise the price that buyers must pay for final or intermediate goods. The effect of changes in multilateral resistance on real GDP can be captured by a linear approximation to the TFP change:

$$-\sum_k \frac{Y_k^j}{\sum_k Y_k^j}\hat{\Pi}_k^j - \sum_k \frac{E_k^j}{\sum_k E_k^j}\hat{P}_k^j$$

In practice it will often be useful to avoid having to solve for the equilibrium quality adjusted efficiency unit costs needed for normalization (3.5). A units choice can always be imposed – for example, $\beta_k^i p_k^{*i} = 1$, $\forall k$ or $p_k^h = 1, \forall k$ for some convenient reference country i or h. (The former convention implies $\left(\prod_k^i\right)^{1-\sigma_k} = Y_k^i/Y_k, \forall k$.) In any case, *relative multilateral resistances are what matters for allocation in conditional general equilibrium.* The normalization choice can be freely made for convenience in calculation and interpretation.

Anderson and Yotov (2008) construct multilateral resistances for Canadian provinces 1992–2003 using these procedures. They first estimate gravity coefficients, then construct the implied t's and then use (3.6)–(3.7) with a normalization to calculate the provincial multilateral resistances for each year and province for eighteen goods classes. They find that outward (sellers' incidence) multilateral resistance is around

---

[6] The demands and supplies of the upper level allocation remain constant, as in the partial equilibrium in Figure 3.2. The aggregation of bilateral t's into Π's at constant $\tilde{p}$ is analogous to the aggregation shown in Figure 3.1.

five times bigger than inward (buyers' incidence) multilateral resistance. The sellers' incidence is negatively related to sellers' market share, and it falls significantly over time due to specialization, despite constant gravity coefficients.

The fall in sellers' incidence over time suggests a powerful and previously unrecognized force of globalization: specialization in production is driving a fall in the sellers' incidence of trade costs despite constant gravity coefficients and hence t's. There is a big fall in Constructed Home Bias. The fall in sellers' incidence results in rises in real GDP that are around 1 per cent per year for star performing provinces. These are big numbers.

4   General equilibrium

Multilateral resistances permit a useful integration of gravity with general equilibrium production and expenditure structures. Consider an iterative process that moves back and forth between the lower level allocation of shipments within sectors and the upper level allocation of resources across sectors. In full general equilibrium computations that simulate equilibria away from the initial conditional equilibrium analyzed in preceding sections, the upper level general equilibrium model at initial Π's and P's yields the new global shares $\{E_k^h / \sum_h E_k^h, Y_k^j / \sum_j Y_k^j\}$ and the normalized quality adjusted efficiency unit costs $\{\beta_k^j \tilde{p}_k^j\}$. The new shares and efficiency unit costs are then inputs into the computation of the new multilateral resistances, the Π's and P's from (3.6)–(3.7) subject to a normalization. The new multilateral resistances are then plugged into the resource allocation module to solve for the new shares and efficiency unit prices. The iterative process continues until convergence.

The determination of supply to the market from each origin and of expenditure at each destination is specified here in general equilibrium using the standard toolkit. It is analytically very convenient to exploit the trade separability property assumed throughout to first describe allocation in each country for given world prices. Subsequently, global market clearance is used to determine the world prices.

4.1   Allocation for given world prices

Total supply from each origin and total expenditure at each destination are determined in an upper stage of general equilibrium. In each country, on the supply side each product class draws resources from the common pool and on the demand side each expenditure class draws from the common income. These total supply and total expenditure variables are taken as given in this stage of the model, in order to focus on the key determinants of the distribution of supply and expenditures across origin-destination pairs.

A tremendous simplification is achieved with the specializing assumption of *trade separability* – the composition of expenditure or production within a product group is independent of prices outside the product group. Separability permits consistent aggregation and a simple solution to the incidence problem.

On the supply side, separability is imposed by the assumption that the goods from j in class k shipped to each destination are perfect substitutes in supply. On the demand side, separability is imposed by assuming that expenditure on goods class k forms a separable group containing shipments from all origins. Goods are differentiated by place of origin, an assumption that has a deeper rationale in monopolistic competition. This setup enables two-stage budgeting. A further specialization to CES structure for the separable groups yields operational multilateral resistance indexes that capture the inward and outward incidence of trade costs.

See Anderson (2008) for a full description of the upper level allocation of expenditure and production and characterization of the global equilibrium pattern of production and trade in the case of the specific factors model of production.

In each country, on the supply side each product class draws resources from the common pool and on the demand side each expenditure class draws from the common income. The simplifying assumption of *trade separability* allows treatment of these allocation decisions at the sectoral level, abstracting from bilateral patterns of shipment. Separability means that the composition of expenditure or production within a product group is independent of prices outside the product group.

Given the separable setup the sellers' incidence Π is conceptually identical to a productivity penalty in distribution. Region j's factors of production are paid less because of distribution frictions: metaphorically a portion $\Pi - 1$ of their pay melts away. Demand for intermediate goods faces a similar productivity penalty P reflecting the trade cost incidence on users of intermediate goods. This link to productivity is exploited by Anderson and Yotov (2008) to convert their incidence results into TFP measures. In final demand the sectoral incidence P acts like a uniform tax on consumption.

The implications are drawn out here in a generic general equilibrium model with final goods only. See Anderson (2008) for a full description of the upper level allocation of expenditure and production and characterization of the global equilibrium pattern of production and trade in the case of the specific factors model of production, including treatment of intermediate goods.

Each country produces and distributes goods to its trading partners. Production is more costly than with best practice by a Hicks neutral multiplier $a_k^j \geq 1$ for product k in country j. In other words, at the factor prices relevant for product k in country j, $a_k^j - 1$ more factors are used than needed with the best practice. Distribution to destination h requires additional factors to be used, in the proportion $t_k^{jh} - 1$ to their use in production (iceberg-melting distribution costs). Otherwise, products sold to all destinations are identical: perfect substitutes in production.[7]

The cost of product k from origin j at destination h is given by $p_k^{jh} = a_k^j t_k^{jh} \tilde{p}_k^j$, where $\tilde{p}_k^j$ is the unit cost of production using best practice techniques, called the "efficiency unit cost." Since the a's and T's enter the model multiplicatively, they combine in a productivity penalty measure $T_k^{jh} = a_k^j t_k^{jh}$ that represents both trade frictions and frictions in the assimilation of technology. The preceding section derives the aggregate supply side incidence of trade costs $\prod_k^j$ for each product category k in each country j. Incorporating the technology penalty a into Π to conserve notation, let Π's now represent both distribution and technology penalties.

The key building block describing the supply side of the economy is the gross domestic product (GDP) function. It is written as $g\left(\tilde{p}^j, \upsilon^j\right)$ where υ^j is the vector of factor endowments. g is convex and homogeneous of degree one in prices, by its maximum value properties. Take P^j as a given vector of "world" prices. Then $\tilde{p}_k^j = p_k^j / \prod_k^j$, $\forall k$. Using Hotelling's lemma, $g_k^j \tilde{p}_k^j \prod_k^j = Y_k^j$, where g_{kj} denotes $\partial g^j / \partial \tilde{p}_k^j$.

Figure 3.3 illustrates. The actual bundle delivered to the market is $(\tilde{y}_1, \tilde{y}_2)$, point A. The value of delivered goods, GDP, is $g\left(p, \Pi\right) = p_1 \tilde{y}_1 + p_2 \tilde{y}_2$. This is also equal to the GDP available if the most efficient technology were to be used facing the prices $(\tilde{p}_1, \tilde{p}_2)$, hence $g\left(p, \Pi\right) = g\left(\tilde{p}, l\right) = p_1 y_1 / \prod_1 + p_2 y_2 / \prod_2$. Point C represents (y_1, y_2), the hypothetical most efficient production and delivery possible based on the resources allocated to achieve the actual deliveries of point A.

Two limiting cases clarify the conceptual basis of productivity used here. The case where trade costs are absent gives the standard TFP

---

[7] The setup can easily be generalized to allow for a separable joint output structure in which products for each destination are imperfect substitutes via a CET structure.

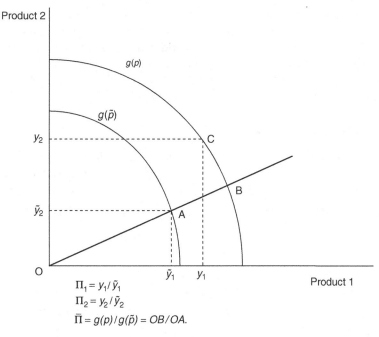

$\Pi_1 = y_1/\tilde{y}_1$
$\Pi_2 = y_2/\tilde{y}_2$
$\bar{\Pi} = g(p)/g(\tilde{p}) = OB/OA.$

Figure 3.3. Incidence and TFP.

measurement. The production possibilities frontier through points C and B represents the most efficient technology where $a_i = 1 = t_{ij}$; $\forall i,j$. With $a_i > 1, t_{ij} = 1$, the production possibilities frontier through point A represents the actual technology frontier. For this case, $\Pi_i = a_i$. The case where productivity frictions are absent in production is the case of pure iceberg trade costs, $a_i = 1, t_{ij} = T_{ij} \geq 1$; $\forall i,j$; and Π_i is the incidence of trade costs on sector i. Point A gives the bundle actually delivered while point C represents the bundle as it leaves the factory gate. The shrinkage is due to the iceberg melting trade costs. Digging into the iceberg metaphor to relate the concepts to national income accounting, gross output in each sector y_1, y_2 (represented by point C) effectively uses some of its own output as an intermediate good in order to achieve deliveries to final demand $\tilde{y}_1, \tilde{y}_2$ (represented by point A). The discussion shows that the metaphor of iceberg melting trade costs can be extended to productivity frictions that "melt" the resources applied to produce before the shipments begin their journey to market.

The illustration in Figure 3.3 emphasizes two separate aspects of the productivity frictions. Along ray OAB, the ratio OB/OA represents the average (across industries) productivity penalty, equivalent to the usual aggregate TFP notion. But point B differs from point C, the bundle that would be produced facing the same world prices that result in actual production A, but with frictionless production and distribution. The difference between B and C is due to $\Pi_1 > \Pi_2$, causing substitution in production away from the relatively penalized good 1.

4.2   Equilibrium world prices

Now turn to the determination of global equilibrium prices. Let the value of shipments at *delivered* prices from origin h in product class k be denoted by Y_k^h. At efficiency production prices, the supply is valued at $g_k^j \tilde{p}_k^j$. Y_k^j is margined up from $g_k^j \tilde{p}_k^j$ to reflect the "average" cost of delivery. Thus

$$Y_k^j = g_k^j \tilde{p}_k^j \prod_k^j .$$

The link of the conditional general equilibrium in (3.6)–(3.7) to full general equilibrium uses the unified world market metaphor and $Y_k^j = g_k^j \tilde{p}_k^j \prod_k^j$. The market clearance conditions in (3.4) can be rewritten as:

$$\left(\beta_k^j \tilde{p}_k^j \prod_k^j \right)^{1-\sigma_k} = \tilde{p}_k^j \prod_k^j g_k^j (.) \left/ \sum_j \tilde{p}_k^j \prod_k^j g_k^j (.) \right. \tag{3.9}$$

For given Π's and β's, (3.9) solves for the $\tilde{p}$'s, the origin prices. The full general equilibrium obtains when the world production shares that arise with equilibrium $\tilde{p}$'s in (3.9) are consistent with the world production shares used to solve for the Π's in (3.6)–(3.7) subject to (3.5) while the Π's that arise from (3.6)–(3.7) for given Y's are consistent with the Π's used in (3.9).

5   Conclusion

This paper describes a framework for decomposing trade costs into their incidence on buyers and sellers, aggregated as if all shipments are made to or from a world market. The results of its implementation for Canada's provinces demonstrate that most incidence falls on sellers. Over time, sellers' incidence is falling due to a previously un-noticed force of globalization – specialization of production. Ongoing work by Anderson and Yotov extends the empirical work to a world of more than a hundred countries and twenty-eight manufacturing goods.

REFERENCES

Anderson, J. E. (1979). "A Theoretical Foundation for the Gravity Equation," *American Economic Review* **69**: 106–16.

(2008). "Gravity, Productivity and the Pattern of Production and Trade," Boston College.

Anderson, J. E. and E. van Wincoop (2003). "Gravity with Gravitas: A Solution to the Border Puzzle," *American Economic Review* **93**: 170–92.

(2004). "Trade Costs," *Journal of Economic Literature* **42**(3): 691–751.

Anderson, J. E. and Y. V. Yotov (2008). "The Changing Incidence of Geography," NBER working paper no. 14423.

Bergstrand, J. H. (1985). "The Gravity Equation in International Trade: Some Microeconomic Foundations and Empirical Evidence," *Review of Economics and Statistics* **67**: 471–81.

Eaton, J. and S. Kortum (2002). "Technology, Geography and Trade," *Econometrica* **70**(5): 1741–79.

Feenstra, R. C. (2004). *Advanced International Trade*, Princeton University Press.

Helpman, E., M. J. Melitz and Y. Rubinstein (2008). "Trading Partners and Trading Volumes," *Quarterly Journal of Economics* **123**: 441–87.

Krugman, P. R. and M. Obstfeld (2006). *International Economics: Theory and Policy*, 7th edition, Boston, MA: Addison-Wesley.

4 Approximating general equilibrium impacts of trade liberalizations using the gravity equation

Applications to NAFTA and the European Economic Area

S. L. Baier and J. H. Bergstrand

1 Introduction

For nearly half a century, the gravity equation has been used to explain econometrically the *ex post* effects of economic integration agreements, national borders, currency unions, immigrant stocks, language, and other measures of "trade costs" on bilateral trade flows. Until recently, researchers typically focused on a simple specification akin to Newton's Law of Gravity, whereby the bilateral trade flow from region i to region j was a multiplicative (or log-linear) function of the two countries' gross domestic products (GDPs), their bilateral distance, and typically an array of bilateral dummy variables assumed to reflect the bilateral trade costs between that pair of regions; we denote this the "traditional" gravity equation. This gravity equation gained acceptance among international trade economists and policy makers in the last twenty-five years for (at least) three reasons: formal theoretical *economic* foundations surfaced around 1980; consistently strong empirical explanatory power (high R^2 values); and policy relevance for analyzing numerous free trade agreements that arose over the past fifteen years.

However, the traditional gravity equation has come under scrutiny. First, the traditional specification ignores that the volume of trade from region i to region j should be influenced by trade costs between regions i and j *relative* to those of the rest of the world (ROW), and the economic sizes of the ROW's regions (and prices of their goods) matter as well. Second, applications of the traditional gravity equation to study bilateral trade agreements often yielded seemingly implausible findings. For instance, coefficient estimates for dummy variables representing the effects of international economic integration agreements (EIAs) on international trade were frequently negative (see Frankel 1997) and estimates of the effects of national borders (i.e. a national EIA) on intra-continental inter-regional trade flows were often seemingly implausibly high (see McCallum 1995). The latter finding – McCallum's "border puzzle" – inspired a cottage industry of papers in the international trade literature to explain this result, see Helliwell (1996, 1997, 1998) and Anderson and Smith (1999a, 1999b).

While two early formal theoretical foundations for the gravity equation with trade costs – first Anderson (1979) and later Bergstrand (1985) – addressed the role of "multilateral prices," a solution to the border puzzle surfaced in Anderson and van Wincoop (2003), which refined the theoretical foundations for the gravity equation to emphasize the importance of accounting properly for the endogeneity of prices.[1] Three major conclusions surfaced from the now seminal Anderson and van Wincoop (henceforth, A-vW) study, "Gravity with Gravitas." First, a complete derivation of a standard Armington (conditional) general equilibrium model of bilateral trade in a multi-region (N>2) setting suggests that traditional cross-section empirical gravity equations have been mis-specified owing to the omission of theoretically motivated *multilateral* (price) resistance terms for exporting and importing regions. Second, to estimate properly the full general equilibrium comparative statics of a national border or an EIA, one needs to estimate these multilateral resistance (MR) terms for any two regions with *and* without a border, in a manner consistent with theory. Third, due to the underlying non-linearity of the structural relationships, A-vW suggest that estimation requires a custom non-linear least squares (NLS) program to account properly for the endogeneity of prices and/or estimate the comparative static effects of a trade cost.

While the A-vW approach yields consistent, efficient estimates of gravity-equation coefficients (in the absence of measurement and specification bias), Feenstra (2004, chapter 5) notes that a "drawback" to the estimation strategy is that it requires a custom NLS program to obtain estimates. One reason the gravity equation has become the workhorse of empirical international trade in the past twenty-five years is that one can use ordinary linear least squares (OLS) to explain trade flows and potentially the impact of policies (such as national borders or EIAs) on such flows. Unfortunately, the need to apply custom NLS estimation has led empirical researchers typically to ignore A-vW's considerations, and will likely continue to impede incorporating these price terms into estimation of gravity equations using the A-vW approach and computation of proper comparative statics.

---

[1] Recently, Balistreri and Hillberry (2007) have questioned some aspects of Anderson and van Wincoop (2003). We address these concerns later in the paper.

Another – and computationally less taxing – approach to estimate potentially unbiased gravity-equation coefficients, which also acknowledges the influence of theoretically motivated MR terms, is to use region-specific fixed effects, as noted by A-vW and Feenstra. An additional benefit is that this method avoids the measurement error associated with measuring regions' "internal distances" for the MR variables. Indeed, van Wincoop himself – and nearly every gravity-equation study since A-vW – has employed this simpler technique of fixed effects, see Rose and van Wincoop (2001) and Rose (2004). Using the case of McCallum's border puzzle as an example, Feenstra (2004, chapter 5 appendix) shows that fixed-effects estimation of the gravity equation can generate unbiased estimates of the *average* border effect of a pair of countries.[2]

Yet, fixed-effects estimation faces two notable drawbacks. First, without the structural system of equations, one still cannot generate region- or pair-specific comparative statics; fixed effects estimation precludes estimating MR terms with *and* without EIAs. However, empirical researchers can use fixed effects to obtain the key gravity-equation parameter estimates, and then simply construct a non-linear system of equations to estimate multilateral price terms with and without the "border." But they don't. Outside of the A-vW Canada-US trade context, researchers have not calculated the full *general-equilibrium comparative-static* effects of a free trade agreement.

Second, many explanatory variables of interest are region specific; using region-specific fixed effects precludes direct estimation of partial effects of numerous potentially important explanatory variables that are often motivated theoretically. For instance, typical gravity studies often try to estimate the effects of exporter and importer populations, foreign aid or internal infrastructure measures on bilateral trade; such variables would be subsumed in the fixed effects; see Egger and Nelson (2007), Nelson and Juhasz Silva (2007), and Melitz (2008). Also, recent analyses of the effects of FTAs on trade using *non-parametric* (matching) econometric techniques require indexes of multilateral resistance that are not derived from a structural model – see Baier and Bergstrand (2009b); an alternative approach is needed. Moreover, recent estimation of economic and political determinants of EIAs between country pairs using probit models of the likelihoods of EIAs require (exogenous) measures of multilateral resistance, see Mansfield and Reinhardt (2003), Baier and Bergstrand (2004), and Mansfield *et al.* (2008).

---

[2] In their robustness analysis, A-vW demonstrate evidence using fixed effects for unbiased estimates of the *average* border effect. Recently, Behrens *et al.* (2007) show that OLS with fixed effects may still result in biased estimates because they fail to capture fully the spatial interdependence among trade flows and their determinants.

Consequently, the empirical researcher faces a tradeoff. A-vW's customized NLS approach can potentially generate consistent, efficient estimates of average border effects *and* comparative statics, but it is computationally burdensome relative to OLS and subject to measurement error associated with internal distance indexes. Fixed-effects estimation uses OLS and avoids internal distance measurement error for MR terms, but one cannot retrieve the multilateral price terms necessary to generate quantitative estimates of comparative-static effects without also employing the structural system of equations. Is there a third way to estimate gravity-equation parameters using *exogenous* measures of multilateral resistance – *and* compute region-specific or pair-specific comparative statics – using "good old" OLS? This paper suggests a method that may be useful when NLS estimation is not suitable.

Following some background, this paper has three major parts (theory, estimation, and comparative statics). First, we provide a method for "approximating" the MR terms based upon theory. In the spirit of the recent literature on general equilibrium macro-economic models, we use a simple first-order log-linear Taylor-series expansion of the MR terms in the A-vW system of equations with bilaterally symmetric trade costs to generate a reduced-form gravity equation that includes theoretically motivated (exogenous) MR terms that can be estimated potentially using "good old" OLS. The paper's theoretical approach is a simpler, but special, case of Baier and Bergstrand (2009a), which allowed asymmetric bilateral trade costs (which required more algebra to solve). However – unlike fixed-effects estimation – this method can *also* generate theoretically motivated general equilibrium comparative statics without estimating a non-linear system of equations.[3]

Second, we discuss numerous contexts for which non-linear estimation is not feasible and we show that our first-order log-linear-approximation method provides *virtually identical* coefficient estimates for gravity-equation parameters. For tractability, we apply our technique first to actual trade flows using the same context and Canadian–US datasets as used by McCallum, A-vW, and Feenstra. However, the insights of our paper have the potential to be used in numerous contexts assessing trade-cost effects, especially estimation of the effects of tariff reductions and free trade agreements on world trade flows – the most common usage of the gravity equation in trade. We show that the linear-approximation approach works even more effectively in the context of *world* (intra- and inter-continental) trade than in the narrower context of regional

---

[3] This paper extends Baier and Bergstrand (2009a) to provide a simpler derivation of the exogenous theoretically motivated MR terms in the case of bilaterally symmetric trade costs.

(intra-continental) trade. Using Monte Carlo techniques we demonstrate – based in this paper upon a linear approximation of multilateral resistance terms using *simple averages* of bilateral trade costs – that the estimated bias (of the distance elasticity) of our method over non-linear least squares for world trade is less than *0.5 of one per cent* – smaller than that for intra-continental trade flows; in Baier and Bergstrand (2009a), linear approximations used GDP-share-weighted averages of bilateral trade costs.

Third, we demonstrate the economic conditions under which our approximation method works well to calculate comparative-static effects of key trade-cost variables... and when it does not. We compare the comparative statics generated using our approach versus those using A-vW's approach for both the Canadian–US context and for world trade flows using the Monte Carlo simulated data. For comparative statics, we use (as more appropriate) GDP-shared-weighted averages of bilateral trade costs to generate multilateral resistance approximations. Two important conclusions surface. First, the approximation errors (for our comparative statics) are largest when the comparative-static changes in the multilateral price terms are largest. Using simulated data from our Monte Carlo analyses, we find that the largest comparative static changes in multilateral price terms are *not necessarily* among the smallest GDP-sized economies (and consequently those with the largest trading partners). Rather, multilateral price terms change the most (for a given change in trade costs) for small countries that are *physically close*. Second, as with any linear Taylor-series expansion, approximation errors increase the further away from the center the change is, see Judd (1998). Since a higher-order Taylor-series expansion can reduce these errors, we discuss – based upon a second-order Taylor expansion – the factors (variances and covariances) that likely explain the approximation errors. Then, using a fixed-point iterative matrix manipulation, we show how the approximation errors can be eliminated, where the key economic insight is an $N \times N$ matrix of GDP shares *relative to bilateral distances*. In this paper, we provide detailed comparative static estimates of the effects of NAFTA and the European Economic Area on trade flows.

The remainder of the paper is as follows. Section 2 discusses the gravity-equation literature and A-vW analysis to motivate our paper. Section 3 uses a first-order log-linear Taylor-series expansion to motivate a simple OLS regression equation that can be used to estimate average effects *and* generate comparative statics. In Section 4, we apply our estimation technique to the McCallum-A-vW-Feenstra dataset and compare our coefficient estimates to these papers' findings and use Monte Carlo simulations to show that estimated border effects using "good old"

OLS are virtually identical to those using A-vW's technique for either *inter-regional* trade flows or *international* trade flows (the typical empirical context). Section 5 examines the economic conditions under which our approach approximates the comparative statics of trade-cost changes well and under which it does not. Section 6 concludes.

2   Background

The gravity equation is now considered the empirical workhorse for studying inter-regional and international trade patterns, see Feenstra (2004). Early applications of the gravity equation – Tinbergen (1962), Linnemann (1966), Aitken (1973), and Sapir (1981) – assumed a specification similar to that used in McCallum (1995):

$$\ln X_{ij} = \beta_0 + \beta_1 \ln GDP_i + \beta_2 \ln GDP_j - \beta_3 \ln DIS_{ij}$$
$$+ \beta_4 EIA_{ij} + \varepsilon_{ij} \qquad (4.1)$$

where: X_{ij} denotes the value of the bilateral trade flow from region i to region j; GDP_i (GDP_j) denotes the nominal gross domestic product of region i (j); DIS_{ij} denotes the distance (typically in miles or nautical miles) from the economic center of region i to that of region j; and EIA_{ij} is a dummy variable assuming the value 1 (0) if two regions share (do not share) an economic integration agreement. In the McCallum Canada–US context, EIA_{ij} would be a national "border" dummy reflecting membership in the same country. In the remainder of this paper, boldfaced regular-case (non-bold italicized) variable names denote observed (unobserved) variables. Traditionally, economists have focused on estimates of, say, β_4, to measure the "average" (treatment) effect of an EIA on trade from i to j. Traditional specification (4.1) typically excludes *price* terms. The rationale in the studies was that prices were endogenous and consequently would not surface in the reduced-form cross-section bilateral trade flow equation.[4]

---

[4] The traditional argument is as follows. Suppose importer j's demand for the trade flow from i to j is a function of j's GDP, the price of the product in i (p_i), and distance from i to j. Suppose exporter i's supply of goods is a function of i's GDP and p_i. Market clearing would require county i's export supply to equal the sum of the $N-1$ bilateral import demands (in an N-country world). This generates a system of N+1 equations in N+1 endogenous variables: $N-1$ bilateral import demands X_{ij}^D ($j = 1, \ldots, N$ with $j \neq i$), supply variable X_i^S, and price variable p_i. This system could be solved for a bilateral trade flow equation for X_{ij} that is a function of the GDPs of i and j and their bilateral distance. Then p_i is endogenous and excluded from the reduced-form bilateral trade flow gravity equation.

However, theoretical foundations in Anderson (1979), Bergstrand (1985), Deardorff (1998), Eaton and Kortum (2002), A-vW (2003), and Feenstra (2004) all suggest that traditional gravity equation (4.1) is likely mis-specified owing to the omission of measures of multilateral resistance (or prices). In reality, the trade flow from i to j is surely influenced by the prices of products in the other $N - 2$ regions in the world, which themselves are influenced by the bilateral distances (and EIAs, etc.) of each of i and j with the other $N - 2$ regions. Bergstrand (1985) provided early empirical evidence of this omitted variables bias, but was limited by crude price-index data. As Feenstra (2004) reminds us, published price indexes probably do not reflect accurately "true" border costs (numerous costs associated with international transactions) and are measured relative to an arbitrary base period.

A-vW raised two important considerations. First, A-vW showed theoretically that proper estimation of the coefficients of a theoretically based gravity equation needs to account for the influence of endogenous price terms. Second, estimation yields partial effects of a change in a bilateral trade cost on a bilateral trade flow, but not *general-equilibrium* effects. A-vW clarified that the comparative-static effects of a change in a trade cost were influenced by the full general-equilibrium framework.

2.1   The A-vW theoretical model

To understand the context, we initially describe a set of assumptions to derive a gravity equation; for analytical details, see A-vW (2003). First, assume a world endowment economy with N regions and N (aggregate) goods, each good differentiated by origin. Second, assume consumers in each region j have identical constant elasticity of substitution (CES) preferences:

$$U_j = \left[\sum_{i=1}^{N} C_{ij}^{(\sigma-1)/\sigma} \right]^{\sigma/(\sigma-1)} \qquad j = 1, ..., N \qquad (4.2)$$

where U_j is the utility of consumers in region j, C_{ij} is consumption of region i's good in region j, and σ is the elasticity of substitution (assuming $\sigma > 1$).[5] Maximizing (4.2) subject to the budget constraint:

$$Y_j = \sum_{i=1}^{N} p_i t_{ij} C_{ij} \qquad (4.3)$$

---

[5] Consumption is measured as a quantity. We can also set up the model in terms of a representative consumer with M_j consumers in each country, but the results are analytically identical.

where p_i is the exporter's price of region i's good and t_{ij} is the gross trade cost (one plus the ad valorem trade cost[6]) associated with exports from i to j, yields a set of first-order conditions that can be solved for the demand for the nominal bilateral trade flow from i to j (X_{ij}):

$$X_{ij} = \left(\frac{p_i t_{ij}}{P_j}\right)^{1-\sigma} Y_j \tag{4.4}$$

where $X_{ij} = p_i t_{ij} C_{ij}$ and P_j is the CES price index, given by:

$$P_j = \left[\sum_{i=1}^{N} (p_i t_{ij})^{1-\sigma}\right]^{1/(1-\sigma)} \tag{4.5}$$

Third, an assumption of market clearing requires:

$$Y_i = \sum_{j=1}^{N} X_{ij} \tag{4.6}$$

Following A-vW, substitution of (4.4) and (4.5) into (4.6) and some algebraic manipulation yields:

$$X_{ij} = \left(\frac{Y_i Y_j}{Y^T}\right) \left(\frac{t_{ij}}{P_i P_j}\right)^{1-\sigma} \tag{4.7}$$

where it follows that

$$P_i = \left[\sum_{j=1}^{N} \left(\theta_j / t_{ij}^{\sigma-1}\right) P_j^{\sigma-1}\right]^{1/(1-\sigma)} \tag{4.8}$$

$$P_j = \left[\sum_{i=1}^{N} \left(\theta_i / t_{ij}^{\sigma-1}\right) P_i^{\sigma-1}\right]^{1/(1-\sigma)} \tag{4.9}$$

under a fourth assumption that bilateral trade barriers t_{ij} and t_{ji} are equal for all pairs. In equations (4.8) and (4.9), Y^T denotes total income of all regions, which is constant across region pairs and $\theta_i(\theta_j)$ denotes $Y_i/Y^T(Y_j/Y^T)$. It will be useful now to define the term "economic density." For country i, the bilateral "economic density" of a trading partner j is the amount of economic activity in j relative to the cost of trade between i and j (scaled by $\sigma - 1 > 0$), or $\theta_j / t_{ij}^{\sigma-1}$.

---

[6] As conventional, we assume that all trade costs consume resources and can be interpreted as goods "lost in transit."

2.2   The econometric model

As is common to this literature, for an econometric model we assume the log of the observed trade flow $(\ln \mathbf{X}_{ij})$ is equal to the log of the true trade flow $(\ln X_{ij})$ plus a log-normally distributed error term (ε_{ij}). Y_i can feasibly be represented empirically by observable $\mathbf{GDP}_i$. However, the world is not so generous as to provide observable measures of bilateral trade costs t_{ij}. Following the literature, a fifth assumption is that the gross trade cost factor is a log-linear function of *observable* variables, such as bilateral distance $(\mathbf{DIS}_{ij})$ and $e^{-\alpha \mathbf{EIA}_{ij}}$, the latter representing the ad valorem equivalent of a common EIA, respectively:

$$t_{ij} = \mathbf{DIS}_{ij}^{\rho} e^{-\alpha \mathbf{EIA}_{ij}} \qquad (4.10)$$

where $e^{-\alpha \mathbf{EIA}_{ij}}$ equals $e^{-\alpha}(< 1)$ if the two regions are in an economic integration agreement (assuming $\alpha > 0$). One could also include a language dummy, an adjacency dummy, etc.; for brevity, we ignore these.

In the McCallum-AvW-Feenstra context of Canadian provinces and US states, $\mathbf{EIA}_{ij} = 1$ if the two regions are in the same country, and 0 otherwise. In the context of the theory, estimation of the gravity equation's parameters should account for the MR terms defined in equations (4.8) and (4.9). A-vW describe one customized non-linear procedure for estimating equations (4.7)–(4.10) to generate unbiased estimates in a two-country world with ten Canadian provinces, thirty US states and an aggregate rest-of-US (the other twenty states plus the District of Columbia), or forty-one regions in total. A-vW also estimate a multicounty model; discussion of that is treated later. This procedure requires minimizing the sum-of-squared residuals of:

$$\ln \left[X_{ij} / \left(\mathbf{GDP}_i \mathbf{GDP}_j \right) \right] = a_0 + a_1 \ln \mathbf{DIS}_{ij} + a_2 \mathbf{EIA}_{ij}$$
$$- \ln P_i^{1-\sigma} - \ln P_j^{1-\sigma} + \varepsilon_{ij} \qquad (4.11)$$

subject to the forty-one market-equilibrium conditions $(j = 1, \ldots, 41)$:

$$P_j^{1-\sigma} = \sum_{k=1}^{41} P_k^{\sigma-1} \left(\mathbf{GDP}_k / \mathbf{GDP}^T \right) e^{a_1 \ln \mathbf{DIS}_{kj} + a_2 \mathbf{EIA}_{kj}} \qquad (4.12)$$

to estimate a_0, a_1, and a_2 where, in the model's context, $a_0 = -\ln \mathbf{GDP}^T$, $a_1 = -\rho(\sigma-1)$ and $a_2 = -\alpha(\sigma-1)$. This obviously requires a custom NLS program.

2.3 Estimating comparative-static effects

As A-vW stress, the MR terms $P_i^{1-\sigma}$ and $P_j^{1-\sigma}$ are "critical" to understanding the impact of border barriers on bilateral trade. Once estimates of a_0, a_1, and a_2 are obtained, one can then retrieve estimates of $P_i^{1-\sigma}$ and $P_j^{1-\sigma}$ for all $j = 1, \ldots, 41$ regions both in the presence and absence of a national border. Let $P_i^{1-\sigma}$ ($P_i^{*1-\sigma}$) denote the estimate of the MR region i with (without) an EIA following NLS estimation of equations (4.11) and (4.12). In the context of the model, A-vW and Feenstra (2004) both show that the ratio of bilateral trade between any two regions *with* an EIA (X_{ij}) and *without* an EIA (X_{ij}^*) is given by:

$$X_{ij}/X_{ij}^* = e^{a_2 \mathbf{EIA}_{ij}} \left(P_i^{*1-\sigma}/P_i^{1-\sigma} \right) \left(P_j^{*1-\sigma}/P_j^{1-\sigma} \right) \qquad (4.13)$$

Comparative-static effects of an integration agreement are then calculated using equation (4.13).

Consequently, A-vW (2003) "resolved" the border puzzle theoretically and empirically. However, the appealing characteristic of the gravity equation, that likely has contributed to its becoming the workhorse for the study of empirical trade patterns, is that it has been estimated for decades using OLS. The A-vW procedure cannot use OLS, which will likely inhibit future researchers from recognizing empirically the MR terms. Moreover, in some instances mentioned earlier and later, one might want to have exogenous measures of the MR terms motivated by theory.

A-vW (2003) and Feenstra (2004) both note that a ready alternative to estimating consistently the *average* border effect is to apply fixed effects. However, while fixed effects can determine gravity-equation parameters consistently, estimation of country-specific border effects *still requires* construction of the structural system of price equations to distinguish MR terms with *and* without borders. We demonstrate in this paper a simple technique that yields virtually identical estimates of the average effects *and* (in many instances) comparative statics surfaces by applying a Taylor-series expansion to the theory.

3 Theory

In this section, we apply a first-order log-linear Taylor-series expansion to the system of price equations above to generate a reduced-form gravity equation – including theoretically motivated exogenous multilateral and world resistance (MWR) terms – that can be estimated using OLS, and will be used later in Section 4. The key methodological insight is the use of

a first-order Taylor-series expansion, not commonly used in international
trade but the *workhorse* for modern dynamic macro-economics. A first-
order Taylor-series expansion of any function $f(x_i)$, centered at x, is given
by $f(x_i) = f(x) + [f'(x)](x_i - x)$. In modern dynamic macro-economics,
the expansion is usually made around the steady-state value suggested by
the underlying theoretical model.[7]

This paper extends Baier and Bergstrand (2009a) to provide a simpler
method to approximate multilateral resistance terms in the special case of
bilaterally *symmetric* trade costs; Baier and Bergstrand (2009a) provide a
method to approximate such terms in the more complex case of bilaterally
asymmetric trade costs. Since the solution to a Taylor-series expansion is
sensitive to how it is centered, we use in our static trade context the
natural choice of an expansion centered around a world with symmetric
trade frictions – $t_{ij} = t$ – but allowing asymmetric economic sizes. We
begin with N equations (4.8) from Section 2. Dividing both sides of
equation (4.8) by $t^{1/2}$ yields:

$$P_i/t^{1/2} = \left[\sum_{j=1}^{N} \theta_j \left(t_{ij}/t^{1/2} \right)^{1-\sigma} / P_j^{1-\sigma} \right]^{1/(1-\sigma)}$$

$$= \left[\sum_{j=1}^{N} \theta_j \left(t_{ij}/t \right)^{1-\sigma} / \left(P_j/t^{1/2} \right)^{1-\sigma} \right]^{1/(1-\sigma)} \tag{4.14}$$

Define $\tilde{P}_i = P_i/t^{1/2}$, $\tilde{P}_j = P_j/t^{1/2}$ and $\tilde{t}_{ij} = t_{ij}/t$. Substituting these
expressions into equation (4.14) yields:

$$\tilde{P}_i = \left[\sum_{j=1}^{N} \theta_j \left(\tilde{t}_{ij}/\tilde{P}_j \right)^{1-\sigma} \right]^{1/(1-\sigma)} \tag{4.15}$$

for $i = 1, \ldots, N$. It will be useful for later to rewrite (4.15) as:

$$e^{(1-\sigma)\ln \tilde{P}_i} = \sum_{j=1}^{N} e^{\ln \theta_j} e^{(\sigma-1)\ln \tilde{P}_j} e^{(1-\sigma)\ln \tilde{t}_{ij}} \tag{4.16}$$

where e is the natural logarithm operator.

---

[7] We find using a Monte Carlo robustness analysis that a first-order Taylor series works well
for estimating gravity-equation coefficients. Higher-order terms are largely unnecessary
for estimation. However, such terms are relevant for subsequent comparative statics; we
address this more later.

In a world with symmetric trade costs ($t > 0$), $t_{ij} = t$, implying $\tilde{t}_{ij} = 1$. In this world, the latter implies:

$$\tilde{P}_i^{1-\sigma} = \sum_{j=1}^{N} \theta_j \tilde{P}_j^{\sigma-1} \qquad (4.17)$$

for all $i = 1, \ldots, N$. Multiplying both sides of equation (4.17) by $\tilde{P}_i^{\sigma-1}$ yields:

$$1 = \sum_{j=1}^{N} \theta_j \left(\tilde{P}_i \tilde{P}_j \right)^{\sigma-1} \qquad (4.18)$$

As noted in Feenstra (2004, p. 158, footnote 11), the solution to equation (4.18) is:

$$\tilde{P}_i = \tilde{P}_j = \tilde{P} = 1 \qquad (4.19)$$

Hence, under symmetric trade costs ($t_{ij} = t$), $\tilde{t}_{ij} = \tilde{P}_i = \tilde{P}_j = 1$ and it follows that $P_i = P_j = t^{1/2}$.

In the following derivations, we assume trade costs are bilaterally *symmetric* ($t_{ij} = t_{ji}$), similar to the case focused upon in A-vW (2003). This is a special case of the derivations in Baier and Bergstrand (2009a) where trade costs are allowed to be bilaterally *asymmetric* (t_{ij} need not equal t_{ji}).

A first-order log-linear Taylor-series expansion of equation (4.16) centered at $\tilde{t} = \tilde{P} = 1$ (and $\ln \tilde{t} = \ln \tilde{P} = 0$) is:

$$1 + \ln \tilde{P}_i^{1-\sigma} = 1 - \sum_{j=1}^{N} \theta_j \ln \tilde{P}_j^{1-\sigma} + (1-\sigma) \sum_{j=1}^{N} \theta_j \ln \tilde{t}_{ij} \qquad (4.20)$$

using $d[e(1-\sigma)\ln \tilde{P}]/d(\ln \tilde{P}) = (1-\sigma)e^{(1-\sigma)\ln \tilde{P}}$. Subtracting 1 from both sides, multiplying both sides by θ_i, and summing both sides over N yields:

$$\sum_{i=1}^{N} \theta_i \ln \tilde{P}_i^{1-\sigma} = -\sum_{i=1}^{N} \theta_i \sum_{j=1}^{N} \theta_j \ln \tilde{P}_j^{1-\sigma} + (1-\sigma) \sum_{i=1}^{N} \sum_{j=1}^{N} \theta_i \theta_j \ln \tilde{t}_{ij}$$

$$(4.21)$$

Noting that the first RHS term can be expressed in alternative ways,

$$-\sum_{i=1}^{N} \theta_i \sum_{j=1}^{N} \theta_j \ln \tilde{P}_j^{1-\sigma} = -\sum_{j=1}^{N} \theta_j \ln \tilde{P}_j^{1-\sigma} = -\sum_{i=1}^{N} \theta_i \ln \tilde{P}_i^{1-\sigma}$$

we can substitute $-\sum_{i=1}^{N} \theta_i \ln \tilde{P}_i^{1-\sigma}$ for $-\sum_{i=1}^{N} \theta_i \sum_{j=1}^{N} \theta_j \ln \tilde{P}_j^{1-\sigma}$ in equation (4.21) to yield:

$$\sum_{i=1}^{N} \theta_i \ln \tilde{P}_i^{1-\sigma} = -\sum_{j=1}^{N} \theta_j \ln \tilde{P}_i^{1-\sigma} + (1 - \sigma) \sum_{i=1}^{N} \sum_{j=1}^{N} \theta_i \theta_j \ln \tilde{t}_{ij}$$

or

$$\sum_{i=1}^{N} \theta_i \ln \tilde{P}_i^{1-\sigma} = \sum_{j=1}^{N} \theta_j \ln \tilde{P}_j^{1-\sigma} = (1/2)(1 - \sigma) \sum_{i=1}^{N} \sum_{j=1}^{N} \theta_i \theta_j \ln \tilde{t}_{ij} \tag{4.22}$$

Substituting equation (4.22) into equation (4.20), after subtracting 1 from both sides of equation (4.20), yields:

$$\ln \tilde{P}_i^{\sigma-1} = -\ln \tilde{P}_i^{1-\sigma}$$

$$= (\sigma - 1) \left[\sum_{j=1}^{N} \theta_j \ln \tilde{t}_{ij} - (1/2) \sum_{i=1}^{N} \sum_{j=1}^{N} \theta_i \theta_j \ln \tilde{t}_{ij} \right] \tag{4.23}$$

Recalling that $\ln \tilde{P}_i^{\sigma-1} = (\sigma - 1) \ln P_i - \frac{1}{2}(\sigma - 1) \ln t$ and $\ln \tilde{t}_{ij} = \ln t_{ij} - \ln t$, then substitution into the equation above and some algebraic manipulation yields:

$$\ln P_i^{\sigma-1} = -\ln P_i^{1-\sigma}$$

$$= (\sigma - 1) \left[\sum_{j=1}^{N} \theta_j \ln t_{ij} - (1/2) \sum_{i=1}^{N} \sum_{j=1}^{N} \theta_i \theta_j \ln t_{ij} \right] \tag{4.24}$$

and it follows that:

$$\ln P_j^{\sigma-1} = -\ln P_j^{1-\sigma}$$

$$= (\sigma - 1)\left[\sum_{i=1}^{N} \theta_i \ln t_{ij} - (1/2)\sum_{i=1}^{N}\sum_{j=1}^{N} \theta_i\theta_j \ln t_{ij}\right] \quad (4.25)$$

Although (by assumption) $t_{ij} = t_{ji}$, $\sum_{i=1}^{N} \theta_i \ln t_{ij}$ need not equal $\sum_{j=1}^{N} \theta_j \ln t_{ij}$.[8]

Equations (4.24) and (4.25) are critical to understanding this analysis. The benefit of the first-order log-linear expansion is that it identifies the *exogenous* actual "multilateral resistance" factors determining the multilateral price terms in equations (4.7)–(4.9) in a manner consistent with the theoretical model. To understand the intuition behind equation (4.25) – analogous for (4.24) – we consider separately each of the two components of the RHS. The first component is a GDP-share-weighted (geometric) average of the gross trade costs facing country j across all regions. The higher this average, the greater overall multilateral resistance in j. Holding constant bilateral determinants of trade, the larger is j's multilateral resistance, the lower are bilateral trade costs relative to multilateral trade costs. Hence, the *larger* the bilateral trade flow from i to j will be.

Now consider the second component on the RHS of equation (4.25). The Taylor-series expansion here makes more transparent the influence of *world resistance*, which is identical for all countries. In A-vW, this second component was also present – see A-vW's equations (14)-(16) – but not emphasized. World resistance lowers trade between *every* pair of countries. This term is constant in cross-section gravity estimation, embedded in and affecting only the intercept. (However, the term cannot be ignored in estimating "border effects.")[9] Together, these terms indicate that the level of bilateral trade from i to j is influenced – not just by the level of *bilateral relative to multilateral* trade costs, but also by *multilateral relative to world* trade costs.

In the context of the theory just discussed, we can obtain consistent estimates of the gravity equations' coefficients – accounting for the

---

[8] For instance, internal distances t_{ii} and t_{jj} will likely differ, as will θ_i and θ_j. For transparency and consistency with A-vW's notation, we note that $\ln P_i^{\sigma-1} = -\ln P_i^{1-\sigma}$; analogously for j.

[9] Moreover, in panel estimation, changes in world resistance over time – along with changes in world income – provide a rationale for including a time trend.

endogenous multilateral price variables – by estimating *using OLS* the reduced-form gravity equation:

$$\ln \mathbf{X}_{ij} = \beta_0' + \ln \mathbf{GDP}_i + \ln \mathbf{GDP}_j - (\sigma - 1) \ln t_{ij}$$

$$+ (\sigma - 1) \left[\left(\sum_{j=1}^{N} \theta_j \ln t_{ij} \right) - \frac{1}{2} \left(\sum_{i=1}^{N} \sum_{j=1}^{N} \theta_i \theta_j \ln t_{ij} \right) \right]$$

$$+ (\sigma - 1) \left[\left(\sum_{i=1}^{N} \theta_i \ln t_{ij} \right) - \frac{1}{2} \left(\sum_{i=1}^{N} \sum_{j=1}^{N} \theta_i \theta_j \ln t_{ij} \right) \right]$$

$$(4.26)$$

where $\beta_0' = -\ln Y^T$ is a constant across country pairs, as is $\sum_{i=1}^{N} \sum_{j=1}^{N} \theta_i \theta_j \ln t_{ij}$. Thus, in the context of the theoretical model, the influence of the endogenous multilateral price variables can be accounted for – once we have measures of t_{ij} – using these theoretically motivated *exogenous* multilateral resistance variables.

We close this section noting that it is useful to exponentiate equation (4.26). After some algebra, this yields:

$$\frac{X_{ij}}{Y_i Y_j / Y^T} = \left(\frac{t_{ij}}{t_i(\theta) t_j(\theta) / t^T(\theta)} \right)^{-(\sigma-1)}$$

$$(4.27)$$

where $t_i(\theta) = \Pi_{j=1}^{N} t_{ij}^{\theta_j}$, $t_j(\theta) = \Pi_{i=1}^{N} t_{ij}^{\theta_i}$, $t^T(\theta) = \Pi_{i=1}^{N} \Pi_{j=1}^{N} t_{ij}^{\theta_i \theta_j}$ and recall $\theta_i = Y_i / Y^T$ and $t_{ij} = t_{ji}$ (by assumption). Our use of the Taylor-series expansion simplifies further the "significantly simplified" gravity equation implied by A-vW's equations (7)–(9); see A-vW (2003, p. 176). Equation (4.27) is a simple reduced-form equation capturing the theoretical influences of bilateral, multilateral, and world trade costs on (relative) bilateral trade. As noted, multilateral and world trade costs are GDP-share weighted. Given data on bilateral trade flows, national incomes, and bilateral trade costs, equation (4.26) can be estimated by "good old" OLS – noting the possible *endogeneity bias* introduced by GDP-share weights in RHS variables.[10] But will this equation work *empirically*? Moreover, even

[10] We ignore here the possibility of "zero" trade flows. Such issues have been dealt with by various means; see, for example, Felbermayr and Kohler (2004).

if our approach yields consistent estimates of gravity-equation parameters, can our approach provide "good" approximations of the MR terms *and* the comparative statics generated using A-vW's non-linear approach? The next two sections address these two questions in turn.

4 Estimation

The goal of this section is to show that one can generate virtually identical gravity-equation coefficient estimates ("partial" effects) to those generated using the technique in A-vW but using instead OLS with exogenous multilateral-resistance terms suggested in the previous section. While the approach should work in numerous contexts, for tractability we apply it first in Section 4.1 to McCallum's US–Canadian case, since this is a popular context. We estimate the McCallum, A-vW, fixed effects, and our versions of the model using the A-vW data provided at Robert Feenstra's website, and compare our coefficient estimates with the other results. We show that A-vW, fixed effects, and our methods can yield similar gravity-equation coefficient estimates, even though both OLS-MR and fixed effects are computationally simpler. In Section 4.2, we provide Monte Carlo analyses for two contexts: Canadian–US flows *and* world trade flows among eighty-eight countries. In Section 4.3, we discuss four contexts in which our method would be useful for estimating gravity-equation parameters instead of using fixed effects.

Before implementing equation (4.26) econometrically, three issues need to be addressed. First, in implementing theoretically the Taylor-series expansion, we needed to assume a "center" for the expansion. In the theory, we centered the expansion around a symmetric trade cost, t. However, OLS generates estimates of coefficients based upon covariances and variances of variables around *all* variables' "means." Consequently, for estimation purposes – but *not* for comparative-static exercises later – a more useful center would be an expansion around a symmetric world, that is, a world symmetric in all variables (trade costs *and* economic sizes). In such a world, the first-order log-linear Taylor expansion of the same system of multilateral price equations yields a reduced-form analogue to equation (4.26) that simply replaces the GDP-share weights (θ_i, θ_j) used in Baier and Bergstrand (2009a) with equal weights (1/N); derivations are available on request.

Second, even if one wanted to generate the econometric specification suggested strictly by theory, another econometric issue arises. As in A-vW, in the estimation trade flows were scaled by the product of GDPs to impose unitary income elasticities and also to avoid an endogeneity bias (running from trade flows to GDPs). Including GDP-share-weighted multilateral trade costs could create an endogeneity bias. Hence, for both reasons mentioned, we use the simple averages of the trade costs for estimation rather than the GDP-share-weighted averages used in Baier and Bergstrand (2009a).[11]

Third, to implement equation (4.26) empirically we need to replace the unobservable theoretical trade-cost variable t_{ij} in ($\mathbf{DIS}_{ij}$) and a dummy representing the presence or absence of an economic integration agreement ($\mathbf{EIA}_{ij}$). We define a dummy variable, $\mathbf{BORDER}_{ij}$, which assumes a value of 1 if regions i and j are *not* in the same nation; hence, $\mathbf{EIA}_{ij} = 1 - \mathbf{BORDER}_{ij}$.[12] Taking the logarithms of both sides of equation (4.10) and then substituting the resulting equation for ln t_{ij} into (4.26) – and using equal weights (1/N) rather than GDP-share weights (θ_i) – yields:

$$\ln \mathbf{X}_{ij} = \beta_0' - \rho(\sigma - 1)\ln \mathbf{DIS}_{ij} - \alpha(\sigma - 1)\mathbf{BORDER}_{ij}$$

$$+ \rho(\sigma - 1)\mathbf{MWRDIS}_{ij} + \alpha(\sigma - 1)\mathbf{MWRBORDER}_{ij}$$

$$+ \varepsilon_{ij} \tag{4.28}$$

where

$$\mathbf{MWRDISij} = \left[\frac{1}{N} \left(\sum_{j=1}^{N} \ln \mathbf{DIS}_{ij} \right) + \frac{1}{N} \left(\sum_{i=1}^{N} \ln \mathbf{DIS}_{ij} \right) \right.$$

$$\left. - \frac{1}{N^2} \left(\sum_{i=1}^{N} \sum_{j=1}^{N} \ln \mathbf{DIS}_{ij} \right) \right] \tag{4.29}$$

---

[11] Monte Carlo analyses confirm that estimates are marginally less biased using the simple averages of RHS variables, rather than the GDP-weighted averages. However, GDP-share-weighted MR terms will generate less biased predicted values of comparative statics. These results are confirmed in Bergstrand *et al.* (2007).

[12] It will be useful now to distinguish "regions" from "countries." We assume that a country is composed of regions (which, for empirical purposes later, can be considered states or provinces). We will assume N regions in the world and n countries, with $N > n$. Our theoretical model applies to a two-country or multi-country ($n > 2$) world. We will assume $n \geq 2$. A "border" separates countries. Also, we use $\mathbf{BORDER}$ rather than $\mathbf{EIA}$ so that the coefficient estimates for $\mathbf{DIS}$ and $\mathbf{BORDER}$ are both negative and therefore are consistent with A-vW (2003) and Feenstra (2004). The model is isomorphic to being recast in a monopolistically competitive framework.

and

$$
\begin{aligned}
\textbf{MWRBORDER}_{ij} = \Bigg[& \frac{1}{N}\left(\sum_{j=1}^{N}\textbf{BORDER}_{ij}\right) \\
+ & \frac{1}{N}\left(\sum_{i=1}^{N}\textbf{BORDER}_{ij}\right) \\
- & \frac{1}{N^2}\left(\sum_{i=1}^{N}\sum_{j=1}^{N}\textbf{BORDER}_{ij}\right)\Bigg]
\end{aligned}
\tag{4.30}
$$

where $x_{ij} = X_{ij}/\textbf{GDP}_i\textbf{GDP}_j$. To conform to our theory, coefficient estimates for ln $\textbf{DIS}$ ($\textbf{BORDER}$) and $\textbf{MWRDIS}$ ($\textbf{MWRBORDER}$) are restricted to have identical but oppositely signed coefficient values. "MWR" denotes multilateral and world resistance. As discussed above, to conform to OLS, only estimation of (4.28) uses equally weighted trade-cost variables; comparative statics will use θ-weighted trade costs.

As readily apparent, equation (4.28) can be estimated using OLS, once data on trade flows, GDPs, bilateral distances, and borders are provided. We note that the inclusion of these additional MWR terms appears reminiscent of early attempts to include – what A-vW term – "atheoretical remoteness" variables, typically GDP-weighted averages of each country's distance from all of its trading partners. However, there are two important differences here. First, our additional (the last two) terms are motivated by theory; moreover, we make explicit the role of *world* resistance. Second, previous atheoretical remoteness measures included only multilateral *distance*, ignoring all other multilateral (and world) "border" variables (such as adjacency, language, etc.).

4.1   Estimation using the McCallum–A-vW–Feenstra dataset for actual Canadian–US trade flows

We follow the A-vW procedure (for the two-country model) of estimating the gravity equation for trade flows among ten Canadian provinces, thirty US states, and one aggregate region representing the other twenty US states and the District of Columbia (denoted RUS). As in A-vW, we do not include trade flows internal to a state or province. We calculate the distance between the aggregate US region and the other regions in the same manner as A-vW. We also compute and use the *internal distances* as described in A-vW for $\textbf{MWRDIS}$. Hence, there are forty-one regions.

Table 4.1. *Estimation results*

Parameters	(1) OLS w/o MR terms	(2) A-vW NLS-2	(3) A-vW NLS-3	(4) OLS with MR terms	(5) Fixed effects	(6) A-vW NLS-2a	(7) A-vW NLS-2b
$-\rho(\sigma - 1)$	−1.06	−0.79	−0.82	−1.26	−1.25	−0.92	−1.15
	(0.04)	(0.03)	(0.03)	(0.04)	(0.04)	(0.03)	(0.04)
$-\alpha(\sigma - 1)$	−0.71	−1.65	−1.59	−1.53	−1.54	−1.65	−1.67
	(0.06)	(0.08)	(0.08)	(0.07)	(0.06)	(0.07)	(0.07)
Avg. Error Terms							
US-US	−0.21	0.06	0.06	−0.01	0.00	0.05	0.04
CA-CA	1.95	−0.17	−0.02	0.03	0.00	−0.22	−0.32
US-CA	0.00	−0.05	−0.04	0.01	0.00	−0.04	−0.02
R^2	0.42	n.a.	n.a.	0.52	0.66	n.a.	n.a.
No. of obs.	1,511	1,511	1,511	1,511	1,511	1,511	1,511

Note: Numbers in parentheses are standard errors of the estimates.

Some trade flows are zero and, as in A-vW, these are omitted. As in A-vW and Feenstra (2004), we have 1,511 observations for trade flows from the year 1993.

Table 4.1 provides the results. For purposes of comparison, column (1) provides the benchmark model (McCallum) results estimating equation (4.28) except *omitting* **MWRDIS** and **MWRBORDER**. Columns (2) and (3) provide the model estimated using NLS as in A-vW for the two-country and multi-country cases, respectively. Column (4) provides the results from estimating equation (4.28). For completeness, column (5) provides the results from estimating equation (4.28), but using region-specific fixed effects instead of **MWRDIS** and **MWRBORDER**.

Table 4.1's results are generally comparable to Table 2 in A-vW. Column (1)'s coefficient estimates for the basic McCallum regression, ignoring multilateral resistance terms, are biased, as expected. This specification can be compared with Feenstra (2004, Table 5.2, column [3]), since it uses US-US, CA-CA, and US-CA data for 1993. Note, however, we report the border dummy's coefficient estimate ("Indicator border") whereas Feenstra reports instead the implied "Country Indicator" estimates.[13] Columns (2) and (3) in Table 4.1 report the estimates (using

[13] In Feenstra's Table 5.2, column (3), he does not report the actual dummy variable's coefficient estimate (comparable to our estimate of 0.71). Instead, he reports only the implied

GAUSS) of the A-vW benchmark coefficient estimates; these correspond exactly to those in A-vW's Table 2 and (for the two-country case) Feenstra's Table 5.2, column (4). The coefficient estimates from our OLS specification (4.28) are reported in column (4) of Table 4.1. While our coefficient estimates differ from the NLS estimates in columns (2) and (3), they match closely the coefficient estimates using fixed effects in column (5). Recall that – as both A-vW and Feenstra note – fixed effects should provide unbiased coefficient estimates of the bilateral distance and bilateral border effects, accounting fully for multilateral-resistance influences in estimation. Our column (5) estimates match exactly those in A-vW and Feenstra (2004).[14]

We now address the difference between bilateral distance coefficient estimates in columns (2) and (3) and those in columns (4) and (5). While Feenstra (2004) omitted addressing this difference, A-vW did address it in their sensitivity analysis (2003, part V, Table 6). As A-vW (2003, p. 188) note, the bilateral distance coefficient estimate using their NLS program is quite sensitive to the calculation of "internal distances." In their sensitivity analysis, they provide alternative coefficient estimates when the internal distance variable values are doubled (or, 0.5 minimum capitals' distance). These are reported in column (6) of our Table 4.1; note that the absolute value of the distance coefficient increases with virtually no change in the border dummy's coefficient estimate. Using the same procedure, we increased the internal distance variables' values by a factor of ten (or, 2.5 times minimum capitals' distance); we see in column (7) that the bilateral distance coefficient estimate is now much closer to those in columns (4) and (5).

These results confirm A-vW's suspicion that the NLS estimation technique is sensitive to both measurement error in internal distances and potential specification error. The main reason is the interaction of the distance and border-dummy variables using NLS. Fixed-effects estimates, of course, do not depend on internal distance measures. Our OLS estimation procedure avoids the potential bias introduced by measurement error and potential specification error better than the non-linear

"Indicator Canada" and "Indicator US" estimates of 2.75 and 0.40, respectively. The implied Indicator Canada and Indicator US estimates from our regression are 2.66 and 0.48, respectively; the difference is that we restrict the GDP elasticities to unity. When we relax the constraints on GDP elasticities, our estimates match those in Feenstra's Table 5.2, column (3) and A-vW's Table 1 exactly.

[14] The coefficient estimates from the fixed-effects regression in A-vW's Table 6, column (viii) are not reported. However, they were generously provided by Eric van Wincoop in email correspondence, along with the other coefficient estimates associated with their Table 6. A-vW's Distance (Border) coefficient estimate using fixed effects was −1.25 (−1.54).

estimation procedure. First, our OLS estimates are insensitive to measures of internal distance. As A-vW note (2003, p. 179), internal distances are only relevant to calculating the multilateral resistance terms (in our context, only the multilateral and world resistance [MWR] terms). Examine equation (4.29) closely. Since **MWRDIS** is linear in logs of distance, a doubling of internal distance simply alters the intercept of equation (4.28). For instance, we can rewrite **MWRDIS**$_{ij}$ as a function of the internal distance measures (ln **DIS**$_{ii}$ for all $i = 1, \ldots, N$) and all other bilateral distances (ln **DIS**$_{ij}$ for all $i \neq j$), which we denote **Other**$_{ij}$:

$$\textbf{MWRDISij} = \left[\frac{\ln \textbf{DIS}_{ii}}{N} + \frac{\ln \textbf{DIS}_{jj}}{N} - \frac{\ln \textbf{DIS}_{11}}{N^2} \right.$$
$$\left. - \cdots - \frac{\ln \textbf{DIS}_{NN}}{N^2} + \textbf{Other}_{ij} \right] \qquad (4.31)$$

Now double all internal distances in equation (4.31). This yields:

$$\textbf{MWRDIS}_{ij}$$
$$= \left[\frac{\ln \textbf{DIS}_{ii}}{N} + \frac{\ln 2}{N} + \frac{\ln \textbf{DIS}_{jj}}{N} + \frac{\ln 2}{N} \right.$$
$$\left. - \frac{\ln \textbf{DIS}_{11}}{N^2} - \cdots - \frac{\ln \textbf{DIS}_{NN}}{N^2} - \frac{N \ln 2}{N^2} + \textbf{Other}_{ij} \right]$$
$$(4.32)$$

This alters **MWRDIS**$_{ij}$ by a constant, $(\ln 2)/N$, for all pairs (i, j). This simply scales **MWRDIS**$_{ij}$ by a constant, and thus will have *no effect* on the coefficient estimates of equation (4.28); measurement error introduced by internal distances in A-vW's structural estimation is avoided using fixed effects or our OLS estimation. Second, OLS avoids potential specification bias, such as one raised by Balistreri and Hillberry (2007) noting A-vW's estimates ignored the constraint that the constant (a_0) needed to equal (the negative of the log of) world income; once this structural constraint is imposed, the A-vW coefficient estimates (especially that for distance) are closer to the fixed-effects estimates and our estimates. OLS and fixed effects avoid this specification error.[15]

---

[15] Our Taylor-series expansion illustrates that the intercept also reflects world resistance and the dispersion of world income. We note that Balistreri and Hillberry (2007) addressed other concerns about the A-vW study as well, including A-vW's exclusion of interstate trade flows and their imposing symmetry on US–Canadian border effects. Due to space limitations, we do not address these issues.

4.2   Monte Carlo analyses

The previous section addressed the question: does OLS estimation with exogenous MR terms work empirically as an approximation to A-vW (allowing for measurement and specification error)? While NLS estimation of the A-vW system of equations, our OLS specification, and a fixed-effects specification should all generate similar estimates of $-\rho(\sigma - 1)$ and $-\alpha(\sigma - 1)$, a comparison of Table 4.1's empirical results for specifications (2)–(5) yield significantly different results. Notably, our OLS (spec. 4) and fixed effects (spec. 5) yield similar results, but both differ sharply from estimation using NLS (spec. 2 or 3), notably for the distance coefficient. Why? As just discussed, A-vW's NLS procedure is highly sensitive to the measurement of internal distances for the multilateral resistance terms and ignoring that the intercept (in theory) equals $- \ln Y^T$. Is there a way to compare the estimation results of A-vW and our approach *excluding* the measurement and potential specification errors?

In this section, we employ a Monte Carlo approach to show that our OLS method yields border and distance coefficient estimates that are virtually identical to those using A-vW's NLS method when we know the "true" model. To do this, in Section 4.2.1 we construct the "true" bilateral international trade flows among forty-one regions using the theoretical model of A-vW described in Section 2. We assume the world is described precisely by equations (4.11) and (4.12), assuming various arbitrary values for α, ρ, and σ under alternative scenarios. Using Canadian–US province and state data on GDPs and bilateral distances and dummy variables for borders, we can compute the *true* bilateral trade flows *and true* multilateral resistance terms associated with these economic characteristics for given values of parameters α, ρ, and σ. We then assume that there exists a log-normally distributed error term for each trade flow equation. We make 5,000 draws for each trade equation and run various regression specifications 5,000 times.[16] We will consider first two different sets of given parameter values and five specifications. We use *GAUSS* in all estimates. In Section 4.2.2, to show that this approach works in the more traditional context of world trade flows, we employ the same Monte Carlo approach and provide the results.

4.2.1   Monte Carlo analysis 1: Canada–US We consider five specifications. Specification (1) is the basic gravity model ignoring multilateral

---

[16] The error terms' distribution is such that the R^2 (and standard error of the estimate) from a regression of trade on GDP, distance, and borders using a standard gravity equation is similar to that typically found (an R^2 of 0.7 to 0.8).

resistance terms, as used by McCallum. The specification is analogous to equation (4.11) excluding the MR terms. In the context of the theory, we should get biased estimates of the true parameters since we intentionally omit the true multilateral price terms or fixed effects. Specification (2) is the basic gravity model augmented with "atheoretical remoteness" terms ($\mathbf{REMOTE}_i$ and $\mathbf{REMOTE}_j$), as in McCallum (1995), Helliwell (1996, 1997, 1998), and Wei (1996). Equation (4.11) would include $\mathbf{REMOTE}_i$ and $\mathbf{REMOTE}_j$, instead of P_i and P_j, where $\mathbf{REMOTE}_i = \ln \Sigma_j^N (\mathbf{DIS}_{ij}/\mathbf{GDP}_j)$ and analogously for $\mathbf{REMOTE}_j$. In the context of the theory, we should get biased estimates of the true parameters since we are using atheoretical measures of remoteness. This specification also ignores other multilateral trade costs. For specification (3), we take the system of equations described in equation (4.12) to generate the "true" multilateral resistance terms associated with given values of $-\rho(\sigma - 1)$ and $-\alpha(\sigma - 1)$. We then estimate the regression (4.11) using the true values of the multilateral resistance terms. In the presence of the true MR terms, we expect the coefficient estimates to be virtually identical to the *true* parameters. Specification (4) uses region-specific fixed effects. As discussed earlier, region-specific fixed effects should also generate unbiased estimates of the coefficients. Specification (5) is our OLS equation (4.28). If our hypothesis is correct, the parameter estimates should be virtually identical to those estimated using specifications (3) and (4).

Initially, we run these five specifications for two different scenarios of values for $a_1 = -\rho(\sigma - 1)$ and $a_2 = -\alpha(\sigma - 1)$. In both cases, we report three statistics. First, we report the average coefficient estimates for a_1 and a_2 from the 5,000 regressions for each specification. Second, we report the standard deviation of these 5,000 estimates. In the last column, we report the fraction of times (from the 5,000 regressions) that the coefficient estimate for a variable was within two standard errors of the true coefficient estimate.[17] All estimation was done using *GAUSS*.

Scenario 1. Assume $-\rho(\sigma - 1) = -0.79$ *and* $-\alpha(\sigma - 1) = -1.65$

For Scenario 1, we use the actual coefficient estimates found in A-vW using their two-country model. Table 4.2a reports the estimated values for the five specifications under this scenario in columns (2)–(4). There are two major results worth noting. First, the first two specifications provide biased estimates of the border and distance coefficient estimates,

---

[17] Note that the standard deviation refers to the square root of the variance of all the coefficient estimates for a specification. We also calculated the standard errors of each coefficient estimate. The last column in each table refers to the fraction of the 5,000 regressions that the estimated coefficient is within two standard errors of the true value.

Table 4.2a. *Monte Carlo simulations: scenario 1*
True border coefficient = −1.65
True distance coefficient = −0.79

Specification	Coefficient estimate average	Standard deviation	Fraction within two standard errors of true value
(1) McCallum			
Border	−0.789	0.026	0.000
Distance	−0.562	0.017	0.000
(2) OLS w/atheoretical remoteness terms			
Border	−0.804	0.026	0.000
Distance	−0.541	0.019	0.000
(3) A-vW			
Border	−1.650	0.051	0.973
Distance	−0.789	0.034	0.950
(4) Fixed effects			
Border	−1.650	0.033	0.967
Distance	−0.790	0.033	0.943
(5) OLS with MR terms			
Border	−1.643	0.033	0.985
Distance	−0.802	0.020	0.978

as expected. Second, both fixed effects and OLS-MR provide estimates very close to those using specification (3), as expected. While the average OLS-MR coefficient estimates depart slightly from the average A-vW estimates, 98 per cent of the border and distance (coefficient) estimates are within two standard errors of true values.

Scenario 2. Assume $-\rho(\sigma - 1) = -1.25$ *and* $-\alpha(\sigma - 1) = -1.54$

Now we choose values for $-\rho(\sigma - 1)$ and $-\alpha(\sigma - 1)$ that are identical to those estimated using fixed effects in Table 4.1. Table 4.2b provides the same set of information as in Table 4.2a, but for this alternative set of true values. The results are robust to this alternative set of parameters. The OLS-MR coefficient estimates are within two standard errors of the true values 99 per cent of the time.

Sensitivity Analysis: Varying $-\rho(\sigma - 1)$ *and* $-\alpha(\sigma - 1)$ *each between* -0.25 *and* -2.00

Given the success of these results, we decided to perform these simulations for a wide range of arbitrary values of the parameters. We considered a range for each variable's "true" coefficient from −0.25 to −2.00. Because of the large number of simulations, we used 1,000 runs

Table 4.2b. *Monte Carlo simulations: scenario 2*
True border coefficient = −1.54
True distance coefficient = −1.25

Specification	Coefficient estimate average	Standard deviation	Fraction within two standard errors of true value
(1) McCallum			
Border	−0.655	0.025	0.000
Distance	−0.952	0.017	0.000
(2) OLS w/atheoretical remoteness terms			
Border	−0.664	0.026	0.000
Distance	−0.940	0.019	0.000
(3) A-vW			
Border	−1.540	0.051	0.977
Distance	−1.250	0.034	0.950
(4) Fixed effects			
Border	−1.540	0.033	0.988
Distance	−1.250	0.033	0.942
(5) OLS with MR terms			
Border	−1.529	0.033	0.999
Distance	−1.276	0.021	0.996

per parameter pair. We basically found the same findings. First, regardless of the true values of the Border and Distance coefficients, the OLS Border coefficient estimate is within two standard errors of the true value no less than *93 per cent* of the time. Second, the OLS Distance coefficient estimate is also within two standard errors of the true value no less than 93 per cent of the time. For brevity, these results are not reported individually.

4.2.2   Monte Carlo analysis 2: gravity equations for world trade flows Of course, the gravity equation has been used over the past four decades to analyze economic and political determinants of a wide range of aggregate "flows." However, the most common usage of the gravity equation has been for explaining *world* (intra- and inter-continental) bilateral trade flows. The issues raised in A-vW (2003) and in this paper have potential relevance for the estimation of the effects of free trade agreements and of tariff rates on world trade flows. In the spirit of "generalizing" our technique to other contexts, we offer another sensitivity analysis.

In this section, we construct a set of "artificial" aggregate bilateral world trade flows among eighty-eight countries for which data on the exogenous

RHS variables discussed above were readily available.[18] Three exogenous RHS variables that typically explain world trade flows are countries' GDPs, their bilateral distances, and a dummy representing the presence (0) or absence (1) of a common land border ("NoAdjacency"). We then estimate the relationship among bilateral trade flows, national incomes, bilateral distances and NoAdjacency among the eighty-eight countries using our OLS method. We simply redo Section 4.2.1's Monte Carlo simulations.[19]

We start with the system of equations (4.11) and (4.12), modified to eighty-eight regions. Initially, we assigned two sets of possible parameters for $-\alpha(\sigma - 1)$ and $-\rho(\sigma - 1)$, the same two sets of values used for Table 4.2. We then calculated the "true" MR terms and "true" trade flows using equations (4.11) and (4.12). We then assume there exists a lognormally distributed error term. We make 1,000 draws for the equation and run various specifications 1,000 times.

For the world dataset, the countries are chosen according to data availability and include the largest of the world's economies. GDPs in thousands of US dollars are from the World Bank's *World Development Indicators*. Bilateral distances were calculated using the standard formula for geodesic, or "great circle," distances (http://mathworld. wolfram.com/GreatCircle.html). NoAdjacency is a dummy variable defined as 0 (1) if the two countries actually share (do not share) a common land border. In the typical gravity equation for world trade flows, adjacency is expected to augment trade; hence, NoAdjacency (like Border in the previous section) has an expected negative relationship with trade.

The notable finding is that the estimation biases for world trade flows are very small, and are *even smaller* than those found using OLS for the intra-continental (Canadian–US) trade flow specifications. For example,

---

[18] The eighty-eight countries are Argentina, Australia, Austria, Bangladesh, Belgium, Bolivia, Brazil, Bulgaria, Canada, Chile, China, Colombia, Costa Rica, Cote d'Ivoire, Cyprus, Denmark, Dominican Republic, Ecuador, Egypt, El Salvador, Finland, France, The Gambia, Germany, Ghana, Greece, Guatemala, Guinea-Bissau, Guyana, Haiti, Honduras, Hong Kong, Hungary, India, Indonesia, Iran, Ireland, Israel, Italy, Jamaica, Japan, Kenya, South Korea, Madagascar, Malawi, Malaysia, Mali, Mauritania, Mauritius, Mexico, Morocco, Mozambique, Netherlands, New Zealand, Nicaragua, Niger, Nigeria, Norway, Pakistan, Panama, Paraguay, Peru, Philippines, Poland, Portugal, Romania, Saudi Arabia, Senegal, Sierra Leone, Singapore, Spain, Sri Lanka, Sudan, Sweden, Switzerland, Syria, Thailand, Trinidad and Tobago, Tunisia, Turkey, Uganda, United Kingdom, United States, Uruguay, Venezuela, Zaire, Zambia, and Zimbabwe.
[19] Naturally, we could also introduce in this exercise an array of other typical bilateral dummies, such as common language, common EIA, etc. However, this would have no bearing on the generality of our results.

consider the results for $-\alpha(\sigma - 1) = -1.65$ and $-\rho(\sigma - 1) = -0.79$. For US–Canadian trade, the average Border estimation bias is 0.42 per cent and the fraction of times the estimate is within two standard errors of the true value is 0.985. The average Distance estimation bias is 1.52 per cent and the fraction of times the estimate is within two standard errors of the true value is 0.978. However, for world trade, the average Border estimation bias is 0.18 per cent and the fraction of times the estimate is within two standard errors of the true value is 0.992. The average Distance estimation bias is 0.13 per cent and the fraction of times the estimate is within two standard errors of the true value is 0.996. The results for $-\alpha(\sigma - 1) = -1.54$ and $-\rho(\sigma - 1) = -1.25$ are similar. In a sensitivity analysis, we have found that the small estimation bias is systematic. In fact, 79.4 per cent of the estimation biases are smaller for world trade flows compared with intra-continental trade flows (although the two "border" variables have different economic interpretations). The distance variable is measured in the same manner for both datasets. For *all* parameter values for the distance variables' coefficients, the estimation bias for world trade flows is less than that for regional trade flows.[20]

These findings provide quantitative support to our hypothesis that our OLS method is not only a good approximation to NLS, but that it works even more effectively in the context in which it is most often used – the analysis of *global* trade flows.

4.3   Potential uses of the approximation method

A question may surface about the potential relevance of estimating equation (4.28) in light of the alternative of fixed effects. If fixed effects yield consistent estimates of gravity-equation parameters, what additional benefit arises from the linear approximation of the MR terms and/or estimation of equation (4.28) using OLS? In the Canadian–US "border-puzzle" cross-section context – or even the more typical gravity-equation analyses of international trade flows – our approximation approach might only provide more "transparency" about understanding the role of MR terms; equation (4.27) does simplify further the "significantly simplified" gravity model of equations (12) and (13) in A-vW (2003, p. 176). However, one may argue that fixed effects allow consistent estimation of cross-section gravity-equation parameters and is easier than estimating equation (4.28). Once one obtains consistent estimates of the

---

[20] The systematically lower estimation bias for the distance coefficients for world relative to regional trade flows is related to the notion of multilateral economic densities, which we address in Section 5.

gravity-equation parameters using fixed effects, is it all that computationally burdensome to run a system of forty-one or eighty-eight non-linear equations to estimate the comparative statics?

Although these are valid questions, we suggest (at least) four potential uses of our approximation method that neither the fixed effects nor the A-vW NLS estimation technique can address. First, in cross-sectional analyses, the use of region- (or country-) specific fixed effects precludes including any region-specific explanatory variables that may be of interest to the researcher. For instance, the levels of foreign aid, domestic populations, and infrastructure levels are all region specific. By including the MR approximation, this allows explicit inclusion of region-specific explanatory variables.

Second, while the context of this paper and A-vW is cross-sectional analysis for a given year, gravity equations are being applied increasingly to *panel data*, with both large cross-sectional and long time-series variation (forty-five years of annual data and increasing). Estimation of gravity equations using country-specific fixed effects to capture the time-varying MR terms for each country in a panel of 200 countries with 45 years would require $8,999 (= (200 \times 45) -)$ dummy variables, which becomes computationally burdensome. Some studies using "huge" panel datasets find the numbers of necessary dummy variables infeasible using "standard computer hardware." Alternatively, one can use the linear approximation method and estimate equation (4.28) using the panel where the *time-varying* relevant MR terms are included explicitly. Three recent applications of our approach in panel contexts are Egger and Nelson (2007), Nelson and Juhasz Silva (2007), and Melitz (2008), for which our OLS method worked successfully.

Third, recent empirical economic and political science research on the determinants of bilateral or regional international economic integration agreements (EIAs) has used probit models to estimate empirically the explanatory role of economic and/or political variables for the likelihood of an EIA between a pair of countries, see Mansfield and Reinhardt (2003), Baier and Bergstrand (2004), and Mansfield *et al.* (2008). For instance, Baier and Bergstrand (2004) examined the role for country pairs' economic determinants of free trade agreements (FTAs). Among other results, they showed theoretically that the welfare of the two countries' representative consumers improved from a regional FTA the more "remote" the two countries were from the rest of the world (e.g. the Australia–New Zealand FTA). In theory this remoteness is economically the *MR terms* we have been addressing; the higher the MR terms for a country pair the more they benefit from bilateral trade, and the greater the welfare improvement from a regional FTA. Like the earlier gravity-equation literature, they measured empirically these MR terms using the *atheoretical remoteness* variables used by McCallum, Helliwell, Wei and others discussed earlier. However, as explanatory variables in a probit regression, the MR terms suggested by our linear approximation would provide instead *theoretically motivated* MR measures.

Fourth, econometric analysis of the *ex post* effects of EIAs on bilateral trade flows has typically been conducted using cross-section gravity equations and OLS; such a method is a parametric approach. However, more recently a few authors have been investigating – using *non-parametric* methods – the effects of EIAs on trade flows, employing econometric considerations more common to labor econometrics, see Egger *et al.* (2008) and Baier and Bergstrand (2009b). For instance, Baier and Bergstrand (2009b) used a (non-parametric) "matching" estimator to generate *ex post* effects of EIAs on country pairs' trade flows, where country pairs with and without EIAs were sorted according to "balancing properties" (i.e. where the distributions of the economic determinants of trade, such as GDPs, bilateral distances, etc., were the "identical"). In order to estimate the effects of EIAs, a necessary variable to address to secure "balancing" was a measure of multilateral resistance. The linear approximation approach provided a theoretically motivated variable to capture the important role of MR terms in order to estimate non-parametrically (using the matching estimator) the effects of EIAs on trade, and secured the balancing properties.

Thus, the linear approximation approach has (at least) four potential uses outside the cross-sectional gravity-equation contexts described earlier and in A-vW.

5   Comparative statics: when does the approximation method work well, and why

The final test of the potential usefulness of the approximation approach is to determine when it works well for conducting comparative statics, and why. In Section 5.1, we compute the comparative statics *analytically* and provide intuition for why the approach provides a "good" approximation of the comparative-static (overall) *country* effects for Canada and the United States provided in A-vW (2003). Yet, MR terms derived from first-order linear approximations are not likely to provide very precise estimates of *region-pair-specific* (such as Alberta–Alabama) comparative statics in the context of the Canadian–US border-puzzle context, and we discuss why. In Section 5.2, we move to other contexts, in particular the most common context – gravity equations of international trade flows among large numbers of countries – to examine under what conditions the approximation method works well for comparative statics – and when it does not – providing the first estimates of the effects of FTAs on international trade flows using the A-vW technique as well as our approximation method. We find that the approximation method works best (for comparative statics) the smaller the comparative-static effect, as would be expected from any linear Taylor-series expansion of a non-linear equation; the further the deviation from the "center" the greater the approximation error, see Judd (1998, chapter 6). However, slightly different from the emphasis in A-vW, the effects of trade costs on multilateral price terms are not *necessarily* the greatest for the smallest countries (with consequently large trading partners); instead we find that the effects are the largest for small countries *that are close* in distance. We go beyond Baier and Bergstrand (2009a) to provide a detailed analysis of the general-equilibrium impacts of NAFTA and the European Economic Area using our approach and A-vW's. In Section 5.3, we extend A-vW to show analytically why small, *close* countries have the largest changes in multilateral price terms. The complexity of the issue requires us to demonstrate this in two parts, an analytical proof and a simulation. Moreover, we show that economic size *relative to* bilateral distance can explain readily the approximation errors of the comparative statics. In other words, as equation (4.8) or (4.9) suggest, the key economic variable to explain differences in comparative statics across country pairs – and the approximation errors – is $\theta_j / t_{ij}^{\sigma-1}$.

5.1   *Analytical estimates of country-specific comparative statics using the approximation approach*

Consistent estimates of the gravity-equation coefficients (and the average border effect) can be obtained estimating a gravity equation adding region-specific fixed effects. However, as A-vW note, one still needs to use the coefficient estimates from OLS with fixed effects along with the non-linear system of equations (4.12) to generate the country-specific border effects. By contrast, our procedure allows one to estimate the country-specific border effects *without* employing the non-linear system of equations. We now demonstrate this.

Recall equation (4.13) to calculate (region-specific) border effects for $\mathbf{x}_{ij}$, using its log-linear form:

$$\mathbf{BB}_{ij} = \ln \mathbf{x}_{ij} - \ln \mathbf{x}_{ij}^* = a_2 - \ln \mathbf{P}_i^{1-\sigma} + \ln \mathbf{P}_i^{*1-\sigma}$$

$$- \ln \mathbf{P}_j^{1-\sigma} + \ln \mathbf{P}_j^{*1-\sigma} \qquad (4.33)$$

where $\mathbf{x}_{ij} = \mathbf{X}_{ij}/\mathbf{Y}_i\mathbf{Y}_j$, a_2 is the estimate of $-\alpha(\sigma - 1)$, and $a_2 < 0$. We substitute equation (4.10) into equations (4.24) and (4.25) to find the MR terms with *and* without national borders. Substituting these results into equation (4.33) yields:

$$\mathbf{BB}_{ij} = \ln \mathbf{x}_{ij} - \ln \mathbf{x}_{ij}^*$$

$$= a_2 \left\{ \left[1 - \left(\sum_{j=1}^{N} \theta_i \mathbf{BORDER}_{ij} \right) - \left(\sum_{i=1}^{N} \theta_j \mathbf{BORDER}_{ij} \right) \right. \right.$$

$$\left. \left. + \left(\sum_{i=1}^{N} \sum_{j=1}^{N} \theta_i \theta_j \mathbf{BORDER}_{ij} \right) \right] \right\} \qquad (4.34)$$

where $\mathbf{BORDER}_{ij} = 1$ if regions i and j are not in the same nation and 0 otherwise and the distance components of the multilateral price terms cancel out. Thus, estimates of the comparative static border barriers do not require estimating the $P_i^{1-\sigma}$, $P_i^{*1-\sigma}$, $P_j^{1-\sigma}$, and $P_j^{*1-\sigma}$ terms using a custom non-linear program.

While we can easily compute these terms using a computer, we can show that the country-specific effects for the Canadian–US data can be readily computed analytically. For the simple Canadian–US case, equation (4.34) can be calculated analytically once we have data on Canadian province and US state GDPs and an estimate of a_2; we use $a_2 = -1.65$. Given the definition of $\mathbf{BORDER}_{ij}$, it turns out that the second term in the large brackets on the RHS in equation (4.34) is simply Canada's share of Canadian and US GDPs ($\theta_{CA} = 0.07$) and the third term in the brackets is simply the US share of Canadian and US GDPs ($\theta_{US} = 0.93$). Consequently, the sum of these terms cancels out the 1 and the effect is -1.65 times the last term in the brackets. The last term simplifies to $2\,\theta_{CA}\theta_{US}$, or 0.13. Hence, the general equilibrium comparative static effect of the national border on the trade between a Canadian province and US state, using our approximation method, is $-1.65 \times 0.13 = -0.21$, implying that the ratio of trade with the barrier (BB) to trade *without* the barrier (NB) is $0.81 (= e^{-0.21})$. This is larger than the A-vW multi-country estimate of 0.56. However, using simple weights (rather than GDP-share weights) our approximation method generates a comparative static effect of 0.54, virtually identical to the A-vW estimate.

5.1.1   A-vW's implication 1 The intuition is similar to A-vW (2003, Section II). As in A-vW's implication 1, trade barriers reduce size-adjusted trade between large countries more than between small ones.

Using the notation just introduced, equation (4.34) can be rewritten as:

$$\mathbf{BB}_{\text{CA,US}} = \ln \mathbf{x}_{ij} - \ln \mathbf{x}^*_{ij} = a_2[1 - \theta_{\text{CA}} - \theta_{\text{US}} + 2\theta_{\text{CA}}\theta_{\text{US}}]$$
(4.35)

When $\theta_{\text{CA}}(\theta_{\text{US}})$ is a fraction, $2\theta_{\text{CA}}\theta_{\text{US}} = 1 - \theta^2_{\text{CA}} - \theta^2_{\text{US}}$. Hence, equation (4.35) can be rewritten as:

$$\mathbf{BB}_{\text{CA,US}} = \ln \mathbf{x}_{ij} - \ln \mathbf{x}^*_{ij} = a_2[1 - \theta_{\text{CA}} - \theta_{\text{US}} + 1 - \theta^2_{\text{CA}} - \theta^2_{\text{US}}]$$
(4.36)

In this case, as in A-vW (2003, p. 176–177), $\theta_{\text{CA}} = 1 - \theta_{\text{US}}$ and $\theta_{\text{US}} = 1 - \theta_{\text{CA}}$. Hence, (4.36) becomes:

$$\mathbf{BB}_{\text{CA,US}} = \ln \mathbf{x}_{ij} - \ln \mathbf{x}_{ij}* = a_2[\theta_{\text{US}} + \theta_{\text{CA}} - \theta^2_{\text{CA}} - \theta^2_{\text{US}}] \quad (4.37)$$

which is identical to equation (15) in A-vW (2003, p. 177). The implications discussed there follow.

5.1.2   A-vW's implication 2 Similarly, A-vW's implication 2 holds also. A national border increases size-adjusted trade within small countries more than within large countries. For instance, using our method, $\mathbf{BB}_{\text{CA,CA}}$ can be calculated as:

$$\mathbf{BB}_{\text{CA,CA}} = \ln \mathbf{x}_{ij} - \ln \mathbf{x}_{ij}* = a_2[0 - \theta_{\text{US}} - \theta_{\text{US}} + 2\theta_{\text{CA}}\theta_{\text{US}}]$$
(4.38)

Since $2\theta_{\text{CA}}\theta_{\text{US}} = 1 - \theta^2_{\text{CA}} - \theta^2_{\text{US}}$ and $\theta_{\text{CA}} = 1 - \theta_{\text{US}}$ and $\theta_{\text{US}} = 1 - \theta_{\text{CA}}$, equation (4.38) can be rewritten as:

$$\mathbf{BB}_{\text{CA,US}} = \ln \mathbf{x}_{ij} - \ln \mathbf{x}^*_{ij} = a_2[-1 + 2\theta_{\text{CA}} - \theta^2_{\text{CA}} - \theta^2_{\text{US}}] \quad (4.39)$$

which is identical to equation (15) in A-vW (2003, p. 177). The implications discussed there follow.

Letting $a_2 = -1.65$, $\theta_{\text{CA}} = 0.07$, and $\theta_{\text{US}} = 0.93$, our method yields a border effect ratio of intra-national Canadian trade with a border to intra-national Canadian trade *without* a border of 17.92, larger than the A-vW multi-country estimate of 5.96. Using simple weights (rather than GDP-share weights) our approximation generates a comparative static effect of 6.60, much closer to the A-vW multi-country estimate for Canada.

5.1.3   A-vW's implication 3 Finally, A-vW's implication 3 follows from implications 1 and 2. The presence of a national border increases intranational *relative to* international trade. The more so, the smaller Canada and the larger the United States are. Letting $a_2 = -1.65$, $\theta_{CA} = 0.07$, and $\theta_{US} = 0.93$, our method yields a ratio of intra-national relative to international trade with a border to that *without* a border of 21.54, much larger than the A-vW multi-country estimate of 10.70. However, using simple weights our approximation generates a ratio of 12.13, closer to the A-vW estimates. In fact, our estimate of 12.13 is within the range of estimates recently reported in a sensitivity analysis by Balistreri and Hillberry (2007).

5.1.4   Limitations of the approximation method While our approximation method can generate border-effect estimates close to those reported in the recent "border-puzzle" debate, a more demanding test of the method is to evaluate the (general equilibrium) comparative statics for specific pairs of regions. In this particular context, the method provides only a crude approximation, since θ_{CA} and θ_{US} are identical for every region pair. Consequently, the "country-wide" border effects are identical to the region-pair border effects. However, using A-vW's NLS system, the region-pair border effects vary from 0.32 to 0.49 with an average of 0.41 (using the A-vW two-country technique). Consequently, for particular pairs of Canadian provinces and US states, the method cannot capture the aspect of A-vW that regions within smaller countries face larger multilateral resistance than regions within larger countries.

5.2   Comparative statics using world trade flows

A-vW motivated the importance of estimating appropriate comparative statics in the context of one specific case: McCallum's Canadian–US "border puzzle." However, for nearly half a century, the gravity equation in international trade has been used *most commonly* to analyze bilateral aggregate international trade flows and – in particular – the effects of free trade agreements (FTAs) on such flows, see Frankel (1997). In this section, we analyze three representative gravity-equation applications to illustrate that our approximation method works in the most common context for the gravity equation and to show when our approximation works well... and when it does not.

5.2.1   NAFTA One of the most common empirical and policy contexts for applying the gravity equation is to analyze the effects of a particular economic integration agreement (EIA) on trade between pairs of countries; the most common type of EIA is a free trade agreement (FTA).

The vast bulk of gravity-equation studies since the early 1960s have estimated the average "treatment" effect of an EIA on trade using dummy variables and OLS, see Tinbergen (1962). However, as A-vW (2003) remind us, the dummy variable's coefficient estimate provides only the "partial" effect, not the full general equilibrium comparative static effect.

In this section we use the same Monte Carlo approach used earlier for our eighty-eight-world simulation (see Section 4.2). We calculated the true trade flows using the A-vW NLS specification including real GDPs, bilateral distance, an adjacency dummy, a language dummy, and a dummy variable representing the presence or absence of an EIA. To keep the approach similar to the literature, we define "NoEIA" as 1 if the EIA does not exist, and 0 if it does; the ratios calculated are then interpreted similar to the effects of "border barriers" discussed earlier. We calculated the effects by pairs of countries of NoEIA using A-vW. We then calculated the same comparative statics using our (GDP-share-weighted) approximation method.

In the first scenario, we considered the effect of the North American Free Trade Agreement. Table 4.3 provides the results of the effect of "NoNAFTA" on the trade between the NAFTA members. Table 4.3 is organized as follows. Column (1) lists various country pairs (i, j) in NAFTA. Column (2) provides the partial effect on the two countries' bilateral trade of NoNAFTA; trade is reduced by 50 per cent by eliminating the FTA between the countries. This value is exogenously assumed based upon evidence to date that (after accounting for endogeneity bias) the average (partial treatment) effect of an FTA on raising trade between two countries is about 100 per cent, see Baier and Bergstrand (2007); hence, removing an FTA reduces trade by 50 per cent. Columns (3) and (4) provide the estimates of how country i's and j's MR terms, respectively, rise as a result of NoNAFTA, computed using the A-vW NLS method. Columns (5) and (6) provide the corresponding estimates of how i's and j's MR terms rise, computed using our approximation method. Column (7) provides our estimate of the "world resistance" term change using our method. Columns (8) and (9) provide the total (full general equilibrium) effects of NoNAFTA on bilateral trade of i and j using the A-vW and our approximation methods, respectively.

Several points are worth noting. First, our example provides (one of) the first application(s) of the A-vW technique outside the context of the Canadian–US data, using a dataset of world trade flows (the most common gravity-equation context for trade). The A-vW results highlight the importance of accounting for *multilateral resistance*. Most notably, the MR terms of the relatively smaller NAFTA members – Canada and Mexico – increase substantively, by 35 and 25 per cent, respectively. Second, all

Table 4.3. *NAFTA comparative statics*

(1) Country pair (i – j)	(2) Partial effect	(3) A-vW MR effect i	(4) A-vW MR effect j	(5) B-B MR effect i	(6) B-B MR effect j	(7) B-B World effect	(8) A-vW Total effect	(9) B-B Total effect
USA – Mexico	0.50	1.02	1.25	1.03	1.19	0.99	0.63	0.60
USA – Canada	0.50	1.02	1.35	1.03	1.19	0.99	0.68	0.60
Canada – Mexico	0.50	1.35	1.25	1.19	1.19	0.99	0.84	0.70

of the approximation-method comparative static total effects are within 15 per cent of the "true" values (i.e. where "true" denotes those computed using the A-vW method). It is important to note that – in the *absence* of estimating the structural price equations using A-vW – our approximation approach provides a *much more accurate* representation of the general equilibrium comparative static effects than simply using the coefficient estimate of the FTA dummy variable from a gravity equation (with or without fixed effects). The USA–Mexico approximation is within 3 per cent of the true value, while the USA–Canada approximation is 8 per cent lower and Canadian–Mexico's is 14 per cent lower. Third, the approximation method distinguishes well between "small" and "large" countries. For instance, A-vW's method suggests that Mexico's MR term should increase by 25 per cent, whereas the approximation method suggests a 19 per cent increase. Fourth, the NAFTA case provides a ready first insight into where the approximation method will work poorly – trade between two countries that are small in economic size but fairly close in distance (here, on the same continent). We will see shortly that this is systematic in simulations, and can be explained economically. Naturally, since the comparative static effect for Canada–Mexico is the largest of the three effects, it has the largest approximation error, as standard to Taylor approximations.

In general equilibrium, bilateral trade among non-members of NAFTA, the vast bulk of the 3,872 country pairs ($88 \times 88/2$) are also affected because of changes in their multilateral resistance terms. However, these effects are small and for these 3,872 non-NAFTA country pairs the approximation method yields comparative statics that are within 2 per cent of the true values 95 per cent of the time.

5.2.2 The European Economic Area The most important economic integration agreement in post-World War Two history has been European economic integration. Consequently, an important context to evaluate

Table 4.4. *European Economic Area comparative statics*

(1) Country pair	(2) Partial effect	(3) A-vW total effect	(4) B-B total effect	(5) Absolute bias
a) 2,871 of 3,872 pairs (74 per cent) have a bias of less than 5 per cent				
France – Germany	0.50	0.62	0.64	0.0124
Spain – Sweden	0.50	0.64	0.67	0.0287
Portugal – UK	0.50	0.66	0.66	0.0029
Netherlands – UK	0.50	0.68	0.66	0.0245
Italy – Norway	0.50	0.69	0.66	0.0373
b) 358 pairs (9 per cent) have a bias between 5 and 10 per cent				
Bulgaria – Germany	0.50	0.70	0.65	0.0548
Netherlands – France	0.50	0.72	0.66	0.0631
Greece – Portugal	0.50	0.74	0.68	0.0605
Denmark – UK	0.50	0.75	0.66	0.0870
Portugal – Romania	0.50	0.75	0.67	0.0804
c) 236 pairs (6 per cent) have a bias between 10 and 15 per cent				
Austria – Germany	0.50	0.77	0.65	0.1202
Poland – Portugal	0.50	0.77	0.67	0.1023
Netherlands – Romania	0.50	0.77	0.67	0.1045
Denmark – Italy	0.50	0.78	0.66	0.1208
Spain – Switzerland	0.50	0.80	0.66	0.1374
d) 407 pairs (11 per cent) have a bias greater than 15 per cent. Every country pair with a bias greater than 15 per cent includes Austria, Belgium, Denmark, Ireland or Switzerland.				
Norway – Denmark	0.50	0.85	0.67	0.1835
Belgium – Netherlands	0.50	0.85	0.67	0.1817
Denmark – Finland	0.50	0.87	0.68	0.1932
Ireland – Romania	0.50	0.89	0.67	0.2170
Denmark – Ireland	0.50	1.01	0.68	0.3348

the approximation method's accuracy is measuring the trade-cost effects of removing the "European Economic Area," or "NoEEA." First, among our 88 countries, the potential number of country pairs that are directly affected by EEA include 165 of the 3,872 country pairs in our sample. Reporting the results for all 165 pairs – much less the *other* 3,707 pairs – is prohibitive in terms of space. Consequently, we summarize the results and provide only some "representative" results in Table 4.4 in the format of the earlier Table 4.3.[21]

---

[21] Since Switzerland is in EFTA, which has an FTA with the EU, we consider here Switzerland to be in the "EEA."

The most notable result from this Monte Carlo experiment is that *74 per cent* of the comparative statics using the approximation method are within 5 per cent of the "true" (A-vW-method-determined) comparative statics. Another 9 per cent of the comparative statics using the approximation method have biases between 5 to 10 per cent of the true values; hence, 83 per cent have biases less than 10 per cent. 92 per cent of the approximation-method comparative statics are within 20 per cent of the true values. As expected using a Taylor approximation, the largest biases occur for the country pairs with the largest changes in their MR terms (and hence in the comparative statics).

However, 8 per cent of the approximation-method comparative statics differ from the true values by more than 20 per cent. The largest error is 38 per cent. Yet, *every single one* of the country pairs with a bias greater than 20 per cent includes either Austria, Belgium, Denmark, Ireland or Switzerland in the pair. Moreover, every single pair where the approximation method performs poorly involves economically small EEA countries that are *close* to one another (and to large trading partners). Consistent with earlier findings, all these countries incur the *highest* increases in their MR terms from "NoEEA" because they are close to each other (and to other large trading partners).

5.2.3   *All FTAs* We also conducted the same analysis for all FTAs in the eighty-eight-country sample. The main three findings from above hold in general. First, similar to the case of the EEA, 86 per cent of pairs have an average bias of less than 20 per cent. Second, the largest approximation errors are for the pairs of countries with the largest increases in their MR terms from having "NoFTA," as one would expect from a Taylor approximation. Third, the country pairs with the largest increases in their MR terms have *small GDPs* and are *close*, e.g. Uruguay–Paraguay in MERCOSUR, the Central American Common Market (CACM) countries, and the EEA countries discussed above.

5.2.4   *Summary* We close this section noting the contrast between the results using our approximation versus using A-vW's method. Given the presence of non-linearities, computing comparative static effects using A-vW's system of non-linear equations is preferable. However, our approximation method provides a ready alternative method for estimating coefficients *and* for calculating (approximations of) *pair-specific* general equilibrium comparative statics. We find in our general setting of world trade flows that our approximation method for computing pair-specific general equilibrium comparative statics is accurate with 10 per cent of the "true" values in *83 per cent* of our 3,872 country pairings. This result – demanding only OLS – is clearly an improvement over simply using the coefficient estimate of an FTA dummy variable, as is typically done.

5.3 Explaining the large MR changes and the approximation errors

In this final section, we address two concerns. First, as with any Taylor expansion, the approximation errors will be largest for the largest changes relative to the center. Since Taylor expansions approximate better (generally) the higher the order, we discuss the factors likely influencing the approximation error, using a second-order Taylor expansion to illustrate them. Second, the Monte Carlo analysis above indicated that the largest MR term changes (from trade costs) were not necessarily for the economically smallest countries (with consequently large trading partners) as A-vW suggested, but rather small countries that are *physically close*. In this part, we present two results. First, we extend A-vW to show analytically in a world with *symmetric* (but positive) trade costs that small countries with large trading partners *relative to* trade costs will tend to have larger MR changes from changing trade costs. Second, because of limitations of the analytical proof, we then demonstrate a simple fixed-point iteration procedure that eliminates the approximation errors without having to use NLS estimation or a higher-order Taylor expansion (which, as for modern dynamic macro-economic models, is very difficult and outside the paper's scope). We show that the *sole* economic variable that explains differences in comparative statics across country pairs and their approximation errors is $\theta_j / t_{ij}^{\sigma-1}$; that is, the approximation errors are largest for small countries that are physically close (i.e. small $t_{ij}^{\sigma-1}$).

5.3.1 A second-order Taylor-series expansion As documented above, the Taylor-series approximations of the MR terms are poorest when the true MR terms are large. As with any Taylor-series expansion, the approximation works best for small changes around the "center"; in our case, this is the average trade cost (t). Judd (1998) discusses the details and shows for a simple exponential function (centered at unity) that the "quality" of the approximation falls as the level of the variable moves further from unity. In general, higher-order Taylor-series expansions can provide better approximations. However, Judd (1998, pp. 197–98) provides an example that shows that the approximation error *can* still increase with the introduction of higher-order terms. It is important to note that the most commonly used expansion in modern dynamic macro-economic models is still the first-order expansion, see Christiano *et al.* (2005). An alternative approach that may work better, but is beyond the scope of this paper, is a Padé approximation.

To understand the economic sources of the Taylor approximation errors, we first consider analytically a *second-order* Taylor-series expansion of equation (4.14), centered around a symmetric world (both trade costs and GDP shares). We report only the first set of derivations, akin to equation (4.20) in Section 3:

$$P^{1-\sigma} + (1-\sigma)P^{1-\sigma}(\ln P_i - \ln P) + \frac{1}{2}(1-\sigma)^2 P^{1-\sigma}(\ln P_i - \ln P)^2$$

$$= \sum_{j=1}^{N} \left[\theta P^{-(1-\sigma)}t^{1-\sigma} - \left(\theta P^{-(1-\sigma)}t^{1-\sigma}\right)(1-\sigma)\left(\ln P_j - \ln P\right) \right.$$

$$+ \left(\theta P^{-(1-\sigma)}t^{1-\sigma}\right)\left(\ln \theta_j - \ln \theta\right)$$

$$+ \left(\theta P^{-(1-\sigma)}t^{1-\sigma}\right)(1-\sigma)\left(\ln t_{ij} - \ln t\right)$$

$$- \frac{1}{2}(1-\sigma)^2 \left(\theta P^{-(1-\sigma)}t^{1-\sigma}\right)\left(\ln P_j - \ln P\right)^2$$

$$+ \frac{1}{2}\left(\theta P^{-(1-\sigma)}t^{1-\sigma}\right)\left(\ln \theta_j - \ln \theta\right)^2$$

$$+ \frac{1}{2}(1-\sigma)^2 \left(\theta P^{-(1-\sigma)}t^{1-\sigma}\right)\left(\ln t_{ij} - \ln t\right)^2$$

$$- 2 \cdot \frac{1}{2}(1-\sigma)^2 \left(\theta P^{-(1-\sigma)}t^{1-\sigma}\right)\left(\ln P_j - \ln P\right)\left(\ln \theta_j - \ln \theta\right)$$

$$- 2 \cdot \frac{1}{2}(1-\sigma)^2 \left(\theta P^{-(1-\sigma)}t^{1-\sigma}\right)\left(\ln P_j - \ln P\right)\left(\ln t_{ij} - \ln t\right)$$

$$\left. + 2 \cdot \frac{1}{2}(1-\sigma)^2 \left(\theta P^{-(1-\sigma)}t^{1-\sigma}\right)\left(\ln \theta_j - \ln \theta\right)\left(\ln t_{ij} - \ln t\right) \right]$$

$$\text{(4.40)}$$

Clearly, this equation cannot be manipulated mathematically to solve for similar terms to the first-order expansion. A comparison of equation (4.40) with equation (4.20) shows that the RHS of the former equation includes three additional terms reflecting variances of the (endogenous) price term and of the (exogenous) GDP shares and trade costs, and three additional terms reflecting covariance among the (endogenous) price terms and (exogenous) GDP shares and trade costs. Thus, GDP shares *relative to* bilateral trade costs $(\theta_j/t_{ij}^{\sigma-1})$ play a critical role.

5.3.2   The role of $\theta_j/t_{ij}^{\sigma-1}$ as the source of approximation errors Examining equation (4.8) or (4.9), it should come as no surprise that the key economic variable influencing outcomes is not just economic size (θ_j) but economic size *relative to* bilateral trade costs, $\theta_j/t_{ij}^{\sigma-1}$.[22] A-vW demonstrated clearly the importance of economic size for influencing MR terms; smaller countries have higher MR terms ceteris paribus and small countries' MR terms increase more for a given shock to trade costs. As A-vW (2003, p. 177) summarized, "For a small country trade is more important and trade barriers therefore have a bigger effect on multilateral resistance." Analogously, trade is more important for *close* countries and therefore border barriers should have a bigger impact on MR terms. In this section, we demonstrate two results. From an initial equilibrium of *symmetric* (but positive) trade costs, we show analytically that MR terms increase more for countries that are economically small *relative to* initial trade costs (t). In this regard, our proof is more general than A-vW's, which assumed an initial frictionless equilibrium. However, unlike A-vW, we cannot prove analytically that the change in MR for a given country (for an increase in trade costs) varies with the level of *pair-specific* trade costs (t_{ij}). To show this, we then turn to a "fixed-point" iteration analysis.

First, we show here that – from an initial equilibrium of symmetric positive trade costs ($t > 0$) – MR terms increase more (for a given increase in trade costs, dt) for countries that are small *relative to* initial trade costs (t). Differentiating (4.8) yields:

$$(1 - \sigma)P_i^{-\sigma}\,dP_i = \sum_{j=1}^{N} \theta_j t_{ij}^{1-\sigma} P_j^{\sigma-2}(-1)(1 - \sigma)dP_i$$

$$+ \sum_{j=1}^{N} \theta_j t_{ij}^{-\sigma} P_j^{\sigma-1}(1 - \sigma)dt + \sum_{i=1}^{N} t_{ij}^{1-\sigma} P_j^{\sigma-1}\,d\theta_j$$

$$\tag{4.41}$$

Dividing by $1/(1 - \sigma)$, setting $t_{ij} = t$ and $P_i = P_j = t^{1/2}$, and some algebraic manipulation yields:

$$dP_i = (1/t^{1/2})[(1/2) - \theta_i + (1/2)\sum_{k=1}^{N} \theta_k^2]dt \tag{4.42}$$

---

[22] One might denote economic size relative to bilateral trade costs as "economic density." Since bilateral distance is a critical empirical variable influencing bilateral trade costs, this is consistent with the literature on "economic densities." Economic density refers, in general, to the amount of economic activity for a given physical area; a large literature exists on its measurement, see Ciccone and Hall (1996). In the trade context, a country's multilateral economic density is high when there is a strong negative correlation between partners' sizes and bilateral distances. For instance, Switzerland has a very multilateral economic density; its largest trading partners are quite close.

Equation (4.42) confirms that for a given shock to trade costs (dt), MR terms increase more for small countries relative to *average* trade costs. However, this does not prove that small *and close* countries' MR terms increase more for a given trade-cost shock.

Given the limitations above of the second-order Taylor-series expansion and the analytical proof, we must turn to an alternative approach to identify the key economic variable that explains the errors. For this, we show that a simple "fixed-point" iteration on a matrix equation can generate precise (in our example, to seven decimal places) estimates of the "true" (or A-vW) MR terms. The key matrix in the equation is an $N \times N$ matrix of GDPs *scaled* by bilateral trade costs, $\theta_j / t_{ij}^{\sigma-1}$ (which we identified earlier as the key determinant of large comparative statics).[23]

We summarize the process briefly, referring the reader to the Appendix for technical details. First, calculate initial estimates of every $P_i^{1-\sigma}(P_i^{*1-\sigma})$ using OLS, denoted $P_{i\ 0}^{1-\sigma}(P_{i\ 0}^{*1-\sigma})$, for every region ($i = 1,\ldots,N$). Denote the $N \times 1$ vector of these MR terms V_0 (V_0^*) and the $N \times 1$ vector of the inverses of each of these MR terms V_0^- (V_0^{-*}). Second, define an $N \times N$ matrix of GDP-share-weighted trade costs, B, where each element, b_{ij}, equals $\theta_j / t_{ij}^{\sigma-1}$. Third, compute V_{k+1} according to:

$$V_{k+1} = zBV_k^- + (1-z)V_k \qquad (4.43)$$

starting at $k = 0$ until successive approximations are less than a predetermined value of ε (say, 1×10^{-9}), where $\varepsilon = \max|V_{k+1} - V_k|$ and z is a dampening factor with $z \in (0,1)$, and analogously for V_k^*. Given the initial estimates of $P_i^{1-\sigma}(P_i^{*1-\sigma})$ using OLS ($i = 1,\ldots,N$), this fixed-point iteration process will converge to the set of multilateral price terms identical to those generated using A-vW's NLS program. In the case where B has no dispersion in $\theta_j / t_{ij}^{\sigma-1}$, convergence will be virtually instantaneous.[24]

We have run this set of matrix calculations and the correlation coefficient between our MR terms (using fixed-point iteration) and A-vW's MR terms (using NLS) is 1.0 (reported to seven decimal places) in both the Canadian–US context and the eighty-eight-country context. In the

---

[23] An advantage of the fixed-point method is that it is computationally much less resource-intensive than the non-linear estimation technique used by A-vW, as it does not require computation of the Jacobian system of equations, nor does it even require that the inverse of the Jacobian *exists*.

[24] We use equation (4.10) to measure $t_{ij}^{\sigma-1}$ using bilateral distance and a coefficient estimate. The results are robust to alternative initial values of $P_i^{1-\sigma}(P_i^{*1-\sigma})$.

Canadian–US case, convergence was achieved in twenty-five iterations (assuming $\rho\,(1-\sigma) = -0.79$ and $\alpha(1-\sigma) = -1.65$ for both cases, with *and* without the border) and the correlation of the multilateral resistance terms with those constructed by A-vW is 1.0. Using parameter values of $\rho\,(1-\sigma) = -1.25$ and $\alpha(1-\sigma) = -1.54$, convergence is achieved after twenty-one iterations.

This method illustrates that the key *economic* variable explaining the approximation errors – as equation (4.8) would suggest – is GDP shares *relative to* bilateral trade costs, $\theta_j / t_{ij}^{\sigma-1}$.

6   Conclusions

Several years ago, theoretical foundations for the gravity equation in international trade were enhanced to recognize the *systematic bias* in coefficient estimates of bilateral trade-cost variables from omitting theoretically motivated "multilateral (price) resistance" (MR) terms. Anderson and van Wincoop (2003) demonstrated that: (i) consistent and efficient estimation of the bilateral gravity equation's coefficients in an N-region world required custom programming of a non-linear system of trade and price equations; (ii) even if unbiased estimates of gravity-equation coefficients could be obtained using fixed effects, general equilibrium comparative statics still required estimation of the full non-linear system; and (iii) the model could be applied to resolve McCallum's "border puzzle."

This paper has attempted to make three potential contributions. First, we have demonstrated that a first-order log-linear Taylor-series expansion of the non-linear system of price equations suggests an alternative OLS log-linear specification that introduces theoretically motivated *exogenous* MR terms. Second, empirical applications and Monte Carlo simulations suggest that the method yields virtually identical coefficient estimates to fixed effects and NLS estimation. Third, we have shown that the comparative statics associated with our approximation method have a bias no more than 5 per cent in 74 per cent of the 3,872 country pairings of 88 countries examined. Moreover, we have identified the size of countries relative to their bilateral trade costs as the key economic variable explaining the approximation errors.

A limitation of the present paper is that our method assumes bilaterally symmetric trade costs; see Baier and Bergstrand (2009a) for an approach allowing asymmetry. However, future work in this direction might consider two issues. First, we have used a standard Taylor-series expansion; however, a Padé approximation may yield better estimates. Second, especially for comparative statics, higher order terms matter, and future work should address their incorporation.

REFERENCES

Aitken, N. D. (1973). "The Effect of the EEC and EFTA on European Trade: A Temporal Cross-Section Analysis," *American Economic Review* 5: 881–92.

Anderson, J. E. (1979). "A Theoretical Foundation for the Gravity Equation," *American Economic Review* 69(1): 106–16.

Anderson, J. E. and E. van Wincoop (2003). "Gravity with Gravitas: A Solution to the Border Puzzle," *American Economic Review* 93(1): 170–92.

Anderson, M. A. and S. L. S. Smith (1999a). "Canadian Provinces in World Trade: Engagement and Detachment," *Canadian Journal of Economics* 32(1): 23–37.

(1999b). "Do National Borders Really Matter? Canada–US Regional Trade Reconsidered," *Review of International Economics* 7(2): 219–27.

Baier, S. L. and J. H. Bergstrand (2004). "Economic Determinants of Free Trade Agreements," *Journal of International Economics* 64(1): 29–63.

(2007). "Do Free Trade Agreements Actually Increase Members' International Trade?" *Journal of International Economics* 71(1): 72–95.

(2009a). "Bonus Vetus OLS: A Simple Method for Approximating International Trade-Cost Effects using the Gravity Equation," *Journal of International Economics* 77(1): 77–85.

(2009b). "Estimating the Effects of Free Trade Agreements on International Trade Flows using Matching Econometrics," *Journal of International Economics* 77(1): 63–76.

Balistreri, E. J. and R. H. Hillberry (2007). "Structural Estimation and the Border Puzzle," *Journal of International Economics* 72(2): 451–63.

Behrens, K., C. Ertur and W. Koch (2007). "Dual Gravity: using Spatial Econometrics to Control for Multilateral Resistance," working paper, June.

Bergstrand, J. H. (1985). "The Gravity Equation in International Trade: Some Microeconomic Foundations and Empirical Evidence," *Review of Economics and Statistics* 67(3): 474–81.

Bergstrand, J. H., P. Egger and M. Larch (2007). "Gravity *Redux*: Structural Estimation of Gravity Equations with Asymmetric Bilateral Trade Costs," working paper.

Christiano, L. J., M. Eichenbaum and C. L. Evans (2005). "Nominal Rigidities and the Dynamic Effects of a Shock to Monetary Policy," *Journal of Political Economy* 113(1): 1–45.

Ciccone, A. and R. E. Hall (1996). "Productivity and Density of Economic Activity," *American Economic Review* 86(1): 54–70.

Deardorff, A. (1998). "Determinants of Bilateral Trade: Does Gravity Work in a Neoclassical World?" in J. Frankel (ed.), *The Regionalization of the World Economy*, University of Chicago Press.

Eaton, J. and S. Kortum (2002). "Technology, Geography, and Trade," *Econometrica* 70(5): 1741–79.

Egger, H., P. Egger and D. Greenaway (2008). "The Trade Structure Effects of Endogenous Regional Trade Agreements," *Journal of International Economics* 74(2): 278–98.

Egger, P. and D. Nelson (2007). "How Bad is Antidumping? Evidence from Panel Data," working paper.

Feenstra, R. C. (2004). *Advanced International Trade*, Princeton University Press.

Felbermayr, G. J. and W. Kohler (2004). "Exploring the Intensive and Extensive Margins of World Trade," working paper, European University Institute and Eberhard Karls University, August.

Frankel, J.(1997). *Regional Trading Blocs in the World Economic System*. Institute for International Economics, Washington DC.

Gerald, C. F. and P. O. Wheatley (1990). *Applied Numerical Analysis* (4th edition). Reading, MA: Addison-Wesley.

Helliwell, J. F. (1996). "Do National Boundaries Matter for Quebec's Trade?" *Canadian Journal of Economics* 29(3): 507–22.

(1997). "National Borders, Trade and Migration," *Pacific Economic Review* 2(3): 165–85.

(1998). *How Much Do National Borders Matter?* Washington DC: Brookings Institution.

Judd, K. L. (1998). *Numerical Methods in Economics*. Cambridge, MA: MIT Press.

Linnemann, H. (1966). *An Econometric Study of International Trade Flows*. Amsterdam: North-Holland.

Mansfield, E. D. and E. Reinhardt (2003). "Multilateral Determinants of Regionalism: The Effects of GATT/WTO on the Formation of Preferential Trading Arrangements," *International Organization* 57(4): 829–62.

Mansfield, E. D., H. C. Milner and J. C. Pevehouse (2008). "Democracy, Veto Players, and the Depth of Regional Integration," in *The Sequencing of Regional Economic Integration*, special issue of *The World Economy*, edited by J. H. Bergstrand, A. Estevadeordal and S. Evenett, January.

McCallum, J. (1995). "National Borders Matter: Canada–US Regional Trade Patterns," *American Economic Review* 85(3): 615–23.

Melitz, J. (2008). "Language and Foreign Trade," *European Economic Review* 52(4): 667–99.

Nelson, D. and S. Juhasz Silva (2007). "Does Aid Cause Trade? Evidence from an Asymmetric Gravity Model," working paper.

Nirenberg, L. (1975). *Functional Analysis: Notes by Lesley Sibner*. Courant Institute of Mathematical Science, New York University.

Rose, A. K. (2004). "A Meta-Analysis of the Effect of Common Currencies on International Trade," NBER working paper no. 10373, National Bureau of Economic Research, Inc.

Rose, A. K. and E. van Wincoop (2001). "National Money as a Barrier to International Trade: The Real Case for Currency Union," *American Economic Review Papers and Proceedings* 91(2): 386–90.

Sapir, A. (1981). "Trade Benefits under the EEC Generalized System of Preferences," *European Economic Review* 15: 339–55.

Tinbergen, J. (1962). *Shaping the World Economy*. New York: The Twentieth Century Fund.

Wei, S.-J. (1996). "Intra-national versus International Trade: How Stubborn Are Nations in Global Integration?" National Bureau of Economic Research (Cambridge, MA) working paper no. 5531.

APPENDIX

The technique described in the paper, OLS-MR, yields virtually identical gravity-equation coefficient estimates to those estimated using region-specific fixed effects (which are unbiased estimates). However, fixed effects cannot be used to generate general equilibrium comparative statics. Because OLS-MR yields linear approximations, it does not provide precise estimates of the region-specific multilateral resistance (MR) terms (with or without borders). However, one need not estimate the entire system of equations using custom non-linear least squares to generate the exact same estimates of the MR terms as with A-vW's NLS estimation. Given initial estimates of the MR terms using OLS-MR, a version of fixed-point iteration can be used to generate *identical* MR terms as under the NLS technique, and fixed-point iteration is computationally much less intensive than the A-vW NLS technique. In particular, even though the system of equations that determines the MR terms is non-linear, our fixed-point iteration method does not require computation of the Jacobian of the system of equations, nor does it require that the inverse of the Jacobian exists. We show that our approach requires nothing more than simple matrix manipulation in *STATA*, *GAUSS* or any similar matrix programming language.

The approach can be calculated for MR terms with or without borders; for demonstration here, we assume borders are present. First, OLS-MR yields estimates of multilateral resistance terms $P_i^{1-\sigma}$ for $i = 1, \ldots, N$ regions (with borders) based upon the log-linear approximation. Denote V_0 as the $N \times 1$ vector of these $P_i^{1-\sigma}$ terms and V_0^- as the $N \times 1$ vector of their inverses ($P_i^{\sigma-1}$). The functional equation we solve is $f(V) = V - BV^-$, where B is an $N \times N$ matrix of GDP-share-weights relative to bilateral trade costs where each element, b_{ij}, equals $\theta_j / t_{ij}^{\sigma-1}$, where t_{ij} are defined in Section 2. Evaluated at the equilibrium values of the MR terms, V^E and V^{-E}, then $f(V^E) = V - BV^{-E} = 0$.

The fixed-point iteration method we use has essentially only two steps. First, use coefficient estimates from OLS-MR to construct the matrix B and use OLS-MR estimates of $P_i^{1-\sigma}$ ($P_i\sigma^{-1}$) to construct the initial value of V_0 (V_0^-). Second, compute V_{k+1} according to:

$$V_{k+1} = zBV_k^- + (1-z)V_k \qquad (4.\text{A}.1)$$

starting at $k = 0$ until successive approximations are less than a predetermined value (e.g. 1×10^{-9}) of $\varepsilon = \max|V_{k+1} - V_k|$, where $\max|V_{k+1} - V_k|$ is the largest error approximation and z is a damping factor with $z \in (0, 1)$. The estimated V_{k+1} satisfying this second step is *identical* to the V estimated using A-vW's custom NLS estimation.

The remainder of this appendix proves in mathematical detail why this version of the fixed-point iteration converges to a solution. First, the standard approach for fixed-point iteration is to start with an initial guess V_0 and iterate on:

$$V_{k+1} = BV_k^- \qquad (4.\text{A}.2)$$

starting at $k = 0$. The above equation converges as long as BV^- is a contraction map; that is, a necessary condition for a fixed-point iteration to converge is that – for each row of the Jacobian of BV^- – the sum of the absolute values of each element is less than unity, see Gerald and Wheatley (1990). This condition is unlikely to hold in general and it certainly does not hold for the McCallum–A-vW–Feenstra data. Even if it is a contraction map, it may not be the case that iterating induces convergence to the fixed point.

To see why this iteration process will not work in this context, consider a simple univariate mapping of:

$$v = (1/2)\, v^{-1} \tag{4.A.3}$$

Trivially, the fixed point of this mapping is $v^E = 1/\sqrt{2}$. Clearly, the Jacobian satisfies the necessary condition for the fixed-point iteration to converge. However, with any initial guess of $v_0 \neq 1/\sqrt{2}$, the iteration produces a periodic cycle. For example, choose $v_0 = 2$ and the "solution" iterates between

$$v_i = \begin{cases} 1/4 \ i \ odd \\ 2 \ i \ even \end{cases}$$

and convergence does not obtain. To induce convergence in this system, we simply add a damping factor $z(z = 0.5)$ and iterate on:

$$v_{k+1} = z(1/2)v_k^{-1} + (1 - z)\, v_k \tag{4.A.4}$$

With an initial estimate of $v_0 = 2$ for $k = 0$, iterating on (4.A.4) causes convergence of v to the true value (within ten decimal places) in three iterations.

Consequently, to induce convergence in our context, we introduce the damping factor z, where $z \in (0, 1)$, and (4.A.2) becomes

$$V_{k+1} = zBV_k^- + (1 - z)\, V_k \tag{4.A.5}$$

Note this implies that $V_{k+1} = V_k - zf(V_k)$. For an initial guess in the range of V^E, the fixed-point iteration will converge to $f(V^E) = 0$ if z is contracting (since z is less than unity), see Nirenberg (1975). Thus, for the class of models discussed in A-vW the solution to the price terms can be obtained by fixed-point iteration with a damping factor of $z \in (0, 1)$. Note how similar this is to the Gauss–Newton iteration scheme discussed in Judd (1998). Unlike the Gauss–Newton iteration, this procedure does not require computing the Jacobian or its inverse, if the latter exists.

We applied this procedure to the McCallum–A-vW–Feenstra Canadian–US dataset, using a stopping rule of $\varepsilon < 1 \times 10^{-9}$ for all elements of V. If we use the parameter values in A-vW of $\rho\,(1 - \sigma) = -0.79$ and $\alpha(1 - \sigma) = -1.65$, convergence is achieved after twenty-five iterations (for both cases, with and without the border) and the correlation of the multilateral resistance terms with those constructed by A-vW is 1.0 (reported to seven decimal places). If we use the parameter values in OLS-MR of $\rho\,(1 - \sigma) = -1.25$ and $\alpha(1 - \sigma) = -1.54$, convergence is achieved after twenty-one iterations (for both cases, with and without the border) and the correlation of the multilateral resistance terms with the multilateral resistance terms constructed by the A-vW NLS methodology is 1.0 (reported to seven decimal places). Given that this methodology replicates perfectly the MR terms calculated by A-vW, the comparative statics are identical to those reported by A-vW (2003, p. 187).

5 An extended gravity model with substitution applied to international trade

J. A. Bikker

1 Introduction

For decades the traditional gravity model has been successfully applied to flows of the most widely varying types, such as migration, flows of buyers to shopping centers, recreational traffic, commuting, patient flows to hospitals, and inter-regional as well as international trade. The model specifies that a flow from origin i to destination j is determined by supply conditions at the origin, by demand conditions at the destination, and by stimulating or restraining forces relating to the specific flow between i and j. In a context of international trade the traditional gravity model usually has the following form:

$$X_{ij} = \beta_0 Y_i^{\beta_1} N_i^{\beta_2} Y_j^{\beta_3} N_j^{\beta_4} D_{ij}^{\beta_5} P_{ij}^{\beta_6} \qquad (5.1)$$

where X_{ij} is the value of trade between countries i and j, Y_k and N_k are the Gross Domestic Product (GDP) and the size of the population, respectively, of country k, and D_{ij} and P_{ij} denote the distance between countries i and j and a possible special preference relationship, respectively. The gravity model of bilateral trade has become the workhorse of applied international economics (Eichengreen and Irwin 1998) and has been used in any number of contexts.[1] Some authors assume that the size of the population has no impact, thus $\beta_2 = \beta_4 = 0$, which renders the resemblance to Newton's Law of Gravity even more obvious.[2]

The author is grateful to an unkown referee, Gert-Jan Linders, and other participants of the Workshop "The Gravity Equation – Or: Why the World is not Flat," Groningen, the Netherlands, October 18–19, 2007, for valuable comments and suggestions and to Jack Bekooij for extensive data support and estimations. This chapter enlarges on Bikker (1987), but all empirical results are new.

[1] Linders (2006) found 200 studies (actually a sample from a much larger set), and provides a selection in his Table 3.1. For an overview, see Anderson and van Wincoop (2004).
[2] E.g. Tinbergen (1962), Pöyhönen (1963a, 1963b), Pulliainen (1963), Geraci and Prewo (1977), Prewo (1978), Abrams (1980), and Bergstrand (1985).

The empirical results obtained with the model have always been judged as very good. Deardorff (1998) argues that the model is sensible, intuitive, and hard to avoid as a reduced theoretical model to explain bilateral trade. Yet the gravity model has some serious imperfections. One is the absence of a cogent derivation of the model, based on economic theory. Several authors have tried to provide the model with such a theoretical basis, using models of imperfect competition and product differentiation, notably Anderson (1979), Bergstrand (1985), Helpman and Krugman (1985), and Anderson and van Wincoop (2003), whereas Deardorff (1998) proves that the model is also consistent with the Heckscher-Ohlin trade theory under perfect competition. However, none of these derivations generates the gravity model exactly as formulated in equation (5.1).[3] This equation could only be approximated under a number of restrictive and unrealistic assumptions, as has been made clear by Bergstrand (1985).

Another imperfection of the gravity model is the absence of substitution between flows.[4] Existence of substitution can be made plausible by economic integration. For example, the accession of Estonia to the European Union (EU) in 2004 is expected to lead to additional imports by other EU countries of "wood, wood products, and paper" (Estonia's major export product) – that is, gross trade creation, see Balassa (1962). However, EU imports of wood products from other countries may very well decline (somewhat). This decline – trade diversion – is not described by the gravity model. In the analysis of economic integration, for which purpose the gravity model is frequently used, trade creation and trade diversion are important phenomena.

This chapter presents an alternative to the gravity model, or rather an extension of it, with substitution between flows. This extended gravity model shows strong similarities to the models of Bergstrand (1985), Anderson and van Wincoop (2003), and Redding and Scott (2003). It can be derived straightforwardly from supply and demand equations, which provides it with a theoretical basis. It appears to be a generalization of the gravity model which permits empirical testing of the assumptions on which the gravity model is based. The extended model generates

[3] The most restrictive theoretical model of Anderson, Bergstrand, as well as Helpman and Krugman, is a gravity model with only GDPs as determinants. A less restrictive model has a different functional form (Anderson, equation [16]) or additional determinants (Bergstrand, equation [14]).

[4] Glejser and Dramais (1969) have attempted to specify a trade model with substitution but, as they admit, their model is not without estimation problems. See also Viaene (1982), whose method, however, becomes very complex when applied to a matrix of trade flows instead of a vector.

estimation results which – due to a substitution structure – deviate widely from the gravity model estimates, which underlines the importance of discerning the substitution structure.

The remainder of this chapter consists of the following sections. Section 2 gives the derivation of the model, called the Extended Gravity Model (EGM), from supply and demand equations. Section 3 compares the EGM with the gravity model, describes its indices of the geo-economic position which establish the model's substitution structure, and treats econometric issues.[5] Section 4 presents estimation results for trade flows between 178 countries in 2005, tests the EGM against the gravity model, and interprets the model parameters and the indices of the geo-economic position. Section 5 concludes.

2   Derivation of the extended gravity model

The next paragraph derives the extended gravity model from a supply and demand system. Alternative derivations from (among other things) constant elasticity of substitution (CES) preference or utility functions are discussed in Section 2.7. The supply and demand system consists of the following four equations:

$$\text{Supply} \quad E_i^s = \omega C_i p_i^\lambda \quad i = 1, \ldots, n \tag{5.2}$$

$$\text{Demand} \quad I_j^d = \gamma B_j q_j^\rho p_j^\pi \quad j = 1, \ldots, m \tag{5.3}$$

$$\text{Allocation} \quad X_{ij}^d \Big/ I_j^d = p_i^\mu D_{ij}^{\varepsilon 1} P_{ij}^{\varepsilon 2} \Big/ \sum\nolimits_{k=1}^n p_k^\mu D_{kj}^{\varepsilon 1} P_{kj}^{\varepsilon 2} \quad i \neq j \tag{5.4}$$

$$\text{Index} \quad q_j = \sum\nolimits_{k=1}^n p_k^\mu D_{kj}^{\varepsilon 1} P_{kj}^{\varepsilon 2} \tag{5.5}$$

2.1   Aggregate supply

E_i^s represents the total foreign supply of country i, C_i, its potential foreign supply and p_i the domestic price of its exports, actually a price index, since the export covers a mix of commodities ($\lambda > 0$). The potential foreign supply depends on, inter alia, the productive capacity for tradeable goods, which is proportional to GDP (Y_i) if the ratio between productive capacity for tradeable and non-tradeable goods were equal in all countries. A theoretical micro-economic foundation of this supply equation can be found in Bergstrand (1985), whose equation (8) is – after summation over j – virtually equal to equation (5.2), under a simplifying assumption – absence of price discrimination (i.e. $p_{ij} = p_i$ for all i). Bergstrand uses the same assumption to obtain an applicable model.

2.2   Aggregate demand

I_j^d denotes the total foreign demand of country j, B_j its potential foreign demand,[6] p_j the price level of domestically produced tradeable goods ($\pi < 0$),[7] and q_j an index indicating the attractiveness of the whole commodity mix offered by all the exporting countries together ($\rho > 0$). This index varies per country because of the different distances between the importing and exporting countries. It also depends on the foreign export prices, and functions in equation (5.3) as a foreign price in the traditional import equation, see Stern et al. (1976).

2.3   Geographical allocation of demand

The supply and demand system consists of n markets, one for each exporting country. These markets are separated from one another by distances. On each market m countries act as demanders. The demand from each importing country is distributed over the n markets. The demand from country j for products of country i is X_{ij}^d. The share of country i in the total demand of country j, X_{ij}^d / I_j^d, depends on price $p_i (\mu > 0)$ and on specific factors promoting or hampering trade between i and j, such as distance, D_{ij}, ($\epsilon_1 < 0$) because of transportation and information costs, etc. and preferential relations, P_{ij}, ($\epsilon_2 > 0$) if any (economic unions, ties with former colonies, etc.). This results in:

$$X_{ij}^d \Big/ I_j^d \propto p_i^\mu D_{ij}^{\epsilon_1} P_{ij}^{\epsilon_2} \tag{5.6}$$

where $\propto$ denotes "proportionate to." The shares of equation (5.6) must add up to 1, due to the restriction $\sum_{i=1}^n X_{ij}^d = I_j^d$ which is automatically met if X_{ij}^d / I_j^d is specified as in equation (5.4). This equation describes the preference of country j to buy products from country i and has the

---

[6] Potential foreign demand depends among other things on national income (Y_j) as a scale factor.
[7] Equation (5.4) assumes imperfect substitutability between domestically and foreign-produced tradeable goods.

form of the multinomial logit model, which is widely applied to specify choice processes and is provided with a theoretical foundation by means of a derivation from utility functions, see Daganzo (1979).

Some or all of the importing and exporting countries may coincide. However, the supply and demand system does not involve domestic supplies and deliveries. So, X_{jj} may be excluded from equations (5.4)–(5.6) and the summations then read: $k = 1, \ldots, n; \ k \neq j$. This will also hold for the following equations.

2.4 Attractiveness index

The index q_j denotes the extent to which producers satisfy consumers of j, see Daganzo (1979). Equation (5.3) which contains q_j is based on the assumption that the reasons *why* country j prefers to buy products from country k (see equation [5.4]) will also play an important role in deciding *how much* will be bought (see equation [5.3]) – *why* depending on the attractiveness of each of the various alternatives and *how much* on the attractiveness of all alternatives together. The index q_j can be regarded as a foreign price index, where the weights $D_{ij}^{\varepsilon 1}$ and $P_{ij}^{\varepsilon 2}$ for $k = 1, \ldots, n$ are proxies for transportation costs and lower tariff rates for preferential trading arrangements, respectively.

2.5 Bilateral demand

The bilateral demand equation follows from substitution of (5.3) and (5.5) into (5.4):

$$X_{ij}^d = \gamma B_j q_j^{\rho-1} p_j^{\pi} p_i^{\mu} D_{ij}^{\varepsilon 1} P_{ij}^{\varepsilon 2} \tag{5.4'}$$

A theoretical foundation of this equation is given by Bergstrand (1985). Under the assumption of absence of price discrimination mentioned above, his equation (4) is in fact equal to equation (5.4'), where $q_j^{\phi} + p_j^{\vartheta}$ is approximated by $q_j^{\eta} p_j^{\xi}$.

2.6 Equilibrium

In export market i price p_i balances total supply and aggregate demand (for each i):

$$E_i^s = \sum_{l=1}^{m} X_{i,l}^d \tag{5.7}$$

The equilibrium prices can be derived from:

$$p_i = [\gamma \omega^{-1} C_i^{-1} \sum_{l=1}^{m} q_l^{\rho-1} p_l^{\pi} B_l D_{il}^{\varepsilon_1} P_{il}^{\varepsilon_2}]^{1/(\lambda-\mu)} \tag{5.8}$$

Equations (5.5) and (5.8) form a simultaneous system: p_i depends on q_l and p_l (note: $1 \neq i$), and q_l on p_i, etc. It can be proven that this system has a unique solution, which provides the equilibrium prices and, by substitution in the other model equations, the equilibrium values of imports, exports, and the index. The equilibrium model obtained in this way cannot be applied empirically in its present form, because the simultaneous set of equilibrium prices p_i from equation (5.8) and index values q_j from equation (5.5) can only be calculated from exogenous variables, given the unknown parameters π, λ, and μ. An empirically useful model can be obtained if the unidentified system of prices and indices is rewritten into an identified set of indices α_i and β_j. These indices are defined as follows:

$$\alpha_i = \sum_{l=1}^{m} q_l^{\rho-1} p_l^{\pi} B_l D_{i,l}^{\varepsilon_1} P_{i,l}^{\varepsilon_2} \quad (= p_i^{\lambda-\mu} C_i^{\omega}/\gamma) \tag{5.9}$$

$$\beta_j = \sum_{k=1}^{n} p_k^{\mu} D_{kj}^{\varepsilon_1} P_{kj}^{\varepsilon_2} \quad (= q_j)$$

The interpretation of these indices is given in the next section. Replacement of p_i and q_j with functions of α_i and β_j yields a system that is expressed exclusively in α_i and β_j, and no longer in p_i and q_j,[8]

$$\alpha_i = \sum_{l=1}^{m} \beta_l^{-1} I_l D_{il}^{\varepsilon_1} P_{il}^{\varepsilon_2} \tag{5.10}$$

$$\beta_j = \sum_{k=1}^{n} \alpha_k^{-1} E_k D_{kj}^{\varepsilon_1} P_{kj}^{\varepsilon_2}$$

with I_j and E_i the equilibrium values of I_j^d and E_i^s. This set is identified because, given ε_1 and ε_2, it can be calculated (iteratively) with observable variables: I_j, E_i, D_{ij}, and P_{ij}, while ε_1 and ε_2 can be estimated without information about α_i and β_j; see equation (5.21) in Section 3.
The equilibrium model expressed in α_i and β_j is:[9]

$$E_i = (\gamma^{\lambda} \omega^{-\mu} \alpha_i^{\lambda} C_i^{-\mu})^{1/(\lambda-\mu)} \tag{5.11}$$

---

[8] For the derivations here and further on, see Bikker (1982, p. 27 ff.).

[9] If all countries are included, importing and exporting countries coincide. In that case country j's own price p_j is endogenous and, according to equation (5.9), a function of α_j. If only a subset of countries is considered, some p_j are exogenous.

$$I_j = \gamma^{1+\pi/(\lambda-\mu)}\beta_j^{\rho}B_j(\alpha_i^{\pi}C_j^{-1}\omega^{-1})^{1/(\lambda-\mu)} \tag{5.12}$$

$$X_{ij} = I_jE_iD_{ij}^{\varepsilon_1}P_{ij}^{\varepsilon_2}/(\gamma\alpha_i\beta_j) \tag{5.13}$$

The properties of this model are analyzed in Section 3.

2.7   Alternative theoretical foundations of the extended gravity model

Anderson and Wincoop (2003), abbreviated to A-vW, derive a comparable EGM from a CES preference function, thereby providing a very elegant micro-economic foundation for that model. The similarity of their results to ours becomes clear when the above equations (5.10) of the indices α_i and β_j are compared to equations (10) and (11) of the A-vW price indices Π_i and P_j. Note that A-vW end up with two (scaled) price indices for each country, reflecting prices of, respectively, imports and exports. Only under a further symmetric trade barrier assumption (discussed below) and a "balanced trade" assumption do the two price indices coincide, that is, $\Pi_i = P_i$ (Anderson, this volume). The symmetric trade barrier assumption, however, is far from trivial, as shown below.

Bergstrand (1985) derives a type of EGM using double constant elasticity of substitution (CES) utility functions for consumers and double constant elasticity of transformation (CET) joint production surfaces for producers. He specifies supply and demand for each trade flow X_{ij}, but links their aggregates over i and j to the respective countries' national incomes. Bergstrand's equilibrium model for X_{ij} resembles equation (5.13) and the model of A-vW, but deviates in that it uses different substitution elasticities on the foreign and domestic markets.

Redding and Scott (2003) and Redding and Venables (2004) derive an EGM rather comparable to that of A-vW and this chapter, using Cobb–Douglas preference and production functions. They define (foreign) market access and (foreign) supplier access identical to our indices α_i and β_j, which can be rewritten in prices and price indices. Their model is more restricted as the exponential parameters of market access, supplier access, and distance are all equal to $\sigma - 1$ or $1 - \sigma$. The "new economic geography" wage level in their model is a function of these access variables, which in turn depend on prices. This approach has also been applied in this volume by Bosker and Garretsen (Chapter 7) and Boulhol and de Serres (Chapter 12). Behrens *et al.* (2007) develop a gravity model, which is a simplification of the various models above, as it contains only one set of indices, supplier access, instead of two (ignoring market access).[10] Similarly, Anderson (1979) presents in equation (16) a gravity model with market access, ignoring supplier access.

For the application of the extended gravity model to world trade, the A-vW foundation is most elegant. However, the derivation in Sections 2.1–2.6 above has two advantages. First, it applies to a wider set of applications. Earlier, the EGM was applied to flows of hospital patients from resident areas to hospitals (Bikker and De Vos 1992a). Other potential applications are the international trade in single commodities (such as oil), commuter traffic, migration flows, and flows of shoppers to shopping centers, students to schools, tourists to holiday destinations, etc. In those cases, origin and destination regions do not coincide, contrary to the symmetry between origin and destination regions commonly found in general international trade.[11]

Second, Sections 2.1–2.6 explain clearly that the attractiveness of a country's trade partners (or "other countries"), given its geographical location, may differ substantially for its imports and its exports. These sections propose the distinct indices α_i and β_j as measures of the geographical attractiveness of, respectively, exports and imports. A-vW come up with two distinct sets of price indices, defined similarly to these indices, but the two sets of price indices coincide under the symmetry trade barrier assumption. Such symmetry is likely with respect to distances and preferential relations due to economic unions, ties with former colonies, etc. International trade between two countries also depends heavily on the correlation between the supply by product types of the exporting country and the demand by product types of the importing country. This applies in particular to commodities. Behrens et al. (2007) and Bergstrand et al. (this volume) stress that trade costs are far from symmetric. Symmetry may also be absent for other omitted variables. This is also evident from the empirical application of the EGM: in 2005, the trade barrier residuals (that is, omitted variables) of the trade flows X_{ij} and $X_{j,i}$ (that is: u_{ij} and $u_{j,i}$) have a markedly low correlation at 0.2, pointing to quite limited symmetry. Particularly in the absence of a variable for the correlation between demanded and supplied goods, this argues for the use of both sets of indices, that is, repudiation of the symmetry trade barrier assumption.

[10] This would be equivalent to imposing $\mu = 0$ in equation (5.4) and (5.5), see Bikker (1982, p. 38).

[11] The symmetric trade barrier assumption does not hold true for the international trade of a commodity with a limited number of supply countries. Furthermore, trade datasets may be incomplete, for instance because some trade flows are reported as zero or are in fact absent.

Finally, we notice a few further, though not essential, differences between A-vW's foundation and the derivation given above. A-vW include demand for and supply to domestic consumption.[12] This inclusion is essential for their derivation, because their (theoretical) model is based on countries' total demand and total supply. Two remarks are in order. First, inclusion of domestic consumption and production is elegant as substitution may be expected between domestic and foreign demand. However, for domestic consumption and production it is quite common to distinguish between tradeables and non-tradeables (e.g. Anderson 1979; Bergstrand 1985). A-vW assume demand substitution among exporter countries to be the same as substitution between foreign and domestic demand, which is less plausible as the substitution between foreign tradeables and domestic non-tradeables is likely to be close(r) to zero. For that reason, Bergstrand assumes different degrees of substitution between demand from various foreign countries and between foreign and domestic demand. In practice, statistics do not exactly distinguish between domestic tradeables and non-tradeables. For that reason, Section 2.2 excludes domestic tradeables (as empirical application goes with practical issues), but includes the price level of domestically produced tradeable goods (p_j) in the demand equation (5.3) so as to take possible substitution into account. This results in a more complex equilibrium equation of imports (5.12), deviating from the A-vW equation.[13]

There is a second argument why inclusion of domestic consumption and production, the diagonal elements of the trade matrix, are often excluded in practice, although they may appear elegant in the theoretical derivations. In the gravity model all trade flows depend on the distances between pairs of exporting and importing countries, but, in practice, the specification of the distance between producers and consumers within a country is a thorny issue (e.g. Anderson and Smith 1999, p. 29; Head and Mayer, this volume). Often no trade costs are assumed; that is, the effect of distance is set at zero ($\ln(D_{ii}) = 0$). For a better solution, see equation (6.15) in Head and Mayer (this volume), and Bosker and Garretsen (this volume). Behrens *et al.* (2007, p. 8) raise the problem that explanatory variable GDP_i is not exogenous to the dependent variable "domestic consumption" (or production) X_{ii}. Note that the diagonal elements of matrix X may be either included in or deleted from the derivations in Sections 2.1–2.6 above without any change in the theoretical results, apart from the respective interpretation: the inclusion implies that total

---

[12] Note that consumption also includes investment goods.
[13] In the empirical application the import equation is used in its simplified form, see equation (5.16) below.

production and consumption are described (in fact, national income),[14] whereas exclusion means that the model refers to imports and exports only.[15] Hence, it is not needed here to make a principle choice.

3   The extended gravity model

For empirical application of the equilibrium model thus obtained, it is necessary to specify the concepts of potential foreign supply, C_i, and demand, B_j. Potential foreign supply depends on productive capacity, proxied by Gross National Product, Y_i, and on market size (approximated by population, N_i). The latter is based on the assumption of economies of scale: the larger N is, the higher is the number of production lines for which the country will meet the minimum market size for efficient market production. The larger N, therefore, the larger the domestic market will be in relation to the foreign market, and the smaller the potential foreign supply. Other lines of reasoning for N_i in the export equations can be found in Leamer and Stern (1970), Krugman (1979, 1980), and Brada and Mendez (1983); see also Linnemann (1966), Leamer (1974), and Chenery and Syrquin (1975). An alternative explanatory variable is the country's surface area A_i, which may reflect size, occurrence of mineral resources, and average distance to foreign countries. Areas are used in variants only. The variables Y_j and N_j determine potential foreign demand, using the same arguments as were applied to potential foreign supply.

Thus, the following equations are obtained.

$$I_j = \delta_0 \beta_j^{\delta_1^*} Y_j^{\delta_2} N_j^{\delta_3} \alpha_j^{\delta_4} \tag{5.14}$$

$$E_i = \gamma_0 \alpha_i^{\gamma_1} Y_i^{\gamma_2} N_i^{\gamma_3} \tag{5.15}$$

Note that equations (5.11)–(5.12) do not impose restrictions on the coefficients in equations (5.14)–(5.15). In our empirical application the variable α_i in equation (5.14) is deleted (or: $\beta_j^{\delta_1^*} \alpha_j^{\delta_4}$ is approximated by $\beta_j^{\delta_1}$). Due to the observed rough symmetry between imports and exports ($E_k \approx I_k$), there appears to be a strong correlation between α_i and β_j (in 2005: 0.92), which may cause multicollinearity. Not only in the empirical

---

[14] Note that if the EGM described all production and consumption (hence include diagonal elements), π, i.e. the elasticity of the (competing) price level of domestically produced tradeable goods, would equal 0 in equation (5.3).

[15] A third option would be to include only (domestic) tradeable goods in the diagonal elements.

section but, for convenience, in this section as well, equation (5.14) is replaced by:

$$I_j = \delta_0 \beta_j^{\delta_1} Y_j^{\delta_2} N_j^{\delta_3} \tag{5.16}$$

Substitution of equations (5.15) and (5.16) into (5.13) produces:

$$X_{ij} = \gamma_0' \alpha_i^{\gamma_1 - 1} Y_i^{\gamma_2} N_i^{\gamma_3} \beta_j^{\delta_1 - 1} Y_j^{\delta_2} N_j^{\delta_3} D_{ij}^{\varepsilon_1} P_{ij}^{\varepsilon_2} \tag{5.17}$$

3.1   Comparison of the extended gravity model to the traditional gravity model

This equation clearly shows that $\gamma_1 = \delta_1 = 1$ corresponds to the standard gravity model, see equation (5.1). The theoretical meaning of these restrictions becomes clear after comparison of equations (5.14) and (5.15) with (5.12) and (5.11): $\delta_1 = \rho$ and $\gamma_1 = \lambda/(\lambda - \mu)$. The restrictions in "background" parameters are $\rho = 1$ and $\mu = 0$ or $\lambda = \infty$, respectively. The interpretation of these parameters follows easily from the rewritten supply and demand system:

$$E_i^s = \omega C_i p_i^\lambda \tag{5.2'}$$

$$X_{ij}^d = \gamma B_j q_j^{\rho - 1} p_j^\pi p_i^\mu D_{ij}^{\varepsilon_1} P_{ij}^{\varepsilon_2} \tag{5.4'}$$

So, $\rho = 1$ means inelasticity of the demand for q_j, the extent to which producers satisfy consumers of country j or, phrased differently, the attractiveness for country j of the goods of all other exporting countries together. The extreme case of perfectly elastic supply, $\lambda = \infty$, relates to another market system where equilibrium is met not by price adjustment but by quantity adjustment. As this is not a likely market system for aggregated trade flows, the relevant restriction is $\mu = 0$, meaning no cross-price elasticity in the demand equation. Therefore, the hypotheses which produce the traditional gravity model are demand inelasticity to the attractiveness index q and cross-price inelasticity of demand. These hypotheses will be tested in Section 4.

3.2   Indices of the geo-economic position

The indices α_i and β_j play a pivotal role in the extended gravity model. They are interpreted as follows: β_j is an index of the attractiveness to country j of the goods offered by the exporting countries, weighted by the distance (see Section 2), or – in other words – a mean distance between country j and the exporting countries, weighted by the attractiveness to country j of the goods offered; an index of the geo-economic position. Because of the symmetry in model structure (with respect to import and export countries), α_i can be called the attractiveness of country i's sales market, weighted by the distance to the importing countries. One may also consider equation (5.9) in which α_i depends upon the weighted potential foreign demand (mainly purchasing power) of the importing countries, B_j. The occurrence of β_j^{-1} in the terms of index α_i can be explained as follows: country j will be the more attractive to country i to sell to as the latter suffers less from competition by other exporting countries. As noted above, α_i and β_j are highly correlated. Equations (5.15) and (5.16) show how exports and imports each depend upon the geo-economic indices concerned. It is to be expected that $\gamma_1 > 0$ and $\delta_1 > 0$. Other names for these indices or closely related indices are (foreign) market access and (foreign) supplier access (Redding and Scott 2003), inward and outward multilateral resistance terms (Anderson and van Wincoop 2003; Anderson, this volume), remoteness indices, balancing factors (Wilson 1967), and spatial competition (Behrens *et al.* 2007).

3.3   Substitution structure

The coefficients $1 - \gamma_1$ and $1 - \delta_1$ are interpreted as the degree of substitution between flows of similar origin and similar destination, respectively. To explain that, we imagine that, owing to economic integration, trade preference between two countries, say i_0 and j_0, doubles, thus $P_{i_0,j_0}^{\varepsilon_2}$ becomes 2 instead of 1, see equation (5.17). The terms of α_{i_0} and β_{j_0}, which correspond to the trade flow between i_0 and j_0, also contain the factor $P_{i_0,j_0}^{\varepsilon_2}$. If $\gamma_1 = \delta_1 = 0$, total exports of country i_0 and total imports of country j_0 – see equations (5.15) and (5.16) – do not change: additional trade between i_0 and j_0 is entirely at the expense of other trade flows of similar origin or similar destination – thus trade diversion without (net) trade creation, or full substitution.[16] By contrast, if $\gamma_1 = \delta_1 = 1$ – the traditional gravity model case – equation (5.17) shows[17] that there will be no substitution at all – trade creation without trade diversion. Doubling of X_{i_0,j_0}, say from x to $2x$, will, if $\gamma_1 = \delta_1 = 1$, lead to more exports from country i_0 to a value of x and more imports by country j_0 to the same

---

[16] It can be proved that the EGM with $\gamma_1 = 0$ and/or $\delta_1 = 0$ corresponds to one of the so-called constrained gravity models originating in regional economics, see Wilson (1967).

[17] As found earlier, these restrictions relate to demand inelasticity to the attractiveness index q and cross-price inelasticity of demand.

amount. Thus we conclude that $1-\gamma_1$ and $1-\delta_1$ reflect the degree of substitution between export flows and import flows, respectively. If γ_1 and δ_1 exceed 1, complementarity between flows will outweigh substitution.

3.4 Econometric issues

To apply the EGM empirically, disturbance terms are added to the logarithms of equations (5.15)–(5.17). These terms must meet the restrictions to which the model is also subjected, i.e. flows X_{ij} should add up over the rows to imports (I_j) and over the columns to exports (E_i). At the same time this means that the sum of the imports equals the sum of the exports: $\Sigma_j I_j = \Sigma_i E_i$. The latter restriction implies that stochastically exports and imports cannot be specified independently. A simple solution of this problem is to specify one of the two equations in terms of deviation from the level, and to let the other one determine the level. For estimation results, predictions, etc., it does not matter which equation is selected. We choose the following specification:

$$\ln E_i = \gamma_0' + \gamma_1 \ln \alpha_i + \gamma_2 \ln Y_i + \gamma_3 \ln N_i + v_i \tag{5.18}$$

$$\ln \tilde{I}_j = \delta_1 \ln \tilde{\beta}_j + \delta_2 \ln \tilde{Y}_j + \delta_3 \ln \tilde{N}_j + \tilde{w}_j \tag{5.19}$$

where $\sim$ denotes "in deviation from the arithmetic mean." In equation (5.19), the transformation $\sim$ refers to, respectively, $\ln I_i$, $\ln \beta_j$, $\ln Y_j$, $\ln N_j$, and w_j (and hence not to I_i, β_j, etc.). Both equations are conditional upon calculated values of α_i and β_j. To keep the estimation procedure simple, E_i and I_j in the formulae of α_i and β_j – see equation (5.10) – are replaced by estimations of the corresponding expectations. The indices are then (re)defined as follows – where, for convenience, the same names are employed for these non-stochastic indices:

$$\alpha_i = \sum_{l=1}^{m} \beta_l^{\delta_1-1} Y_l^{\delta_2} N_l^{\delta_3} D_{il}^{\varepsilon_1} P_{il}^{\varepsilon_2} \tag{5.20}$$

$$\beta_j = \sum_{k=1}^{n} \alpha_k^{\gamma_1-1} Y_k^{\gamma_2} N_k^{\gamma_3} D_{kj}^{\varepsilon_1} P_{kj}^{\varepsilon_2}$$

Under one restriction, say $\prod_{j=1}^{m} \beta_j = 1$, this iterative system is unique for given parameter values.

The restrictions on X_{ij} imply that, after taking logarithms, the arithmetic means over i and, subsequently, over j can be subtracted from equation (5.17) without losing any statistical information. This eliminates all the terms which depend solely on i or solely on j:

$$\ln \tilde{X}_{ij} = \varepsilon_1 \ln \tilde{D}_{ij}^{\varepsilon_1} + \varepsilon_2 \ln \tilde{P}_{ij}^{\varepsilon_2} + \tilde{u}_{ij} \tag{5.21}$$

in which $\approx$ denotes "in deviation from the arithmetic means over i and, subsequently, over j." In equation (5.21), the transformation $\approx$ refers to, respectively, $\ln X_{ij}$, $\ln D_{ij}$, $\ln P_{ij}$, and u_{ij}. Equation (5.21) only reflects the geographical distribution or a (gravity) model with two sets of fixed effects for import and export countries (compare to Feenstra 2002, 2004). Statistically equation (5.21) corresponds to the traditional analysis-of-variance model. Equations (5.18)–(5.21) add up to the Extended Gravity Model (EGM), which will be applied to international trade in the next section. Note that equations (5.18), (5.19), and (5.21) successively determine n, $(m-1)$ and $(n-l)$ $(m-1)$ degrees of freedom, therefore together exactly nm.

The three model equations can be estimated with OLS. The estimation procedure is as follows:

(1) first ε_1 and ε_2 are estimated with OLS: $\hat{\varepsilon}_1$ and $\hat{\varepsilon}_2$;[18]
(2) α and β are calculated iteratively given $\hat{\varepsilon}_1$ and $\hat{\varepsilon}_2$, given initial values for the gammas and deltas, e.g. from the estimation of a gravity model. Moreover, α_i will then be conditional on the values of β_j and vice versa;
(3) Equations (5.18) and (5.19) are estimated, given values of α and β, with which new OLS estimates of the gammas and deltas are obtained;
(4) Steps (2) and (3) are repeated until given convergence criteria are met.

If the disturbance terms are normally distributed, the total likelihood function can be formulated and therefore the most likely estimates can be calculated. These estimates may depart slightly from the OLS estimates, since through the indices in equation (5.20) the imports and exports equations may contain information about the estimates of ε_1 and ε_2 from the allocation equation (5.21). Maximum likelihood estimates can be calculated with a numerical estimation procedure.

4   Estimation results

This section applies both the traditional gravity model and the EGM to international aggregated trade flows between 178 countries. As diagonal elements relate to domestic supplies and deliveries, they have not been included here, so there are in principle 178 x 177 individual trade flows.

---

[18] OLS estimates are Best Linear Unbiased, as is shown for a special case by Teekens and Jansen (1977). This follows from the Law of Aitken, see Theil (1971).

Part of the flows (12,156) have been recorded as zero due to rounding or to actual absence of trade, leaving 19,350 non-zero flows.[19] The figures date back to 2005. Information about the data used is given in Appendix A.

Table 5.1 shows estimation results of the common gravity model and our extended version of it. A number of preference variables have been added to the model, which will be explained below. We present results of two variants of the EGM, the EGM with standard α and β, as introduced above, and the EGM based on α and β which include the allocation residuals $\tilde{\tilde{u}}_{ij}$:

$$\alpha_i(\tilde{u}) = \sum\nolimits_{l=1}^{m} \beta_l^{\delta_1-1} Y_l^{\delta_2} N_l^{\delta_3} D_{il}^{\varepsilon_1} P_{il}^{\varepsilon_2} \exp(\tilde{u}_{il}) \qquad (5.22)$$

$$\beta_j(\tilde{u}) = \sum\nolimits_{k=1}^{n} \alpha_k^{\gamma_1-1} Y_k^{\gamma_2} N_k^{\gamma_3} D_{kj}^{\varepsilon_1} P_{kj}^{\varepsilon_2} \exp(\tilde{u}_{kj})$$

The latter can be seen as more precise, because they include also the information about the geographical allocation as contained in the omitted variables, such as the correlation between the composition in terms of products between supply of the export country and demand of the import country. Bosker and Garretsen (this volume) show how extremely sensitive the (market access) indices are with respect to the specification of the trade costs model (or geographical allocation model) when applied in a new-economic-geography wage function. Inclusion of the allocation errors would solve that problem to a large extent. Estimates of the models including also the surface area of importing and exporting countries can be found in Appendix B. The parameter estimates of both the traditional and the extended gravity model seem to correspond fairly reasonably to what has been found by other authors. However, the interpretation of the EGM will appear to be quite different. Before examining the parameter estimates in detail, we will discuss the major difference between the gravity model and the EGM.

4.1   Comparison of the gravity model with the EGM

The gravity model is a special case of the EGM. The models are equal if two sets of restrictions are imposed on the latter. The first set concerns the substitution between flows, which is lacking in the gravity model, owing to the two restrictions $\gamma_1 = \delta_1 = 1$. The second set regards the error structure. Comparison of equations (5.18), (5.19), and (5.21) with

---

[19] Bikker and De Vos (1992b) aim at solving estimation bias due to zero trade flows.

Table 5.1. *Estimation results of the traditional and extended gravity model (2005)*

	Parameters	Traditional gravity model Coeff.	t-values	EGM (standard α and β) Coeff.	t-values	EGM (α and β with residuals $\tilde{\tilde{u}}_{ij}$) Coeff.	t-values
				Export model			
Intercept	γ'_0	−10.62	(−41.5)	−2.377	(−7.5)	−3.369	(−8.2)
Alpha (market access)	γ_1			0.106	(1.5)	0.197	(3.8)
GDP	γ_2	1.25	(113.4)	1.101	(28.5)	1.148	(32.4)
Population	γ_3	−0.04	(−3.1)	−0.122	(−2.9)	−0.119	(−3.0)
Number of observations				178		178	
R-squared, adjusted				90.4		91.0	
				Import model			
Beta (supplier access)	δ_1			0.230	(4.1)	0.121	(2.0)
GDP	δ_2	0.89	(80.7)	0.908	(33.5)	0.944	(36.2)
Population	δ_3	0.02	(2.0)	−0.086	(−2.8)	−0.110	(−3.5)
Number of observations				178		178	
R-squared, adjusted				93.4		92.9	
				Allocation model			
Distance	ε_1	−1.30	(−55.4)	−1.699	(−71.3)		
Neighbors	ε_2	0.99	(8.1)	0.568	(5.4)		
Common language, off.	ε_3	0.36	(4.4)	0.641	(8.3)		
Common language, eth.	ε_4	0.65	(8.3)	0.156	(2.0)		
Former colonial relations	ε_5	0.60	(4.5)	0.738	(6.0)		
Commonwealth	ε_6	1.07	(13.2)	0.448	(5.2)		
French territorial areas	ε_7	0.66	(2.8)	1.244	(5.8)		
Communist past	ε_8	0.15	(1.6)	0.933	(9.8)		
Soviet Union	ε_9	2.16	(10.6)	2.411	(12.7)		
Warsaw Pact	ε_{10}	0.02	(0.1)	0.345	(1.2)		
EU6	ε_{11}	−0.94	(−2.1)	−2.813	(−7.3)		
EU9-6	ε_{12}	−0.88	(−9.9)	−1.080	(−1.3)		
EU12-9	ε_{13}	−0.23	(−0.2)	−0.315	(−0.4)		
EU15-12	ε_{14}	0.11	(0.1)	−0.629	(−0.8)		
EU25-15	ε_{15}	0.69	(2.6)	0.514	(2.2)		
Number of observations		19,350		19,350			
R-squared, adjusted		63.5		33.0			

(5.13) shows that the EGM has an error with a variance components structure: $\tilde{u}_{ij} + \tilde{w}_j + v_i$. This error structure reduces to an ordinary one (u_{ij}) only if a special relation between the standard deviations σ_v, σ_w, and σ_u holds:[20]

$$m\sigma_v = n\sigma_w = \sigma_u \tag{5.23}$$

A Wald test on the two restrictions $\gamma_1 = \delta_1 = 1$ (that is, a gravity model with a variance components error structure) makes clear that these restrictions (and thus the traditional gravity model) are rejected in favor of the EGM with a well-nigh maximum conviction. Earlier calculations have revealed that the – from an economic point of view – less crucial restrictions on the standard deviations of the errors terms are rejected with even more confidence, supporting the rejection of the traditional gravity model (Bikker 1987).

The EGM has also been compared with the gravity model in a second way. This way is inspired by the fact that interest in total imports and exports per country is often greater than in individual trade flows. When the country aggregates of the gravity model are compared to those of the EGM, the gravity model again proves to be strongly defeated by the EGM – for their standard deviations of total exports and total imports residuals appear to be well over 50 per cent higher than those of the EGM. Moreover, the gravity model rather heavily overestimates the actual totals, but this could be due in part to problems of interpreting the constant in a log-linear model, see Teekens and Koerts (1972).

4.2   *Interpretation of the EGM parameter estimates*

On the face of it, most parameter values of the gravity model and of the EGM do not differ much, especially not in the equations for imports and exports, whereas it is exactly here that some differences might be expected, because of the diverging coefficients of the indices (0.106 versus 1 and 0.230 versus 1, see Table 5.1, standard α and β). Closer examination, however, shows that the EGM parameters clearly have a different meaning from those of the gravity model. This is because each

---

[20] Some elements of the analysis become a little more complex if observations are lacking, as is the case here. One element is the restriction (5.24) which in this empirical application is actually formulated somewhat differently. Another is the reduction of equation (5.18) to (5.22): the transformation $\approx$ now requires more calculations. A third relates to the Jacobian required to transform the dependent variables of the EGM into those of the gravity model. In all cases the problems are purely technical and have been fully solved, see Bikker (1982).

explanatory variable also occurs in both indices and therefore affects the modeled trade flow along three channels. Therefore, the overall effect is not immediately apparent. Of course, the effect of a variable can always be determined with a model simulation. However, it is also possible to interpret the parameter estimates analytically. For it can be demonstrated that the effect of (changes in) Y or N from the export equation on X_{ij} equals γ_2 or γ_3, respectively, each multiplied by:

$$\delta_1/(\gamma_1 + \delta_1 - \gamma_1\delta_1) \tag{5.24}$$

that is, provided there is an equal proportional change in Y or N in all exporting countries. We call the coefficients multiplied by (5.24) overall-effect elasticities. They are immediately comparable with the parameters β_1 and β_2 from the gravity model. The overall effect elasticities of the import equation (apart from δ_1 itself) and the distribution model are obtained analogously by multiplying the corresponding parameters with, respectively:

$$\gamma_1/(\gamma_1 + \delta_1 - \gamma_1\delta_1) \text{ and } \gamma_1\delta_1/(\gamma_1 + \delta_1 - \gamma_1\delta_1) \tag{5.25}$$

The overall effect elasticities are shown in column (3) of Table 5.2. The effects on trade flows of GDP and population of the imports and exports model have been added together because in this empirical example importing and exporting countries coincide, so that a change in e.g. all GDPs will affect the modeled trade flow along the import side as well as the export side. Remarkably, nearly all overall effects of the EGM are much smaller than those of the gravity model. Owing to substitution, part of the initial effects leak away. This effect is similar to the lower "border effect" between the USA and Canada measured by the EGM of Anderson and van Wincoop (2003), including the multilateral resistance terms, compared to the traditional gravity model of McCallum (1995); see also Behrens et al. (2007, p. 8).

If we recalculate the elasticities in Table 5.2 on the EGM with α and β with residuals $\tilde{u}_{ij}$ instead of the standard EGM α and β, we obtain largely identical results (see third and fourth row in Table 5.2). This illustrates that different values of the coefficients of α and β (that is, γ_1 and δ_1) should not be considered separately but together.

4.3   Individual parameter estimates

The estimated coefficients of α_i and β_j of the standard EGM are 0.106 (γ_1) and 0.230 (δ_1), respectively. They prove that the EGM provides a better description of international trade than the gravity model, as $\gamma_1 < 1$

Table 5.2. *Elasticities between explanatory variables and trade flows (standard α and β; 2005)*

Column	Traditional gravity model (1)	EGM Initial effect (2)	EGM Overall effect[a] (3)	3 as % of 1 (4)
	standard α and β			
GDP (import & export)	2.140	2.010	1.122	0.524
Population (import & export)	−0.020	−0.210	−0.119	5.958[b]
	α and β with residuals			
GDP (import & export)	2.140	2.090	1.101	0.515
Population (import & export)	−0.020	−0.230	−0.123	6.149[b]
Distance	−1.300	−1.700	−0.137	0.105
Neighbours	0.990	0.570	0.046	0.046
Common language, official	0.360	0.640	0.051	0.143
Common language, ethnic	0.650	0.160	0.013	0.020
Former colonial relations	0.600	0.740	0.059	0.099
Commonwealth	1.070	0.450	0.036	0.034
French territorial areas	0.660	1.240	0.100	0.151
Communist past	0.150	0.930	0.075	0.498
Soviet Union	2.160	2.410	0.194	0.090
Warsaw Pact	0.020	0.350	0.028	1.407
EU6	−0.940	−2.810	−0.226	0.240
EU9-6	−0.880	−1.080	−0.087	0.099
EU12-9	−0.230	−0.320	−0.026	0.112
EU15-12	0.110	−0.630	−0.051	−0.460
EU25-15	0.690	0.510	0.041	0.059

[a] For the allocation based on standard α and β; [b] Quotient is high due to nominator value close to zero.

and δ_1 < 1. On the other hand, they show that countries' exports and imports depend significantly on the geo-economic position, because γ_1 > 0 and δ_1 > 0 holds jointly. As is made clear in Section 3, $1 - \gamma_1$ and $1 - \delta_1$ denote the degree of substitution between flows from exporting country i and between flows to importing country j, respectively. The observed value of $1 - \gamma_1$ is 0.894. Additional exports stemming from new trade possibilities due to e.g. economic integration, newly introduced products or the opening of a new trade route (e.g. the Panama canal),[21] go with

[21] Or the reopening of the Suez canal in 1975 after the closure in 1956, or the newly navigable North-West Passage (North of Canada) or, in the near future, the North-East Passage (North of Russia).

a decrease in export flows to less attractive destinations by 89 per cent of the additional sales (i.e. gross trade creation). Similarly, additional imports due to new attractive import possibilities go with a 77 per cent decrease in competitive import flows. Apparently, ignoring substitution would generate disastrous model forecasts.

The EGM coefficients of the GDPs of import and export countries suggest that a 1 per cent growth of the world economy leads to a somewhat more than proportional increase in international trade flows of 1.22 per cent, see column (3) of Table 5.2. This corresponds to past observations. This contrasts, however, with the more than "quadratic" increase in trade suggested by the gravity model; see column (1). Remarkably, exports outgrow GDP (γ_2 is 1.10), whereas import growth lags behind GDP growth ($\delta_2 = 0.91$). The size of the population reflects scale economies: large countries are more autarkic. Their effects are in line with expectations, but the population coefficients are small compared to the values observed in the past. Apparently, the optimal scale becomes larger over time: even large countries cannot afford to produce for the domestic market alone.

Distance is the major allocation variable. Its coefficient in the EGM approaches the parameter in Newton's law. The coefficient is higher than observed in the past, as also found in a survey by Linders (2006). Our value is at the highest end of the observed estimates. This may reflect a worldwide convergence of prices, so that transportation costs count more heavily (Estevadeordal et al. 2003 and Anderson and van Wincoop 2004). Further, the allocation model includes the following preferential dummy variables, which reflect the intangible barriers to trade related to cultural differences, institutional conditions and differences other than those embodied by mere distance (Obstfeld and Rogoff 2000; Deardorff 2004): whether or not two countries are contiguous, share a common official language, have a common language due to ethnic composition of the population, have ever had a colonial link, are both members of the Commonwealth or the Francophone "Communauté Financière Africaine" (CFA), are both former communist countries, are both former members of the Soviet Union or the former Warsaw Pact, or, finally, are both EU Member States, with a further distinction by membership of the 6, 9, 12, 15, or 25 Member Community. For instance, EU9-6 refers to (additional) trade of Denmark, Ireland, and the UK with the first six EU Member States as well as their mutual trade. Most preferential coefficients are in line with expectations, that is, have positive signs; many are more or less consistently significant. Many ex-colonial preferences are weaker than observed in the past. Apparently, ex-colonial ties have worn thinner in the course of time. A remarkable exception in the expected effects is EU membership, where the older cohorts have negative rather than positive signs.[22] This might be due to measurement errors: even a minor error in the determination of the – relatively small – distances between EU countries would greatly affect the EU coefficients, as the EU countries lie closely together (see Head and Mayer, this volume). Comparisons over time could reveal the true EU impact on international trade.[23] The R-squares make clear that we are able to explain only a minor part of the variation in the allocation ($R^2 = 33.0$), compared to that in the imports ($R^2 = 92.9$) and exports ($R^2 = 91.0$).

4.4   The indices of the geo-economic position

The index α_i can be called the attractiveness of country i's sales market, weighted by the distances to the respective importing countries, whereas β_j is an index of the attractiveness to country j of the goods offered by the respective exporting countries, again weighted by distance. Table 5.3 presents regional means for both indices, with and without allocation residuals, all expressed in deviation from their geometric worldwide mean. We first discuss the indices without residuals, reflecting best the geographical position of countries. The location of the European countries clearly is a favorable one – with, in economic terms, many countries with a large economy situated closely together. This holds even more for Central and Eastern Europe and the former Soviet Union (former Soviet Union members have strong mutual preferences), which lie near Western Europe. North American countries benefit from the USA with its gigantic economy, while the USA itself lies less favorably. South America, Africa and, particularly, Oceania, have more isolated locations, whereas the Middle East and the Rest of Asia take intermediate positions.

The allocation residual $\tilde{u}_{ij}$ reflects mainly the correlation between the composition in terms of products between the supply of country i and the demand of country j. If they are included in the indices, the alphas of countries with sought-after products rise. Oil-producing countries in the

[22] Intra-EU trade is larger than the trade between the other countries in Western Europe, as shown by Aitken (1973), Abrams (1980), and Bergstrand (1985), who used European trade flow figures only. Negative EU coefficients point to a level of EU trade which is nevertheless lower than the level of world trade, after correction for the size of the countries (Y and N), for distances, etc.

[23] Comparison of earlier estimates for 1974 and 1959 – before the EU could make any considerable contribution towards economic integration – shows that the relative preference for other EU countries over 1959–74 rose by 76 per cent (Bikker 1987). In other words, it is not the level of the EU dummy, but the change therein that provides quantitative information about economic integration. However, such a shift has not been observed over 1975–2005.

Table 5.3. *Geo-economic trade positions of exports (α)
and imports (β) per region*

	Without residuals $\tilde{\tilde{u}}_{ij}$		With residuals $\tilde{\tilde{u}}_{ij}$	
	Alphas	Betas	Alphas	Betas
Western Europe	1.86	1.73	0.40	1.36
Central and Eastern Europe[a]	3.23	2.27	1.67	2.89
Former Soviet Union	4.46	2.70	1.20	1.96
North and Central America	0.98	1.59	0.81	1.14
South America	0.51	0.63	0.43	1.00
Middle East	1.13	0.80	2.82	0.91
Rest of Asia	0.93	1.17	0.56	0.60
Oceania	0.32	0.47	1.22	0.50
North-Western Africa	0.60	0.57	1.77	0.74
South-Eastern Africa	0.38	0.37	1.05	0.56

[a] Excluding the former Soviet Union Member countries.
Explanation: The indices are from the EGM without area and are
expressed in deviation from their world-wide geometric mean.

Middle East and countries producing raw material in Africa become more
attractive, whereas regions with less mineral resources, such as Europe
and Asia, lose attraction. The position of importing countries is affected
less strongly.

5   Conclusions

The Extended Gravity Model (EGM) proves to be a useful extension
of the traditional gravity model. A test of 2005 figures on international
trade flows quite convincingly rejects the gravity model in favor of the
more generalized EGM. Apparently, the EGM's substitution structure,
which does not preclude a relatively simple estimation procedure, is a
much more realistic model for international trade. In general, the degree
of substitution between trade flows appears to be around 80 per cent or
more. This structure, in principle, allows for an analysis of economic
integration in terms of trade diversion and trade creation. The EGM
leads to conclusions regarding the effect of the determinants of trade
flows, which deviate clearly from those reached by means of the gravity
model: the traditional gravity model strongly overestimates the effects of
changes in determinants. In addition, the EGM provides index values
of the geo-economic trade position for all countries concerned, both of
the attractiveness of a country's sales market, weighted by the distances

to the respective importing countries, and of the attractiveness to each country of the goods offered by the respective exporting countries, again weighted by distance.

The EGM can be applied usefully to a wide variety of subjects, see e.g. Bikker and De Vos (1992a) on patient flows to hospitals. Apart from the log-linear regression model, the EGM also encompasses the production-constrained, the attraction-constrained and the so called doubly constrained gravity models originating in regional economics – see Wilson (1967) – and of the analysis-of-variance model; see Cesario (1973) and Wansbeek (1977). From a statistical point of view, the EGM has well-defined properties. Empirical application requires more calculations than in the case of the traditional gravity model. However, the applications show clearly that the effort pays off.

REFERENCES

Abrams, R. K. (1980). "International Trade Flows under Flexible Exchange Rates," Federal Reserve Bank of Kansas City *Economic Review*, 3–10.

Aitken, N. D. (1973). "The Effect of the EEC and EFTA on European Trade: A Temporal Cross-Section Analysis," *American Economic Review* 63: 881–92.

Anderson, J. E. (1979). "A Theoretical Foundation for the Gravity Equation," *American Economic Review* 69: 106–16.

Anderson, J. E. and E. van Wincoop (2003). "Gravity with Gravitas: A Solution to the Border Puzzle," *American Economic Review* 93: 170–92.

(2004). "Trade Costs," *Journal of Economic Literature* 42(3): 691–751.

Anderson, M. A. and S. L. S. Smith (1999). "Canadian Provinces in World Trade: Engagement and Detachment," *Canadian Journal of Economics* 32: 22–38.

Balassa, B. (1962). *The Theory of Economic Integration*, London: Allen and Unwin.

Behrens, K., C. Ertur and W. Koch (2007). "Dual Gravity: Using Spatial Econometrics to Control for Multilateral Resistance," CORE discussion paper no. 2007/59.

Bergstrand, J. H. (1985). "The Gravity Equation in International Trade: Some Microeconomic Foundations and Empirical Evidence," *Review of Economics and Statistics* 67: 471–81.

Bikker, J. A. (1982). *Vraag-aanbodmodellen voor stelsels van geografisch gespreide markten. toegepast op de internationale handel en op ziekenhuisopnamen in Noord-Nederland* (Supply-demand Models for Systems of Geographically Dispersed Markets, with Applications to International Trade Flows and Hospital Admissions in the North of the Netherlands; in Dutch). Amsterdam: Free University Press.

(1987). "An International Trade Flow Model with Substitution: An Extension of the Gravity Model," *Kyklos* 40: 315–37.

Bikker, J. A. and A. F. De Vos (1982). "Interdependent Multiplicative Models for Allocation and Aggregates: A Generalization of Gravity Models," research paper no. 80, Actuarial Science and Econometrics Department, Amsterdam: Free University.

(1992a). "A Regional Supply and Demand Model for Inpatient Hospital Care," *Environment and Planning A* **24**: 1097–1116.

(1992b). "An International Trade Flow Model with Zero Observations: An Extension of the Tobit Model," *Cahiers Economiques de Bruxelles* **135**: 379–404.

Brada, J. C. and J. A. Mendez (1983). "Regional Economic Integration and the Volume of Intra Regional Trade: A Comparison of Developed and Developing Country Experience," *Kyklos* **36**: 589–603.

Cesario, F. J. (1973). "A Generalized Trip Distribution Model," *Journal of Regional Science* **13**: 223–47.

Chenery, H. and M. Syrquin (1975). *Patterns of Development, 1950–1970*, World Bank, Oxford University Press.

Daganzo, C. (1979). *Multinomial Probit, the Theory and its Application to Demand Forecasting*, New York: Academic Press.

Deardorff, A. (1998). "Determinants of Bilateral Trade: Does Gravity Work in a Neoclassical World?," in J. Frankel (ed.), *The Regionalization of the World Economy*, University of Chicago Press, pp. 7–28.

(2004). "Local Comparative Advantage: Trade Costs and the Pattern of Trade," Research Seminar in International Economics discussion paper, no. 500, University of Michigan.

Eichengreen, B. and D. A. Irwin (1998). "The Role of History in Bilateral Trade Flows," in J. Frankel (ed.), *The Regionalization of the World Economy*, University of Chicago Press, pp. 33–57.

Estevadeordal, A., B. Frantz and A. M. Taylor (2003). "The Rise and Fall of World Trade, 1870–1939," *Quarterly Journal of Economics* **68**: 359–408.

Feenstra, R. C. (2002). "Border Effects and the Gravity Equation: Consistent Methods for Estimation," *Scottish Journal of Political Economy* **49**: 491–506.

(2004). *Advanced International Trade*, Princeton University Press.

Geraci, V. J. and W. Prewo (1977). "Bilateral Trade Flows and Transport Costs," *Review of Economics and Statistics* **59**: 67–74.

Glejser, H. and A. Dramais (1969). "A Gravity Model of Interdependent Equations to Estimate Flow Creation and Diversion," *Journal of Regional Science* **9**: 439–49.

Head, K. and T. Mayer (2002). "L'effet frontière: une mesure de l'intégration économique," *Economie et Prévision* **152–53**: 71–92.

Helpman, E. and P. R. Krugman (1985). *Market Structure and Foreign Trade: Increasing Returns, Imperfect Competition, and the International Economy*, Cambridge, MA.

Krugman, P. R. (1979). "Increasing Returns, Monopolistic Competition and International Trade," *Journal of International Economics* **9**: 469–79.

(1980). "Scale Economies, Product Differentiation and the Pattern of Trade," *American Economic Review* **70**: 950–59.

Leamer, E. E. and R. M. Stern (1970). *Quantitative International Economics*. Boston: Allyn and Bacon.

Leamer, E. E. (1974). "Nominal Tariff Averages with Estimated Weights," *Southern Economic Journal* **41**: 34–45.

Linders, G. J. M. (2006). "Intangible Barriers to Trade: The Impact of Institutions, Culture and Distance on Pattern of Trade," Tinbergen Institute Research Series no. 371.

Linnemann, H. (1966). *An Econometric Analysis of International Trade Flows.* Amsterdam: North-Holland.

McCallum, J. (1995). "National Borders Matter: Canada–US Regional Trade Patterns," *American Economic Review* **85**: 615–23.

Obstfeld, M. and K. Rogoff (2000). "The Six Major Puzzles in International Macro-economics: Is There a Common Cause?" in *NBER Macro-economics Annual* **15**, 339–90, Cambridge, MA: MIT Press.

Pöyhönen, P. (1963a). "A Tentative Model for the Volume of Trade between Countries," *Weltwirtschaftliches Archiv* **90**: 93–100.

———— (1963b). "Toward a General Theory of International Trade," *Economiska Samfundets Tidskrift* **16**: 69–77.

Prewo, W. (1978). "Determinants of the Trade Pattern among OECD Countries from 1958 to 1974," *Jahrbücher für Nationalökonomie und Statistik* **193**: 341–58.

Pulliainen, K. (1963). "A World Trade Study: An Econometric Model of the Pattern of the Commodity Flows of International Trade in 1948–60," *Economiska Samfundets Tidskrift* **16**: 78–91.

Redding, S. and P. K. Scott (2003). "Distance, Skill Deepening and Development: Will Peripheral Countries Ever Get Rich?" *Journal of Development Economics* **72**: 515–41.

Redding, S. and A. J. Venables (2004). "Economic Geography and International Inequality," *Journal of International Economics* **62**: 53–82.

Stern, R. M., J. Francis and B. Schumacher (1976). *Price Elasticities in International Trade,* London and Basingstoke: Macmillan.

Teekens, R. and R. Jansen (1977). "A Note on the Estimation of a Multiplicative Allocation Model," research report no. 7703, Econometric Institute, Rotterdam: Erasmus University.

Teekens, R. and J. Koerts (1972). "Some Statistical Implications of the Log Transformation of Multiplicative Models," *Econometrica* **40**: 793–813.

Theil, H. (1971). *Principles of Econometrics.* New York: John Wiley & Sons.

Tinbergen, J. (1962). *Shaping the World Economy.* New York: Twentieth Century Fund.

Viaene, J. M. (1982). "A Customs Union between Spain and the EEC," *European Economic Review* **18**: 345–68.

Wansbeek, T. (1977). "Least Squares Estimation of Trip Distribution Parameters: A Note," *Transportation Research* **11**: 429–31.

Wilson, A. G. (1967). "A Statistical Theory of Spatial Distributed Models," *Transportation Research* **1**: 253–69.

APPENDIX A: EXPLANATION OF THE DATA USED

The trade flow figures are from Direction of Trade Statistics (DOTS) of the International Monetary Fund (IMF) and date back to 2005. They solely concern trade of goods, as figures of flows of services were not available. The trade flows are recorded in the exporting countries and are expressed in free-on-board (fob) prices, so that the data are not affected by transportation costs. We also applied our models on imports data, yielding fully similar results. The trade data are expressed in millions of US dollars. In 2005, the DOTS database included 181 countries.

Three countries, Turkmenistan, Serbia and Montenegro, and the Democratic Republic of Congo, were dropped as they could not be linked to the distances from the Centre d'Etudes Prospectives et d'Information Internationales (CEPII; see below), so that 178 countries remain. A large number of the flows (39 per cent) are reported as missing or zero, and are either really zero or rounded to zero. The rounding thresholds vary and depend on the statistics of the exporting country.

The GDP and population figures are from the International Financial Statistics (IFS) of the IMF. GDP data in national currencies are converted to millions of US dollars, using IFS exchanges rates. The GDP figures are nominal ones, being a scaling factor of the nominal trade flows. Population figures are expressed in millions. Missing values of GDP and population are replaced by observations from the 2007 edition of the CIA *World Factbook*.[24] Surface area of land, exclusive of inland water, is expressed in ten squared kilometres and dates back from 2002 (source: UNSTAT[25]).

Distances between countries are expressed in kilometres and stem from CEPII.[26] Distances are weighted measures, based on all principal cities of the respective countries in order to assess the geographic distribution of population inside each nation. Hence, the distance between two countries is based on bilateral distances between the largest cities of those two countries, those inter-city distances being weighted by the share of the city in the overall country's population. Latitudes, longitudes, and population data of main agglomerations of all countries available are from www.world-gazetteer.com. The distance formula used is a generalized mean of city-to-city bilateral distances developed by Head and Mayer (2002; Chapter 6 of this volume), where we take the arithmetic mean and not the harmonic mean.

CEPII provides also dummy variables indicating whether two countries are contiguous, share a common language, have had a common colonizer after 1945, have ever had a colonial link, have had a colonial relationship after 1945, or are currently in a colonial relationship (the dist_cepii.xls file). There are two common languages dummies; the first one based on the fact that two countries share a common official language, and the other set to one if a language is spoken by at least 9 per cent of the population in both countries. Trying to give a precise definition of a colonial relationship is obviously a difficult task. Colonization is here a fairly general term that we use to describe a relationship between two countries, independently of their level of development, in which one has governed the other over a long period of time and has contributed to the current state of its institutions. Other dummy variables for Common Wealth Membership, CFA Membership, formerly communistic countries, former Members of the Soviet Union, former Members of the Warsaw Pact, and Membership of the EU6, 9, 12, 15, or 25 are from various sources (e.g. Wikipedia).

---

[24] Source: https://www.cia.gov/library/publications/the-world-factbook/index.html.
[25] Source: FAOSTAT (Rome), http://unstats.un.org/unsd/cdb/cdb_series_xrxx.asp? series_code =3700.
[26] Source: www.cepii.fr/anglaisgraph/bdd/distances.htm.

APPENDIX B: ESTIMATES OF VARIANTS ON THE MAIN MODELS

Table 5.A.1. *Estimation results of the traditional gravity model including surface areas (2005)*

	Coefficients	t-values
Intercept	−9.08	(−32.4)
GDP export country	1.24	(112.7)
Population export country	0.06	(3.3)
Area export country	−0.09	(−8.0)
GDP import country	0.87	(79.6)
Population import country	0.16	(9.0)
Area import country	−0.13	(−10.8)
Distance	−1.28	(−54.5)
Neighbors	1.09	(9.0)
Common language, official	0.44	(5.4)
Common language, ethnic	0.58	(7.3)
Former colony relations	0.58	(4.4)
Commonwealth	1.00	(12.3)
French territorial areas	0.79	(3.4)
Communist past	0.17	(1.8)
Soviet Union	2.25	(11.1)
Warsaw Pact	0.03	(0.1)
EU6	−1.17	(−2.6)
EU9-6	−0.94	(−1.0)
EU12-9	−0.26	(−0.3)
EU15-12	0.08	(0.1)
EU25-15	0.63	(2.4)
Number of observations	19,350	
R-squared, adjusted	63.8	

Table 5.A.2. *Estimation results of the imports and exports models including surface areas (2005)*

	EGM without residuals $\tilde{\tilde{u}}_{ij}$		EGM with residuals $\tilde{\tilde{u}}_{ij}$	
	Coefficients	t-values	Coefficients	t-values
Export model				
Intercept	−3.10	(−7.0)	−3.60	(−7.7)
GDP	1.10	(28.8)	1.15	(32.4)
Population	−0.22	(−3.8)	−0.18	(−3.1)
Area	0.10	(2.5)	0.06	(1.5)
Alpha (market access)	0.14	(2.0)	0.18	(3.4)
Number of observations	178		178	
R-squared, adjusted	90.7		91.1	
Import model				
GDP	0.91	(34.4)	0.93	(36.7)
Population	0.00	(0.1)	0.01	(0.1)
Area	−0.09	(−3.4)	−0.10	(−3.9)
Beta (supplier access)	0.19	(3.5)	0.13	(2.3)
Number of observations	178		178	
R-squared, adjusted	93.7		93.4	

Table 5.A.3. *Regional geo-economic trade positions of the EGM including surface areas*

	Without residuals $\tilde{\tilde{u}}_{ij}$		With residuals $\tilde{\tilde{u}}_{ij}$	
	Alphas	Betas	Alphas	Betas
Western Europe	1.97	1.62	0.42	1.32
Central and Eastern Europe[a]	3.42	2.10	1.85	2.72
Former Soviet Union	3.78	3.32	1.21	1.95
North and Central America	0.91	1.69	0.80	1.20
South America	0.46	0.69	0.41	1.06
Middle East	1.16	0.78	2.91	0.89
Rest of Asia	1.21	0.89	0.60	0.58
Oceania	0.29	0.51	0.98	0.55
North-Western Africa	0.60	0.57	1.79	0.72
South-Eastern Africa	0.38	0.37	1.06	0.55

[a]Exclusive of the Former Soviet Union.
Explanation: The indices are expressed in deviation from their geometric worldwide mean.

Part II

Distance in the gravity model

6 Illusory border effects

Distance mismeasurement inflates estimates of home bias in trade

K. Head and T. Mayer

1 Introduction

The measured effect of national borders on trade seems too large to be explained by the apparently small border-related trade barriers. This puzzle was first presented by McCallum (1995) and has gone on to spawn a large and growing literature on so-called border effects. The original finding was that Canadian provinces traded over twenty times more with each other than they did with states in the USA of the same size and distances. Subsequent studies of North American, European, and OECD trade also found somewhat smaller but still very impressive border effects.[1] Obstfeld and Rogoff (2000) referred to the border effect as one of the "six major puzzles in international macro-economics."

There are three basic ways to solve the border effect puzzle. First, one might discover that border-related trade barriers are actually larger than they appear. This approach might emphasize unconventional barriers such as the absence of good information.[2] Second, it might be that there is a high elasticity of substitution between domestic and imported

We thank an anonymous referee for helpful comments. The paper also benefited from comments by Henry Overman and participants at the ETSG 2001 conference in Brussels, and at the CREST seminar held in Paris in September 2001.

[1] Helliwell (1996) and Anderson and Smith (1999) further investigate province-state trade. Wei (1996) and Helliwell (1998) examine OECD trade. Nitsch (2000) looks at aggregate bilateral flows within the European Union while Head and Mayer (2000) examine industry level border effects in the EU. Wolf (1997 and 2000) also considers the case of trade between and within each American state. Anderson and van Wincoop (2003) found much smaller Canada–US border effects in their estimations using a theory-derived specification. Balistreri and Hillberry (2007) argue that these results derive more from the inappropriate inclusion of US commodity flow data and the imposition of symmetric border effects.

[2] Rauch (2001) provides a comprehensive survey of this emerging literature.

goods, leading to high responsiveness to modest barriers.[3] Finally, the border effects may have been *mismeasured* in a way that leads to a systematic overstatement. This paper takes the third approach and argues that illusory border effects are created by the standard methods used for measuring distance between and within nations.

Hundreds of papers have estimated gravity equations to investigate the determinants of bilateral trade after controlling for the sizes of trading partners and the geographic distances separating them. The data used in these studies generally aggregate the trade conducted by individual actors residing within two economies. However, distances between economies have customarily been measured from one point in a country to another point.

Wei (1996) showed how the gravity equation could be used to estimate border effects in the absence of data on trade flows by sub-national units. He measured "trade with self as production minus exports to other countries. He then added a dummy variable that takes a value of one for the observations of trade with self and interpreted its coefficient as the border effect. This approach has been widely emulated. However, it only works if one measures distance within and between nations in an accurate and comparable manner. Most of the literature has used point-to-point measures for internal and external distances.

We are concerned in this paper with situations in which point-to-point distances may give misleading estimates of the relevant geographic distance between and within geographic units. Our goal here is to develop a correct measure distance for economies that are not dimensionless points. This measure differs from the average distance measures developed in Head and Mayer (2000) and Helliwell and Verdier (2001). We then show how use of the existing methods for calculating distance leads to "illusory" border and adjacency effects. We then apply our methods to data on interstate trade in the USA and international trade in the EU. We find that our new distance measure reduces the estimated border and adjacency effects but does not eliminate them.

Correct measurement of a region or country's distance to itself has relevance beyond estimating border effects. For example, studies of how market potential (or "access") affects wages – such as Bosker and Garretsen and Boulhol and de Serres in this volume – necessarily must consider the local contribution to market potential. The size of that contribution depends on internal distance. Also in this volume, Anderson (equation

---

[3] Head and Ries (2001) estimate large (between eight and eleven) elasticities of substitution affecting Canada–US trade but still find barriers other than tariffs have the effect of at least a 27 per cent tariff.

3.9) shows that a country's "openness" depends, among other things, on its trade costs with self (t^{ii}). These trade costs clearly depend on distance to self, underlining the importance of measuring such distances appropriately.

2 Prior measures of distance

Here we review the different methods used in the literature for the calculation of distances between and within economies.

2.1 Between-unit distances

The gravity-equation literature almost always calculates between country distances as the great-circle distance between country "centers." In practice the centers selected are usually capitals, largest cities or occasionally a centrally located large city. In some cases, such as France, the same city accomplishes all three criteria. In a case like the United States, one could arguably choose Washington DC, New York City or St Louis but in practice most studies use Chicago. The selection of cities is not particularly important in cases where countries are small and/or far apart or alternatively if economic activity is very much concentrated in the city chosen. Then the variance due to city choice is probably swamped by the basic imprecision of using geographic distance as a proxy for a whole host of trade costs (freight, time, information transfer).

When countries are close together and economic actors within those countries are geographically dispersed, there is greater cause for concern with the practice of allocating a country's entire population to a particular point. Most studies include a dummy variable indicating when two countries are adjacent. Since this variable is rarely of interest, many authors include it without an explanation, simply out of deference to common practice. However, it might be related to freight costs (adjacent countries are directly connected via train and highway) or to political costs (there may be costs entailed every time one crosses a national border). However, neither argument really justifies an adjacency dummy. The freight costs argument suggests rather that the available modes of transport between two economies be interacted with the distance. The political argument suggests one should count the number of border crossings between two trade partners.

We argue later that adjacency will tend to have a positive measured effect on trade because effective distance between nearby countries is systematically lower than average distance and on average it is lower than center-to-center distance as well.

2.2   Within-unit distances

There has been remarkably little consensus on the appropriate measure
of internal distance. Those discrepancies are a particular source of concern in the border effects literature as the level of internal distance chosen
directly affects the estimated border effect. As described below, the border
effect measures the "excessive" trade volumes observed within a nation
compared with what would be expected from a gravity equation: this is
interpreted as a negative impact of the existence of the border on international trade flows. Recalling that gravity relates negatively trade flows
with distance, the border effect is crucially dependent on how distances
within a country and between countries are measured. More precisely,
an overestimate of internal distance with respect to international distance
will mechanically inflate the border effect which will compensate for the
large volumes of trade observed within a nation not accounted for by the
low distance between producers and consumers inside a country.[4]

In this section we survey the literature on this topic. Our central argument is that most measures of internal distances overestimate them with
respect to international distances because they try to calculate average
distances between consumers and producers without taking into account
the fact that, inside countries, goods tend to travel over smaller distances.

1. The initial papers in the literature employed fractions of distances
   to the centers of *neighbor* countries. Nitsch (2000, 2001) vigorously
   criticizes this approach and so far as we know there is no defense other
   than it represented a first attempt at solving an intrinsically difficult
   problem.
   a. Wei (1996) proposes $d_{ii} = .25 \min_j d_{ij}$, i.e. one-quarter the dis-
      tance to the nearest neighbor country, with distance d_{ij} between two
      countries being calculated with the great circle formula. Anderson
      and van Wincoop (2003) follow Wei's approach but report that it
      seems to underestimate internal distances.
   b. Wolf (1997, 2000) uses measures similar to Wei's except for multi-
      plying the neighbor distance by one-half instead of one-quarter and
      Wolf (1997) averaged over all neighbors rather than taking only the
      nearest one.
2. A second strand in the literature uses area-based measures. Those
   try to capture an average distance between producers and consumers
   located on a given territory. They therefore require an assumption

---

[4] An important caveat is provided in the empirical section. If use of overestimated internal
distances results in lower estimated coefficients on distance, then it is not clear what the
final impact on estimated border effects will be.

on the shape of a country and on the spatial distribution of buyers and sellers. Their advantage is that they can be calculated with only a single, readily available datum, the region's area.

  a. Uniform disks: Leamer (1997) and Nitsch (2000) use the radius of a hypothetical disk, i.e. $\sqrt{area/\pi}$. Both authors assert that this is a good approximation of the average distance between two points in a population uniformly distributed across a disk. Redding and Venables (2004) also intend to use "the average distance between two points in a circular country" but use the formula $d_{ii} = .33\sqrt{area/\pi}$. Bettstetter *et al.* (2004) demonstrate that the expected distance between two random points on a disk is given by 0.9054 times the radius, implying $d_{ii} \approx 0.51\sqrt{area}$, somewhat less than the $0.56\sqrt{area}$ implied by Leamer.

  b. Disks with production or transportation hubs: Head and Mayer (2000) also work with the disk approximation but assume that production in sub-national regions is concentrated at a single point at the center of the disk and that only consumers are uniformly distributed across the disk. As will be demonstrated later, this can be shown analytically to lead to the following distance formula: $d_{ii} = (2/3)\sqrt{area/\pi} \approx 0.38\sqrt{area}$. This result implies that under the extreme assumption that all shipments must flow through a transport hub at the center of the country, the average internal transport distance between randomly drawn points on the disk would be approximately $0.75\sqrt{area}$.

  c. Uniform rectangles: Helliwell and Verdier (2001) consider internal distances of cities which are represented as square grids. Calculating distances between any two points on the grid, they report that the internal distance is $d_{ii} \approx 0.52\sqrt{area}$. Analytical results in Bettstetter *et al.* (2004) imply that $d_{ii} = 0.5214\sqrt{area}$ for squares and $d_{ii} = 0.5685\sqrt{area}$ for rectangles that are twice as long as they are wide.

3. Geometric approximations, while stingy in their data requirements, impose what appear to be flagrantly unrealistic assumptions on the shape and population distributions of regions. When feasible, it makes more sense to use actual data on the spatial distribution of economic activity with nations. These *sub-unit-based weighted averages* require geographically disaggregated data on activity, area, longitude, and latitude.

  a. Wolf (1997) uses the distance between the two largest cities, which we shall denote $d_{i;\,12}$, to calculate internal distance of American states. This is akin to estimating the average distance with a single draw. It ignores intra-city trade. Wolf (2000) amends the earlier formula by adding a weight for the share of the population in the top two cities accounted for by the smaller city, $w_{i:2}$. He sets $d_{ii} = 2w_{i:2}d_{i:12}$, which forces the internal distance to lie between zero (if the entire population were concentrated in the largest city) and $d_{i:12}$ if the cities were equally sized.[5]

b. Head and Mayer (2000) use a simple weighted arithmetic average over *all* region-to-region distances inside a country. They use GDP shares as the weights, w_j. With R denoting the number of regions, country i's distance to itself is given by

$$d_{ii} = \sum_{j=1}^{R} w_j \left(\sum_{k=1}^{R} w_k d_{jk} \right).$$

For regions' distances to themselves Head and Mayer use the area approximation described above.

c. For internal distances of Canadian provinces, Helliwell and Verdier (2001) use urban agglomerations and two or three rural areas as their sub-provincial geographic units. Their internal distance is given by a "weighted average of intra-city distances, inter-city distances, the average distance between cities and rural areas, and the average distance from one rural area to another." Although their algebraic expression for obtaining average distances is more complicated than the one displayed in the previous item, we believe it to be essentially the same, except for using population weights instead of GDP shares.

We conclude from this review of the literature that the desired measure of internal distance has been some form of "average" distance between internal trading partners. It may be calculated directly using sub-national data on the geographic distribution of activity or by making various simplifying geometric assumptions. Nitsch (2001) compares the two methods and concludes that the area-based approximations may be good enough indicators of the averages of sub-national distances.[6]

[5] Note that Zipf's law, described in Fujita *et al.* (1999), suggests that the second-largest city in a country will have half the population of the largest city. This implies $w_{i:2} = 1/3$. If $d_{i:12}$ is an unbiased estimate of the distance between randomly selected individuals, then Wolf's measure is about 67 per cent of that representative distance. Indeed, Wolf (2000) reports an average value of 95 for his d_{ii} which is 62 per cent of the average 153 miles separating first and second cities in the continental forty-eight states.

[6] He also warns that center-to-center distances are very fragile for countries that are near each other and illustrates with the example of Germany and Austria.

We will argue that average distances are not the appropriate measures of distance within or between geographically dispersed economies. Rather we argue for a constant elasticity of substitution (CES) aggregation that takes into account that desired trade between two actors is inversely related to the distance between them.

3   Effective distances between "states"

Trade is measured between "states" where we denote the exporting state with i and the importing state with j. In the empirical section states correspond to either the States that comprise the United States or the nation-states that comprise the European Union. Each state consists of geographic sub-units that we will refer to as districts. This will correspond to counties in the United States. For the EU nation-states, counties will correspond to NUTS1 regions for most countries except Portugal where we use NUTS2 and Ireland, where we use NUTS3 (these smaller countries are single NUTS1 regions).

Trade flows between and within districts are presumed to be unmeasured by official data-collecting agencies. Of course the degree of geographic disaggregation for trade data is a decision variable of statistical agencies and varies across jurisdictions and time. The key idea is that a "state" is defined here as the smallest unit for which trade flows are measured. Districts are defined as a smaller unit for which only basic geographic information (area, longitude, and latitude of the center) and economic size (gross product or population) are available.

We identify exporting and importing districts respectively with the indexes k and l. Thus trade flows from district k to district l are given by x_{kl}. Therefore state-to-state trade is given by

$$x_{ij} = \sum_{k \in i} \sum_{l \in j} x_{kl}.$$

Suppose x_{kl} is a function, $f_{kl}(\cdot)$ of distance between districts, d_{kl}. We define effective distance between states i and j as the solution to the following equation:

$$f_{ij}(d_{ij}) = \sum_{k \in i} \sum_{l \in j} f_{kl} d_{kl}. \tag{6.1}$$

Thus, effective distances between two states replicate the sum of trade as a function of district-to-district distances.

For the purposes of deriving the effective distance measure between states i and j, we will assume trade between districts is governed by a simple gravity equation:

$$x_{kl} = G y_k y_l d_{kl}^{\theta} \qquad (6.2)$$

where the y variables represent the total income (or GDP) of each district, the d represents distance between districts, and θ is a parameter that we expect to be negative. The parameter G is a "gravitational constant." While it used to be said that gravity equation lacked theoretical foundations, there are now about a half dozen papers establishing conditions for equations that closely resemble (6.2).[7] As a general rule, however, G must be replaced with more complex terms that vary across exporters and importers. In the derivation that follows we are assuming that those indexes terms do not vary much.

Using the gravity-equation formula we find

$$x_{ij} = \sum_{k \in i} \sum_{l \in j} G y_k y_l d_{kl}^{\theta} = G \sum_{k \in i} y_k y_j d_{kj}^{\theta},$$

where $y_i = \sum_{l \in j} y_l$ and $d_{kj} = \left(\sum_{l \in j} (y_l/y_j) d_{kl}^{\theta} \right)^{1/\theta}$. Thus the distance from district k to state j is a constant elasticity of substitution (CES) index of the distance to each individual district in state j. In mathematics, this function is also referred to as a "general mean." It takes the weighted arithmetic mean as a special case when $\theta = 1$ and the harmonic mean as a special case when $\theta = -1$ and each district is of equal size. Continuing, we find $x_{ij} = G y_i y_j d_{ij}^{\theta}$, where d_{ij}, the effective distance is given by

$$d_{ij} = \left(\sum_{k \in i} (y_k/y_i) \sum_{l \in j} (y_l/y_j) d_{kl}^{\theta} \right)^{1/\theta} \qquad (6.3)$$

This formula satisfies our definition of effective distance. It reduces to the average distance formula used by Head and Mayer (2000), Helliwell and Verdier (2001), and Anderson and van Wincoop (2003, footnote 16) for $\theta = 1$.[8] Unfortunately for that formula, there are hundreds of gravity-equation estimates of θ that show θ is not equal to one. Disdier and Head's (2008) meta-analysis of the gravity-equation literature finds that

---

[7] Van Bergeijk and Brakman's (2009) introduction to this volume presents a history of the papers that derived theoretical foundations for the gravity equation.

[8] All three papers appear to have arrived at this measure independently.

the mean of θ is -0.95 for studies based on data since 1990. This suggests that the harmonic mean, $9 = -1$ might be a useful approximation. Since the harmonic mean is known to be less than the arithmetic mean whenever there is variation, this implies that arithmetic mean distances overstate effective distances.

4   Geometric examples

We now consider a few concrete, highly stylized, but analytically tractable, examples. These will allow us to illustrate the differences between our effective distance and other possible metrics.

4.1   States along a line

Suppose there are two identical states comprising a continuum of districts with uniformly distributed incomes. State i is centered at the origin and extends from $-R$ to R whereas state j begins at $\Delta - R$ and extends to $\Delta + R$. The density of income in each state is given by $1/(2R)$. Center-to-center distance is Δ. This geometry is illustrated in Figure 6.1.

Let us first consider state-to-state distance. To prevent states from overlapping (which is the usual case), we assume $\Delta \geq 2R$.

$$d_{ij} = \left(\int_{-R}^{R} (1/(2R)) \int_{\Delta-R}^{\Delta+R} (1/(2R))(l-k)^{\theta} \, dl \, dk \right)^{1/\theta}$$

Solving the double integral we obtain

$$d_{ij} = \left(\frac{(\Delta - 2R)^{\theta+2} + (\Delta + 2R)^{\theta+2} - 2\Delta^{\theta+2}}{(\theta+1)(\theta+2)(2R)^2} \right)^{1/\theta}$$

Let us now express the ratio of center-to-center distance (Δ, which is also the average distance, as can be checked when setting θ equal to one) to

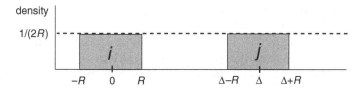

Figure 6.1. Two states on a line.

effective distance as

$$\Delta/d_{ij} = \lambda \left(\frac{(\lambda - 1)^{\theta+2} + (\lambda + 1)^{\theta+2} - 2\lambda^{\theta+2}}{(\theta + 1)(\theta + 2)} \right)^{-1/\theta}$$

where $\lambda = \Delta/(2R)$. This equation shows the factor by which center-to-center distances inflate effective state-to-state distances. While the expression is fairly compact, it is not easy to analyze directly. Evaluating it numerically for the case of $\theta = -1.0001$ (trade is inversely proportionate to distance as is commonly observed in the data) and $\lambda = 1$ (adjacent states), we find that center-to-center distances (which equal average distances in this case) overstate effective distance by 39 per cent. As λ increases, the inflation declines quickly and for $\lambda > 2$, distance inflation lies under 5 per cent.

Let us now consider intra-state distance. States, generally, totally overlap, in the sense that they have a continuous geography. In that case, following the state-to-state method, we find state i's distance from self is given by

$$d_{ii} = \left(\int_{-R}^{R} (1/(2R)) \int_{-R}^{k} (1/(2R))(k - l)^{\theta} dl \right.$$

$$\left. + \int_{k}^{R} (1/(2R))(l - k)^{\theta} dldk \right)^{1/\theta}$$

Integrating, we obtain

$$d_{ii} = R \left(\frac{2^{\theta+1}}{(\theta + 1)(\theta + 2)} \right)^{1/\theta}$$

The average distance in this case is then equal to 23R. The ratio of average to effective distance is thus now much higher than in the inter-state distance. Indeed, for $\theta = -0.99$, we obtain an inflation factor of 69 here against 1.38 for inter-state. The overestimate of existing measures of distance (like the average distance, which we chose here because it is one of the most sophisticated) is thus much higher for internal distances. As emphasized first by Wei (1996) and as will be apparent formally in the next section, an overestimate of internal distance relative to the external one will mechanically translate into an overestimate of the border effect.

4.2   States on a plane

Locating states along a line allows us to compute effective distance by evaluating a double integral. However, real states occupy (at least) two dimensions. We first consider a simplified case that is analytically feasible before considering a few numerical examples. Suppose state i consists of a single point located at the center of a disk of radius R. Let state j consist of economic activity that is uniformly distributed across that disk. Thus, $y_l/y_j = (2\pi d_{il})/(\pi R^2)$. We denote da as r. The distance of state i to state j is given by

$$d_{ij} = \left(\int_0^R [(2\pi r)/(\pi R^2)]r^\theta \right)^{(1/\theta)} = (2/(\theta + 2))^{1/\theta} R.$$

Substituting $\theta = 1$, we obtain the arithmetic average distance of $(2/3)R$. Using $\theta = -1$ we obtain $d_{ij} = (1/2)R$. Note that this implies that average distances inflate the effective distance by a factor 4/3 or 33 per cent.

Now let us compare average and effective *within* state distances for some two-dimensional geometric representations of an economy. Table 6.1 shows the ratio of average to effective distance for different distance-decay parameters, θ. The first two columns work with disk-shaped economies and the second two use rectangles. Column (1) works with analytical results from the previous section for the case of a core point at the center of the disk trading with a set of actors uniformly distributed across the rest of the disk.[9] Column (2) contains results of simulations of 2,500 actors randomly distributed across the disk.[10] Column (3) follows Helliwell and Verdier in considering a grid. Column (4) changes the dimensions of the grid so that it is three times as long as it is wide.[11]

Comparisons for a given θ show that the nature of the geometric approximation does matter for determining average and effective distances. In particular, concentration of producers in column (1) gives rise to low distances while the elongated rectangle of column (4) gives larger distances. Squares and disks are approximately the same. For any given geometry, smaller values of θ, i.e. greater trade impeding effects of distance, causes lower effective distances. The reasoning is that a higher

[9] Note that we could also think of this as one-half the effective distance between any two points on the disk if we restricted all transport to pass through the center point.
[10] The program used was http://sauder.ubc.ca/head/border/disksimu.do.
[11] The program used was http://sauder.ubc.ca/head/border/gridsimu.do.

Table 6.1. *Average distance relative to effective (CES) distance in two dimensions*

Method:	(1)	(2)	(3)	(4)
Shape:		Disk		Rectangle
Distribution:	Core-periphery	2,500 draws	50X50 grid	90X30 grid
avg/CES ($\theta = -0.5$)	1.186	1.305	1.302	1.436
avg/CES ($\theta = -1.0$)	1.333	1.545	1.513	1.730
avg/CES ($\theta = -1.5$)	1.679	2.133	1.8445	2.184
avg/$\sqrt{area}$	0.376	0.514	0.522	0.642

Table 6.2. *Inter-state border effects in friction regressions*

Model:	Dependent Variable: Ln Ξ (friction) in 1997					
	(WOLFD)			(AREA)	(AVGD)	(CESD)
Cross border	2.14*	2.56*	2.62*	2.32*	2.23*	1.85*
	(0.02)	(0.03)	(0.03)	(0.04)	(0.04)	(0.05)
Ln distance (see note)	0.65*	0.47*	0.45*	0.54*	0.63*	0.55*
	(0.01)	(0.01)	(0.02)	(0.02)	(0.02)	(0.02)
Adjacent states		−0.62*	−0.53*	−0.47*	−0.42*	−0.41*
		(0.03)	(0.03)	(0.03)	(0.03)	(0.03)
States in same census division			−0.25*	−0.14*	−0.20*	−0.17*
			(0.03)	(0.03)	(0.03)	(0.03)
Border effect[†]	8.5–8.5	6.9–12.9	6.3–13.7	5.5–10.2	5–9.3	3.6–6.3
N	5,841	5,841	5,841	5,841	5,841	5,841
R^2	0.325	0.37	0.377	0.364	0.386	0.380
RMSE	0.817	0.79	0.785	0.793	0.78	0.783

Notes: Standard errors in parentheses with * denoting significance at the 1% level. Distances are calculated using two major cities in columns (1) through (3) (WOLFD), area-based internal distances in (4) (AREA), average distance in columns (5) (AVGD), effective distance (CESD) in column (6).
[†]The first border effect is imports from home relative to imports from an adjacent state in same census division. The second is relative to a non-adjacent state in a different division.

marginal effect of distance on trade causes individuals to concentrate their trading activity locally. This is not taken into account in the average distances. The implication is that the more negative is true θ, the more average distances will overstate effective distances.

5   Estimating border effects

The simplest form of the gravity equation is useful for determining the appropriate method of creating a distance index for trade between and within states that are geographically dispersed aggregates of smaller units. However, as emphasized by Anderson and van Wincoop (2003), the simple gravity equation is not a reliable tool for estimating border effects. In that paper the authors carefully develop a theoretically consistent method for identifying national border effects when one has data on sub-national units.

Using similar but somewhat more general assumptions we develop an alternate method that appears to have two advantages. First, it is appropriate for aggregate and industry-level trade flows. Second, it can be estimated using ordinary least squares.

Denote quantity consumed of variety v originating in state i by a representative consumer in state j as c_{vij}. Following virtually all derivations of bilateral trade equations we assume that import volumes are determined through the maximization of a CES utility function subject to a budget constraint. We use a utility function that is general enough to nest the Dixit-Stiglitz approach taken by Krugman (1980) and its descendants as well as Anderson (1979) and related papers by Deardorff (1998) and Anderson and van Wincoop (2003). We follow the notation of the latter paper whenever appropriate. We represent the utility of the representative consumer from country j as

$$U_j = \left(\sum_i \sum_{v=1}^{n_j} (S_{ij} C_{vij})^{\frac{\sigma-1}{\sigma}} \right)^{\frac{\sigma-1}{\sigma}} \tag{6.4}$$

The s_{ij} can be thought of as the consumer j's assessment of the quality of varieties from country i, measured in "services" per unit consumed. The budget constraint is given by

$$y_j = \sum_i \sum_{v=1}^{n_j} p_{ij} C_{vij}.$$

The Anderson approach assumes a single variety (or good, depending on interpretation) per state, i.e. $n_j = 1$, that is perceived the same by all consumers, i.e. $s_{ij} = s_i$. The Krugman approach identifies varieties with symmetric firms and sets $s_{ij} = 1$.

The solution to the utility maximization problem specifies the value of exports from i to j as

$$x_{ij} = \frac{n_i(p_{ij}/S_{ij})^{1-\sigma}}{\sum_h n_h(p_{hj}/S_{hj})^{1-\sigma}} y_j. \tag{6.5}$$

Thus, the fraction of income, y_j, spent on goods from i depends on the number of varieties produced there and their price per unit of services compared to an index of varieties and quality-adjusted prices in alternative sources.

The next step is to relate delivered prices and service levels to those in the state of origin. Again following standard practice we assume a combined transport and tariff cost that is proportional to value, that is $p_{ij} = t_{ij} p_i$. We further allow for an analogous effect of trade on perceived quality. In particular the services offered by a good delivered to state j are lower than those offered in the origin i by a proportional decay parameter $\gamma_{ij} \geq 1$. The decay may be attributed to damage caused by the voyage (for instance if a fraction $\gamma - 1$ of the products shipped break or spoil due to excessive motion or heat in the vessel) or to time costs or even to more exotic factors such as cultural differences or communication costs. We expect pairs of states that speak different languages to have higher values, γ_{ij}. Combining both types of trade cost we obtain

$$p_{ij}/S_{ij} = (t_{ij}\gamma_{ij})(p_i/S_i)$$

We now follow Baldwin *et al.* (2003) in defining a new term, ϕ, that measures the "free-ness," or phi-ness as a mnemonic, as $\phi_{ij} = (t_{ij}\gamma_{ij})^{1-\sigma}$. The parameter ϕ is conceptually appealing because it ranges from zero (trade is prohibitively costly) to one (trade is completely free). Note that ϕ depends on both the magnitude of trade costs (through t and γ) and the responsiveness of trade patterns (through σ). After making the substitutions into equation (6.5), we obtain

$$x_{ij} = \frac{n_i(p_i/S_i)^{1-\sigma}\phi_{ij}}{\sum_h n_h(p_h/S_h)^{1-\sigma}\phi_{hj}} y_j \tag{6.6}$$

Since our goal is to determine (and then decompose) the ϕ_{ij} parameters, the term $n_i(p_i/S_i)^{1-\sigma}$ is simply a nuisance. The number of varieties in each country and their qualities are un-observable and good cross-sectional price information is difficult to obtain. Hence, we would like to use theory to eliminate these parameters and obtain a relationship between exports and ϕ_{ij} that does not depend on unobservables.

Anderson and van Wincoop (2003) accomplish this by imposing a "market-clearing" condition and assuming symmetric trade costs. Formally, this means first setting income in the importing country equal to the sum of its exports to all markets (including itself); making i the importer this means $y_i = \sum_j x_{ij}$. Second, it means $\phi_{ij} = \phi_{ji}$. Applying both assumptions, Anderson and van Wincoop obtain

$$x_{ij} = \frac{y_i y_j}{y_w} \frac{\phi_{ij}}{(P_i P_j)^{1-\sigma}},$$

where y_w is world income and the P terms are referred to as the multilateral trade resistance of each country and given by the solution to $P_j^{1-\sigma} = \sum_i (y_i/y_w)\phi_{ij}P_i^{\sigma-1}$.

This solution is compact and intuitively appealing and relates closely to the simple gravity equation. However, it has two drawbacks. First, the market clearing assumption sets GDP (y_i) equal to the sum of all trade flows from i. This balanced trade equation is not appropriate for industry-level data where we expect states with high numbers of varieties of low quality-adjusted prices to be net exporters.[12] A second drawback of the Anderson and van Wincoop specification is that the non-linear specification of the resistance terms necessitates the use of non-linear least squares.

We now develop a method to calculate ϕ_{ij} directly and then ordinary least squares can decompose the ϕ_{ij} into parameters corresponding to distance and border effects. This method is simply a many-country generalization of the method introduced in Head and Ries (2001). The basic idea is combine the odds of buying domestic relative to foreign in country i, x_{ii}/x_{ji}, with the corresponding odds in the other country, x_{jj}/x_{ij}. Our "nuisance" term, $n_i(p_i/S_i)^{1-\sigma}$, will cancel out as it appears in the numerator of the odds term for country i and the denominator for country j. The multilateral resistance terms also disappear in this transformation.

Define Ξ_{ij} as the geometric mean of the two odds-ratios. It relates to ϕ_{ij} as follows:

$$\Xi_{ij} = \sqrt{\frac{x_{ii}}{x_{ji}} \frac{x_{jj}}{x_{ij}}} = \sqrt{\frac{\phi_{ii}\phi_{jj}}{\phi_{ij}}}. \tag{6.7}$$

---

[12] Even for aggregate data, the market-clearing assumption must be used cautiously since GDP (the measure for y_i) includes services and sums value-added flows whereas most trade flows comprise gross shipments of merchandise.

If trade within regions was costless the free-ness of trade would be given by the *inverse* of Ξ_{ij}.

We decompose the determinants of the free-ness of trade into distance and border-related components:

$$\phi_{ij} = (\mu \xi_{ij})^{-B_{ij}} d_{ij}^\theta,$$

where $B_{ij} = 1$ if $i \neq j$ and zero otherwise. The ξ_{ij} reflect log-normal variation in the border effect around a central tendency of μ. By construction, $\Xi_{ii} = 1$, $\forall i$. Regressions using Ξ_{ij} as a dependent variable therefore only retain observations where $i \neq j$, which means that in practice, B_{ij} is always one in the estimated sample. We can then express cross-border observations as

$$\Xi_{ij} = \mu \xi_{ij} \left(\frac{d_{ij}}{\sqrt{d_{ii} d_{jj}}} \right)^{-\theta} \quad \forall i \neq j \tag{6.8}$$

Taking logs, we obtain our regression equation:

$$In \Xi_{ij} = In\mu - \theta In \left(\frac{d_{ij}}{\sqrt{d_{ii} d_{jj}}} \right) + In \xi_{ij}. \tag{6.9}$$

We will refer to $\ln \Xi_{ij}$ using the term "friction" as it represents the barriers to external trade which are zero when both distance and borders do not matter for trade patterns ($\mu = 1$ and $\theta = 0$). The mean border effect, μ, is obtained by exponentiating the constant term in the regression. One may determine the ad valorem tariff equivalent of the trade costs due to the border, denoted $b - 1$ by Anderson and van Wincoop, by raising the estimate of μ to the power of $1/(\sigma - 1)$ (which has to be taken from another source, as a cannot be identified in the present setting) and subtracting 1.

This method for calculating ϕ and estimating border effects is easy to use and imposes relatively few assumptions. To review, we need CES preferences and trade costs that are (i) multiplicative, (ii) power functions of distance, and (iii) symmetric between trade partners. As with all studies based on Wei (1996) our method does require data on exports to self, x_{ii}, and accurate estimates of the internal distances, d_{ii}.

We now return to the issue of distance measurement. Let us define $\bar{d}_{ij}$ as the average distance, or equation (6.3) evaluated at $\theta = 1$. The corresponding estimate of the border effect will be called $\bar{\mu}$. For simplicity, take the case of symmetric countries, i.e. where $d_{ii} = d_{jj}$. Using equation (6.8), we define the *illusory border effect*, or the magnitude of border inflation due to distance mismeasurement, as

$$\bar{\mu}/\mu = \left(\frac{\bar{d}_{ij}/\bar{d}_{ii}}{d_{ij}/d_{ii}}\right)^{\theta} \tag{6.10}$$

Consider again the relatively simple case of two states that are identical except for their position along a line. In that case we can obtain an analytic solution for border inflation as a function of λ, the ratio of the distance between county centers over the distance within a country from border to border.

$$\bar{\mu}/\mu = \frac{2(3\lambda)^{\theta}}{(\lambda - 1)^{\theta+2}(\lambda + 1)^{\theta+2} - 2\lambda^{\theta+2}}. \tag{6.11}$$

We plot this function for cases of θ equal to -0.9, -0.7, and -0.5 in Figure 6.2. We see that use of average distance causes substantial inflation of the estimated border effects. The illusory border arises because average distances overmeasure internal distance to a much greater extent than they overmeasure external distance. The inflation factor is smallest for adjacent states. This is because average distance also substantially overestimates distance to nearby states.

In summary, use of average distances (or similar methods) instead of effective distances will lead to biased upwards border effects. Furthermore the more negative is θ, the distance-decay parameter for trade, the greater the bias.

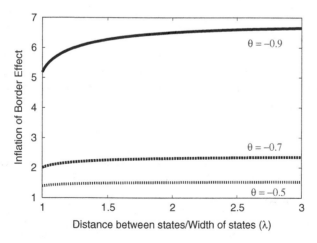

Figure 6.2. Distance mismeasurement causes border inflation in "Lineland."

6   Empirical applications

We apply our new measure of state-to-state distances to two distinct datasets that have recently been subject to empirical analysis in the literature on border effects. The first sample uses trade flows between American States as used by Wolf (1997 and 2000) except that he used 1993 data at the aggregate level and we use industry-level 1997 data. The second one focuses on trade between and within European nations between 1993 and 1995 (Head and Mayer 2000). The two datasets use quite different sources of information for trade flows: transportation data (the 1997 Commodity Flow Survey) for the US sample and more traditional trade data from customs declarations for the EU sample.[13]

In each case we present first the results of the estimated equation (6.9). Our focus is here to see how the estimated border effect varies according to the measure of distance used in the regressions. We use various measures of distance that are precisely defined in Section 2. For the US sample, we use the method initiated by Wolf (which we will note WOLFD) which provides a natural benchmark as the samples used here and in Wolf (2000) are very comparable. We also use the disk-area-based measure (which we will note AREA) where $d_{ii} = .67\sqrt{area/\pi}$. For the EU sample, we choose to take the AREA distance as a benchmark. For both samples, we compare those distances with two versions of the key distance measure developed in this paper: $d_{ij} = \left(\sum_{k \in i}(y_k/y_i)\sum_{l \in j}(y_l/y_j)d_{kl}^{\theta}\right)^{1/\theta}$. A first version sets $\theta = 1$, which is the arithmetic weighted average distance (noted AVGD) used in Head and Mayer (2000). A second version sets $\theta = -1$, which appears to be a very frequent finding of the gravity equations run in the literature. This is the distance measure we will focus on as the previous sections showed that its use should reveal the illusory part of the border effect.

To keep results comparable to previous papers and as a robustness check, we also present results of "standard gravity equations" in each case. We regress then imports of a destination economy on its total consumption, the production of the origin economy,[14] our various measures

---

[13] The US data can be downloaded easily from www.bts.gov/ntda/cfs/cfs97c. The EU trade data comes from the COMEXT database provided by Eurostat but requires much more manipulation to reach the form used in our estimation (see Head and Mayer 2000, for more information).

[14] For the EU data, production data is directly available at the industry level considered which enables us to compute industry level production and consumption. For the US data, we use the sum of flows departing from a state (destinations include the state itself) as its production for the considered industry and the total inflows (including from self) as its consumption.

of distance, and a dummy indicating when the origin and destination are the same, i.e. when trade takes place *within borders*. Those regressions also include industry fixed effects.

In both the friction and gravity type regressions, we add controls for adjacency, same Census Division (US data only), and same language (EU data only). We define these last three dummy variables so that they *only take values of one on inter-economy trade*. This means that the border effect is interpreted as the extra propensity to trade within borders relative to trade with an economy that is not adjacent, in the same Division, or sharing the same language. This is a different specification from that employed by Wei and Wolf. It is the one advocated by Helliwell (1998). Near the bottom of the results tables we provide McCallum-style border effects for both types of dummy specification. We emphasize that the issue is one of interpretation, not estimation.

6.1   The impact of "borders" within the United States

Wolf (2000) points out that if border effects were caused exclusively by real border-related trade barriers then they should not operate on state-to-state trade. The reason is that the US constitution expressly prohibits barriers to inter-state commerce. There are no tariffs, no customs formalities, or other visible frontier controls. Nevertheless Wolf finds significant border effects, albeit smaller than those reported for province-state trade by McCallum and Helliwell's studies. That is, state borders give a case of a political border that should have no economic significance based on trade barriers. Furthermore, even informal barriers due to cultural difference or imperfect information seem unlikely to apply. These factors might enter into the effect of distance but we would expect no discontinuities at the border.

Could the border effects estimated by Wolf be "illusory"—the consequence of improper distance measures? Table 6.3 investigates this hypothesis. The main results are obtained by comparing columns (5) and (6). We find that effective distances sharply reduce the estimated border effect relative to average distances (the fall is about one-third of the initial border effect, going from 9.3 to 6.3; compared to the distance measure used by Wolf, the border effect is roughly divided by 2).[15] Furthermore, adjacency effects decline as well. This is just as predicted. However, these

---

[15] These border effect estimates are notably larger than those reported by Wolf (2000). This seems to come from the fact that we are using a different year of the CFS data. Robustness checks not reported here show that a regression of trade flows, using exactly the same variables as the first column of Table 6.1 on page 176, gives extremely close

Table 6.3. *Inter-state border effects in gravity specifications*

Model:	Dependent Variable: Ln shipments in 1997					
	(WOLFD)			(AREA)	(AVGD)	(CESD)
Ln origin Production	0.79*	0.81*	0.81*	0.81*	0.82*	0.82*
	(0.01)	(0.01)	(0.01)	(0.01)	(0.01)	(0.01)
Ln destination	0.75*	0.76*	0.76*	0.76*	0.77*	0.77*
consumption	(0.01)	(0.01)	(0.01)	(0.01)	(0.01)	(0.01)
Ln distance (see note)	−0.73*	−0.51*	−0.47*	−0.48*	−0.56*	−0.54*
	(0.01)	(0.01)	(0.01)	(0.01)	(0.01)	(0.01)
Within state (home)	2.35*	2.94*	3.05*	2.96*	2.85*	2.40*
	(0.03)	(0.03)	(0.03)	(0.03)	(0.03)	(0.04)
Adjacent states		0.80*	0.72*	0.70*	0.68*	0.61*
		(0.02)	(0.02)	(0.02)	(0.02)	(0.02)
States in same			0.28*	0.27*	0.29*	0.27*
census div.			(0.02)	(0.02)	(0.02)	(0.02)
Border effect[†]	10.4–10.4	8.4–19	7.7–21.1	7.3–29.6	7.5–17.2	4.5–11
N	21,394	21,394	21,394	21,394	21,394	21,394
R^2	0.716	0.735	0.738	0.738	0.741	0.742
RMSE	0.908	0.876	0.872	0.872	0.866	0.865

Notes: Standard errors in parentheses with * denoting significance at the 1% level. Distances are calculated using two major cities in columns (1) through (3) (WOLFD), area-based internal distances in (4) (AREA), average distance in columns (5) (AVGD), effective distance (CESD) in column (6).
[†] The first border effect is imports from home relative to imports from an adjacent state in same census division. The second is relative to a non-adjacent state in a different division.

effects do not disappear. Moreover, we find small but statistically significant effects for trade within Census Divisions. These are nine regional groups of states that have no political significance.

The results in Table 6.3 suggest that there are positive neighborhood effects on trade that are just not being captured by distances, even our preferred effective distances. One partial explanation may be found in Hillberry and Hummels (2003). They point out that the publicly available CFS data we use includes shipments from wholesalers to retailers. When they exclude such flows, the estimates of the state border effect fall. This is because wholesale trade patterns may be influenced by exclusive territories (for market segmentation purposes) that align with state borders.

The standard gravity specification yields qualitatively similar results. Border effects fall by 36 per cent when using our preferred measure of

results for all coefficients except the border coefficient which is 1.48 in his study for 1993 and 2.13 here for 1997.

distance instead of the arithmetic average one as can be seen in the two last columns of Table 6.3.

6.2   The impact of borders within the European Union

Head and Mayer (2000) and Nitsch (2000) found results on the extent of border effects for the European Union (EU) that revealed that the level of fragmentation was still quite high within it despite the progressive removal of formal and informal barriers to trade during the economic integration process. We now draw on the same data used in Head and Mayer (2000) to investigate the extent to which the impact of borders was in fact inflated by average distance measures used. In order to get most comparable results possible with the US dataset, we restrict the sample to the three years of data we have post 1992 (1993–95). We chose those years because the Single Market Programme was supposed to be fully implemented and therefore the border effects should not reflect any tariff (since 1968) or non-tariff (since January 1, 1993) barriers to trade.

The most important result of those regressions estimating border effects in the EU is the fall in the estimated effect of borders when adopting our improved measure of effective distance. The border effect estimated in the friction specification (Table 6.4) goes from $\exp(2.64) = 14$ to $\exp(1.44) = 4.2$ when passing from simple arithmetic average distance (AVGD) to effective distance (CESD). Compared to a more traditional area-based distance measure (AREA), the impact of distance measurement is even more impressive, the impact of the border being divided by 6.6 and adjacency being also drastically less important in trade patterns. The traditional gravity-equation results are almost identical in both the estimated magnitudes and falls of the considered coefficients (Table 6.5). While we just showed that our effective distance measure can help to understand how the effect of borders is globally overestimated because of the mismeasurement in distance, there is still some evidence of significant border effects in our sample. We will now see that the differences in border effects among industries can also be explained by the same reasoning we used in deriving our effective distance measure, that is a systematic overstatement of border effects in goods that are difficult to ship compared to others.

6.3   Transportability

The additional cost needed to transport an item varies greatly across goods. We have just seen that accounting for the fact that distance matters inside countries too considerably alters the magnitude of global border effects. A related question is how does it matter across industries. Authors

Table 6.4. *EU border effects in friction regressions*

Model:	Dependent variable: Ln Ξ (friction)		
	(AREA)	(AVGD)	(CESD)
Cross Border	3.35*	2.64*	1.44*
	(0.18)	(0.21)	(0.25)
Ln Distance	1.05*	1.38*	1.27*
	(0.05)	(0.08)	(0.07)
Share language	−0.72*	−0.92*	−0.74*
	(0.14)	(0.13)	(0.14)
Adjacency	−0.70*	−0.48*	−0.40*
	(0.07)	(0.08)	(0.07)
Border effect[†]	6.8–28	3.4–14	1.3–4.2
N	7,213	7,213	7,213
R^2	0.265	0.258	0.276
RMSE	1.685	1.694	1.672

Notes: Standard errors in parentheses with * denoting significance at the 1% level. Distances are calculated using the area approximation in columns (1) (AREA), the arithmetic weighted average in columns (2) (AVGD), the CES aggregator in column (3) (CESD). Standard errors are robust to correlated industry residuals.
[†] The first border effect is imports from home relative to imports from an adjacent country speaking the same language. The second is relative to a non-adjacent country speaking a different language.

who have been able to work at the industry level on this topic have systematically found that industries such as oil refining, construction materials, wooden products, clay, and metal containers were characterized by very high border effects, despite industry-specific distance variables. For example, Chen (2004) finds a clear, positive relationship between the border effect of an industry and the weight-to-value ratio of trade in that industry. Table 6.6 reflects this tendency. The ten highest border effects expressed as McCallum's ratio are shown industry by industry for the two samples. Those products appearing in the top list of border effects are also the ones that are presumably the harder to transport over long distances as it appears in the last column of the table. This last column shows the ratio of the average distance covered by the considered good over the same distance for the whole manufacturing industry (the precise construction of this variable is described below). As expected, those ratios are well below one, except for one of those industries. Typical examples are cement, concrete, and soft drinks, all those products covering very low distances (between 10 and 15 per cent of the average manufacturing product) and having a very high border effect.

Table 6.5. *EU border effects in gravity specifications*

Model:	Dependent Variable: Ln Imports					
	(AREA)	(AVGD)	(CESD)	(AREA)	(AVGD)	(CESD)
Ln importer's consumption	0.53*	0.60*	0.59*	1	1	1
	(0.03)	(0.03)	(0.03)			
Ln exporter's production	0.89*	0.98*	0.96*	1	1	1
	(0.05)	(0.05)	(0.06)			
Ln distance	−0.94*	−1.20*	−1.17*	−0.74*	−1.07*	−1.01*
	(0.04)	(0.05)	(0.05)	(0.04)	(0.05)	(0.05)
Share language	0.66*	0.55*	0.55*	1.13*	0.88*	0.90*
	(0.07)	(0.06)	(0.06)	(0.07)	(0.07)	(0.07)
Adjacency	0.72*	0.54*	0.39*	0.60*	0.40*	0.28*
	(0.06)	(0.06)	(0.06)	(0.06)	(0.06)	(0.06)
Within border	3.34*	2.72*	1.45*	3.56*	2.82*	1.71*
	(0.15)	(0.16)	(0.17)	(0.16)	(0.16)	(0.18)
Mills ratio	1.76	3.06	2.58	5.74*	5.26*	5.28*
	(1.65)	(1.58)	(1.56)	(0.73)	(0.67)	(0.65)
N	20,376	20,376	20,376	20,376	20,376	20,376
R^2	0.777	0.779	0.782	0.671	0.681	0.684
RMSE	1.381	1.373	1.4	1.477	1.453	1.447

Notes: Standard errors in parentheses with * denoting significance at the 1% level. Distances are calculated using the area approximation in columns (1) and (4) (AREA), the arithmetic weighted average in columns (2) and (5) (AVGD), the CES aggregator in columns (3) and (6) (CESD). In columns (4)–(6) a unit elasticity is imposed on exporter production and importer consumption by passing them to the left hand of the regression equation. Standard errors are robust to correlated industry residuals.
† The first border effect is imports from home relative to imports from an adjacent country speaking the same language. The second is relative to a non-adjacent country speaking a different language.

This result is very confusing at first sight. In industry-by-industry regressions, goods that are difficult and/or expensive to transport over long distances like cement or carpentry should simply exhibit larger negative effects of distance and therefore transportability should not affect border effects. The development of our improved measure of distance clarifies the link between transportability and border effect and explains why those goods for which transportability is very low will exhibit border effects that are very much biased upwards. Indeed, the θ should be very high (in absolute value) for those industries which will cause internal distances of countries to be even more overestimated than for other goods because products in those industries cover very low distances in reality.

In order to test for this conjecture, we would ideally want to collect an independent estimate of θ for each industry and use it to calculate

Table 6.6. *High border effects industries*

USA		EU		
Industry	Border effect	Industry	Border effect	Miles
Coal	498.3	Tobacco	2870.3	0.5
Natural sands	277.43	Cement	960.78	0.15
Gravel and crushed stone	243.38	Oil refining	730.31	0.24
Logs and other wood in the rough	49.76	Carpentry	718.76	0.66
Alcoholic beverages	32.21	Wood containers	284.37	1.67
Coal and petroleum products, n.e.c.	32.14	Food n.e.s	235.18	0.34
Other agric. products	30.61	Concrete	213.68	0.15
Gasoline and aviation turbine fuel	21.49	Soft drinks	164.36	0.1
Mixed freight	18.47	Wood-sawing	153.05	0.34
Wood products	17.19	Grain milling	112.83	0.25

effective distance shown in equation (6.3). We would then expect the link between transportability and the border effect to disappear. We are unfortunately unable to do that because our model does not enable us to get a prior estimate of θ before distance calculations.

We therefore proceed in an indirect way by using separate information that gives us the average distance covered by goods in different industries. This data comes from the CFS data used in the above section and we match the industries used in that dataset to our NACE industries in the EU data. We therefore suppose that distance covered by a particular good within the USA is roughly similar to distance covered in the EU for that same good. This does not appear to us as a highly unrealistic assumption, especially since the important aspect is the *relative* transportability of goods and how it affects the estimated border effect.

We calculate a transportability variable that uses the average mileage covered by goods in each industry. We divide that figure by the average mileage for aggregated flows to get a relative transportability index ranging from 0.10 for soft drinks (lowest transportability) to 2.6 for clocks (highest transportability). We plug in this variable in the regression and also interact it with the distance variable and the adjacency variable.

The results presented in Table 6.7 show that transportability indeed strongly affects border effects as expected. This is true for all distance measurements but is especially strong in the case of our effective distance. The resulting mean border effect is $\exp(1.14) = 3.12$, which falls to $\exp(1.14 - 1.22\ln(1.5)) = 1.9$ for an industry with a transportability

Table 6.7. *How transportability influences distance, adjacency, and border effects*

Model:	Dependent Variable: Ln S (friction)					
	(AREA)		(AVGD)		(CESD)	
Cross border	3.35*	3.06*	2.64*	2.33*	1.44*	1.14*
	(0.18)	(0.17)	(0.21)	(0.17)	(0.25)	(0.21)
Ln distance	1.05*	1.07*	1.38*	1.41*	1.27*	1.29*
	(0.05)	(0.05)	(0.08)	(0.08)	(0.07)	(0.06)
Share language	−0.72*	−0.83*	−0.92*	−1.01*	−0.74*	−0.84*
	(0.14)	(0.14)	(0.13)	(0.13)	(0.14)	(0.14)
Adjacency	−0.70*	−0.63*	−0.48*	−0.40*	−0.40*	−0.32*
	(0.07)	(0.06)	(0.08)	(0.07)	(0.07)	(0.06)
Transportability		−1.00*		−1.22*		−1.22*
		(0.16)		(0.17)		(0.21)
Ln distance X transportability		0.08		0.20∼		0.12
		(0.05)		(0.09)		(0.06)
Adjacency X transportability		0.27*		0.38*		0.33*
		(0.07)		(0.09)		(0.08)
N	7,213	7,213	7,213	7,213	7,213	7,213
R²	0.265	0.38	0.258	0.371	0.276	0.39
RMSE	1.685	1.548	1.694	1.56	1.672	1.536

Notes: Standard errors in parentheses with * denoting significance at the 1% level. Distances are calculated using the area approximation in columns (1) and (2) (AREA), the arithmetic weighted average in columns (3) and (4) (AVGD), the CES aggregator in columns (5) and (6) (CESD). Standard errors are robust to correlated industry residuals.

index 50 per cent higher than average. For the most easily transportable good, the border effect is about nil and even slightly negative (exp(1.14 − 1.22 ln(2.6)) = 0.97). Note also that the adjacency effect vanishes for this industry (exp(−0.32 + 0.33 ln(2.6)) = 0.99).

Transportability issues and the way they affect distance mismeasurement therefore seem totally crucial in the estimation of the impact of the borders on trade flows. With an appropriate measure of distance, it seems that European markets were, in those years following the completion of the Single Market Program, only marginally fragmented, with a border effect of 3.12.

7   Conclusion

Statistical institutes report trade flows at a geographical level (usually the national level) that is far more aggregated than the level at which trade flows actually take place.

We develop in this paper a new measure of "effective" distance between and within geographical units for which we can observe trade flows that takes into account underlying trade patterns at a more disaggregated level. More precisely, it is calculated so as to ensure that bilateral trade flows between geographical units like nations are equal to the sum of bilateral trade flows between their sub-units. Our major finding is that the existing measures used in the literature overestimate effective distances and that this distance inflation is stronger the closer the two nations are to each other.

One important consequence of this finding has to do with border effects. Since conventional methods overestimate internal distances more than external ones, the negative impact of borders will be magnified in regressions trying to explain why trade is so "local." Following the same idea, adjacency effects are also very likely to be overestimated. We show that those two problems are most severe for goods that are costly to ship over long distances.

We investigate empirically these findings using trade flows between states in the USA for the year 1997 and between countries in the EU during the years 1993–95. Those two samples offer the advantage of being free of any effect of formal border-related barriers to trade. We thus want to see if the estimated impact of borders on trade flows can be totally brought to zero by the use of our improved distance measurement, that is if border effects of those samples are totally "illusory."

The use of the effective distance leads to smaller estimates of border effects and adjacency effects in the two samples; the reductions in the estimates are particularly important in the EU sample where the border effect is divided by more than six when using effective distance over a standard measurement. However it does not eliminate these effects. Thus the use of average and area-based measures of internal distance in the previous literature caused inflated border effect estimates but not illusory borders.

Finally, we investigate our conjecture about how the mismeasurement of distance causes easily transportable goods to have low border effects and goods like cement to have very large ones. Transportability issues and the way it affects distance mismeasurement indeed seem central in the estimation of the impact of the borders on trade flows. With our measure of distance, we find that post-single market Europe in 1992–95 was only marginally fragmented, with a border effect of 3.12. The most easily transportable industries have no border effect nor positive effect of adjacency.

REFERENCES

Anderson J. E. (1979). "A Theoretical Foundation for the Gravity Equation," *American Economic Review* **69**(1): 106–16.

Anderson J. E. and E. van Wincoop (2003). "Gravity with Gravitas: A Solution to the Border Puzzle," *American Economic Review* **93**(1): 170–92.

Anderson, M. and S. Smith (1999). "Do National Borders Really Matter? Canada–US Regional Trade Reconsidered," *Review of International Economics* **7**(2): 219–27.

Baldwin, R., R. Forslid, P. Martin, G. Ottaviano and F. Robert-Nicoud (2003). "The Core-Periphery Model: Key Features and Effects," Chapter 2 of *Economic Geography and Public Policy*, Princeton University Press.

Balistreri, E. J. and R. H. Hillberry (2007). "Structural Estimation and the Border Puzzle," *Journal of International Economics* **72**(2): 451–63.

Bettstetter, C., H. Hartenstein and X. Perez-Costa (2004). "Stochastic Properties of the Random Waypoint Mobility Model," *Wireless Networks* **10**(5): 555–67.

Chen, N. (2004). "Intra-national versus International Trade in the European Union: Why Do National Borders Matter?" *Journal of International Economics* **63**(1): 93–118.

Deardorff, A. (1998). "Determinants of Bilateral Trade: Does Gravity Work in a Neoclassical World?" in J. Frankel (ed.), *The Regionalization of the World Economy*, University of Chicago Press, pp. 7–28.

Disdier, A.-C. and K. Head (2008). "The Puzzling Persistence of the Distance Effect on Bilateral Trade," *Review of Economics and Statistics*.

Fujita, M., P. Krugman and A. J. Venables (1999). *The Spatial Economy: Cities, Regions, and International Trade*, Cambridge, MA: MIT Press.

Head, K. and T. Mayer (2000). "Non-Europe: The Magnitude and Causes of Market Fragmentation in the EU," *Weltwirtschaftliches Archiv* **136**(2): 285–314.

Head, K. and J. Ries (2001). "Increasing Returns versus National Product Differentiation as an Explanation for the Pattern of US–Canada Trade," *American Economic Review* **91**(4): 858–76.

Helliwell, J. (1996). "Do National Borders Matter for Quebec's Trade?" *Canadian Journal of Economics* **29**(3): 507–22.

(1998). *How Much Do National Borders Matter?* Washington DC: Brookings Institution.

Helliwell, J. and G. Verdier (2001). "Measuring Internal Trade Distances: A New Method Applied to Estimate Provincial Border Effects in Canada," *Canadian Journal of Economics* **34**(4): 1024–41.

Hillberry, R. and D. Hummels (2003). "Intranational Home Bias: Some Explanations," *The Review of Economics and Statistics* **85**(4): 1089–92.

Krugman, P. (1980). "Scale Economies, Product Differentiation, and the Pattern of Trade," *American Economic Review* **70**: 950–59.

Leamer, E. (1997). "Access to Western Markets, and Eastern Effort Levels," in S. Zecchini, *Lessons from the Economic Transition: Central and Eastern Europe in the 1990s*, Dordrecht; Boston: Kluwer Academic Publishers.

McCallum, J. (1995). "National Borders Matter: Canada–US Regional Trade Patterns," *American Economic Review* **85**(3): 615–23.

Nitsch, V. (2000). "National Borders and International Trade: Evidence from the European Union," *Canadian Journal of Economics* **22**(4): 1091–1105.

(2001). "It's Not Right But It's Okay: On the Measurement of Intra- and International Trade Distances," mimeo, Bankgesellschaft Berlin.

Obstfeld, M. and K. Rogoff (2000). "The Six Major Puzzles in International Macroeconomics: Is There a Common Cause?" National Bureau of Economic research paper no. 7777.

Rauch, J. (2001). "Business and Social Networks in International Trade," *Journal of Economic Literature* **39**(4): 1177–1203.

Redding, S. and A. J. Venables (2004). "Economic Geography and International Inequality," *Journal of International Economics* **62**(1): 53–82.

Wei, S.-J. (1996). "Intra-National versus International Trade: How Stubborn are Nations in Global Integration?" National Bureau of Economic Research working paper no. 5531.

Wolf, H. C. (1997). "Patterns of Intra- and Inter-State Trade," National Bureau of Economic Research working paper no. 5939.

(2000). "Intranational Home Bias in Trade," *Review of Economics and Statistics* **82**(4): 555–63.

7 Trade costs, market access, and economic geography

Why the empirical specification of trade costs matters

E. M. Bosker and H. Garretsen

1 Introduction

Trade or transport costs are a key element of new economic geography (NEG) models in determining the spatial distribution of economic activity (see e.g. Krugman 1991; Venables 1996 and Puga 1999). Without trade costs there is no role for geography in NEG models. It is therefore not surprising that trade costs are also an important ingredient of empirical studies in NEG (see Redding and Venables 2004; Hanson 2005 or Head and Mayer 2004). They are a vital ingredient of a region's or country's (real) market potential, which measures the ease of access to other markets (Redding and Venables 2004; Head and Mayer 2006). In the empirical trade literature at large, trade costs are also a main determinant of the volume of trade between countries (see e.g. Limao and Venables 2001; Anderson and van Wincoop 2004).

The empirical specification of trade costs is, however, far from straightforward.[1] Problems with the measurement of trade costs arise because between any pair of countries they are very hard to quantify. Trade costs most likely consist of various sub-components that potentially interact, overlap, and/or supplement each other. Obvious candidates are transport costs, tariffs, and non-tariff barriers (NTBs), but also less tangible costs

The authors would like to thank the participants of the conference on "The Gravity Equation – Or: Why the World is not Flat," October 18–19 2007, University of Groningen, the Netherlands as well as an anonymous referee, Steven Brakman, Joppe de Ree, and Marc Schramm for useful comments and suggestions. The present paper is an abridged version of the 2007 CESifo working paper with the same title (see www.cesifo.de) which can also be found in Bosker (2008, chapter 2). For an extended and rather different analysis of the main issues covered in the present paper based on the same dataset see Bosker and Garretsen (2010).

[1] The specification of trade costs may also be not that straightforward from a theoretical point of view, see McCann (2005) or Fingleton and McCann (2007).

194   Bosker and Garretsen

arising from cross-border trade, due to institutional and language differences for example, have been incorporated in previous studies (Limao and Venables 2001). An additional difficulty arises with what is arguably the most obvious measure of trade costs, transport costs. Accurate transport cost data between country pairs are very difficult to obtain and almost completely unavailable when considering transport costs between regions.[2] In principle, between-country transport costs can be inferred from cif / fob ratios. The IMF provides for instance extensive trade data on the basis of which these cif / fob ratios can be calculated, see e.g. Limao and Venables (2001) and Baier and Bergstrand (2001). However, as put forward by Hummels (1999, p. 26) these data "suffer from severe quality problems and broad inferences on these numbers may be unwarranted."[3]

The problems of measuring trade costs that beset the empirical trade literature also apply to empirical studies into the relevance of NEG since any attempt to shed light on the empirical relevance of NEG calls for the availability of bilateral trade costs between a sufficiently large number of countries or regions (e.g. Redding and Venables 2004; Hanson 2005; Brakman et al. 2006; Knaap 2006). Given the lack of a direct measurement of bilateral trade costs, all NEG studies turn to the indirect measurement of trade costs. In doing so, they closely follow the empirical trade literature (see Anderson and van Wincoop 2004 for a very good survey of the latter) and assume a so-called trade cost function. This aims to proxy the unobservable trade costs by combining information on observable trade cost proxies such as distance, common language, tariffs, adjacency, etc. with assumptions about the unobservable trade cost component. The assumptions made about this trade cost function, e.g. functional form, parameter hetero- or homogeneity across country pairs, which observable cost proxies to include or how to estimate each cost proxy's effect, all potentially have a (crucial) effect on the results of any empirical NEG study.

---

[2] Where actual transport cost data are used in the empirical literature the coverage in terms of the number of country pairs is very limited (e.g. costs of shipping a standard forty-foot container from Baltimore (USA) to sixty-four different countries in Limao and Venables 2001) or only the evolution of average (by world-region) transport costs over time is available (e.g. Norwegian and German shipping indices and air cargo rates in Hummels 1999). The only study that we are aware of that constructs very detailed transportation statistics at the regional level is Combes and Lafourcade (2005). Their method is very useful to obtain accurate transportation cost data; however, how to incorporate intangible costs like cultural and/or language differences, that become much more important when considering international trade, is much less straightforward.
[3] Hummels infers transport costs by making use of more accurate data, but these data are only available for very few countries.

In the empirical NEG literature, the measurement of trade costs is only a means to an end, and as a result the relevance of the preferred trade costs specification for the conclusions with respect to the NEG hypotheses under consideration is typically ignored. Virtually all studies just pick a trade cost specification and do not (or only marginally) address the sensitivity of their results to their chosen approximation of trade costs. This paper aims to overcome this lack of attention by systematically estimating and comparing trade cost functions that have been used in the empirical NEG literature. We use various trade cost functions to estimate a standard NEG wage equation for eighty countries and look into the importance of the trade costs specification for the relevance of market access, the central NEG variable when it comes to cross-country spatial interdependencies, as a determinant of the difference in GDP per capita between countries. It turns out that the way trade costs are proxied has substantial effects when it comes to the conclusions about the relevance of market access. Trade costs matter not only in terms of the size (and sometimes also the significance) of the market access effect, but also in terms of the spatial reach of economic shocks. The main message of our paper is that the empirical specification of trade costs really matters for the conclusions reached with respect to the empirical relevance of NEG models.[4] Our analysis in this chapter complements the analysis by Keith Head and Thierry Mayer in Chapter 6. They focus on a related but rather different issue: the (mis)measurement of the distance effect on trade and how to handle the distance effect correctly at different spatial scales. Our chapter focusses on the relevance of various specifications of trade costs, and where distance between locations is a key element of these specifications, we stress the implications of the handling of the functional form of the trade cost function. What both chapters have in common is that they show that the (empirical) trade literature on gravity models or, in our case, NEG, takes the specification of trade costs far too lightly.

Our chapter is organized as follows. In the next section we first introduce the basic NEG model with a focus on the equilibrium wage equation and the role of trade costs. Next we discuss the two estimation strategies that have been used in the literature to estimate the wage equation, both of which require the specification of a trade cost function. Section 3 discusses the main conceptual difficulties involved in the approximation of trade costs by specifying a trade cost function. Section 4 introduces our

---

[4] Hereby corroborating the suspicion expressed by Combes and Lafourcade (2005) who state that "using the correct impedance function to measure them (accessibility measures, i.e. market access) ... appears ... crucial in this field (NEG)."

dataset. In Section 5 we present our estimation results for the NEG wage equation, hereby focusing in detail on the impact of the choice of trade cost approximation used and of the chosen estimation strategy on the key explanatory NEG variable, market access. It turns out that the relevance of market access, or in other words of spatial interdependencies between countries, depends strongly on the choice of trade cost approximation. Section 6 concludes.

2   Trade costs and the wage equation in NEG

The need to have a measure of trade costs when doing empirical work on NEG models immediately becomes clear when discussing the basic NEG model on which most empirical studies are based. This section first develops the theory behind the widely used wage equation that serves as the vehicle for our empirical research too (e.g. Krugman 1991; Venables 1996 and Puga 1999). Our exposition is largely based on the seminal paper by Redding and Venables (2004).[5] In the second part of this section, we move from theory to empirics by introducing the two different estimation strategies that have to date been used to estimate the parameters of the NEG wage equation (see Head and Mayer 2004), focusing explicitly on the specification of trade costs.

2.1   The basic NEG model

Assume the world consists of $i = 1, \ldots, R$ countries, each home to an agricultural and a manufacturing sector. In the manufacturing sector, firms operate under internal increasing returns to scale, represented by a fixed input requirement $c_i F$ and a marginal input requirement c_i. Each firm produces a different variety of the same good under monopolistic competition using the same Cobb–Douglas technology combining three different inputs. The first is an internationally immobile primary factor (labor), with price w_i and input share β, the second is an internationally mobile primary factor with price v_i and input share γ, and the third is a composite intermediate good with price G_i and input share α, where $\alpha + \gamma + \beta = 1$.

Manufacturing firms sell their variety to all countries and this involves shipping the goods to foreign markets. This is where the trade costs come in; these are assumed to be of the iceberg kind and the same for each variety produced, i.e. in order to deliver a quantity $x_{ij}(z)$ of variety z

[5] See also Puga (1999) or Fujita *et al.* (1999, chapter 14) for more details.

produced in country i to country j, $x_{ij}(z)T_{ij}$ has to be shipped from country i. A proportion $(T_{ij} - 1)$ of output "is paid" as trade costs ($T_{ij} = 1$ if trade is costless). Note that this relatively simple iceberg specification (introduced mainly for ease of modeling purposes) does not specify in any way what trade costs are composed of. It is precisely the need to specify T_{ij} more explicitly in empirical research, see below, that motivates our paper. Taking these shipping costs into account gives the following profit function for each firm in country i,

$$\pi_i = \sum_j^R p_{ij}(z)x_{ij}(z)/T_{ij} - G_i^\alpha w_i^\beta v_i^\gamma c_i \left[F + \sum_j^R x_{ij}(z) \right] \quad (7.1)$$

where $p_{ij}(z)$ is the price of a variety produced in country i.

Turning to the demand side, each firm's product is both a final (consumption) and an intermediate (production) good. It is assumed that these products enter both utility and production in the form of a CES-aggregator with σ the elasticity of substitution between each pair of product varieties. Given this CES-assumption about both consumption and intermediate production, it follows directly that in equilibrium all product varieties produced in country i are demanded by country j in the same quantity (for this reason varieties are no longer explicitly indexed by (z)). Denoting country j's expenditure on manufacturing goods (coming from both firms and consumers) as E_j, country j's demand for each product variety produced in country i can be shown to be (following utility maximization and cost minimization on behalf of consumers and producers respectively),

$$x_{ij} = p_{ij}^{-\sigma} E_j G_j^{(\sigma-1)} \quad (7.2)$$

where G_j is the price index for manufacturing varieties that follows from the assumed CES-structure of both consumer and producer demand for manufacturing varieties. It is defined over the prices, p_{ij}, of all goods produced in country $i = 1, \ldots, R$ and sold in country j,

$$G_j = \left[\sum_i^R n_i p_{ij}^{1-\sigma} \right]^{1/(1-\sigma)} \quad (7.3)$$

Maximization of profits (7.1) combined with demand as specified in (7.2) gives the well-known result in the NEG literature that firms set their fob price at p_i, i.e. depending only on the location of production (so that price differences between countries of a good produced in country i only arise from differences in trade costs, i.e. $p_{ij} = p_i T_{ij}$), where p_i is a markup over marginal costs:

$$p_i = G_i^\alpha w_i^\beta v_i^\gamma c_i \sigma / (\sigma - 1) \tag{7.4}$$

Next, free entry and exit drive (maximized) profits to zero, which pinpoints equilibrium output per firm at $\bar{x} = (\sigma - 1)F$. Finally combining this equilibrium output with equilibrium price (7.4) and equilibrium demand (7.2), and noting that in equilibrium the price of the internationally mobile primary factor of production will be the same across countries ($v_i = v$ for all i), gives the equilibrium wage of the composite factor of immobile production, i.e. labor,

$$w_i = A G_i^{-\alpha/\beta} c_i^{-1/\beta} \left(\sum_j^R E_j G_j^{(\sigma-1)} T_{ij}^{(1-\sigma)} \right)^{\frac{1}{\beta\sigma}} \tag{7.5}$$

where $A = v^{-\gamma/\beta}[(\sigma - 1)^{(\sigma-1)/\sigma} F^{(-1/\sigma)} / \sigma]^{1/\beta}$ is a constant.

Equation (7.5) is the wage equation that is at the heart of those empirical studies in NEG that try to establish whether, as equation (7.5) indicates, there is a spatial wage structure with wages being higher in economic centers (e.g. Redding and Venables 2004; Mion 2004; Hanson 2005; Brakman *et al.* 2006 and Knaap 2006). More precisely, the wage equation (7.5) says that the wage level a country is able to pay its manufacturing workers is a function of that country's technology, c_i, the price index of manufactures in that country, G_i, and so-called real market access, the sum of trade cost-weighted market capacities.[6]

Note that trade costs play a crucial role in (7.5), most visibly in the real market access term. It also plays a role in the price index of manufactures (7.3), i.e. using $p_{ij} = p_i T_{ij}$:

$$G_j = \left[\sum_i^R n_i p_i^{1-\sigma} T_{ij}^{1-\sigma} \right]^{1/(1-\sigma)} \tag{7.6}$$

Wages are relatively higher in countries that have easier access to consumer markets in other countries when selling their products and that

---

[6] The actual wage equation estimated may differ slightly from the one presented here in each particular empirical study, but the basic idea behind it is always the same, i.e. with wages depending on real market access and the price index of manufactures, which to a very large extent depend on the level of trade costs between a country (or region) and all other countries (regions).

have easier access to products produced in other countries (producer markets). The lower trade costs, the easier access to both producer and consumer markets abroad, the higher the wages that firms can offer their workers to remain profitable. Trade costs are thus of vital importance in determining the spatial distribution of income.

We now turn to the discussion of the two different ways by which the wage equation has been estimated in the literature so far, hereby particularly emphasizing the way in which trade costs are dealt with.

2.2   Estimating the wage equation

Taking logs on both sides of (7.5) gives the following non-linear equation that can be estimated:

$$\ln w_i = \alpha_1 + \alpha_2 \ln G_i + \alpha_3 \ln \left(\sum_j^R E_j G_j^{(\sigma-1)} T_{ij}^{(1-\sigma)} \right) + \eta_i \quad (7.7)$$

where η_i captures the technological differences, c_i, between countries that typically consist of both variables that are correlated (modeled by including e.g. measures of physical geography or institutional quality) and/or variables that are uncorrelated (modeled by an i.i.d. log-normal disturbance term) with market and supplier access. The α's are the estimated parameters from which in principle the structural NEG parameters can be inferred (see e.g. Redding and Venables 2004 or Hanson 2005). There are basically two different ways in which wage equation (7.7) has been estimated in the empirical NEG literature.

2.2.1   Direct non-linear estimation of the wage equation The first empirical strategy to estimate the wage equation was introduced by Hanson (2005) and can be discussed rather briefly. It involves direct non-linear estimation of the wage equation (7.7). Authors that have subsequently followed this direct non-linear estimation strategy include Brakman et al. (2004, 2006) and Mion (2004).[7]

To deal with the lack of directly measurable trade costs, all papers in the "Hanson" tradition assume a trade cost function to deal with the need to specify T_{ij} for empirical research (see the next section).[8] What

---

[7] The first version of this paper was already available as an NBER working paper (no. 6429) in February 1998. This explains why others have used his methodology and have published their work earlier than Hanson himself.

[8] Besides information on trade costs, T_{ij}, also the data on the price index, G_i, is unavailable at the regional level. Very briefly, the problems with the lack of data on regional price

is important here is that this trade cost function is subsequently directly substituted for T_{ij} in (7.7). Its parameters are jointly estimated along with the parameters of the wage equation. This is rather different from the second estimation strategy.

2.2.2 Two-step linear estimation of the wage equation making use of trade data The second strategy comes from the work by Redding and Venables (2004) and involves a two-step procedure where in the first step the information contained in (international) trade data is used to provide estimates of so-called market and supplier capacity and bilateral trade costs that are subsequently used in the second step to estimate the parameters of the wage equation. Other papers using this strategy include inter alia Breinlich (2006); Head and Mayer (2006); Hering and Poncet (2006) and Knaap (2006).

Instead of directly estimating (7.7), this estimation strategy makes use of the following definition of bilateral trade flows between countries that follows directly from aggregating the demand from consumers in country j for a good produced in country i (7.2) over all firms producing in country i:

$$EX_{ij} = n_i p_i x_{ij} = n_i p_i^{1-\sigma} T_{ij}^{1-\sigma} E_j G_j^{\sigma-1} \qquad (7.8)$$

Equation (7.8) says that exports from country i to country j depend on the "supply capacity," $n_i p_i^{1-\sigma}$, of the exporting country that is the product of the number of firms and their price competitiveness, the "market capacity," $E_j G_j^{\sigma-1}$ of the importing country, and the magnitude of bilateral trade costs T_{ij} between the two countries. Taking logs on both sides of (7.8) and replacing market and supply capacity by an importer and exporter dummy respectively, i.e. $s_i = n_i p_i^{1-\sigma}$ and $m_j = E_j G_j^{\sigma-1}$, results in the following equation that is estimated:

$$\ln EX_{ij} = \ln s_i + (1 - \sigma) \ln T_{ij} + \ln m_j + \varepsilon_{ij} \qquad (7.9)$$

where ε_{ij} is an i.i.d. log-normal disturbance term.

In the second step, the estimated country-specific importer and exporter dummies and the predicted value of bilateral trade costs that result from the estimation of (7.9) are then used to construct so-called

indices are solved by either using, besides the wage equation, other (long run) equilibrium conditions (Brakman *et al.* 2004; Mion 2004; Hanson 2005) *or* by assuming away the use of intermediates in manufacturing production ($\alpha = 0$) and approximating each region's price index by the average wage level in the economic centers that are closest to that region (Hanson 2005; Brakman *et al.* 2006), see also Head and Mayer 2004, p. 2624.

market and supplier access. These are defined as follows respectively; see Redding and Venables (2004, pp. 61–62) for more details:

$$MA_i = \sum_{j}^{R} E_j G_j^{\sigma-1} T_{ij}^{1-\sigma} = \sum_{j}^{R} m_j T_{ij}^{1-\sigma}$$

$$SA_j = \sum_{i}^{R} n_i p_i^{1-\sigma} T_{ij}^{1-\sigma} = \sum_{i}^{R} s_i T_{ij}^{1-\sigma}$$

(7.10)

The predicted values of market and supplier access are subsequently used to estimate the wage equation, i.e. rewriting (7.5), using (7.6) and (7.10) and taking logs on both sides gives:

$$\ln w_i = \alpha_1 + a_2 \ln SA_i + \alpha_3 \ln MA_i + \eta_i \tag{7.11}$$

where η_i, α_1 and α_3 are as specified in (7.7) and a_2 captures a somewhat different combination of structural parameters than α_2 in (7.7).

The problem of the lack of a direct measurement of trade costs when using this estimation strategy enters in the first step. All papers solve this problem by assuming a trade cost function (see next section). The parameters of this trade cost function are jointly estimated with the importer and exporter dummies and subsequently used in the construction of the predicted values of market and supplier access. Different from the direct estimation of the wage equation, the parameters of the distance function are thus not jointly estimated with the parameters of the NEG wage equation.

The motivation for Redding and Venables (2004) to use this two-step strategy is that "this approach has the advantage of capturing relevant country characteristics that are not directly observable but are nevertheless revealed through trade performance" (Redding and Venables 2004, p. 75). Still, they have to assume an empirical specification for the trade cost function, and moreover the country dummies may be capturing "too much" relevant country characteristics (see Section 3 for more detail). In Bosker and Garretsen (2010) the idea that actual trade data can be used as a foundation for market and supplier access in the wage equation is taken one step further by letting trade data determine total trade costs (following the idea of Head and Ries 2001) thereby circumventing the need to explicitly specify a trade cost function for T_{ij}. In this chapter we, however, restrict ourselves to using a trade cost function, focusing in detail on the explicit and implicit assumptions made when specifying a trade cost function and on the impact of the choice of trade cost function on the estimated size and significance of the impact of market access on GDP per capita.

3   The trade cost function

All papers using either the direct or two-step estimation strategy deal with the lack of a direct measure of trade costs by specifying a trade cost function. In its most general form the trade cost function is:

$$T_{ij} = f(X_{ij}, X_j, X_i, \upsilon_{ij}) \tag{7.12}$$

The trade costs involved in shipping goods from country i to country j are a function f of cost factors that are specific to the importer or the exporter (X_j and X_i respectively), such as infrastructure, institutional setup or geographical features of a country (access to the sea, mountainness), bilateral cost factors related to the actual journey from j to i, X_{ij}, such as transport costs, tariffs, sharing a common border, language barriers, membership of a free trade union, etc., and unobservable factors, υ_{ij}. Given the aforementioned lack of transport cost data between a sufficient number of countries, these are in turn also proxied by most notably bilateral distance, but sometimes also actual travel times or population-weighted distance measures are used.

The trade cost function that is used in estimating the wage equation in NEG studies, is typically chosen on the basis of the "older" empirical literature on international trade, more specifically on the estimation of the so-called gravity equation of which (7.9) is an example (see Anderson and van Wincoop 2004 for an extensive discussion of the gravity equation). Usually, and probably mostly for ease of estimation (see Hummels 2001), the trade cost function takes the following (multiplicative) form,

$$T_{ij} = \prod_{m=1}^{M} X_{ij}^{\gamma_m} \prod_{k=1}^{K} (X_i^{\gamma_{1k}} X_j^{\gamma_{2k}}) \upsilon_{ij} \tag{7.13}$$

where the unobservable part, υ_{ij}, of the trade cost function is modeled by a disturbance term (that is usually assumed to be i.i.d.). To give an idea about the type of trade cost function used in the NEG wage equation studies, Table 7.1 shows the trade cost function used in several NEG papers.

As can be seen from Table 7.1, the trade cost function imposed differs quite a bit between these papers and between the two estimation strategies. Or, to quote Anderson and van Wincoop (2004): "A variety

Table 7.1. *Trade cost functions used in the empirical literature*

Paper	Sample	Trade cost function
Direct estimation		
Hanson (2005)	US counties	$T_{ij} = \exp(\tau D_{ij})$
Brakman *et al.* (2006)	European regions	$T_{ij} = \tau D_{ij}^{\delta}$
Mion (2004)	Italian regions	$T_{ij} = \exp(\tau D_{ij})$
Two-step estimation		
Redding and	World countries	$T_{ij} = D_{ij}^{\delta} \exp(\alpha B_{ij})$ or
Venables (2004)		$T_{ij} = D_{ij}^{\delta} \exp(\alpha B_{ij}) \exp(\beta_1 isl_i + \beta_2 isl_j$
		$+ \beta_3 llock_i + \beta_4 llock_j + \beta_5 open_i + \beta_6 open_j)$
Knaap (2006)	US states	$T_{ij} = D_{ij}^{\delta} \exp(\alpha B_{ij})$
Breinlich (2006)	European regions	$T_{ij} = D_{ij}^{\delta} \exp\left(\alpha_1 L_{ij} + \sum_i \alpha_{2i} B_{ij}^i\right)$
Hering and Poncet (2006)	Chinese cities	$T_{ij} = D_{ij}^{\delta} \exp(\alpha_1 B_{ij}^f + \alpha_2 B_{ij}^C + \alpha_3 B_{ij}^{fC})$

Notes: D_{ij} denotes a measure of distance, usually great-circle distance, but sometimes also other measures such as travel times (e.g. Brakman *et al.* 2004) or population-weighted great-circle distance (e.g. Breinlich 2006) have been used. B_{ij} denotes a border dummy, either capturing the (alleged positive) effect of two countries/regions being adjacent (e.g. Redding and Venables 2004; Knaap 2006) or the (possibly country-specific) effect of crossing a national border (e.g. Breinlich 2006; Hering and Poncet 2006).

of ad hoc trade cost functions have been used to relate the unobservable cost to observable variables" (p. 706) and "Gravity theory [*read: new economic geography theory*] has used arbitrary assumptions regarding functional form of the trade cost function, the list of variables, and regularity conditions" (p. 710, phrase in italics added). To a large extent based on Anderson and van Wincoop (2004), our discussion of the (implicit) assumptions underlying the use of a trade cost function concerns six issues: i) functional form; ii) variables included; iii) regularity conditions; iv) modeling costs involved with internal-trade; v) the unobservable component of trade costs; vi) estimating the trade cost function's parameters.[9]

[9] Although this is already a fairly extensive list of issues, there are additional important issues when it comes to the handling and specification of trade costs. One issue is how to deal with (distance related) trade costs at different spatial scales; see the contribution by Head and Mayer in chapter 6. Another issue, and see the vast literature on transport economics, is that trade or transport costs are a function of the transport cost system (issues of modal choice). In the NEG literature the literature on transport economics is typically ignored which may be one reason why the depiction of transport or trade costs

i. *Functional form*. All papers in Table 7.1 *have* to assume a specific functional form for the trade cost function. As can be seen from Table 7.1, empirical papers in NEG opt for a functional form as shown in (7.13); all cost factors enter multiplicatively. As in the international trade literature (see Hummels 2001), the main reason for doing so is probably ease of estimation. Although being by far the most common functional form used in the empirical NEG and the international trade literature, its implications are usually not given much attention. As pointed out by Hummels (2001), the multiplicative form implies that the marginal effect of a change in one of the trade cost components depends on the magnitude of all the other cost factors included in the trade cost function. As this may not be that realistic he argues that a more sensible trade cost function combines the different cost factors *additively*, i.e.

$$T_{ij} = \sum_m^M \gamma_m X_{ij} + \sum_k^K (\gamma_{1k} X_i + \gamma_{2k} X_j) + \upsilon_{ij} \qquad (7.14)$$

where X_{ij}, X_i, X_j, and υ_{ij} are defined as in (7.12). Using this specification avoids the above-mentioned problem, as each cost factor's marginal effect does no longer depend on the magnitude of the other cost factors.

Also the specific distance funtion chosen is of concern. Some papers take an exponential distance function (Brakman *et al.* 2004; Mion 2004 and Hanson 2005), hereby following the theoretical NEG literature (e.g. Krugman 1995 and Fujita *et al.* 1999). The other papers shown in Table 7.1 opt for the power function instead, which is also the standard choice in the empirical trade literature. As argued by Fingleton and McCann (2007) the latter function has the virtue of allowing for economies of distances,[10] so that transport costs are concave in distance (standard in the transportation and logistics literature, see e.g. McCann 2001), whereas the exponential distance function implies that transport costs are convex in distance. It also implicitly imposes a very strong distance decay, which may not be wanted (see Head and Mayer 2004).

ii. *Variables included*. The number and composition of variables included in the trade cost function differs quite substantially across the papers in Table 7.1. The papers employing the direct estimation strategy only include distance in the trade cost function. The impact of assuming a more elaborate trade cost function when applying the direct estimation

---

in NEG has been criticized by those who take insights from transport economics more seriously, see McCann (2005) and Fingleton and McCann (2007).
[10] The estimated distance parameter lies between zero and minus one.

strategy is shown in Section 6. Studies employing the two-step estimation strategy usually also take other bilateral trade cost proxies into account besides distance; see the variables L_{ij} and B_{ij} in Table 7.1, capturing the effect of language similarity and the border effect respectively.[11]

When it comes to the inclusion of potentially relevant variables capturing country-specific trade costs, a drawback of the second estimation strategy as outlined in Section 2 is that the inclusion of the importer and exporter dummies (recall equations [7.9] and [7.10]) wipes out all importer-specific and exporter-specific variation so that the effect of country-specific trade cost proxies cannot be estimated. As a result, the constructed market (supplier) access term (7.10) includes only the exporter- (importer-) specific trade costs and misses those trade costs specific to the importer (exporter).[12] Implicitly all the papers using the two-step estimation strategy *cum* dummies approach mentioned in Table 7.1 assume that country-specific trade costs are zero. Redding and Venables (2004, pp. 76–77) take note of this by also estimating the trade equation (7.9) without capturing the market and supplier capacity terms by importer and exporter dummies but by using importer and exporter GDP instead, hereby allowing for a more elaborate trade cost function. We will do the same in our estimations.

Besides the above discussion on which variables to include, also the way to measure a certain included variable differs between papers. The best example is the distance variable that shows up in all the assumed trade cost functions. Usually this is measured as great-circle distance between capital cities (e.g. Redding and Venables 2004), but others have used

---

[11] Even though these papers include some more variables in the trade cost function, many additional variables have been shown to be of importance in the empirical trade literature. Examples are tariffs, colonial ties, quality of infrastructure, degree of openness, being member of a common currency union, the World Trade Organization or some preferential trade agreement (NAFTA, EU, Mercosur) and many more (see Anderson and van Wincoop 2004).

[12] The estimated exporter/importer dummy would in this case also pick up the exporter/importer specific trade costs so that market and supplier access would implicitly look like (in case of a multiplicative trade cost function):

$$M\hat{A}_i = \sum_{j}^{r} \left[\hat{m}_j \prod_{k=1}^{K} (X_j^{\hat{\gamma}2k}) \prod_{m=1}^{M} X_{ij}^{\hat{\gamma}m} \right] \text{ and}$$

$$S\hat{A}_j = \sum_{i}^{r} \left[\hat{s}_i \prod_{k=1}^{K} (X_i^{\hat{\gamma}1k}) \prod_{m=1}^{M} X_{ij}^{\hat{\gamma}m} \right]$$

Note that MA_i and SA_j fails to capture the trade costs specific to country j and country i respectively.

great-circle distance between countries'/regions' largest commercial centers or counties'/regions' centroids, population-weighted distances (e.g. Breinlich 2006) or travel times (e.g. Brakman *et al.* 2004). It is difficult to give a definitive answer to what measure of distance to include and the same applies for other variables (e.g. the border dummy, proxies of infrastructure quality). However, we think two recommendations can be made.

Regarding the general question of which variables to include, one should be careful with the inclusion of variables that are very likely endogenous. Examples are travel times, population-weighted distance measures, quality of infrastructure, institutional setup or even being a member of a free trade union. Especially when estimating the parameters of the NEG wage equation, that is itself already (by construction) plagued by endogeneity issues, adding more endogeneity through the trade cost function should in our view be avoided (or properly addressed but this is usually not so easy). The use of proxy variables such as great-circle distance, border and language variables, and countries' geographical features such as having direct access to the sea, that can more confidently be considered to be exogenous, should be preferred.

iii. Regularity conditions. All papers in Table 7.1, implicitly or explicitly, make assumptions about the extent to which the impact of each variable included in the trade cost function is allowed to be different for different (pairs of) countries. Most papers assume that the effect of distance, sharing a common border or trading internationally on trade costs is the same for all countries or regions included in the sample. It is however likely that there exists some heterogeneity in the effect of different cost factors (see e.g. Limao and Venables 2001). Some authors do allow these effects to differ between countries or regions (e.g. Breinlich 2006 and Hering and Poncet 2006) but usually do so by imposing ad hoc assumptions regarding the way they are allowed to differ.[13] An advantage of the assumption(s) made about the regularity conditions (compared to e.g. assumptions about functional form) is that they can be tested. This has so far not been done; we argue that this should receive much more attention.

iv. Internal trade costs. The modeling of the costs associated with within-country trade is another "problematic" feature in the empirical NEG papers.[14] The need to incorporate some measure of internal trade

---

[13] Note that assuming the effect to be the same for all countries/regions is also an ad hoc assumption.

[14] Some empirical papers in the international trade literature also deal with this issue (e.g. Helliwell and Verdier 2001) focusing largely on how to measure internal distances, but in general internal trade costs are not dealt with in this literature.

costs follows directly from the functional form of the wage equation (7.5). There it is the sum of trade cost-weighted market capacities (real market access) that consists of on the one hand *foreign* real market access, $\sum_{j \neq i}^{R} E_j G_j^{(\sigma - 1)} T_{ij}^{(1-\sigma)}$ but also of *domestic* real market access, $E_i G_i^{(\sigma - 1)} T_{ii}^{(1-\sigma)}$, which is a measure of own market capacity weighted by internal trade cost. Theoretically these internal trade costs are usually set to zero ($T_{ii}, = 1$). In contrast, all empirical NEG papers proxy the internal trade cost by using an internal trade cost function that solely depends on so-called internal distance, D_{ii}, excluding other country-specific factors that could influence internal trade costs (see Redding and Venables 2004, p. 62). More formally:

$$T_{ii} = f(D_{ii}), \text{ where almost exclusively } D_{ii} = 2/3 (area_i / \pi)^{1/2}$$

$$(7.15)$$

This often-used specification of D_{ii} reflects the average distance from the center of a circular disk with $area_i$ to any point on the disk (assuming these points are uniformly distributed on the disk). Basically own trade costs are simply a function of a country's or region's area, the larger the country or region, the higher the internal trade costs.

Also most papers, regardless of estimation strategy, do not allow internal distance to have a different effect than bilateral distance (an exception are Redding and Venables (2004), who make the ad hoc assumption that the internal distance parameter is half that of the bilateral distance parameter). In Section 6 we explicitly *estimate* a different parameter on internal and bilateral trade and allow own trade costs to depend on other factors than simply internal distance. This and the use of own trade data gives us some indication into the (un)importance of explicitly modeling internal trade costs.

v. The unobservable component of trade costs. In the direct estimation strategy this component is ignored, thereby implicitly positing that the assumed trade cost function is *the* actual trade cost function (Breinlich 2006, also notes this). Taking account of the unobserved component using this strategy is not straightforward. Even if the unobservable component is assumed to be of the simplest kind, i.e. distributed i.i.d. and uncorrelated with any other compenent of either the trade cost function or the wage equation, the non-linear fashion in which it enters the wage equation makes it difficult to determine the appropriateness of the inference on the structural parameters when simply assuming it away (or equivalently assuming it is nicely incorporated into the error component of the wage equation itself). Using simulation-based inference methods could (and maybe should) be a way to shed more light on this issue. More generally – see also Anderson and van Wincoop (2004) on this issue – it is unclear how the error structure should be modeled in gravity like trade costs specifications. Behrens *et al.* (2007) is one of the few papers to date which actually try to tackle this issue.

When using the two-step estimation strategy the unobserved trade cost component(s) is (are) more explicitly taken into account. They are usually assumed to be uncorrelated with the other (observable) trade cost components and to be independent draws from a log-normal distribution, so that they can be incorporated as a (possibly heteroskedastic) normal error term in the first-step estimation of the gravity equation (7.9). Next the use of bootstrapped standard errors in the second-step estimation aims to take account of the fact that the market and supplier access terms (constructed on the basis of the estimated parameters of the first step) implicitly contain the unobservable trade cost component as well, i.e. they are both generated regressors.

vi. Estimating the trade cost function's parameters and dealing with zero trade flows. This is only an issue when using the two-step estimation strategy, where, as explained in Section 2, the parameters of the trade cost function are estimated in the first step by making use of a gravity-type equation. A well-known problem with the estimation of gravity equations is the presence of a substantial number of bilateral trade flows that are zero (i.e. countries not trading bilaterally at all). To deal with this different estimation strategies have been put forward. These can be grouped into two categories, i.e those estimating the log-linearized trade equation (7.9) and those estimating the non-linear trade equation (7.8). Because taking logs of the zero trade flows is problematic, the log-linearized version of the trade equation (7.9) is usually estimated using OLS and the non-zero trade flows only, or, by first adding 1 (or e.g. the smallest non-zero trade flow) to all or only the zero trade flows, and subsequently estimating the trade cost function's parameters by OLS or Tobit. When estimating the non-linear trade equation (7.8) instead, either NLS (Coe *et al.* 2002) or the recently proposed Poisson pseudo maximum likelihood (PPML) estimator (Santos Silva and Tenreyro 2006) can be used; in this case all trade flows can be used (the zero trade flows can now also be used as there is no need to take logs). Arbitrarily adding 1 (or some other positive number) to trade flows in order to be able to take logs of all (also the zero) trade flows is in our view highly unsatisfactory. The subsequent results obtained depend quite strongly on the actual amount that is added to the zero trade flows. Using the non-linear techniques solves this issue and can therefore be considered as a preferred way to estimate the trade function's parameters. This is why we opt for the estimation of the non-linear trade

Table 7.2. *Trade cost functions and the two estimation strategies*

| Issue | (Possible) solution | Ability to deal with issue raised | |
		Two-step	Direct
functional form	experiment with different functional forms	+	− (non-linearity)
regularity conditions	test the assumptions	+	+
variable inclusion	significance of inclusion can be tested	+ − (difficulty with exporter/importer specific trade costs when using dummies)	+
variable measurement	include exogenous variables	+	+
internal trade cost	include more than simply area	+ − (lack of internal trade data)	+
unobservable component	most hidden issue, deserves more explicit care	+	− (implicitly assumed away)
estimating the parameters	non-linear estimation techniques (PPML, NLS) or two-step estimation	− (non-zero trade flows)	+ (NLS should do the job, given the other assumptions)

Notes: + and − indicate the ability of the corresponding estimation strategy to deal with the issue raised w.r.t. to the choice of trade cost function that is used (compared to the other strategy).

equation (7.8) using the PPML estimator.[15] To summarize, Table 7.2 lists the issues that one has to face when approximating trade costs by a trade cost function, while also providing possible ways to deal with these issues.

The remainder of our paper deals with the impact of using different ways to proxy trade costs when estimating the NEG wage equation using

---

[15] An alternative method that also takes account of the issue of the zero trade flows is a two-step estimation procedure (see e.g. Bosker 2007; Helpman *et al.* 2007). Poisson estimates are known to suffer from the so-called excess zero problem, i.e. underpredicting the number of zero observations. When faced with a sample containing a large number of zeroes, the two-step estimation can be preferable.

either the direct or two-step estimation strategy. Hereby we focus in particular on the way conclusions about the effect of real market access, a key NEG variable, on wages may differ when using different methods to proxy trade costs.

4   Data

Our empirical results are based on a sample of ninety-seven countries (see the Appendix for a complete list of these countries) for the year 1996. In order to be able to estimate the wage equation, we have collected data on *GDP*, *GDP per capita* (as wage data are not available for all countries in our sample, we follow Redding and Venables (2004), and use GDP per capita as a proxy) and the *price index* of GDP (as a proxy for G_i in (7.7)[16]) from the *Penn World Tables*. We also need data to calculate the various trade cost proxies. To this end, we have collected data on *bilateral distances, contiguity, common language*, and indicators of a country being *landlocked*, an *island* nation, or a *Sub-Saharan African country*. All these variables are chosen because of their exogeneity (at least in terms of reverse causality). Complementing these data, we also need *trade data* to be able to infer the trade cost function's parameter(s) when using the two-step estimation strategy. These we have collected from the *Trade and Production 1976–1999 database* provided by the French institute CEPII,[17] which enables the use of both bilateral trade and internal trade data for most of the countries in our sample.

5   Estimation results: trade costs and market access

In line with the discussion so far, we discuss our results in two stages. First, we focus on inferring trade cost proxies from bilateral trade data. We estimate the parameters of the trade cost function and illustrate how the results differ when using different trade cost functions (Section 5.1). Subsequently, we turn to our main point of interest, i.e. the way in which a particular trade cost approximation affects conclusions about the relevance of real market access in determining GDP per capita (Section 5.2). This is done by estimating the wage equation using the different trade cost proxies, and by comparing the size and significance of the parameter on market access (α_3) in equation (7.11) for each of the trade cost proxies used. Moreover, we look at how the choice of trade cost specification

---

[16] Note that theoretically the price index should only refer to that of tradeable goods. Using the overall price index as a proxy does also capture the price of non-tradeables.

[17] www.cepii.org/anglaisgraph/bdd/TradeProd.htm.

Table 7.3. *Trade cost functions used*

Abbreviation	Trade cost function
RV 2004	$T_{ij} = D_{ij}^{\delta} \exp(\alpha B_{ij})$
Hanson 2005	$T_{ij} = \exp(\tau D_{ij})$
Multiplicative	$T_{ij} = D_{ij}^{\delta} \exp(\alpha_1 B_{ij} + \alpha_2 L_{ij}) \exp(\beta_1 isl_i + \beta_2 isl_j + \beta_3 llock_i + \beta_4 llock_j$ $+\beta_5 ssa_i + \beta_6 ssa_j + \beta_7 ssa_{ij})$

Note: See Table 7.1 for the definition of the variables.

affects the spatial reach of economic shocks to market access by simulating the effects of a 5 per cent GDP shock in Belgium on GDP per capita in other countries (Section 5.3). In this way, we can gauge the importance of varying the trade costs specifications for the relevance of spatial interdependencies, the backbone of the empirical NEG literature.

We distinguish between three different types of trade cost functions, see Table 7.3. The first two are chosen as they are the ones used by the two papers (Redding and Venables [RV] 2004 and Hanson 2005) that introduced the two-step and direct estimation strategy respectively. The multiplicative function is chosen as it allows trade costs to depend not only on bilateral variables but also on importer/exporter-specific trade cost factors, more specifically those associated with being landlocked (*llock*), being an island nation (*isl*) and, because it is often found to be significant in related gravity studies, being a Sub-Saharan African country (*ssa*). As mentioned before, such a multiplicative function is quite common in the empirical trade literature (see e.g. Limao and Venables 2001).[18]

We also allow for the distance parameter to be different for bilateral and internal distance, hereby estimating (instead of imposing) the different impact of distance when considering intra- or international trade. Estimating instead of assuming the coefficient on internal distance should in our view be preferred compared to making ad hoc assumptions about the impact of internal distance.

5.1   Inferring trade costs from trade flows

To infer the trade cost function's parameters from bilateral (and internal) trade flows we estimate equation (7.8) by using the PPML estimation

---

[18] A fourth option – see Hummels (2001) – and this really refers back to our discussion of the trade cost function in Section 3, would be to use an additive trade cost function (see the CESifo working paper version of this paper).

strategy. This estimation strategy is – see Section 3 – able to take account of the zero trade flows in a way that (contrary to NLS) also deals with the heteroskedasticity that is inherently present in trade flow data (see Santos Silva and Tenreyro 2006). It gives the PPML method an advantage over the heavily used Tobit and/or OLS methods.[19] Table 7.4 shows our estimation results.

To allow for the more elaborate multiplicative cost function and following Redding and Venables 2004, p. 76 – see their equation (22) – we substituted the importer and exporter dummies with importer and exporter GDP.[20] In all specifications the distance coefficient is significant: the further apart two countries are, the higher trade costs are as a result.

Also, sharing a common border (contiguity) significantly lowers trade costs (except in the additive specification), a finding consistent with earlier studies (e.g. Limao and Venables 2001 and Redding and Venables 2004). When estimating the multiplicative specification, the results show the importance of also considering country-specific trade cost proxies. Being landlocked or a Sub-Saharan African country raises trade costs, whereas being an island lowers these costs. These findings are very much in line with the results reported in Limao and Venables (2001) and show that these country-specific trade cost proxies cannot a priori be ignored.

Of special interest here is the coefficient on internal distance (the coefficient shown reflects the difference of the internal distance coefficient with that of bilateral distance). When using the RV or the multiplicative specification we find no evidence that internal distance affects trade costs significantly differently than bilateral distance does. Only when using the Hanson specification do we find that internal distance affects trade costs significantly differently from bilateral trade; the estimated coefficient suggests that internal distance increases trade costs to a much larger extent than bilateral distance does, which is contrary to what one would expect.

---

[19] Note that PPML itself also requires assumptions that may not be met when dealing with international trade flows (most notably that the same process, i.e. the gravity equation, drives the zero and the non-zero observations), see e.g. Bosker 2007 or Helpman et al. 2007.

[20] For sake of comparison we have also estimated the trade equation including importer and exporter dummies while using the corresponding RV trade cost function (equation 16 in their paper). The results were very similar to the results shown here when including importer and exporter GDP, also in terms of explanatory power (R^2) and in terms of the implication in the second step estimation on the effect of market access. Results are available upon request.

Table 7.4. *Trade cost functions and trade flows –*
PPML estimation

Trade cost function:	RV	Hanson	Multiplicative
Distance	−0.721	−0.0002	−0.712
	0.000	0.000	0.000
Internal distance	0.034	−0.001	0.050
	0.745	0.000	0.650
Contiguity	0.746	—	0.930
	0.000	—	0.000
Common language	—	—	0.007
	—	—	0.962
Landlocked importer	—	—	−0.441
	—	—	0.045
Landlocked exporter	—	—	−0.257
	—	—	0.003
Island importer	—	—	0.285
	—	—	0.000
Island exporter	—	—	0.526
	—	—	0.000
ssa importer	—	—	−0.801
	—	—	0.000
ssa exporter	—	—	−1.052
	—	—	0.000
ssa importer and exporter	—	—	0.950
	—	—	0.004
GDP importer	0.751	0.743	0.733
	0.000	0.000	0.000
GDP exporter	0.851	0.838	0.841
	0.000	0.000	0.000
exporter dummies	No	No	No
importer dummies	No	No	No
own trade dummy	1.599	3.810	2.431
	0.008	0.000	0.000
(pseudo) R^2	0.953	0.943	0.956
nr. obs.	8774	8774	8774
importer = exporter?			
– landlocked	—	—	0.386
– island	—	—	0.192
– ssa	—	—	0.275

Notes: p-values underneath the coefficient; importer = exporter?
shows the p-value of a test of equality of the importer and exporter
variant of a certain country-specific variable.

214   Bosker and Garretsen

5.2   Varying trade costs and the impact on market access

We are now finally in a position to turn to our main point of interest, the way in which the various trade cost approximations affect the conclusions regarding the relevance of real market access in determining GDP per capita levels in our sample. To this end, we estimate wage equation (7.7) using both the direct and the two-step estimation strategies introduced in Section 2, i.e. to refresh our memory:

$$\ln w_i = \alpha_1 + \alpha_2 \ln G_i + \alpha_3 \ln \left(\sum_j^R E_j G_j^{(\sigma-1)} T_{ij}^{(1-\sigma)} \right) + \eta_i \quad (7.7')$$

We focus on the size and significance of the parameter on market access (α_3) when using the different trade cost proxies (this section) as well as when looking at the spatial reach of economic shocks (next section). For the direct estimation strategy as developed by Hanson (2005), we use NLS to estimate the parameters whereby we proxy G_i by a country's price index and E_i by a country's GDP level. When using the two-step estimation method as developed by Redding and Venables (2004), we construct market access as specified in (7.10) on the basis of the results shown in Table 7.5 and estimate (7.7) by simple OLS, again proxying G_i by a country's price index.[21] We could have instead used more sophisticated GMM or 2SLS techniques that have been used in the empirical NEG literature and/or have proxied G_i by, for example, a constructed measure of supplier access. But we decided to use OLS and a simple proxy of G_i, to be able to focus entirely on the effect of the trade cost proxy used on the estimated effect of market access. The use of more sophisticated ways of estimating (7.7') would make it far more difficult to ascribe different outcomes to the differences in the way trade costs are proxied. For the same reasons, we also assume that the technological differences between countries, as measured by η_i, can be adequately captured by a simple i.i.d. error term that is uncorrelated with the other regressors instead of also adding additional variables.

The results of the various estimations are shown in Table 7.5a. Each column gives first the estimation strategy used (two-step or direct) and below the trade cost approximation that was used. So, *direct-RV* refers for instance to a direct estimation of the wage equation with the Redding and Venables trade cost specification. Similarly, *two-step-Hanson* (column 2

[21] Results are very similar when we exclude the price index, G_i, from (7.7').

Table 7.5a. *Market access and GDP per capita*

Strategy: Trade costs:	2-step RV	2-step Hanson	2-step multiplicative	direct RV	direct Hanson	direct multiplicative
α_3	0.634	0.303	0.642	0.262	0.236	0.248
	0.003	0.047	0.000	0.002	0.008	0.000
a_2	0.969	1.114	0.804	0.879	1.090	0.942
	0.000	0.000	0.000	0.002	0.000	0.000
R^2	0.644	0.586	0.731	0.706	0.654	0.736
nr obs	80	80	80	80	80	80

Notes: p-values underneath the coefficient.

in Table 7.5a) indicates a two-step estimation of $(7.7')$ with the Hanson trade cost function.

The first thing to note is that *market access is always significant.*[22] But the size of the α_3 coefficient differs quite a bit across the trade cost proxies and the estimation strategies! The impact of a 1 per cent increase in a region's market potential on GDP per capita ranges from 0.24 per cent to 0.64 per cent. When comparing results for each estimation strategy separately, the differences are smaller but still the impact of a 1 per cent change in market access ranges from 0.24 per cent to 0.26 per cent (0.30 per cent to 0.64 per cent) when using the direct (two-step) estimation strategy[23].

Table 7.5b shows additional evidence on the impact of the type of trade cost proxy used. Here we abstracted from the thorny issue of internal trade costs and estimated the effect of only *foreign* market access (FMA), that is market access excluding a region's own internal distance-weighted GDP, on a region's GDP per capita level. This allows one to focus more specifically on the way spatial interdependencies between countries matter for an individual country's prosperity.[24]

---

[22] Notwithstanding differences in the exact specifications used our estimation results for market access in Tables 7.5a and 7.5b are at least for the RV case (column [1]) similar to those in Redding and Venables (2004), see for instance their Table 3.

[23] Note that the difference in size could also be due to the different ways in which market access is constructed. The thought experiment in the next section, which more explicitly describes the spatial reach of an income shock, implicitly shows, by calculating the marginal effects, that this is probably not the case.

[24] As rightfully pointed out by our referee, whether or not to focus on a measure of market access that also includes own-country market access is no trivial matter. From a theoretical perspective—see also our setup of the NEG model in Section 2 – a good market access signals to firms that this is an attractive location to set up their production because of the large home market effect but it also implies stiffer competition. The balance

Table 7.5b. *Foreign market access and GDP per capita*

Strategy: Trade costs:	2-step RV	2-step Hanson	2-step multiplicative	direct RV	direct Hanson	direct multiplicative
FMA	0.425	0.232	0.669	0.098	0.102	0.153
	0.031	0.132	0.001	0.133	0.201	0.071
a_2	1.142	1.203	0.958	1.092	1.120	1.042
	0.000	0.000	0.000	0.000	0.000	0.000
R^2	0.592	0.571	0.708	0.628	0.607	0.645
nr obs	80	80	80	80	80	80

Notes: p-values underneath the coefficient.

As can be clearly seen from Table 7.5b, the estimated impact of foreign market access differs much more when using different trade cost functions: a 1 per cent increase in foreign market access raises GDP per capita from a mere 0.1 per cent to 0.67 per cent depending on the trade cost proxy used. *This clearly indicates that the choice of trade costs specification makes quite a difference.* Its impact is even estimated to be insignificant at the 5 per cent level in four out of six cases. The latter is especially the case for the direct estimation strategy when estimating the trade cost parameters jointly with the NEG parameters (columns [4] to [6])[25].

Based on the estimation results in Tables 7.5a and 7.5b, we conclude that both the size and significance of (foreign) market access does depend on the type of trade cost approximation used. This is not the only way to illustrate why the empirical specification matters for NEG empirics. As trade costs are key to the strength of spatial interdependencies, the spatial or geographical reach of income shocks can potentially be very different when comparing different trade costs specifications. It is to this topic that we turn next.

5.3   Trade costs and the spatial reach of an income shock in Belgium

To address this issue we conducted the following thought experiment. Suppose that Belgium, a country in the heart of Europe, experiences a

---

between those forces may be quite different for own-country market access compared to foreign market access.

[25] As mentioned already in the previous section, this probably is to a large extent due to the non-linear estimation process. The use of more elaborate trade cost functions makes it even "more non-linear" increasing the difficulties with pinpointing the parameters.

positive 5 per cent GDP shock. To what extent will this shock, given our estimation results in Table 7.5, spill over to the other countries in our sample through the market access variable? The 5 per cent increase in GDP increases the demand for goods from potentially all countries; however the actual magnitude of this increase in a specific country depends crucially on the strength of the spatial linkages and thus on the measurement of trade costs, i.e. the lower trade costs with Belgium, the larger the impact on a country's GDP per capita.

Based on the estimation results from Table 7.5a and the various trade cost approximations, we have calculated the resulting GDP per capita changes as experienced by all other countries in response to the increased demand for their products from Belgium. Figure 7.1 visualizes four of these correlations in some more detail. It turns out that the correlation coefficients for GDP per capita differ markedly across the various different trade cost proxies used.

Figure 7.1 plots the different GDP per capita changes for the two basic estimation strategies in estimating equation (7.7′), direct (= han) or indirect (= rv) and for three different trade cost specifications (i.e.

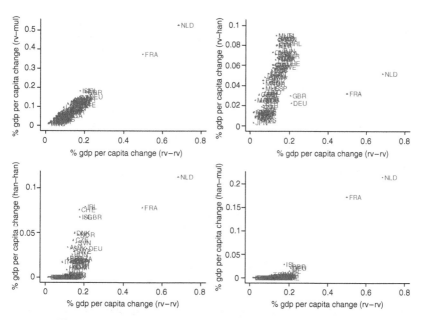

Figure 7.1. Correlations visualized.
Notes: The corresponding correlations are from upper-left to lower-right: 0.98, 0.42, 0.83, 0.89.

Redding Venables (rv), Hanson (han), the multiplicative trade costs function (mul)) against each other. So, for instance, the GDP per capita change (rv-rv) on the horizontal axis in Figure 7.1 refers to the indirect estimation of (7.7′) using the Redding and Venables trade cost function from Table 7.3. Similarly, GDP per capita change (han-mul), see vertical axis in lower-right panel, refers to a direct estimation of equation (7.7′) using the multiplicative trade cost function. Figure 7.1 visualizes that the spatial impact of our localized (Belgium) GDP shock differs quite a bit across trade cost specifications. Note for instance the difference between the "han-han" results and the "rv-rv" outcomes in the lower left panel, but also note the difference in size of the estimated impact of the shock.

Figure 7.2 focuses explicitly on the spatial reach of the Belgian GDP shock. It plots the percentage GDP per capita change against log distance for the same three different trade cost approximations as shown in Figure 7.1: again the conclusions differ on the basis of the type of trade cost function used.

In, for instance, the Hanson case (lower left panel), where market access (MA) is based on a direct estimation of equation (7.7′) using the

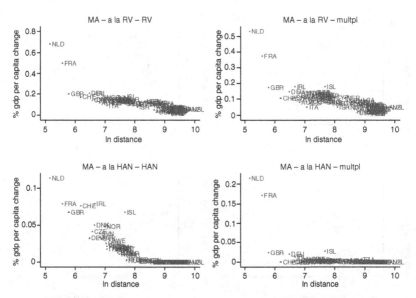

Figure 7.2. GDP per capita changes, 5 per cent GDP shock in Belgium and distance.
Notes: The corresponding correlations are from upper left to lower right: −0.77, −0.76, −0.84, −0.48.

Hanson trade cost function (hence the han-han notation), the distance decay is very strong and also the size of the GDP per capita changes is relatively small. Take for instance the case of the Netherlands (NLD). In the Redding and Venables specifications (upper left and right panels), the GDP per capita change is about seven times as large as in the Hanson case.[26] Figure 7.2 also shows that a more elaborate or heterogeneous trade costs specification (see the upper right panel) increases the variation of the GDP shock for countries at a similar distance to Belgium. Moreover this heterogeneity in differences in spatial reach corresponds to the type of trade cost specification used.

When using the Hanson (2005) exponential trade cost function that depends solely on distance, the size and spatial reach of the Belgian income shock also depends heavily on distance. The correlation between the shock and log distance is the largest in this case. Moreover due to the exponential distance function used, the effect of the income shock quickly peters out; there is no discernable effect any more in countries lying farther from Belgium than Egypt (in the RV specification Egypt still experiences a 0.1 per cent increase in GDP per capita; this is about the size of the wage increase in the most heavily affected country, the Netherlands, when using the Hanson specification!).

The Redding and Venables (2004) specification also allows contiguity to have its effect on trade costs. Consequently the effect of the Belgian income shock is less correlated with distance and has a larger effect on its contiguous neighbors. The shock now for example has a larger effect on Germany than on the closer (as measured by distance between capital cities) United Kingdom. Also the less extreme distance decay as implied by the estimated distance coefficient (compared to the exponential Hanson specification) ensures that the income shock peters out much more slowly and affects all countries in the sample in some way (Japan, with only a 0.02 per cent increase in its GDP per capita, is affected the least).

All countries are also affected when allowing for country-specific trade cost factors in the multiplicative trade cost function. However, the correlation of the income shock with distance decreases somewhat further. Moreover the estimated positive (negative) effect of being an island (land-locked or a Sub-Saharan African country), has a clear effect on the effect of the Belgian income shock. Landlocked Switzerland and Sub-Saharan Côte d'Ivoire are relatively much less affected by the income shock

---

[26] This seems to reaffirm the conclusion of Head and Mayer (2004, p. 2626) that the strong distance decay in Hanson (2005) "may be a consequence of the functional form of the distance decay function." See also Fingleton and McCann (2007).

for example, whereas island nations such as Ireland and New Zealand experience a relatively larger GDP per capita increase.

To sum up, based on the evidence in Tables 7.5a and b as well as in Figures 7.1 and 7.2, we have to conclude that the way trade costs are approximated when doing empirical work has the potential to shape the overall conclusions about the empirical relevance of NEG and thus of the strength and the geographical reach of spatial interdependencies. The lesson for future NEG research is therefore that the topic of (the approximation of) trade costs should be given much more attention (see also Combes and Lafourcade (2005) and Bosker and Garretsen (2010) for a discussion). Also the robustness of the results to the use of a particular trade cost proxy warrants much more explicit attention.

6   Conclusions

Trade costs are a crucial element of new economic geography (NEG) models; without trade costs geography does not matter. The impact of trade costs crucially determines the strength of regions' spatial interdependencies and thereby the relevance of market access. The lack of actual trade costs data hampers empirical research in NEG and it requires the approximation of trade costs. Notwithstanding the importance of trade costs in NEG models, most empirical NEG studies do not pay attention to the ramifications of the particular trade costs specification used. This chapter shows that it matters how trade costs are specified. Estimations of an NEG wage equation for a sample of eighty countries shows that the relevance of a key NEG variable, market access, and hence of spatial interdependencies hinges non-trivially upon the trade costs specification. Using two estimation strategies and various trade cost specifications, the main conclusion is that NEG needs to (re-)examine the sensitivity of its empirical findings to the handling of trade costs.

New economic geography is, of course, not the only theory around in spatial economics. But compared to urban and regional economics, NEG prides itself on the way it focuses on spatial interdependencies. These interdependencies come to the fore in the role that market access and trade costs play in NEG whereas they are for instance typically neglected in urban economics (Combes et al. 2005, p. 320). Whether spatial interdependencies and hence market access and trade costs really matter is ultimately an empirical question. This chapter argues that the answer to that (from an NEG perspective) crucial question can depend rather strongly on the empirical specification of trade costs. Future empirical research in NEG should therefore pay far more attention to the way trade costs are dealt with. Our chapter provides a useful overview of the explicit and/or implicit assumptions made when approximating trade costs, hereby facilitating the choice of trade cost approximation when doing empirical work on NEG. Just as in chapter 6 by Head and Mayer, the general message is that again that more attention should be paid to the implications of the way trade costs and its key determinants, like distance, are handled. This is no easy task as theory offers little guidance (yet) in this respect and the choices made may matter a great deal for the empirical results.

REFERENCES

Anderson, J. E. and E. van Wincoop (2004). "Trade Costs," *Journal of Economics Literature* **42**(3): 691–751.
Baier, J. and J. Bergstrand (2001). "The Growth of World Trade: Tariffs, Transport Costs, and Income Similarity," *Journal of International Economics* **53**: 1–27.
Behrens, K., C. Ertur and W. Koch (2007). "Dual Gravity: Using Spatial Econometrics to Control for Multilateral Resistance," CORE discussion paper no. 2007/59, Louvain-la-Neuve.
Bosker, E. M. (2007). "Sub-Saharan Africa's Manufacturing Trade: Trade Costs, Zeroes, and Export Orientation," mimeo, Utrecht University.
   (2008), *The Empirical Relevance of Geographical Economics*, unpublished Ph.D. thesis, Utrecht University.
Bosker, E. M. and H. Garretsen (2010). "Trade Costs in Empirical New Economic Geography," *Papers in Regional Science* (forthcoming).
Brakman, S., H. Garretsen and M. Schramm (2004). "The Spatial Distribution of Wages: Estimating the Helpman-Hanson Model for Germany," *Journal of Regional Science* **44**(3): 437–66.
   (2006). "Putting New Economic Geography to the Test," *Regional Science and Urban Economics* **36**(5): 613–35.
Breinlich, H. (2006). "The Spatial Income Structure in the European Union – What Role for Economic Geography," *Journal of Economic Geography* **6**: 593–617.
Coe, D. T., A. Subramanian, N. T. Tamirisa and R. Bhavnani (2002). "The Missing Globalization Puzzle," IMF working paper no. 02/171.
Combes, P.-P. and M. Lafourcade (2005). "Transport Cost: Measures, Determinants, and Regional Policy Implications for France," *Journal of Economic Geography* **5**: 319–49.
Combes, P.-P., G. Duranton and H. Overman (2005). "Agglomeration and the Adjustment of the Spatial Economy," *Papers in Regional Science* **84**(3): 311–49.
Fingleton, B. and P. McCann (2007). "Sinking the Iceberg? On the Treatment of Transport Costs in New Economic Geography," in B. Fingleton (ed.), *New Directions in Economic Geography*, Edward Elgar, pp. 168–204.
Fujita, M., P. Krugman and A. J. Venables (1999). *The Spatial Economy*, Cambridge, MA: MIT Press.
Hanson, G. (2005). "Market Potential, Increasing Returns and Geographic Concentration," *Journal of International Economics* **67**(1): 1–24.

Head, K. and T. Mayer (2004). "The Empirics of Agglomeration and Trade," in V. Henderson and J.-F. Thisse (eds.) *The Handbook of Regional and Urban Economics*, volume IV, Amsterdam: North-Holland, pp. 2609–65.

(2006). "Regional Wage and Employment Responses to Market Potential in the EU," *Regional Science and Urban Economics* **36**(5): 573–94.

Head, K. and J. Ries (2001). "Increasing Returns versus National Product Differentiation as an Explanation for the Pattern of US – Canada Trade," *American Economic Review* **91**(4): 858–76.

Helliwell, J. and A.-C. Verdier (2001). "Measuring Internal Trade Distances: A New Method Applied to Estimate Provincial Border Effects in Canada," *Canadian Journal of Economics* **34**: 1024–41.

Helpman, E., M. Melitz and Y. Rubinstein (2007). "Estimating Trade Flows: Trading Partners and Trading Volumes," NBER working paper no. 12927, Cambridge, MA.

Hering, L. and S. Poncet (2006). "Market Access Impact on Individual Wages: Evidence from China," working paper, CEPII.

Hummels, D. (1999). "Have International Transportation Costs Declined?" manuscript, University of Chicago.

(2001). "Toward a Geography of Trade Costs," mimeo, Purdue University.

Knaap, T. (2006). "Trade, Location, and Wages in the United States," *Regional Science and Urban Economics* **36**(5): 595–612.

Krugman, P. (1991). "Increasing Returns and Economic Geography," *Journal of Political Economy* **3**: 483–99.

(1995). *Development Geography and Economic Theory*, Cambridge, MA: MIT Press.

Limao, N. and A. J. Venables (2001). "Infrastructure, Geographical Disadvantage, Transport Costs, and Trade," *The World Bank Economic Review* **15**: 451–79.

McCann, P. (2001). "A Proof of the Relationship between Optimal Vehicle Size, Haulage Length and the Structure of Distance-Transport Costs," *Transportation Research*, **35A**: 671–93.

(2005). "Transport Costs and New Economic Geography," *Journal of Economic Geography* **5**: 305–18.

Mion, G. (2004). "Spatial Externalities and Empirical Analysis: The Case of Italy," *Journal of Urban Economics* **56**: 97–118.

Puga, D. (1999). "The Rise and Fall of Regional Inequalities," *European Economic Review* **43**: 303–34.

Redding, S. and A. J. Venables (2004). "Economic Geography and International Inequality," *Journal of International Economics* **62**(1): 53–82.

Santos Silva, J. and S. Tenreyro (2006). "The Log of Gravity," *The Review of Economics and Statistics* **88**: 641–58.

Venables, A. J. (1996). "Equilibrium Locations of Vertically Linked Industries," *International Economic Review* **37**: 341–59.

APPENDIX

Countries included			
Albania	Egypt	Latvia	Portugal
Algeria	El Salvador	Lithuania	Romania
Argentina	Estonia	Macau	Russia
Armenia*	Ethiopia*	Macedonia	Saint Lucia
Australia	Finland	Malawi*	Senegal
Austria	France	Malaysia	Singapore
Bahamas*	Germany	Malta	Slovakia
Bangladesh*	Greece	Mauritius	Slovenia
Barbados*	Guatemala*	Mexico	South Africa
Belgium	Honduras	Moldova*	Spain
Bolivia	Hong Kong	Mongolia	Sri Lanka*
Brazil	Hungary	Morocco	Sweden
Bulgaria	Iceland	Nepal*	Switzerland
Cameroon	India	Netherlands	Taiwan
Canada	Indonesia	New Zealand	Tanzania
Cape Verde*	Ireland	Niger	Thailand
Chile	Israel	Nigeria	Trinidad and Tobago*
China	Italy	Norway	Tunisia
Colombia	Japan	Oman	Turkey
Costa Rica	Jordan*	Pakistan*	United Kingdom
Côte d'Ivoire	Kenya*	Panama	United States of America
Cyprus	Korea	Peru	Uruguay
Czech Republic	Kuwait*	Philippines	Venezuela
Denmark	Kyrgyzstan	Poland	Zimbabwe*
Ecuador			

Note: * means the country is excluded in the wage equation estimation.

8   Intangible barriers to international trade

A sectoral approach

L. J. Möhlmann, S. Ederveen, H. L. F. de Groot, and
G.-J. M. Linders

1   Introduction

International trade flows have increased impressively in the last few decades. Data from the United Nations, which have been edited by Feenstra *et al.* (2005), suggest that the aggregate nominal value of reported international trade increased from about US$130 billion in 1962 to more than US$6.5 trillion in 2000. This corresponds to an annual growth rate close to 11 per cent. With an estimated world population of about 6 billion in 2000, this implies that international trade per capita was over US$1,000 or about 15 per cent of the average Gross Domestic Product (GDP) per capita.

The growing importance of international trade has led to an increased need for sound analyses of its determinants. The gravity model has been the workhorse model to explain international trade flows for nearly half a century now. The main idea behind this model is that the magnitude of bilateral trade flows can be explained by the economic size of the two trading countries and the distance between them (Deardorff 1998). The model has sound theoretical foundations, yields almost invariantly plausible parameter estimates, and has a strong explanatory power.

Although the basic framework of the gravity model is unaltered throughout the years, new insights have contributed to its increasing popularity by improving its theoretical underpinnings (see, e.g. Feenstra 2004) and addressing econometric issues concerning the correct specification of the model (see, e.g., Anderson and van Wincoop 2004). These include the correct specification of the multilateral resistance (price) effect, the specification of panel gravity equations, and the treatment of zero-valued bilateral trade flows.

We are grateful to Andrés Rodríguez-Pose, an anonymous referee, and participants of the 2007 conference "The Gravity Equation – Or: Why the World is Not Flat" in Groningen for useful comments on an earlier version of this chapter. The usual disclaimer applies.

Despite the rapid growth of trade and the popular discussions on the "death of distance" (e.g., Cairncross 1997; Friedman 2005), many studies estimating gravity equations of bilateral trade confirm that the impact of geographic distance is still substantial and has not shown a clear tendency to decline over time (e.g. Linders 2006; Disdier and Head 2008). Thus, distance still matters for the patterns of trade. Given the decline in transport and communication costs over time, this finding provides support for the view that intangible trade barriers are persistent and are important in explaining the resistance to trade (Obstfeld and Rogoff 2000; Anderson and van Wincoop 2004).

Substantiating the effect of intangible trade barriers has been another important recent extension of the gravity model. Most of the early gravity model studies consider only geographical distance. However, it is likely that there are significant additional costs involved in trading besides transport costs. Deardorff (2004) suggests that the current amount of global trade is far below the level that would prevail if transport costs were the only costs of trading. Furthermore, Trefler (1995) and Davis et al. (1997) find that the factor proportions theory of trade would predict trade flows that are missing from actual observations. They argue that home bias in preferences may explain this "mystery of missing trade." But the missing trade flows might also partly originate from alternative dimensions of distance in trade. These other dimensions of distance could include cultural and institutional distances. Den Butter and Mosch (2003) and Anderson and van Wincoop (2004) state that the transaction costs of trading can include many aspects including transport costs, tariffs, search costs, information costs regarding the product and the reliability of the trading partner, and contract enforcement costs. These transaction costs are likely to increase with cultural dissimilarities between countries because firms will have less knowledge about foreign cultures and markets. Moreover, the costs of negotiation will be higher when the trading partners do not speak the same language (see Anderson and Marcouiller 2002). This is why more recent studies include measures for cultural and institutional distance (see, for example, den Butter and Mosch 2003; de Groot et al. 2004; Linders et al. 2005) in their gravity model specifications.

What has remained unchanged in the application of the gravity model is the strong focus on total trade flows. This is surprising, as there are good reasons to believe that the effects of distance and GDP on the value of bilateral trade differ between different product groups. An important exception is the seminal study by Rauch (1999) in which a network/search view of international trade is developed. He argues that search costs present a major barrier to trade in differentiated products, whereas distance only increases transport costs for trade in homogeneous products without principally preventing trade. These hypotheses are empirically tested by estimating models for both homogeneous and heterogeneous products, providing empirical support for the hypotheses.

In this study we build on the work of Rauch (1999) by estimating the gravity model for different product groups. We improve and extend his empirical work in a number of directions. First, we incorporate recent econometric insights. More specifically, we use the Heckman selection model to estimate the gravity equation. This model is able to deal with zero trade flows in a more satisfactory way, which becomes particularly relevant when studying disaggregate trade because of the increased absence of trade of specific products between pairs of countries. Second, we use a broader view on the different dimensions of distance. Rauch (1999) hypothesises that networks are an important factor in trade transactions and that a common language or a shared colonial history will make networks more likely to exist. Besides geographical distance, Rauch uses a dummy variable indicating whether two countries share a common language or a shared colonial history to test this view. However, this variable does not capture the idea that transaction costs increase when firms have less knowledge about foreign cultures and markets due to cultural differences. In this study we include additional cultural indicators to test this hypothesis as well. Third, we explore the importance of using different product categories for the parameters of the gravity equation. For that purpose we extend the analysis of Rauch by exploring the impact on different sectors of the economy and on specific products. In addition we use data covering a more recent time period (viz. 2000).

The remainder of this chapter is organized as follows. The next section discusses the basic concept of the gravity model for bilateral trade. Section 3 elaborates on the importance of intangible barriers to trade, with a special focus on cultural and institutional distance. Data and estimation method are discussed in Section 4. Section 5 presents the results. This section consists of three parts. The first part strictly follows the distinction made by Rauch (1999) between homogeneous and heterogeneous products and considers the impact of more recent data and different estimation techniques on the key results obtained by Rauch. The second part focuses on the importance of intangible barriers to trade. The last part applies the gravity model to more detailed product groups. Finally, Section 6 presents the conclusions and provides some further discussion.

2   The gravity model in international trade

The gravity model of bilateral trade has become the workhorse model of applied international economics (Eichengreen and Irwin 1998). It was originally inspired by Newton's gravity equation in physics, in which the gravitational forces exerted between two bodies depend on their mass and distance. The basic idea of gravity can be used to model spatial interaction in social sciences as well. The gravity model has been used extensively in regional science to describe and analyze spatial flows of information, goods, and persons (see, e.g., Greenwood 1975; Nijkamp and Reggiani 1992; Isard 1999), and was pioneered in the analysis of international trade by Tinbergen (1962), Pöyhönen (1963) and Linnemann (1966).

The traditional gravity model relates bilateral trade flows to the GDP levels of the countries and their geographic distance. The levels of GDP reflect the market size in both countries, as a measure of "economic mass." The market size of the importing country reflects the potential demand for bilateral imports, while GDP in the exporting country represents the potential supply of goods from that country; geographic distance reflects resistance to bilateral trade. The familiar functional form from physics is then used to relate bilateral trade to these variables of economic mass and distance.

Usually, the gravity equation is expressed in logarithmic form, for the purpose of empirical estimation. The extended gravity equation, used in estimation, then looks as follows:

$$\ln T_{ij} = \ln K + \alpha \ln Y_{ij} + \beta \ln y_{ij} + \lambda \ln D_{ij} + \delta M_{ij} + \theta_1 CD_{ij}$$
$$+ \theta_2 ID_{ij} + \varepsilon_{ij}, \tag{8.1}$$

where T_{ij} stands for exports from country i to country j; K is a scalar; Y_{ij} and y_{ij} represent the product of GDP and GDP per capita of country i and j; and D_{ij}, CD_{ij}, and ID_{ij} reflect physical, cultural, and institutional distance between the countries. The matrix M_{ij} contains additional variables that may affect the ease of trading bilaterally, such as a common border, linguistic or colonial links, and common trade bloc membership (such as the EU and NAFTA). In specifying this basic structure of the model, we largely follow the model set out in Rauch (1999). In estimating the model, we conform as much as possible to the country sample of Rauch (1999). This serves to facilitate the comparison of results. Our key parameters of interest are θ_1 and θ_2, capturing the effect of, respectively, cultural and institutional distance on trade. Finally, ε_{ij} is a disturbance term that reflects the impact of other factors (assumed orthogonal) that have not been included in the model.

The recent literature has provided extensions to the theoretical foundations of the gravity model (see, for example, Anderson and van Wincoop 2003; Feenstra 2004; Anderson, this volume). This has resulted in a modification of the gravity equation (8.1), to account for omitted variable bias related to the omission of multilateral resistance terms P_i and P_j, which are themselves a function of all regressor variables (e.g. Y_k, Y_l, M_{kl}, and D_{kl}) for all countries k and l.

The resulting equation, also indicated as the theoretical gravity equation, is of the form:

$$\ln T_{ij} = \ln K + \alpha \ln Y_{ij} + \beta \ln y_{ij} + \lambda \ln D_{ij} + \delta M_{ij} + \theta_1 CD_{ij}$$

$$+ \theta_2 ID_{ij} - \ln P_i^{1-\sigma} - \ln P_j^{1-\sigma} + \varepsilon_{ij}, \tag{8.2}$$

where σ stands for a preference parameter (in the theoretical derivations equal to the elasticity of substitution between goods from different countries). Because the logged multilateral resistance terms are non-linear functions of the variables and parameters in the model, this gravity equation cannot be estimated by OLS. A number of solutions has been proposed for estimation. In our analysis, we will proceed in line with Feenstra (2004) to estimate a gravity equation in which the multilateral resistance terms are estimated as country-specific fixed effects. We assume that trade costs are symmetric, implying that we assume the existence of a single country-specific multilateral resistance term for each country.[1]

3   Multidimensional distance: institutions, culture, and trade

The point of departure for our analysis is the observation that trade costs are important to understand the patterns of bilateral trade. Bilateral resistance to trade can arise from formal barriers (tariffs, NTBs) and transport costs, but also from informal barriers such as differences in institutional quality and in cultural norms and values. Moreover, these barriers to trade may be more important for some products than for others. This chapter focuses on these intangible barriers to trade, and asks the question: "Do institutional and cultural distance affect trade differentially across different (groups of) products?"

3.1   *The network view on trade*

To understand how trade patterns evolve, recent research points at the importance of networks, rather than atomistic markets (e.g. Rauch 1999,

---

[1] Allowing for asymmetric trade costs (and hence for different multilateral resistance terms for exports and imports) does not lead to major changes in the OLS estimation results. With the Heckman selection model we had to rely on a single indicator of multilateral resistance per country for technical reasons.

2001). The search/network view starts from the observation that a majority of products is not traded on organized exchanges. Therefore, search processes are important in order to match buyers and sellers. Networks serve to facilitate the search for suitable trade partners. As a result, understanding the characteristics and development of networks is important to explain the observed patterns of trade.

Rauch (1999) classifies products according to product type. Homogeneous products differ from differentiated goods in the use of "markets" as opposed to "networks" for exchange. Homogeneous goods can be compared exclusively on the basis of price differences. Several homogeneous products are traded on an organized exchange where supply and demand are directly matched. Many other homogeneous products are sold on a decentralized market where the "invisible hand" of the price mechanism takes care of coordination. Although not frictionless, matching resembles a perfectly competitive centralized market, where the comparison is based on prices as the only relevant characteristic. For these products, reference prices are often published, illustrating that the price mechanism guides allocation through the possibility for international arbitrage of price differences. Differentiated products cannot be compared on the basis of prices alone. Price differences must be adjusted for differences in characteristics and quality between the varieties. The relative importance of the various characteristics differs across countries depending on the available supply and preferences that prevail (Rauch 1999). In the end, each variety has its own unique blend of characteristics. The product is "branded," and has its own supplier. Because of the difficulty of comparing differentiated products, they cannot be traded on organized exchanges. Moreover, information costs are so high that international arbitrage by specialized traders across varieties is not feasible either. Instead, differentiated products are traded through networks by search and match between traders, customers, and suppliers. Rauch (1999) argues that the process of search is facilitated by factors that improve the information flow and knowledge of foreign markets. He refers to shared language, colonial links, and geographical proximity as search-enabling factors, because they increase bilateral familiarity and decrease "psychic distance" (see Frankel 1997).

Rauch (1999) identifies three product groups that reflect the "network versus market" distinction in trade. Homogeneous products comprise two groups: products traded on an organized exchange and reference-priced articles; the third group consists of differentiated goods. The network theory of trade hypothesizes that search costs are most important for the pattern of trade in differentiated products and least important for organized-exchange products.

3.2   Insecurity of property and trade

An alternative explanation for unobserved trade costs focuses on variation in institutional effectiveness across countries. A poor institutional environment, in terms of property rights protection and contract enforceability, entails negative externalities for private transactions and consequently raises transaction costs. As a result, the quality of governance is an important determinant of economic growth and development (see, e.g., Olson 1996). Institutional economics has recently been extended into the field of international economics (e.g. Wei 2000; Anderson and Marcouiller 2002; Dixit 2004). This approach states that insecurity of property and contract enforcement imposes high costs on trade. Rodrik (2000) argues that the transaction-costs problem of contract enforcement is aggravated for international trade, compared to domestic exchange. International trade involves at least two jurisdictions, which makes contract enforcement more difficult. This discontinuity in the political and legal system increases uncertainty and the risk of opportunistic behavior by either party to the exchange. Accordingly, differences in the effectiveness of legal and policy systems in providing law and order, securing contract enforcement and facilitating trade is an important determinant of bilateral trade costs. Besides the level of the quality of institutions, the similarities of institutions between two countries could also affect bilateral trade costs. With more similar institutions enforcement of international contracts is easier and uncertainty is reduced (see, for example, de Groot *et al.* 2004).

In this chapter, we investigate whether the impact of differences in institutional quality on bilateral trade depends on the type of product that is being traded. We would generally expect the costs of insecurity and differences in contract enforceability to be lowest for organized-exchange products. Specialized traders can diversify systemic risk of opportunistic behavior by ordering from many different suppliers, without any concern left for final customers. For reference-priced commodities, the need for more case-specific search raises search costs and creates an incentive to enter into closer relations. Trade will increasingly avoid environments with very different institutional settings. The largest effect is expected for trade in differentiated goods.

3.3   Cultural differences as trade barrier

Many studies have extended the basic trade-flow gravity equation with (dummy) variables indicating whether the trading partners share a common language, religion, and/or colonial past (e.g. Geraci and Prewo 1977;

Boisso and Ferrantino 1997; Frankel 1997; Yeyati 2003; Guiso *et al.* 2004). Most studies find that these variables have significant positive effects on the magnitude of international trade flows. Although this indicates that these variables matter, they only capture cultural familiarity, in the sense that the trading partners will have more knowledge of each other's culture and will find it easier to communicate and share information (Rauch 1999, 2001).

We go beyond cultural familiarity by focusing on cultural distance, which is defined as the extent to which the shared norms and values in one country differ from those in another (Kogut and Singh 1988; Hofstede 2001). It is generally acknowledged that a large cultural distance raises the costs of international trade, as significant cultural differences make it difficult to understand, control, and predict the behavior of others (Elsass and Veiga 1994). This complicates interactions (Parkhe 1991), thus impeding the realization of business deals. Some of the most notable difficulties associated with cross-cultural interaction include those associated with understanding, and particularly those associated with differences in perceptions of the same situation. Differences in perceptions complicate interactions, make them prone to fail, and hinder the development of rapport and trust, which are factors that generally facilitate the interaction process and lower the costs of trade (Neal 1998). This suggests that a large cultural distance between countries reduces the amount of trade between them.

However, cultural differences can also have a positive impact on trade. When entering foreign markets, companies have to decide whether to export products to another country or open a factory to start local production. The tradeoff between producing locally and producing at a single site to benefit from scale advantages is known as the proximity-concentration tradeoff. The literature on trade and horizontal foreign direct investment (FDI) suggests that the tradeoff between various modes of serving foreign markets may result in a positive effect of cultural and institutional distance on trade (Brainard 1997; Helpman *et al.* 2004). An increase in cultural distance is likely to raise the costs of bilateral FDI more than the costs of bilateral trade, because FDI involves a higher stake in the local foreign market. Resource commitment, in the form of asset specific investments, is higher for FDI than for trade. Moreover, cultural differences are likely to affect the variable costs of direct local presence via FDI more than the cost of trading, as the transaction costs of managing and producing locally are relatively more substantial. If the costs resulting from cultural differences rise, companies may therefore prefer to focus on exports rather than FDI. This may lead to a substitution of local presence by trade. The total effect of cultural distance on trade then consists of a direct, negative effect and a positive substitution effect from FDI to trade. The total effect could therefore be either positive or negative.[2]

Cultural diversity can also have a positive influence on international trade through specialization. Wherever there are big differences between countries, there are larger opportunities for specializing in the production of specific goods, which can be exchanged via international trade. In the end, the effect of cultural distance on trade is an empirical question.

4   Data and estimation method

4.1   Trade data

As the dependent variable we use bilateral exports between two countries measured in thousands of US dollars. For this variable we used the database compiled by Feenstra *et al.* (2005), which is based on trade data from the United Nations. The database covers bilateral trade between 1962 and 2000. For the purpose of this study only cross-section data are required, so we only used data for the year 2000.

The data are classified according to the Standard International Trade Classification (SITC) revision 2 at the four-digit level. The SITC is a system that provides codes for product types. At the four-digit level there can be a maximum of 10,000 different codes. In practice there are less than 10,000 because not all numbers are being used.

To compare our results with those of Rauch (1999) we used the same set of countries as he did, as far as possible. The fifty-five remaining countries are listed in the Appendix. It is possible that the value of a trade flow reported by the exporter differs from the trade flow reported by the importer. When this is the case the value reported by the importer is used because these data are generally more reliable (Feenstra *et al.* 2005). When there is no record from the importing country available we use the record from the exporting country.

According to the database, the total amount of trade in 2000 between the fifty-five countries used in this study was about US$5.3 trillion. The three Rauch groups, viz. differentiated goods (N), reference priced goods (R), and goods that are traded on an organized exchange (W) account

---

[2] Export and FDI can be substitutes in case of horizontal FDI (sales to the local market). Although the bulk of FDI is horizontal in nature (see, for example, Brakman *et al.* in this volume), vertical FDI has increased due to fragmentation of production. In this case, trade and FDI act as complements. Hence we would expect a negative effect of cultural and institutional distance on both vertical FDI and trade. Therefore, this type of FDI does not lead to a positive substitution effect from FDI to trade. A similar reasoning applies to international outsourcing and resulting trade.

Table 8.1. *Shares of differentiated goods, reference priced goods, and goods traded on organized exchanges in one-digit SITC product groups*

Product group	Trade value billions US$		Share of N in %		Share of R in %		Share of W in %		Share of not classified %	
0: food and live animals	282	[5]	19	[2]	46	[15]	34	[17]	1	[1]
1: beverages and tobacco	46	[1]	10	[0]	79	[4]	9	[1]	2	[0]
2: crude materials, inedible, except fuels	178	[3]	31	[2]	48	[10]	21	[7]	0	[0]
3: mineral fuels, lubricants and related materials	430	[8]	1	[0]	12	[6]	78	[60]	9	[7]
4: animal and vegetable oils, fats and waxes	14	[0]	9	[0]	10	[0]	63	[2]	18	[0]
5: chemicals and related products	513	[10]	46	[7]	53	[32]	1	[1]	0	[0]
6: manufactured goods	721	[14]	45	[10]	39	[33]	9	[12]	7	[10]
7: machinery and transport equipment	2,310	[44]	85	[59]	0	[0]	0	[0]	15	[66]
8: miscellaneous manufactured articles	697	[13]	95	[20]	0	[0]	0	[0]	5	[7]
9: commodities and transactions n.e.s.	101	[2]	50	[2]	0	[0]	5	[1]	45	[9]
Total	5,292	[100]	64	[100]	16	[100]	10	[100]	10	[100]

Notes: N = Differentiated goods, R = Reference priced goods, and W = goods traded on an organized exchange. Numbers between square brackets show the importance (in percentages) of each one-digit SITC group for the whole category, whereas the main figures in each column show the total value of trade for each four-digit SITC-group and its subdivision in per cent. For example, when we look at SITC-group 0, total trade value is 282 billion, which can be subdivided in 19% N, 46% R, 34% W, and 1% not classified. Trade in the SITC-group 0 accounts for 5% of total trade, 2% of N, 15% of R, 17% of W, and 1% of not classified.

for, respectively, 64 per cent, 16 per cent, and 10 per cent of total trade. These shares do not add up to 100 per cent, because not all four-digit SITC codes are attributed to one of the three categories. Table 8.1 shows information on total trade flows, classified according to one-digit SITC codes and the three Rauch groups.

Table 8.1 reveals that SITC group 7 (machinery and transport equipment) is by far the most important SITC group in terms of trade: 44 per cent of total trade value is in this category. As the whole group falls under the category of heterogeneous products, it even accounts for almost 60 per cent of total trade in heterogeneous products. Second largest are the manufactured goods (SITC 6), which are more or less equally divided over the heterogeneous and reference priced goods. Manufactured goods together with chemicals (SITC 5) are the most important reference priced goods and cover about two-thirds of trade in that category. Goods traded on world exchange are predominantly mineral fuels (SITC 3, 60 per cent).

4.2   Multidimensional distance

A main contribution of our analysis of trade patterns at the product group level is the introduction of multiple dimensions of distance, with an explicit distinction between cultural and institutional differences. We use these distance measures in addition to the links variable used by Rauch (1999), which indicates whether or not two countries share a language or have colonial ties.

Regarding the role of cultural differences, previous research has typically used measures of cultural *(un)familiarity*, such as dummy variables indicating whether the trading partners share a common language, religion, and colonial past (e.g. Srivastava and Green 1986; Anderson and Marcouiller 2002; de Groot *et al.* 2004). We also distinguish the separate effect of cultural *(dis)similarity* across countries, which is based on the well-established cultural framework of Hofstede (1980, 2001). Our measure for cultural distance combines its four original cultural dimensions: (i) power distance, (ii) uncertainty avoidance, (iii) individualism, and (iv) masculinity.[3] Cultural distance captures the extent of differences in norms and values between countries, and hence allows us to go beyond more traditional measures of cultural familiarity.

Previous research has measured the institutional dissimilarity between trading partners through a dummy variable indicating whether the partners had comparable governance quality levels (de Groot *et al.* 2004). We apply a measure that captures the *extent* to which these quality levels differ. Institutional distance is calculated on the basis of a database compiled by Kaufmann *et al.* (2003). They combined cross-country indicators on governance from different sources in a factor analysis, and constructed six indicators for the quality of institutions. These indicators are (i) voice

---

[3] Later Hofstede added long-term orientation as a fifth dimension, but this dimension is available for only a few countries and therefore not included here.

and accountability, (ii) political stability, (iii) government effectiveness, (iv) regulatory quality, (v) rule of law, and (vi) control of corruption.
Bilateral cultural and institutional distance are both measured using the Kogut-Singh (1988) index. This index provides a single comparative measure based on the differences between two countries in multiple dimensions. It is constructed by taking a weighted average of the squared difference in each dimension. With D distinct dimensions this yields:

$$KS_{ij} = \frac{1}{D} \sum_{d=1}^{D} \frac{(S_{di} - S_{dj})^2}{V_d}, \tag{8.3}$$

where KS_{ij} is the (Kogut-Singh) distance variable, S_{di} is the value of dimension d for country i, S_{dj} is the value of dimension d for country j, and V_d is the sample variance in dimension d.
A complete description of the data and data sources of all variables included in our gravity model is provided in the Appendix.

4.3   Estimation method

Although most countries do trade with each other, they do not necessarily trade in every product category. Given our focus on trade at a disaggregate level, this implies that there is a number of zero trade flows in our sample. Simply neglecting the zero flows may seriously bias the results of an OLS regression analysis based on a log-linear transformation of the gravity equation. The fifty-five countries from our sample have 2,752 bilateral trade flows, out of a possible 2,916. When only the products traded on organized exchanges are considered, only 2,265 country pairs with a positive trade flow remain. This amount of zero flows can get much larger as more specific product groups are considered. At a one-digit SITC level as much as 60 per cent (SITC 4) of the country pairs do not trade.
In order to address the potential bias caused by the neglect of zero flows, we estimate a sample selection model to take into account zero-valued bilateral trade flows in the sample. This model, also known as the Tobit II model (Verbeek 2004), specifies a probit selection equation for the decision whether or not to trade, in addition to the standard log-linear gravity equation that models the volume of bilateral trade.[4]

---

[4] Alternatively, some authors estimate the gravity model using Poisson regression (e.g. Santos Silva and Tenreyro 2006). However, Poisson regression pertains mostly to a context in which data are counts, rather than (essentially continuous) monetary values. Furthermore, Poisson estimation does not work well if outcomes are (very) large. So far, the discussion on the appropriateness and value-added of Poisson methods in this context

236 Möhlmann *et al.*

Economic reasoning suggests that the selection equation should at least contain those explanatory variables also included in the gravity equation. The sample selection model can be estimated using two different approaches. First, the parameters in both parts of the model can be jointly estimated using maximum likelihood. Alternatively, the model can be estimated in two steps (Heckman 1979). The first step estimates a probit selection equation using maximum likelihood. From the parameter estimates in the selection equation, we can compute the inverse Mill's ratio for each country pair, denoted λ_{ij} (also known as Heckman's lambda). If we include Heckman's lambda as an additional regressor in the second-stage estimation of the gravity equation, the remaining residual is uncorrelated with the selection outcome, and the gravity model parameters can be estimated consistently with OLS. The parameter estimated for Heckman's lambda in the second-stage regression captures initial selection bias in the residual of the gravity equation.

In our estimations, we use the first approach, based on full maximum likelihood estimation of the parameters in the sample selection model. There are two reasons for this, as described by Verbeek (2004). First, the two-step estimator is generally inefficient and the OLS regression provides incorrect standard errors, because the remaining residual is heteroskedastic, and λ_{ij} is not directly observed but estimated from the first-stage regression equation. Second, the two-step approach will not work very well if λ_{ij} varies only to a limited extent across observations and is close to being linear in the regressors. This is related to potential identification problems that occur if the explanatory variables in the selection and regression equation are identical. In this case, the two-stage sample selection model is only identified because λ_{ij} is a non-linear function of the regressors whereas these regressors enter (log-) linearly in the gravity equation (see Vella 1998). The full maximum likelihood estimation provides an integrated approach to estimate the parameters in both the selection and regression equations, instead of relying on the second-stage estimation of an extended (log-) linear gravity equation using OLS. To conform to earlier empirical applications in trade modeling, we have included an additional regressor in the selection equation nevertheless.

On the matter of identification, Verbeek (2004, p. 232) notes that: "the inclusion of [regressor] variables in [the selection equation] in addition to

---

remains an open issue in the literature. See, for example, Martinez-Zarzoso *et al.* (2007) for a critique of Poisson regression in the context of modeling bilateral trade patterns. Therefore, we prefer to pertain to the conventional log-linear specification and concomitant estimation methods, using a selection model to explicitly acknowledge the special nature of zero flows.

those [already in the regression model] can be important for identification in the second step," but adds: "often there are no natural candidates and any choice is easily criticized." We follow Helpman *et al.* (2007) in using an indicator for common religion as an additional regressor in the selection equation for this purpose. However, if this regressor is incorrectly omitted from the gravity equation, the estimation results may suffer from omitted variables bias and lead to spurious conclusions on the existence of sample selection bias (Verbeek 2004). To perform some sensitivity analysis on the implied exclusion restriction with respect to the religion variable, we also estimate a sample selection model including the religion indicator in the gravity equation as well.

5   Results

This section discusses the results of our analyses. Section 5.1 updates the analysis by Rauch (1999) by (i) considering a more recent time period and (ii) applying recently developed estimation techniques. Section 5.2 then continues by elaborating on the importance of other intangible barriers to trade. In Section 5.3, we look at more disaggregate product groups.

5.1   An update of Rauch (1999)

The results in Table 8.2 are obtained using a specification similar to that used by Rauch (1999). Our analysis is based on data for 2000, whereas Rauch used data for 1990. A minor difference in specification is that we include a generic dummy for common trade bloc membership while Rauch (1999) included a dummy for common membership of the EEC and for common membership of the EFTA. Table 8.2 shows the results for the total amount of trade, the trade in heterogeneous goods (N), trade in referenced priced goods (R), and trade in goods which are traded on organized exchanges (W). The coefficients are estimated using Ordinary Least Squares (OLS) with a balanced sample. Only the country pairs that have a positive amount in all four groups are included in the analysis. From the 2,970 possible country pairs, 2,142 (72 per cent) have a positive amount of trade in each of these categories.

The results in Table 8.2 are comparable with those obtained by Rauch (1999) for the year 1990, which is the most recent year he used. The explained variation of trade is of the same order of magnitude, ranging from around 0.4 for homogeneous goods to around 0.7 for heterogeneous goods and aggregate trade. Also the signs and sizes of the estimated coefficients are comparable. We find a similar pattern for the GDP and per capita GDP coefficients, which tend to decrease as one moves from trade

Table 8.2. *An update of Rauch's analysis – I*

Dependent variable:	ln(total trade value)	ln(trade value N)	ln(trade value R)	ln(trade value W)
Specification	Total Rauch	Differentiated Rauch	Reference priced Rauch	Organized exchange Rauch
ln(GDP product)	0.83***	0.96***	0.81***	0.74***
	(0.01)	(0.02)	(0.02)	(0.02)
ln(per capita GDP product)	0.57***	0.74***	0.51***	0.16***
	(0.02)	(0.03)	(0.03)	(0.04)
ln(distance)	−0.66***	−0.81***	−0.67***	−0.66***
	(0.03)	(0.04)	(0.03)	(0.05)
Adjacency	0.22**	−0.03	0.33***	0.75***
	(0.11)	(0.15)	(0.10)	(0.17)
Links	0.56***	0.66***	0.60***	0.61***
	(0.06)	(0.08)	(0.08)	(0.10)
Common trade bloc membership	0.68***	0.78***	0.89***	0.82***
	(0.05)	(0.07)	(0.07)	(0.10)
Method	OLS	OLS	OLS	OLS
Country dummies	No	No	No	No
R^2-Adjusted	0.75	0.69	0.67	0.40
Total observations	2,142	2,142	2,142	2,142

Notes: Robust standard errors in parentheses. Statistical significance at a 10%, 5% or 1% level is indicated by *, ** or ***, respectively.

in heterogeneous goods towards trade in goods that are traded on organized exchanges. However, we do not find a clear pattern for the effect of links. The size of the adjacency effect is clearly increasing as the products become more homogeneous. For goods traded on organized exchanges the adjacency effect is particularly high.

In Table 8.3 we expand the previous analysis by adding country-specific dummies to control for country-specific multilateral trade resistance, consistent with Anderson and van Wincoop (2003). The effects of GDP and distance tend to increase whereas the effect of a common trade bloc membership decreases. The effect of links now also has a clear pattern, being high for heterogeneous goods and relatively small for goods traded on organized exchanges. It is also interesting to see that the effect of sharing a common border becomes much smaller for referenced price goods and for goods traded on organized exchanges. At the same time, distance decay becomes more pronounced. The estimators for distance and for the adjacency dummy are closely related to each other, as the positive

Table 8.3. *An update of Rauch's analysis – II (including country dummies)*

Dependent variable:	ln(total trade value)	ln(trade value N)	ln(trade value R)	ln(trade value W)
	Total	Differentiated	Reference priced	Organized exchange
Specification	Rauch + country dummies	Rauch + country dummies	Rauch + country dummies	Rauch + country dummies
ln(GDP product)	0.79***	0.90***	0.85***	0.73***
	(0.03)	(0.04)	(0.03)	(0.05)
ln(per capita GDP product)	1.04***	1.22***	0.69***	0.68***
	(0.05)	(0.06)	(0.06)	(0.09)
ln(distance)	−0.72***	−0.78***	−0.86***	−0.95***
	(0.04)	(0.05)	(0.05)	(0.07)
Adjacency	0.23*	0.17	0.14	0.37*
	(0.13)	(0.16)	(0.13)	(0.20)
Links	0.53***	0.66***	0.60***	0.36***
	(0.07)	(0.08)	(0.08)	(0.12)
Common trade bloc membership	0.60***	0.68***	0.64***	0.69***
	(0.06)	(0.08)	(0.08)	(0.12)
Method	OLS	OLS	OLS	OLS
Country dummies	54	54	54	54
R^2-Adjusted	0.82	0.78	0.76	0.49
Total observations	2,142	2,142	2,142	2,142

Notes: Robust standard errors in parentheses. Statistical significance at a 10%, 5% or 1% level is indicated by *, ** or ***, respectively.

result for a common border is partly caused by mismeasurement of the distance (Head and Mayer, this volume). This may suggest that the distance effect can be estimated more accurately, or that the functional form works better when including country dummies.

We now apply the sample selection model instead of OLS. The results are depicted in Table 8.4. The use of the selection model only marginally changes the results.

There is a clear pattern present for five variables: GDP, GDP per capita, distance, links, and common trade bloc membership. The GDP coefficient for differentiated goods (0.88) is higher than for referenced priced goods (0.85) and for goods traded at organized exchanges (0.72). A similar pattern was found by Rauch (1999). The pattern for the GDP per capita is even more pronounced, ranging from 1.26 for heterogeneous goods to 0.65 for homogeneous goods. This suggests that heterogeneous goods are income elastic while homogeneous goods are income

Table 8.4. *An update of Rauch's analysis – III (Heckman selection model)*

Dependent variable:	Ln(total trade value)	ln(trade value N)	ln(trade value R)	ln(trade value W)
Specification	Total Rauch + country dummies	Differentiated Rauch + country dummies	Reference priced Rauch + country dummies	Organized exchange Rauch + country dummies
ln(GDP product)	0.82***	0.88***	0.85***	0.72***
	(0.03)	(0.04)	(0.03)	(0.06)
ln(per capita GDP product)	1.09***	1.26***	0.67***	0.65***
	(0.06)	(0.07)	(0.06)	(0.10)
ln(distance)	−0.85***	−0.81***	−0.92***	−0.95***
	(0.04)	(0.05)	(0.05)	(0.08)
Adjacency	0.08	0.12	0.06	0.39*
	(0.14)	(0.16)	(0.15)	(0.23)
Links	0.61***	0.69***	0.63***	0.31**
	(0.07)	(0.08)	(0.08)	(0.12)
Common trade bloc membership	0.56***	0.63***	0.65***	0.71***
	(0.08)	(0.09)	(0.08)	(0.13)
Method	Heckman	Heckman	Heckman	Heckman
Country dummies	54	54	54	54
Uncensored obs.	2,752	2,627	2,586	2,265
Censored obs.	164	289	330	651

Notes: Robust standard errors in parentheses. Statistical significance at a 10%, 5% or 1% level is indicated by *, ** or ***, respectively.

inelastic. Since we use the product of GDP per capita of the exporter and the importer, it is also possible that high-income countries export relatively more heterogeneous goods than homogeneous goods. This could be caused by comparative advantages of high-income countries for heterogeneous goods.

For the links variable we also find the same pattern as Rauch (1999). For all three product categories trade will be higher when the trading partners have colonial links or share a common language. The size of this effect increases with the extent of differentiation of the products. This is one of the main conclusions of Rauch (1999) and is consistent with his network/search theory.

According to the network/search view, distance would reduce trade in heterogeneous goods more than it would reduce trade in homogeneous goods. The results of Rauch (1999) confirmed this hypothesis and are consistent with those found in Table 8.2. However, when we add country dummies (Table 8.3) and apply the Heckman selection model (Table 8.4), the results suggest the opposite effect. Physical distance reduces trade more for homogeneous goods. A possible explanation for this is that for homogeneous goods, exactly the same good can be imported from many countries. Because of the nature of these goods, it does not matter where the goods come from. Heterogeneous goods are probably produced in fewer places. Moreover, if similar but differentiated goods are produced in multiple places, they may vary in quality, giving more reason to trade the goods over a larger distance. Second, when goods are traded on organized exchanges, intangible trade costs probably play a smaller role. There is less need for negotiation over the properties of the product or the price. Therefore, the importance of tangible costs like transportation costs, relative to the importance of intangible transaction costs, is likely to be higher for homogeneous goods than it is for heterogeneous goods. This may either increase or decrease distance decay, depending on the relative importance of transportation costs and intangible transaction costs in explaining the marginal effect of distance on trade.

Tariffs are also a form of tangible trade costs. The idea behind the common trade bloc variable is that it acts as a proxy for tariffs and other forms of trade protection, which should be lower when both countries are a member of the same trade bloc. Common trade bloc membership can therefore be expected to be more important for homogeneous goods. This is confirmed by the pattern for the trade bloc coefficient. This coefficient is, like the distance coefficient, higher for the group of products that is traded on organized exchanges (0.71) than for referenced priced goods (0.65), and for differentiated goods (0.63). An alternative explanation is that trade protection is more severe for goods traded on organized exchanges.

5.2   The impact of cultural and institutional distance

We now turn to the impact of cultural and institutional dissimilarities. Table 8.5 extends the specification with two variables reflecting these intangible barriers to trade. The coefficients for the other variables, that were already included in Table 8.4, are hardly affected by the inclusion of institutional and cultural distance, so we will focus on the results for institutional and cultural distance. Based on the discussion in Section 3, the expected sign of the effect of cultural and institutional distance is ambiguous. On the one hand a negative effect on bilateral trade could be expected, because trade costs increase with cultural and institutional distance. Then the negative effect is expected to be more pronounced for

Table 8.5. *The role of cultural and institutional distance*

Dependent variable:	ln(total trade value)	ln(trade value N)	ln(trade value R)	ln(trade value W)
	Total	Differentiated	Reference priced	Organized exchange
Specification	Rauch + country dummies	Rauch + country dummies	Rauch + country dummies	Rauch + country dummies
Ln(GDP product)	0.83***	0.88***	0.85***	0.71***
	(0.03)	(0.04)	(0.03)	(0.06)
Ln(per capita GDP	1.08***	1.24***	0.71***	0.67***
product)	(0.06)	(0.06)	(0.06)	(0.10)
Ln(distance)	−0.86***	−0.82***	−0.91***	−0.93***
	(0.05)	(0.05)	(0.05)	(0.08)
Adjacency	0.09	0.13	0.00	0.39*
	(0.14)	(0.16)	(0.15)	(0.23)
Links	0.62***	0.71***	0.62***	0.25*
	(0.07)	(0.08)	(0.08)	(0.13)
Common trade	0.57***	0.62***	0.60***	0.78***
bloc membership	(0.08)	(0.09)	(0.08)	(0.13)
Cultural distance	0.02	0.04	−0.02	−0.11***
	(0.02)	(0.02)	(0.02)	(0.04)
Institutional	0.01	−0.01	−0.06***	0.10***
distance	(0.02)	(0.02)	(0.02)	(0.03)
Method	Heckman	Heckman	Heckman	Heckman
Country dummies	54	54	54	54
Uncensored obs.	2,752	2,627	2,586	2,265
Censored obs.	164	289	330	651

Notes: Robust standard errors in parentheses. Statistical significance at a 10%, 5% or 1% level is indicated by *, ** or ***, respectively.

goods that are more differentiated, because higher asset-specific invest-ments in trade relations imply a greater risk of exposure to differences in culture and institutional quality. However, on the other hand, high cultural and institutional differences lower the attractiveness of serving foreign markets with FDI and may lead to substitution by trade flows. The total effect of cultural and institutional distance on trade could then even be positive. The empirical analysis is needed to assess the relative importance of both opposite powers.

The empirical findings reported in Table 8.5 provide support for the latter explanation. Cultural and institutional distance are statistically insignificant determinants for total trade and trade in group N (which accounts for the bulk of the total trade). Furthermore, the coefficient of cultural distance is becoming more negative as the product groups become more homogeneous. This result contradicts the expectation from the first explanation that cultural distance is especially important for heterogeneous goods and that cultural distance is less important for goods that are traded on organized exchanges, because trade occurs at arm's length. This latter group is the only product group where cultural distance has a statistically significant negative effect on trade. For institutional distance the results do not confirm the traditional hypothesis either. This variable is statistically insignificant for aggregate bilateral trade and trade in heterogeneous goods, significant and negative for reference priced goods, and significant and positive for goods traded on organized exchanges.

Substitution between trade and FDI provides a possible explanation for the pattern of cultural distance that we find. As cultural distance increases, substitution from FDI to trade may occur, under the assumption that cultural distance is more harmful for FDI than for trade. Bergstrand and Egger (this volume) studied the determinants of trade in final goods, trade in intermediate goods, and FDI stocks. Their results suggest that language is much more important for FDI than for trade, which indicates that cultural barriers are indeed more important for FDI. The findings for the three product groups could be interpreted, according to this line of thought, as follows: the substitution effect from FDI to trade appears to increase as products are less homogeneous. This could actually reflect that the substitutability of different suppliers in trade is smaller for more differentiated goods, implying that the bilateral relation changes form in the face of higher cultural and institutional distance. For homogeneous goods, on the other hand, importers may rely on exporters that are relatively close in terms of culture and institutions. Substituting away in *both* trade *and* FDI relations from suppliers that are more distant is easier. This line of reasoning is consistent with the findings for the effect of cultural distance on trade across product groups. A qualification on this explanation should be that, ceteris paribus, we expect FDI to be a more attractive option for differentiated types of goods. Because trade costs related to search and insecurity are expected to be higher for more differentiated goods, FDI becomes relatively more attractive. Because these trade costs increase more with distance and other barriers, while FDI costs increase similarly for all types of goods, we would expect a smaller percentage substitution from FDI to trade for differentiated goods.

The pattern for institutional distance does not correspond to the hierarchy following from the FDI-trade substitution, however. It could be expected that institutional distance does not have a strong effect on trade in group W, because country-specific institutions are not that relevant for goods that are traded on organized exchanges. Organized exchanges form an institutional framework in itself. The effect, however, is actually significantly positive, suggesting a high substitution from FDI to trade. A possible explanation for this is that homogeneous goods are generally produced by countries with relatively low institutional quality and exported to countries with relatively high institutional quality.[5]

5.3   More detailed product groups

The above results clearly reveal that the effects of tangible and intangible barriers to trade vary according to the type of product that is being traded. As a final extension to the analysis we now look at even more disaggregate product groups. We consider the ten one-digit product categories distinguished in the SITC classification. The results are presented in Table 8.6.

A result that stands out is the substantial heterogeneity in the estimated coefficients for the different product groups. The GDP variable, for example, ranges from 0.51 to 0.90. The GDP per capita variable has an even larger range, between 0.47 and 1.54. The variation is also striking in the impact of physical distance, ranging from −0.56 for beverages and tobacco to −1.42 for mineral fuels, lubricants, and related materials. The markets for the latter goods can thus be characterized as highly localized.

There are three product groups (SITC 0, 2, and 4) that have a relatively low coefficient for GDP per capita and a relatively high coefficient for the trade bloc variable. As such, the results for these three categories strongly resemble those of the goods traded on organized exchanges (see Table 8.5). As shown in Table 8.1, these three product groups also contain relatively high shares of homogeneous products.

An interesting result is that cultural distance has a negative coefficient for all one-digit product groups, except for machinery and transport equipment (SITC 7), for which it is significantly positive. This product group has a particularly large share in total trade. Table 8.1 shows that machinery and transport equipment account for over 40 per cent of

---

[5] We have also included institutional quality as a separate explanatory variable (although it is strongly correlated with GDP per capita). Institutional quality especially stimulates trade for the differentiated product group, which accounts for the bulk of the total trade. For reference-priced goods and goods that are traded on organized exchanges, the institutional quality does not significantly increase trade. This confirms the prediction of the *insecurity view* on trade costs that the effectiveness of the formal institutional framework of a country in enforcing property rights matters particularly for differentiated products and not so much for homogeneous goods. In specifications that include country dummies, the level of institutional quality is controlled for by the dummy parameters.

Table 8.6. Results for SITC 1 product groups (dependent variable: log of exports)

Product group	0: food and live animals	1: beverages and tobacco	2: crude materials, inedible, except fuels	3: mineral fuels, lubricants and related materials	4: animal and vegetable oils, fats and waxes	5: chemicals and related products	6: manufactured goods	7: machinery and transport equipment	8: miscellaneous manufactured articles	9: commodities and transactions n.e.s.
Specification	Rauch + country dummies	Rauch + country dummies	Rauch + country dummies	Rauch + country dummies	Rauch + country dummies	Rauch + country dummies	Rauch + country dummies	Rauch + country dummies	Rauch + country dummies	Rauch + country dummies
ln(GDP product)	0.82***	0.53***	0.90***	0.51***	0.80***	0.81***	0.86***	0.83***	0.90***	0.64***
	(0.05)	(0.05)	(0.04)	(0.09)	(0.08)	(0.04)	(0.03)	(0.05)	(0.04)	(0.07)
ln(per capita GDP product)	0.67***	1.14***	0.47***	0.77***	0.54***	0.94***	0.58***	1.54***	1.31***	1.42***
	(0.08)	(0.11)	(0.08)	(0.15)	(0.14)	(0.07)	(0.06)	(0.08)	(0.08)	(0.13)
ln(distance)	−0.62***	−0.56***	−0.66***	−1.42***	−0.64***	−1.02***	−0.93***	−0.70***	−0.77***	−0.53***
	(0.06)	(0.08)	(0.06)	(0.12)	(0.10)	(0.05)	(0.05)	(0.06)	(0.06)	(0.11)
Adjacency	0.36*	0.48**	0.30*	0.54*	0.64***	0.02	0.15	0.32	0.18	0.49*
	(0.19)	(0.23)	(0.17)	(0.30)	(0.24)	(0.16)	(0.15)	(0.19)	(0.17)	(0.30)
Links	0.54***	0.64***	0.44***	−0.22	0.45***	0.56***	0.49***	0.61***	0.83***	0.15
	(0.10)	(0.14)	(0.10)	(0.18)	(0.16)	(0.09)	(0.08)	(0.11)	(0.10)	(0.17)
Common trade bloc membership	0.99***	0.54***	0.70***	0.37*	0.79***	0.40***	0.60***	0.74***	0.53***	0.91***
	(0.11)	(0.14)	(0.10)	(0.20)	(0.16)	(0.09)	(0.09)	(0.11)	(0.10)	(0.17)
Cultural distance	−0.05*	−0.16***	−0.03	−0.16***	−0.10**	−0.04	−0.06**	0.05*	−0.03	−0.09*
	(0.03)	(0.04)	(0.03)	(0.05)	(0.05)	(0.03)	(0.02)	(0.03)	(0.03)	(0.05)
Institutional distance	0.06	−0.05	0.00	0.05	0.09**	−0.07***	−0.05***	−0.02	−0.04	−0.05
	(0.02)	(0.04)	(0.02)	(0.05)	(0.04)	(0.02)	(0.02)	(0.03)	(0.02)	(0.05)
Method	Heckman	Heckman	Heckman	Heckman	Heckman	Heckman	Heckman	Heckman	Heckman	Heckman
Country dummies	54	54	54	54	54	54	54	54	54	54
Uncensored obs.	2,373	1,368	2,250	1,425	1,122	2,321	2,467	2,307	2,223	1,283
Censored obs.	543	1,548	666	1,491	1,794	595	449	609	693	1,633

Notes: Robust standard errors in parentheses. Statistical significance at a 10%, 5% or 1% level is indicated by *, ** or ***, respectively.

the total trade between the countries in our sample. This implies that this product group is probably responsible for the statistically insignificant effect which was found for total trade and trade in heterogeneous goods. For the other product groups, culture does seem to impose a barrier to trade.[6] When ignoring all trade in SITC 7, cultural distance has a coefficient of -0.04, with a p-value of 0.1.

6   Conclusions

This chapter has focused on the importance of intangible barriers to trade in explaining variation in bilateral trade. As such, the analysis expands in several ways upon the seminal work by Rauch (1999). The new elements as compared to Rauch are that (i) we consider a more recent time period, (ii) we apply more appropriate estimation techniques, (iii) we consider intangible barriers to trade in much more detail, and (iv) we consider more refined product categories.

Our results confirm the network/search theory specified in Rauch (1999) with respect to the effect of linguistic or colonial links. The effect of linguistic or colonial links is larger for more differentiated goods. However, geographical distance shows the opposite pattern when we control for omitted variable bias due to multilateral resistances and account for selection bias due to zero-valued trade flows: it is most important for trade in homogeneous goods. This qualifies the importance of distance for search costs relative to more traditional transportation barriers. The analysis of additional cultural and institutional distance variables suggests that these effects are rather different for different product types. Cultural distance exercises a negative influence and institutional distance a positive influence on goods traded on organized exchanges, while both variables are statistically insignificant for trade in differentiated goods. A possible explanation for the positive effect can be found in the tradeoff between FDI and trade. Zooming in on more disaggregated product groups provides further insights on the effect of different dimensions of distance. An interesting result is that for nine out of ten groups cultural distance does have a negative effect on trade.

Although some clear patterns are discernible from the presented evidence, our results also point to a number of opportunities for future research. Particularly promising is to delve deeper into the determination of more homogeneous product groups, extending the classification into

---

[6] The effect of cultural distance on food and live animals (SITC 0) is not particularly large, even though this product group is generally considered as a culture-specific product. This could be explained by a preference for variety. Since some food-related products are only produced in certain countries, they can only be imported from countries with a different culture. This effect would reduce the negative effect of cultural distance on trade.

three groups proposed by Rauch (1999). An interesting way forward could be to consider trade for more refined product groups and classify them into homogeneous groups based on key characteristics of gravity equations estimated for these groups. Such classifications should acknowledge the multidimensionality of distance. Analyses for more refined product groups will further increase our understanding of the product-specific barriers to trade and as such have substantial policy implications in view of the continued attempts to further enhance free trade and exploit the returns from specialization. More attention should also be devoted to the proximity-concentration tradeoff. So far, we have considered trade in isolation and thus neglected foreign direct investments as an alternative mode of entering foreign markets. Also for foreign direct investments, the payoff from considering investments at a disaggregate level is likely to be substantial, although data problems are particularly severe in this research domain.

REFERENCES

Anderson, J. E. and D. Marcouiller (2002). "Insecurity and the Pattern of Trade: An Empirical Investigation," *Review of Economics and Statistics* **84**: 342–52.
Anderson, J. E. and E. van Wincoop (2003). "Gravity with Gravitas: A Solution to the Border Puzzle," *American Economic Review* **93**: 170–92.
(2004). "Trade Costs," *Journal of Economic Literature* **42**: 691–751.
Boisso, D. and M. Ferrantino (1997). "Economic Distance, Cultural Distance, and Openness in International Trade: Empirical Puzzles," *Journal of Economic Integration* **12**: 456–84.
Brainard, S. L. (1997). "An Empirical Assessment of the Proximity-Concentration Trade-off between Multinational Sales and Trade," *American Economic Review* **87**: 520–44.
Cairncross, F. (1997). *The Death of Distance: How the Communications Revolution Will Change Our Lives*, Boston, MA: Harvard Business School Publications.
Davis, D. R., D. E. Weinstein, S. C. Bradford and K. Shimpo (1997). "Using International and Japanese Regional Data to Determine when the Factor Abundance Theory of Trade Works," *American Economic Review* **87**: 421–46.
Deardorff, A. (1998). "Determinants of Bilateral Trade: Does Gravity Work in a Neoclassical World?" in J. Frankel (ed.), *The Regionalization of the World Economy*, University of Chicago Press: 7–28.
(2004). "Local Comparative Advantage: Trade Costs and the Pattern of Trade," Research Seminar in International Economics discussion paper no. 500, University of Michigan.
De Groot, H. L. F., G. J. M. Linders, P. Rietveld and U. Subramanian (2004). "The Institutional Determinants of Bilateral Trade Patterns," *Kyklos* **57**: 103–23.
Den Butter, F. A. G. and R. H. J. Mosch (2003). "Trade, Trust and Transaction Costs," Tinbergen Institute discussion paper no. 2003–082/3, Amsterdam–Rotterdam.

Disdier, A. and K. Head (2008). "The Puzzling Persistence of the Distance Effect on Bilateral Trade," *Review of Economics and Statistics* **90**: 37–48.

Dixit, A. K. (2004). "Lawlessness and Economics: Alternative Modes of Governance," The Gorman Lectures in Economics, Princeton and Oxford, NJ: Princeton University Press.

Eichengreen, B. and D. A. Irwin (1998). "The Role of History in Bilateral Trade Flows," in J. Frankel (ed.), *The Regionalization of the World Economy*, Chicago and London: University of Chicago Press: 33–57.

Elsass, P. M. and J. F. Veiga (1994). "Acculturation in Acquired Organizations: A Force-Field Perspective," *Human Relations* **47**: 431–53.

Feenstra, R. C. (2004). *Advanced International Trade*, Princeton University Press.

Feenstra, R. C., R. E. Lipsey, H. Deng, A. C. Ma and H. Mo (2005). *World Trade Flows: 1962–2000*, NBER working paper no. 11040, Cambridge, MA.

Frankel, J. (1997). *Regional Trading Blocs in the World Economic System*, Washington DC: Institute for International Economics.

Friedman, T. L. (2005). *The World is Flat*, London: Penguin.

Geraci, V. J. and W. Prewo (1977). "Bilateral Trade Flows and Transport Costs," *Review of Economics and Statistics* **59**: 67–74.

Greenwood, M. (1975). "Research on Internal Migration in the United States: A Survey," *Journal of Economic Literature* **13**: 397–433.

Guiso, L., P. Sapienza and L. Zingales (2004). *Cultural Biases in Economic Exchange*, NBER working paper no. 11005, Cambridge, MA.

Heckman, J. J. (1979). "Sample Selection Bias as a Specification Error," *Econometrica* **47**: 53–161.

Helpman, E., M. Melitz and S. Yeaple (2004). "Export versus FDI with Heterogeneous Firms," *American Economic Review* **94**: 300–16.

Helpman, E., M. Melitz and Y. Rubinstein (2007). "Estimating Trade Flows: Trading Partners and Trading Volumes," NBER working paper no. 12927, Cambridge, MA.

Hofstede, G. (1980). *Culture's Consequences: International Differences in Work-Related Values*, Beverly Hills, CA: Sage Publications.

    (2001). *Culture's Consequences: Comparing Values, Behaviors, Institutions, and Organizations across Nations*, Thousand Oaks, CA; London; New Delhi: Sage Publications.

Isard, W. (1999). "Regional Science: Parallels from Physics and Chemistry," *Papers in Regional Science* **78**: 5–20.

Kaufmann, D., A. Kraay and M. Mastruzzi (2003). "Governance Matters III—Governance Indicators for 1996–2002," World Bank Policy Research Department working paper no. 3106, Washington DC.

Kogut, B. and H. Singh (1988). "The Effect of National Culture on the Choice of Entry Mode," *Journal of International Business Studies* **19**: 411–32.

Linders, G. J. M. (2006). *Intangible Barriers to Trade: The Impact of Institutions, Culture, and Distance on Patterns of Trade*, Tinbergen Institute Research Series, 371, Amsterdam: Thela Thesis Academic Publishing Services.

Linders, G. J. M., A. H. L. Slangen, H. L. F. de Groot and S. Beugelsdijk (2005). "Cultural and Institutional Determinants of Bilateral Trade Flows," Tinbergen Institute discussion paper no. 2005–074/3, Amsterdam–Rotterdam.

Linnemann, H. (1966). *An Econometric Study of International Trade Flows*, Amsterdam: North-Holland.

Martinez-Zarzoso, I., F. D. Nowak-Lehman and S. Vollmer (2007). "The Log of Gravity Revisited," CEGE discussion paper no. 64, Göttingen.

Neal, M. (1998). *The Culture Factor: Cross-National Management and the Foreign Venture*, Houndmills, UK: Macmillan.

Nijkamp, P. and A. Reggiani (1992). *Interaction, Evolution and Chaos in Space*, Berlin: Springer-Verlag.

Obstfeld, M. and K. Rogoff (2000). "The Six Major Puzzles in International Macroeconomics: Is There a Common Cause," NBER working paper no. 7777, Cambridge, MA.

Olson, M. (1996). "Big Bills Left on the Sidewalk: Why some Nations are Rich, and Others Poor," *Journal of Economic Perspectives* **10**: 3–24.

Parkhe, A. (1991). "Interfirm Diversity, Organizational Learning, and Longevity in Global Strategic Alliances," *Journal of International Business Studies* **22**: 579–601.

Pöyhönen, P. (1963). "A Tentative Model for the Volume of Trade between Countries," *Weltwirtschaftliches Archiv* **90**: 93–99.

Rauch, J. E. (1999). "Networks versus Markets in International Trade," *Journal of International Economics* **48**: 7–35.

——— (2001). "Business and Social Networks in International Trade," *Journal of Economic Literature* **39**: 1177–1203.

Rodrik, D. (2000). "How Far Will International Integration Go?" *Journal of Economic Perspectives* **14**: 177–86.

Santos Silva, J. and S. Tenreyro (2006). "The Log of Gravity," *Review of Economics and Statistics* **88**: 641–58.

Srivastava, R. K. and R. T. Green (1986). "Determinants of Bilateral Trade-Flows," *Journal of Business* **59**: 623–40.

Tinbergen, J. (1962). *Shaping the World Economy*, New York: Twentieth Century Fund.

Trefler, D. (1995). "The Case of Missing Trade and Other Mysteries," *American Economic Review* **85**: 1029–46.

Vella, F. (1998). "Estimating Models with Sample Selection Bias: A Survey," *Journal of Human Resources* **33**: 127–69.

Verbeek, M. (2004). *A Guide to Modern Econometrics* (2nd edition), Chichester, UK: John Wiley & Sons.

Wei, S. J. (2000). "Natural Openness and Good Government," NBER working paper no. 7765, Cambridge, MA.

Yeyati, E. L. (2003). "On the Impact of a Common Currency on Bilateral Trade," *Economics Letters* **79**: 125–29.

APPENDIX: DESCRIPTION OF THE DATASET

The variables included in the analysis and their respective sources are as follows:

- For the size of the countries we use the Gross Domestic Product (GDP). Additionally we include a variable for the GDP per capita. Both GDP and GDP per capita are obtained for the year 2000 from the Penn World Table, Mark 6.2.
- The distance between each pair of countries is obtained from the Centre d'Etudes Prospectives et d'Information Internationales (CEPII). This database offers several measures of distance. This study uses the simple distances, which

are obtained from the latitudes and longitudes of the city with the largest population count in the country. This distance is measured "as the crow flies" by the great circle formula and is measured in kilometres. Alternative measures for distance use the capital city rather than the city with the largest population or take the population distributions into account. The city with the largest population is chosen here because it is expected to be a better indicator for economic activity than the capital city.

- The adjacency variable is a dummy which equals 1 when the two countries included in the country pair are adjacent. Countries are considered to be adjacent when they have a land border or a small body of water as a border. The adjacency variable is also obtained from the CEPII database.
- The data on trade blocs are obtained from OECD data. A distinction is made between twenty-four different trade blocs. A dummy variable is constructed which equals 1 if both countries are a member of at least one mutual trade bloc in the year 2000 and 0 otherwise. The trade blocs considered are: EU, CANUS, NAFTA, APEC, ANDEAN, CACM, MERCOSUR, GR3, LAIA, CARICOM, CBI, EAC, EMCCA, ECOWAS, CMESA, IOC, SADC, ECWA, WAEMU, SACU, ECCGL, ASEAN, GCC, and SAARC.
- The links variable is a dummy variable that equals 1 if both countries share a common official language or one country has ever colonized the other country. Countries may have multiple official languages. The data on languages and colonial ties have been compiled by CEPII.
- The data on cultural dimensions are obtained from Hofstede (2001). Data on additional countries have been kindly provided after personal correspondence (see Linders 2006). His indicators for (i) power distance, (ii) uncertainty avoidance, (iii) individualism, and (iv) masculinity are used to construct a Kogut-Singh index for cultural distance.
- The data on institutional indicators are obtained from Kaufmann et al. (2003). The Kogut-Singh index for institutional distance is constructed using their indicators for (i) voice and accountability, (ii) political stability, (iii) government effectiveness, (iv) regulatory quality, (v) rule of law, and (vi) control of corruption.
- The instrument we use in the Heckman selection model (see also Section 4.3) is a variable that indicates whether two countries have the same main religion. This dummy variable is constructed using data from the CIA *World Factbook*. These data are obtained from surveys at different points in time. The surveys are not all taken in the year 2000, but this should not have a significant effect because the main religion of a country is very persistent over time. The CIA *World Factbook* provides data on the fraction of the population that practice certain religions. Since there are many similar religions, for this study they have been aggregated into seven groups: Buddhists, Catholics, Hindus, Jews, Muslims, Orthodox-Christians, and Protestants. For each country the religion practiced by the highest portion of the population is marked as the main religion. The dummy variable is constructed by assigning a value of 1 if the countries have the same main religion and a value of 0 if they do not.

The countries included in the analysis (in alphabetical order) are Argentina, Australia, Austria, Belgium and Luxembourg customs union, Brazil, Canada,

Chile, China, Colombia, Denmark, Ecuador, Egypt, Ethiopia, Finland, France, Germany, Ghana, Greece, Hong Kong, Hungary, India, Indonesia, Iran, Ireland, Israel, Italy, Japan, Kenya, Republic of Korea, Kuwait, Libya, Malaysia, Mexico, Morocco, Netherlands, New Zealand, Nigeria, Norway, Pakistan, Peru, Philippines, Poland, Portugal, Saudi Arabia, Singapore, South Africa, Spain, Sweden, Switzerland, Thailand, Turkey, United Kingdom, United States of America, Uruguay, and Venezuela.[7]

[7] Compared to the set of countries used by Rauch, our sample does not contain Yugoslavia, which no longer existed in 2000. Algeria, Bolivia, Iceland, Taiwan, Paraguay, Sudan, and Tunisia are excluded because of a lack of data on the cultural indicators.

Part III

Specific applications

9 International environmental arrangements and international commerce

A. K. Rose and M. M. Spiegel

1 Introduction

Countries protect the environment mostly for their own benefit. Similarly, they also engage in international trade (of goods, services, and assets) for their own advantage. But there are also ancillary benefits to a country that protects the environment; it may well find international trade easier. Countries that are involved in international environmental arrangements (IEAs) find it easier to engage in the international exchange of goods and assets (a multilateral effect). Further, a pair of countries with a joint interest in the environment also finds it easier to engage in international commerce, since each can punish the other in one domain for transgressions in a different sphere (a bilateral effect). In this paper, we formalize such theoretical notions, and then test and confirm them, using a recent cross-section of international asset holdings and environmental commitments. In practice, participation in non-economic partnerships turns out to enhance international economic relations.

In a recent and related paper of ours (Rose and Spiegel 2009), we demonstrate that IEA activity can facilitate international portfolio borrowing. Our analysis begins with an extension of the "reputation spillover" concept introduced by Cole and Kehoe (1997). With differing discount rates, more patient governments choose to join a greater number of environmental treaties; this sends a credible signal concerning a country's debt capacity. Creditors respond by granting the country more trade credit. The predictions of this model are *multilateral*, since membership in IEAs is easily accessible common knowledge. A country that joins more IEAs enhances its reputation with all nations. We then extend the model to accommodate *bilateral* spillovers. We allow a creditor to respond to default by reducing the debtor's gains from involvement in mutual IEAs. This extended model demonstrates that cross-country economic interaction can be a function of *solo* and/or *joint* participation in environmental treaties. Succinctly, the more international environmental commitments that countries make individually and in common, the easier economic exchange is between the countries.

While this model allows for bilateral flows between countries, it does not impose enough structure to motivate the relationship between the bilateral flows in the data and the willingness of creditors to extend funds bilaterally in our theoretical model. In this paper, we extend the analysis to consider a specific form of economic engagement to more explicitly tie down the relationship between IEA engagement and the magnitude of predicted bilateral flows. In particular, we consider trade credit as the form of bilateral lending taking place. This allows us to model bilateral gains from trade as the formal mechanism by which IEA engagement enhances market discipline bilaterally.

We then take these ideas to the data. Using a gravity model to control for other phenomena, we find that participation in IEAs is indeed positively associated with the international exchange of assets.[1] This confirms the notion of positive spillovers between environmental cooperation and economic exchange. Moreover, we find that multilateral IEA participation is not a sufficient statistic to explain bilateral economic exchange; joint IEA participation is also related to asset cross-holdings. The data therefore support our extended model with both a multilateral reputation effect and some sort of bilateral punishment mechanism.

A brief survey of the literature section is provided next, while our theoretical framework is developed in the following section. The empirical work is presented in Section 4. The paper ends with a brief conclusion.

2   Literature survey

The concept of reputation spillovers arose as a response to the Bulow and Rogoff (1989) challenge to the sovereign debt literature. In their seminal paper, Bulow and Rogoff cast doubt on the possibility of sustainable sovereign lending based solely on the desire of borrowers to maintain their reputations. They demonstrated that such relationships would not be sustainable, because a borrower would eventually prefer to default on its debt and "self-finance" its consumption-smoothing.

This challenge was addressed in a series of papers by Cole and Kehoe (1995, 1997, 1998). They show that the problem with reputation-based borrowing stems from the fact that a borrower able to replicate

---

[1] Our analysis therefore extends the standard gravity specification by adding in membership in IEAs as an additional explanatory variable. Afman and Maurel (chapter 10), use a similar extension of the gravity model to examine the impact of diplomatic relations on bilateral trade.

interactions with other creditors receives only *transient* benefits from such relationships. At some point, the benefits of maintaining a reputation fall sufficiently that default and subsequent self-finance is the rational response. However, Cole and Kehoe (1995) show that the desire to maintain *other* interactions with creditor nations may support debt, provided that these other relationships are not transient but *enduring*. Cole and Kehoe (1998) demonstrate that the desire to maintain reputations in enduring relationships can support a debt relationship with transient benefits. Cole and Kehoe (1997) show that the desire to maintain an enduring relationship can support a transient debt relationship in a simple trigger-strategy model, where a creditor responds to default by breaking off the debtor-relationship even if such a relationship would have enduring benefits. We borrow this modeling strategy below in our theoretical work.

A different literature of relevance concerns the formation and characteristics of IEAs; references here include Barrett (1994), Carraro and Siniscalco (1998), and Finus *et al* (2005). Most of the literature is skeptical about the ability of voluntary self-enforcing IEAs to improve on non-cooperative outcomes. The intuition is that the level of any attainable environmental objective – say, abatement of a certain pollutant – is limited in a heterogeneous group by the preferences of the nation least interested in the problem. While there has been some discussion about encouraging greater participation in IEAs through cooperation in other dimensions such as R&D activity (e.g. Carrero and Siniscalco 1998), the literature is discouraged by the fact that such agreements are not explicitly found in practice (Barrett 2003).

3   Theory

This section introduces a simple model of the extension of bilateral trade credit and participation in IEAs. We model IEA activity as we did in Rose and Spiegel (2009). As such, we first introduce a model where IEA activity signals a country's type multilaterally, and then consider the implications of bilateral penalties for sovereign default.

3.1   Pure reputation model

We begin with a reputation-based model, where a government's choices concerning membership in IEAs send a credible signal concerning its type to creditors; this, in turn, influences the country's borrowing constraint.

We assume that each of $k + 1$ countries are endowed with x units of a perishable good in each period, $t = 0, 1, \ldots, \infty$. We model decisions in terms of a representative country i. Decisions are made by a national government that maximizes the discounted utility of a representative consumer. We assume utility is linear in consumption, so country i is interested in maximizing:

$$U_t^i = \sum_{j=t}^{\infty} (\beta^i)^j c_t^i \qquad (9.1)$$

where β^i represents the country's discount rate, $0 < \beta^i < 1$. We order the countries such that i is increasing in impatience, the key parameter of the model, i.e. $\beta^i \leq \beta^{i+1}$. We assume that the discount rate is private information. For notational simplicity, we drop the i superscript and analyze a representative country.

As in Rose and Spiegel (2009), there are $\mathcal{J}$ categories of environmental issues, numbered $j = 1, \ldots, \mathcal{J}$. Each category is covered by an IEA (which we refer to interchangeably as a "treaty") that requires participants to contribute a fixed amount of their consumption good e in each period, including period 0, towards improving the environment. IEA$_j$ then yields a benefit, y_j, in each of the following periods $t > 0$. We number the treaties such that $y_j \geq y_{j+1}$ and assume that y_j is a continuous twice-differentiable function of j that satisfies $y_j' < 0$, $y_j'' > 0$, and $\lim_{j \to \infty} y_j = 0$.

Since effort levels are constant across treaties, while payoffs are decreasing in j, participation by country i in treaty j implies participation by i in IEAs 0 through $j - 1$. We therefore concentrate on the government's choice of j^*, the number of treaties to join.

We model bilateral economic interactions in terms of goods trade facilitated by the extension of bilateral trade credit. We model trade in terms of a representative bilateral partner country, k, and assume that there are K such countries with whom each country engages in trade. We assume that this trade is facilitated by a bilateral exchange of trade credit. In particular, the gains from bilateral trade between countries i and k in period t satisfy $T_t^k = T(\eta_t^k, d_t^k)$, where $T' \geq 0$, $T'' \leq 0$ in both arguments and η_t^k is a vector of characteristics of the two countries (we later associate this with arguments that enter the standard bilateral gravity equation). The payment due in period t on trade credit extended in period $t - 1$ from country i to country k is represented by d_t^k, where $\partial T / \partial d_t^k \geq 0$ below an upper limit $T \leq \overline{T}$.[2]

---

[2] As the benefits from trade are enduring and the endowment is constant by assumption, the Bulow-Rogoff critique concerning the unsustainability of reputation-based borrowing does not apply here.

The timing of the model is as follows: in period 0, the government chooses j^*, the number of IEAs to join. It then chooses whether or not to comply with the terms of these treaties. Next, the representative competitive creditor in country k chooses its repayment d_1^k. Finally, country i consumes the unused portion of its endowment. In subsequent periods, the government again decides whether to comply (or not) with the treaty. In addition, it decides whether or not to service its debt d_t^k, while country k chooses how much credit to extend and thus d_{t+1}^k. The country then consumes, subject to any penalties for default or shirking on its environmental commitments.

To insure sub-game perfection, we solve the model backwards, beginning in a representative period $t \geq 1$. Initially, we treat default and IEA penalties as separate; below, we also consider an extension which allows punishment through environmental treaties.

3.2   Solving the model

We solve the model in inverse sequential order for: a) the default decision; b) the IEA compliance decision; and c) the choice of participation in IEAs.

Consumption by country i in period $t > 0$ is equal to the country's endowment, plus the net gains from international trade (the gains from trade minus debt service) and environmental improvement, minus any penalties incurred for debt default or shirking on IEA commitments.[3] These are:

$$(c_t | t > 0) = x + \sum_{k=1}^{K} \left[T(\eta_t^k, d_t^k) - \tilde{d}_t^k \right] + \sum_{j=1}^{j^*} \tilde{y}_j \qquad (9.2)$$

where: $\tilde{y}_j$ represents the net payoff from participation in treaty j (which equals $y_j - e$ under compliance, and $-\phi$ under non-compliance; the latter represents the penalty for reneging on an IEA),[4] and $\tilde{d}_t^k$ represents the

---

[3] There are also flows from lending activity by private creditors in country i with the rest of the world. However, as creditors are risk neutral by assumption, the expected (and realized in this deterministic model) sum of these flows reflecting activity by private agents in country i are zero. In particular, we maintain the assumption that the validity of private claims by agents in country i are independent of that country's default decision on its sovereign debt.

[4] For simplicity, we assume that the penalty for shirking on environmental obligations is homogeneous across treaties. This drives none of our results, but allows treaties to differ only in their payoffs.

debt service payment (which equals d_t^k under debt service, and 0 under default).[5]

We assume that when the representative country services its debts it continues to obtain funds from all k countries in each period in the future. Discounted utility under debt service then satisfies

$$U_t = \left(\frac{1}{1-\beta}\right)\left\{x + \sum_{i=1}^{K}[T(\eta_t^i, d_t^i) - d_t^i] + \sum_{i=1}^{j^*}(y_i - e)\right\}. \quad (9.3)$$

If the country chooses to default on its credit obligations to country k, we assume that it loses access to trade credit with that country in the future. Assuming that it fulfills its environmental treaty obligations and debt obligations to other creditors, discounted utility subsequent to default on credit obligations to country k satisfies

$$\widehat{U}_t = T(\eta_t^k, d_t^k) + \left(\frac{1}{1-\beta}\right)$$

$$\times \left\{\left(x + \sum_{m=1}^{K}[T(\eta_t^m, d_t^m) - d_t^m]|m \neq k\right) + \sum_{j=1}^{j^*}(y_j - e)\right\}.$$

$$(9.4)$$

By (9.3) and (9.4), the representative country will choose to default unless

$$d_t^k \leq \beta T(\eta_t^k, d_t^k). \quad (9.5)$$

By (9.5), the credit ceiling will be a function of the creditor's perception of the discount rate of the host country government. This raises the possibility that a country might join more than its optimal number of IEAs to misleadingly signal that it is more patient, and thus ease its credit ceiling. To address this issue, we first consider the decision problem faced in a separating equilibrium, where governments reveal their true types through their IEA participation decisions. We then derive the conditions necessary to rule out pooling in the Appendix.

---

[5] Our specification implicitly sets a zero penalty on debt default for notational simplicity. However, we could easily extend our analysis to include penalties for debt default as well. Under this alternative specification, countries could sustain some level of positive borrowing without any IEA participation, but the amount of borrowing that could be sustained would still be increasing in both unilateral and multilateral IEA participation as described in Propositions 1 and 2.

We next turn to the IEA compliance decision. In any period $t \geq 1$, the country is a member of treaties 1 through j^*. If its government chooses to comply with the terms of treaty j^*, it is easy to demonstrate that it will also comply with all treaties $j \leq j^*$. Under compliance, and given debt service, the government's discounted utility again satisfies (9.3). Alternatively, given non-compliance, the country suffers a direct penalty of ϕ in every future period. Discounted utility under violation of treaty j^* then satisfies

$$
\widehat{U}_t = y_{j^*} - \left(\frac{\beta}{1-\beta} \right) \phi + \left(\frac{1}{1-\beta} \right)
$$

$$
\times \left\{ x + \sum_{i=1}^{K} [T(\eta_t^i, d_t^i) - d_t^i] + \sum_{z=1}^{j^*-1} (y_z - e) \right\}. \tag{9.6}
$$

In the first period, the government chooses j^*, the number of IEAs to join. Consumption in period 0 is equal to the endowment minus the initial IEA effort.

$$
c_0 = x - j^* e \tag{9.7}
$$

For any IEA j, the government has three choices: 1) it can choose not to join the treaty; 2) it can choose to join the treaty and comply with its terms; and 3) it can choose to join the treaty but to violate its terms. However, since the payoff from joining and shirking on a marginal treaty is negative due to the cost of non-compliance, no country will choose the last option; a country can always do better by simply not signing the IEA. The relevant choice is thus whether to join an IEA and comply with its terms, or never sign the treaty. By (9.3), (9.6), and (9.7), it follows that the representative country will choose to join (and comply with) treaty j if and only if

$$
e \leq \beta (y_j + \phi). \tag{9.8}
$$

Equation (9.8) demonstrates that the treaty compliance decision is based upon the difference between the single-period gain from shirking on the treaty commitment, and the discounted sum of future gains from remaining in the treaty and avoiding the shirking penalty. Compliance is more desirable the higher are ϕ, y_{j^*}, and β, and the lower is e.[6]

---

[6] A more realistic approach to environmental policy would make the benefits – y_j in our model – rise over time, so that pollution abatement is viewed as an investment project

By (9.3) and (9.8), the discounted net benefit of joining any treaty j and complying satisfies

$$\Omega \equiv \left(\frac{1}{1 - \beta} \right) (\beta y_j - e) \tag{9.9}$$

It can be seen by inspection in (9.9) that Ω is increasing in β. This leads to proposition 1.

3.2.1   Proposition 1 Under a separating equilibrium, d^k is increasing in j^*. The proof is in the Appendix.

Proposition 1 demonstrates that in a separating equilibrium, the number of IEAs in which a country participates is a credible signal concerning its discount rate. Creditors respond to this signal by offering more credit to a country whose government joins more environmental treaties. Succinctly, the model implies that higher international environmental involvement is associated with more international exchange of credit.

3.3   Adding punishment via international environmental arrangements

The prediction of the analysis above is *multilateral*; when Ruritania signs its IEAs, *all* its potential trade partners see this signal. We now add *bilateral* linkages across countries, consistent with the framework of Cole and Kehoe (1997). We assume that if Ruritania defaults, its creditors punish it in the environmental sphere. We then demonstrate that this possibility increases economic integration over and above the level sustained through multilateral IEA membership. In the next section, we take this prediction to the data to verify the empirical importance of reputation spillovers.

Formally, we specify the bilateral punishment to debt default as reducing the net gains in each period from membership in IEAs in which both countries i and k are members by some fraction γ, $0 < \gamma \leq 1$, so that the gains from being in treaty j are equal to $(1 - \gamma)(y_j - e)$. An intermediate value of γ may reflect a loss in co-operation between the two nations, while $\gamma = 1$ would involve a "grim strategy," where the creditor nation responds to a default by its debtor by rescinding the treaty altogether. For simplicity, we assume that the value of γ is constant across countries.[7]

---

where the costs are borne immediately for later benefits. Adding such time-variation in the net benefits of IEAs would only strengthen our results.

[7] The capacity to punish partners may differ across countries. For example, a large country may be able to influence treaty policies more than a small one. However, as influence may differ in a number of unknown dimensions, we do not attempt to introduce any explicit heterogeneity in punishment technology across countries, although we do condition for other attribute differences, such as country size, in our empirical specification.

Define m^k as the highest-numbered treaty which contains both countries i and k. With the addition of the bilateral treaty-based default penalty, the value of discounted utility under default satisfies

$$\widehat{U}_t = T(\eta_t^k, d_t^k) + \left(\frac{1}{1-\beta}\right)\left(x + \sum_{i=1}^{K}[T(\eta_t^i, d_t^i) - d_t^i]|i \neq k\right)$$

$$+ \sum_{z=1}^{j^*}\left[1 + \left(\frac{\beta}{1-\beta}\right)(1 - \varphi\gamma)\right](y_z - e) \qquad (9.10)$$

where φ is an indicator variable that takes value 1 if $z \leq m^k$, and value 0 otherwise.

By (9.3), (9.9), (9.10), and $\Omega \geq 0$, the credit constraint from country k satisfies

$$d_t^k \leq \frac{e}{y_{j^*}}\left[T(\eta_t^k, d_t^k) + \varphi\gamma\sum_{z=1}^{j^*}(y_z - e)\right] \qquad (9.11)$$

Comparing (9.11) and (9.5), it can be seen that the capacity to levy bilateral treaty penalties under default eases the credit ceiling faced by country k. This leads to Proposition 2.

3.3.1   Proposition 2 Under a separating equilibrium, and given the bilateral treaty-based default penalty γ, d_t^k is increasing in j^*. Moreover, d_t^k is also increasing in m^k. The proof is in the Appendix.

Both our models predict that the international exchange of trade credit (and thus d_t^k) will be increasing in the number of IEAs, j^*. Proposition 2 shows that the inclusion of bilateral penalties adds the prediction that international economic exchange d_t^k is also increasing in the number of joint treaties, m^k. Below, we test for the presence of both effects.

The addition of the bilateral default penalty potentially adds a distortion to the treaty-joining decision, as it increases the rate at which the credit ceiling eases when joining an additional treaty holding all else equal. This alters the condition for a separating equilibrium. We therefore also derive the augmented sufficient condition for a separating equilibrium in the presence of these bilateral penalties in the Appendix.

4   Empirics

We think of the model above as illustrative rather than one to be taken literally. We have made a host of assumptions to keep the model stripped down to its bare essentials. For instance, the model assumes: no production, no uncertainty (and thus no renegotiation), much symmetry (and thus no net debtors or creditors), limited interactions between countries, and so forth. We think the analysis points to two key predictions (each summarized in a proposition). First, a country's non-economic commitments (which we model as the number of IEAs in which a country participates) should have a positive effect on its ability to conduct international economic exchange (which we model as trade credit)). Second, bilateral non-economic interactions may also matter; the level of multilateral IEA participation may not be a sufficient statistic for the level of environmental engagement. The number of IEAs common to both countries is also relevant to their bilateral economic interactions if there are "bilateral penalties." We now take these predictions to the data.

4.1   Specification

Our pure reputation model characterized by Proposition 1, predicts that the level of international asset cross-holdings between two nations will be increasing in the number of IEAs in which each of them participates, while the extended bilateral penalty model, characterized by Proposition 2, predicts that the number of IEAs in which they are joint members is also relevant. Our goal in this section is to check these predictions.

Our empirical specification of international cross-holdings of assets is a generalization of the standard bilateral "gravity" model. While gravity specifications have been primarily applied to bilateral trade patterns, they have also been shown to explain bilateral financial flows (e.g. Rose and Spiegel 2007, 2009 and Portes and Rey 2005) and M&A activity (e.g. di Giovanni 2008 and Brakman et al., chapter 11) surprisingly well. Since transportation costs of moving assets are likely to be negligible, motivations for gravity specifications of financial flows in the literature have concentrated on information asymmetries. Our specification satisfies:

$$
\begin{aligned}
\ln(A_{ij}) = {} & \beta_1 \ln(D_{ij}) + \beta_{2i} \ln(Y_i) + \beta_{2j} \ln(Y_j) + \beta_{3i} \ln(Pop_i) \\
& + \beta_{3j} \ln(Pop_j) + \beta_4 RTA_{ij} + \beta_5 CU_{ij} + \beta_6 Lang_{ij} \\
& + \beta_{7i} \ln(Area_i) + \beta_{7j} \ln(Area_j) + \beta_8 Cont_{ij} + \beta_{8i} Landl_i \\
& + \beta_{8j} Landl_j + \beta_{9i} Island_i + \beta_{9j} Island_j + \beta_{10} ComCol_{ij} \\
& + \gamma_1 IEA_{ij} + \gamma_2 IEA_i + \beta_{11} IEA_j + \varepsilon_{ij} \qquad (9.12)
\end{aligned}
$$

where i denotes the host country, j denotes the source country, and the variables are defined as:

- A_{ij} denotes asset cross-holdings held in host country i and sourced from j, measured in (millions of) dollars;
- D_{ij} is the distance between i and j;
- Y_i is real GDP of i;
- Pop_i is population of i;
- RTA_{ij} is a binary variable which is unity if i and j belong to the same regional trade agreement and zero otherwise;
- CU_{ij} is a binary variable which is unity if i and j use the same currency at time t;
- $Lang_{ij}$ is a binary variable which is unity if i and j have a common language;
- $Area_i$ is the total area of i;
- $Cont_{ij}$ is a binary variable which is unity if i and j share a land border;
- $Landl_i$ is a binary variable which is unity if country i is landlocked;
- $Island_i$ is a binary variable which is unity if country i is an island nation;
- $Comcol_{ij}$ is a binary variable which is unity if i and j were ever colonies after 1945 with the same colonizer;
- IEA_i is the number of environmental treaties that i has ratified at t;
- IEA_{ij} is the number of environmental treaties that i and j have both ratified at t;
- β is a vector of "nuisance" coefficients which are not of direct interest; and
- ε_{ij} represents the other influences on bilateral credit, assumed to be well behaved.

The coefficients of interest to us are $\{\gamma\}$. γ_1 represents the effect on international economic exchange of host country i's participation in international environmental treaties; γ_2 is the analogous effect of joint IEA participation by i and j.

While we examine a gravity specification for asset flows, we acknowledge that other aspects of "distance" that have been found to explain trade flows, such as market and supplier access and measures of "market potential" (see Boulhol and de Serres, chapter 12, for details), and other "intangible barriers" to trade (see Möhlmann et al. in this volume), might also apply here. While we do not control for all of these other potential channels here, our specification does include dyadic fixed effects, which should account for time-invariant differences across countries in these broader concepts of distance. Similarly, the caution raised by Bosker and Garretsen (chapter 7) that results for trade flow gravity specifications are likely to be dependent on the empirical specification of trade costs clearly also applies to our asset flow gravity specification.

4.2   Data

Our regressand is asset cross-holdings. We use the *Coordinated Portfolio Investment Survey* (CPIS) dataset, available annually for 2001, 2002, and 2003 from the IMF.[8] This records cross-holdings of asset stocks between up to 68 source and 221 host "countries" measured in millions of US dollars. The countries in the dataset are listed in Appendix Table 9.A.1. Asset cross-holdings are a good measure of economic exchange, but not a perfect measure of trade credit. Accordingly, and to check the sensitivity of our results, we also use trade flows as a regressand. We do this by merging into the CPIS dataset bilateral data on exports and imports, measured in American dollars taken from the IMF's *Direction of Trade* dataset. To smooth the data out, we average our series across the years available, so that our data become a single bilateral cross-section.

As control variables, we merge in data on population and real GDP data (in constant dollars) taken from the World Bank's *World Development Indicators*. We exploit the CIA's *World Factbook* extensively for data on other regressors.[9] From it we find series on: latitude and longitude, land area, landlocked and island status, physically contiguous neighbors, language, colonizers, and dates of independence. We use these to create great-circle distance and other controls. We obtain data from the World Trade Organization to create an indicator of regional trade agreements, including some 178 regional trade agreements. Finally, we add the Glick and Rose (2002) currency union dummy variable.

The coefficients of interest measure the effect of solo (multilateral) and joint (bilateral) participation in environmental treaties. Our dataset on environmental treaties is the Environmental Treaties and Resource Indicators (ENTRI) dataset produced by Columbia University.[10] The ENTRI dataset contains country-by-country indicators of participation in up to 464 treaties. The treaties range from the "Act regarding Navigation and Economic Co-operation between the States of the Niger Basin" through the "Vienna Convention on the Law of Treaties." The dataset includes the usual suspects, including e.g. CITES (the "Convention on International Trade in Endangered Species of Wild Fauna and Flora"); Biodiversity ("Convention on Biological Diversity"); and the Kyoto Protocol (to the United Nations Framework Convention on Climate Change).

---

[8] www.imf.org/external/np/sta/pi/cpis.htm. The CPIS dataset has its foibles; for instance, a number of entries are missing. Since a large number of asset cross-holdings are reported to be zero, we add 0.0001 to these observations. Future researchers might want to take account of the possibility of censoring and selection bias.
[9] www.cia.gov/cia/publications/factbook/.
[10] http://sedac.ciesin.columbia.edu/entri/.

ENTRI provides data for individual countries on: 1) which agreements the country has signed (so that a country is a "signatory" to a treaty); 2) which agreements are in force (where the country is a "party" to an agreement); as well as 3) agreements denounced (so that the country is a "former party" to a treaty). There are only a small number of the latter; almost one hundred countries have not denounced any agreements (the United States has denounced three agreements; and the United Kingdom has denounced the largest number of treaties, ten).

For our multilateral regressor IEA_i (as well as IEA_j, which we use simply as a control symmetrically), we simply sum up the number of agreements either signed or in force, and subtract from this the number of denounced agreements. For our bilateral regressor (IEA_{ij}) we sum up the number of agreements that are either signed or in force by both countries and subtract from this the number of jointly denounced agreements. Simply adding up the number of international environmental treaties is obviously a crude starting point, since treaties are not all of equal importance. We consider a more careful weighting of participation in different treaties to be an interesting topic for future work.[11]

We do not think there is much cause for concern with simultaneity. The key variables – individual and joint participation in environmental treaties by the source and host countries – are plausibly exogenous. There is certainly little evidence from the literature that countries take into account their potential attractiveness as a potential recipient for capital flows when contemplating environmental negotiations.[12] Nevertheless, we pursue instrumental variable estimation in Rose and Spiegel (2009), and find supportive results taking such issues into account.

Descriptive statistics for the key variables are presented in Appendix Table 9.A.2.

4.3   Results

Our results are presented in Table 9.1; all are estimated with OLS. The first column presents a specification in which there are no environmental treaties entered at all. The next two columns add: first, the number

---

[11] In the model above, our ability to monotonically order the IEAs in terms of desirability implied that if $j^* \geq j_i^*$ an increase in j^* would have no impact on m^i. In the data, however, countries are likely to have heterogeneous preferences across treaties for a variety of reasons, allowing j^* and m^i to vary independently. We therefore treat these variables as independent in our empirical analysis.

[12] This is in contrast to participation in security alliances and/or international organizations, which are sometimes linked to international trade of goods, services, and assets. Indeed, this is one of the reasons for our focus on IEAs as opposed to some other form of non-economic international partnership.

of treaties to which each of the host and source countries separately belong (multilateral measures); and second, the number of environmental treaties to which both countries belong (a bilateral measure). The most important column is that on the right, which includes both the bilateral and multilateral measures of environmental treaties.

While the control variables are not of direct interest, it is reassuring to see that the default gravity model seems to work well. Countries that are further apart have fewer asset cross-holdings, while countries with greater economic mass (as measured by GDP) have more. Holding GDP constant, countries with larger population (i.e. lower GDP per capita) exchange fewer assets. A number of sensible features seem to raise cross-holdings, including a common language, currency, land border, colonizer or regional trade agreement. Some of the purely geographic features (the physical size of a country, whether it is landlocked, and whether it is an island nation) also matter. The equation fits well, with an impressive R^2 of 0.61 on a purely cross-sectional basis.

Is there space for environmental commitment to matter above and beyond these factors? Yes. Both the multilateral and bilateral number of environmental commitments have a positive effect on asset cross-holdings. If one examines the column on the extreme right (which gives the weakest results since it examines multilateral and bilateral effects simultaneously), for each additional jointly signed environmental treaty, asset cross-holdings increase by 0.03%. This effect is small but seems intuitively plausible, and is statistically significant at any reasonable confidence level. If a pair of countries were to move from the twenty-fifth percentile (with seven jointly signed environmental treaties) to the seventy-fifth percentile (with fifty-four joint treaties) holding other factors constant, asset cross-holdings would be expected to rise by around 1.5 per cent. Similarly, the effect of a host country's environmental commitment also has a small positive and statistically significant effect on asset holdings; a one standard deviation increase in the number of environmental treaties signed raises asset cross-holdings by around 0.65 per cent.[13]

We consider these results to be supportive of the idea that non-economic partnerships play a small but positive role in supporting economic exchanges such as international cross-holdings of assets. Moreover, as we find that both multilateral and joint IEA memberships are significantly positive, the results appear to support some level of bilateral punishment as well. That said, we have not thoroughly explored

---

[13] Rose and Spiegel (2009) present further sensitivity analysis that confirms the robustness of our key results.

Table 9.1. *Results*

# Environmental Treaties, Host		0.024**		0.013**
		(0.001)		(0.002)
# Environmental Treaties, Joint			0.048**	0.032**
			(0.003)	(0.004)
Log Distance	−1.07**	−0.85**	−0.49**	−0.59**
	(0.08)	(0.09)	(0.09)	(0.09)
Log Host Real GDP	3.51**	2.83**	2.95**	2.76**
	(0.05)	(0.07)	(0.06)	(0.07)
Log Source Real GDP	2.73**	2.33**	2.14**	2.26**
	(0.09)	(0.12)	(0.10)	(0.12)
Log Host Population	−2.27**	−1.72**	−1.84**	−1.67**
	(0.07)	(0.08)	(0.08)	(0.08)
Log Source Population	−2.12**	−1.79**	−1.53**	−1.67**
	(0.10)	(0.12)	(0.11)	(0.12)
Regional Trade Agreement	1.13**	1.20**	0.69**	0.89**
	(0.16)	(0.16)	(0.16)	(0.16)
Currency Union	3.17**	1.77**	0.83**	0.90**
	(0.21)	(0.24)	(0.25)	(0.26)
Common Language	1.83**	2.06**	1.97**	2.00**
	(0.16)	(0.16)	(0.16)	(0.16)
Log Host Area	0.13**	0.01	−0.00	−0.03
	(0.04)	(0.04)	(0.04)	(0.04)
Log Source Area	−0.26**	−0.28**	−0.44**	−0.36**
	(0.03)	(0.03)	(0.03)	(0.04)
Common Land Border	0.97**	0.87*	0.56	0.61
	(0.36)	(0.38)	(0.39)	(0.39)
Host Landlocked	−0.56**	−0.48**	−0.29*	−0.36*
	(0.14)	(0.14)	(0.14)	(0.14)
Source Landlocked	0.35*	0.43*	0.28	0.38*
	(0.18)	(0.18)	(0.18)	(0.18)
Host Island Nation	0.61**	0.57**	0.31**	0.38*
	(0.18)	(0.18)	(0.17)	(0.18)
Source Island Nation	1.37**	1.43**	1.27**	1.33**
	(0.17)	(0.17)	(0.17)	(0.17)
Common Colonizer	1.00**	1.81**	1.37**	1.66**
	(0.41)	(0.40)	(0.39)	(0.40)
# Environmental Treaties, Source		0.009**		0.003
		(0.001)		(0.001)
Observations	6,432	6,354	6,432	6,354
R^2	0.61	0.63	0.63	0.63
Root MSE	4.227	4.131	4.116	4.111

Notes: Dependent variable: log asset cross-holdings. Columns estimated separately. OLS with robust standard errors in parentheses. Data averaged over 2001–03. Intercept included but not tabulated. Coefficients that are significantly different from zero at 0.05 (01) are marked with one (two) asterisk(s).

the linkages between IEA and economic exchange; we model the asset cross-holdings, but trade linkages are also of potential importance. Indeed, the entire production structure of the economy might change as a result of IEA membership; there is plenty of future research to be done.

We conclude that there is indeed a link between environmental engagement – as proxied through environmental treaty obligations – and international exchanges of assets. Moreover, this link appears to reflect both overall and joint IEA participation, suggesting that both the pure reputation and bilateral punishment channels for reputation spillovers play a role in the determination of cross-holdings of assets.

5   Summary

Membership in international environmental arrangements (IEAs) yields costs and benefits. A country can gain directly from such interactions; its air might be cleaner, or there might be more fish in the sea. However, some gains can be indirect. For instance, countries with long horizons and low discount rates might be more willing both to protect the environment and to maintain a reputation as a good credit risk. If they can signal their discount rate through IEA activity, participation in IEAs may indirectly yield gains from improvements in credit terms. Alternatively, countries that are tightly tied into a web of international relationships may find that withdrawing from one domain (such as environmental cooperation), may adversely affect activities in an unrelated area (such as finance). The fear of these spillovers may then encourage good behavior in the first area. In this paper, we have modeled these ideas theoretically, and confirmed their empirical relevance. We have focused on the environmental sphere, but see no reason why the basic logic could not be extended to other facets of international relations such as security.

Important questions remain to be examined. For instance, there is little evidence that bad behavior in the economic sphere (e.g. debt default) actually leads to retaliation outside the economic domain. Why not? Indeed, are there any costs at all of violating IEAs? If not, why do they matter? We leave such questions for future research.

REFERENCES

Barrett, S. (1994). "Self-Enforcing International Environmental Arrangements," *Oxford Economic Papers*, Special Issue on Environmental Economics, **46**, 878–94.
    (2003). *Environment and Statecraft*, New York: Oxford University Press.
Bulow, J. and K. Rogoff (1989). "Sovereign Debt: Is to Forgive to Forget?" *American Economic Review* **79**, 43–50.

Carraro, C. and D. Siniscalco (1998). "International Environmental Agreements: Incentives and Political Economy," *Journal of Public Economics* **42**, 561–72.

Cole, H. L. and P. J. Kehoe (1995). "The Role of Institutions in Reputation Models of Sovereign Debt," *Journal of Monetary Economics* **35**: 45–64.

(1997). "Reviving Reputation Models of International Debt," *Federal Reserve Bank of Minneapolis Quarterly Review* **21**(1): 21–30.

(1998). "Models of Sovereign Debt: Partial vs. General Reputations," *International Economic Review* **39**(1): 55–70.

Di Giovanni, J. (2008). "What Drives Capital Flows? The Case of Cross-Border Mergers and Acquisitions Activity and Financial Deepening," *Journal of International Economics* **65**: 127–49.

Finus, M., J.-C. Altamirano-Cabrera and E. C. van Ierland (2005). "The Effect of Membership Rules and Voting Schemes on the Success on International Climate Arrangements," *Public Choice* **125**: 95–127.

Glick, R. and Rose, A. K. (2002). "Does a Currency Union Affect Trade? The Time-series Evidence," *European Economic Review* **46**(6): 1125–51.

Portes, R. and H. Rey (2005). "The Determinants of Cross-Border Equity Flows," *Journal of International Economics* **65**(2): 269–96.

Rose, A. K. and M. M. Spiegel (2007). "Offshore Financial Centres: Parasites or Symbionts?" *Economic Journal* **117**(523): 1310–35.

(2009). "Non-Economic Engagement and International Exchange: The Case of Environmental Treaties," *Journal of Money, Credit and Banking* **41**(2–3): 337–63.

APPENDIX

9.A.1 Proof of proposition 1

By definition, j^* is the largest value of j for which $\Omega \geq 0$ in (9.9). By (9.9), since $\Omega \geq 0$ is required for an IEA to be joined voluntarily, and since y_{j*} is decreasing in j^*, an increase in j^* requires an increase in the minimum value of β. As more credit is desirable, competition among creditors will then imply that they set the debt ceiling such that (9.5) is binding for the minimum value of β that satisfies $\Omega \geq 0$. Let d_t^k represent the credit constraint given that the representative country joins j treaties. d_t^k satisfies

$$d_t^k \leq \frac{e}{y_{j*}} T(\eta_t^k, d_t^k) \tag{9.A.1}$$

An interior solution for d_t^k requires that $T' \leq y_{j*}/\bar{e}$, where $T' \equiv \partial T/\partial d^k$, which we adopt. Totally differentiating d_t^k with respect to j^* yields

$$\frac{dd_t^k}{dj^*} = -\frac{eTy_{j*}'}{(y_{j*} - \bar{e}T')y_{j*}} \geq 0 \tag{9.A.2}$$

where $y_j' \equiv \partial y/\partial j$, and the denominator is positive when we have an interior solution. This completes the proof.

9.A.2   Proof of proposition 2

If $j^* = m^k$, by (9.11)

$$\frac{dd_t^k}{dj^*} = \frac{-e\left[T + \gamma \sum_{i=1}^{j^*}(y_i - e)\right]y'_{j^*} + e\gamma\,(y_{j^*})^2}{(y_{j^*} - eT')y_{j^*}} \geq 0 \qquad (9.A.3)$$

where the denominator can again be signed as positive given an interior solution.

Alternatively, if $m^k < j^*$, by (9.11) dd_t^k/dj^* is the same as in (9.14) and positive, since the bilateral penalty is unaffected by the increase in j^* in this case. Finally, by (9.11) dd_t^k/dm^k satisfies

$$\frac{dd_t^k}{dm^k} = \frac{e\gamma y_{j^*} y_{m^k}}{(y_{j^*} - eT')y_{j^*}} \geq 0 \qquad (9.A.4)$$

where the denominator is again be signed as positive given an interior solution. This completes the proof.

9.A.2.1   Conditions for separating equilibrium

We can rule out a pooling equilibrium if no individual country would choose to deviate from its separating equilibrium solution to mimic a more patient government. We first examine the case where there are no bilateral penalties. Suppose that instead of joining j^* treaties, an individual government chose to join $j^* + 1$ treaties. Under a separating equilibrium, the country would receive a credit extension that exceeded its borrowing constraint and it would then default on all K countries. By (9.3) and (9.8), its discounted utility would satisfy

$$U_{j^*} = x - (j^* + 1)e + \beta\sum_{i=1}^{K}T(\eta_t^i, d_t^i(j^* + 1))$$

$$+ \left(\frac{\beta}{1-\beta}\right)\left\{x + \sum_{i=1}^{j^*+1}(y_i - e)\right\} \qquad (9.A.5)$$

so that the gain in utility from joining an additional treaty relative to playing the separating equilibrium strategy is equal to

$$U_{j^*+1} - U_{j^*} = \left\{\left(\frac{1}{1-\beta}\right)[\beta y_{j^*+1} - e]\right\}$$

$$+ \beta\sum_{i=1}^{K}\{T(\eta_t^i, d_t^i(j^* + 1)) - T(\eta_t^i, d_t^i(j^*))\} \qquad (9.A.6)$$

The first term is negative, reflecting the loss from entering into an excessive number of IEA treaties, while the second term is positive, reflecting the gains from easing country i's credit constraint.

To evaluate the condition needed to rule out pooling, we also need to consider infra-marginal choices of j. We first demonstrate that the utility from mimicking a more patient government by choosing to join more than the number of treaties that would be optimal under the separating equilibrium, $\hat{j} > j^*$, is decreasing in $\hat{j}$. By (9.A.6)

$$U_{\hat{j}+1} - U_{\hat{j}} = \left(\frac{1}{1-\beta}\right) [\beta y_{\hat{j}+1} - e]$$

$$+ \beta \sum_{i=1}^{K} [T(\eta_t^i, d_t^i(\hat{j}+1)) - T(\eta_t^i, d_t^i(\hat{j}))] \qquad (9.A.7)$$

Differentiating with respect to $\hat{j}$ yields

$$\frac{\partial}{\partial \hat{j}}(\hat{U}_{\hat{j}+1} - \hat{U}_{\hat{j}}) = \beta \left\{ \frac{\partial y_{\hat{j}+1}}{\partial \hat{j}} + \sum_{i=1}^{K} \left[\left(\frac{\partial T}{\partial j} \middle| j = \hat{j} + 1 \right) - \left(\frac{\partial T}{\partial j} \middle| j = \hat{j} \right) \right] \right\}.$$
$$(9.A.8)$$

The entire term will be negative if T is concave in j, i.e. if

$$\frac{\partial^2 T}{\partial j^2} = T'' \left(\frac{\partial d^k}{\partial j}\right)^2 + T' \left(\frac{\partial^2 d^k}{\partial j^2}\right) < 0 \qquad (9.A.9)$$

By (9.14)

$$\frac{\partial^2 d^k}{\partial j^2} = \frac{eT}{(y_{j^*} - eT')y_{j^*}} \left[\frac{(2y_{j^*} - eT')(y'_{j*})^2}{(y_{j^*} - eT')y_{j^*}} - y''_{j*} \right] \qquad (9.A.10)$$

which is ambiguous in sign. Substituting (9.14) and (9.22) into (9.21), T is concave in j if

$$\frac{\partial^2 T}{\partial j^2} = \left\{ \frac{T''eT + T'(2y_{j^*} - eT')}{(y_{j^*} - eT')y_{j^*}} (y'_{j*})^2 - T'y''_{j*} \right\} \left[\frac{eT}{(y_{j^*} - eT')y_{j^*}} \right] < 0$$
$$(9.A.11)$$

This condition will be satisfied if T is sufficiently concave in d^k. A sufficient, but not necessary, condition is

$$|T''| \geq \frac{T'(2y_{j^*} - eT')}{eT} \qquad (9.A.12)$$

which we take as a parameter restriction.

Given the parameter restriction in (9.A.12), the gain from joining an additional treaty relative to any $\hat{j} > j^*$ is decreasing in $\hat{j}$. A separating equilibrium will then obtain if no country would choose to join j^*+1 treaties, i.e. if the term in equation (9.A.6) is negative.

The necessary and sufficient condition is

$$\sum_{i=1}^{K}\{T(\eta_t^i, d_t^i(j^* + 1)) - T(\eta_t^i, d_t^i(j^*))\} \leq \left(\frac{1}{1-\beta}\right)[y_{j^*} - y_{j^*+1}]$$

(9.A.13)

which we adopt. Satisfaction of conditions (9.A.11) and (9.A.13) then guarantee a separating equilibrium.

Finally, we examine the conditions for a separating equilibrium in the presence of bilateral default penalties. The gain from joining an additional treaty relative to any $\widehat{j} > j^*$ will be the same as in (9.A.7), with the exception that d_t^k will now also be a function of m^k if $m^k < j^*$. As before, this gain will be decreasing in $\widehat{j}$ if $\partial^2 T / \partial j^2 \leq 0$. However, the components of $\partial^2 T / \partial j^2$ now incorporate the impact of bilateral penalties.

To derive a sufficient, but not necessary, condition for a separating equilibrium, we evaluate the case where adding an additional treaty yields the largest impact possible. This would be the case where joining an additional treaty increase m^{ik} for all k creditor nations, i.e. where $j^* = m^k \forall k \in K$. $\partial d^k / \partial j$ would then satisfy (9.A.3).

The second derivative now satisfies

$$\frac{\partial^2 d^k}{\partial j^2} = \frac{\{y_{j^*}''(y_{j^*} - eT')y_{j^*} - (y_{j^*}')^2(2y_{j^*} - eT')\} - e\gamma(y_{j^*})^3 y_{j^*}'}{[(y_{j^*} - eT')y_{j^*}]^2} \cdot \left(-e\left[T + \gamma\sum_{i=1}^{j^*}(y_i - e)\right]\right)$$

(9.A.14)

T will then be concave in j if T is sufficiently concave in d_t^k. The necessary and sufficient condition is

$$|T''| \geq \frac{T'\left\{\frac{-e\left[T + \gamma\sum_{i=1}^{j^*}(y_i - e)\right]}{\{y_{j^*}''(y_{j^*} - eT')y_{j^*} - (y_{j^*}')^2(2y_{j^*} - eT')\} - e\gamma(y_{j^*})^3 y_{j^*}'}\right\}}{\left\{-e\left[T + \gamma\sum_{i=1}^{j^*}(y_i - e)\right]y_{j^*}' + e\gamma(y_{j^*})^2\right\}^2}$$

(9.A.15)

As before, we can rule out a pooling equilibrium if a government would not choose to join an additional treaty relative to its undistorted choice. The formal condition is again that in (9.A.13), with d_t^k now corresponding to (9.11). This condition is more restrictive. An increase in the number of joint treaties between countries i and k raises the penalty for default on obligations to country k. It therefore follows that satisfaction of conditions (9.A.13) and (9.A.15) with d_t^k corresponding to (9.11) are sufficient, but not necessary, to rule out pooling in the nested model, i.e. with or without bilateral penalties.

Table 9.A.1. *Countries in CPIS dataset*

Afghanistan	Albania	Algeria	American Samoa	Andorra
Angola	Anguilla	Antigua and Barbuda	Argentina*	Armenia
Aruba*	Australia*	Austria*	Azerbaijan	Bahamas*
Bahrain*	Bangladesh	Barbados	Belarus	Belgium*
Belize	Benin	Bermuda	Bhutan	Bolivia
Bosnia and Herzegovina	Botswana	Brazil	British Virgin Islands	Brunei Darussalam
Bulgaria*	Burkina Faso	Burundi	Cambodia	Cameroon
Canada*	Cape Verde	Cayman Islands*	Central African Rep.	Chad
Chile*	China	Colombia*	Comoros	Congo (Zaire/Kinshasa)
Congo (Brazzaville)	Cook Islands	Costa Rica*	Côte d'Ivoire	Croatia
Cuba	Cyprus*	Czech Republic*	Denmark*	Djibouti
Dominica	Dominican Republic	Ecuador	Egypt*	El Salvador
Equatorial Guinea	Eritrea	Estonia*	Ethiopia	Falkland Islands
Faeroe Islands	Fiji	Finland*	France*	French Guiana
French Polynesia	Gabon	Gambia	Georgia	Germany*
Ghana	Gibraltar	Greece*	Greenland	Grenada
Guadeloupe	Guam	Guatemala	Guernsey*	Guinea
Guinea-Bissau	Guyana	Haiti	Honduras	Hong Kong*
Hungary*	Iceland*	India	Indonesia*	Iran
Iraq	Ireland*	Isle of Man*	Israel*	Italy*
Jamaica	Japan*	Jersey*	Jordan	Kazakhstan*
Kenya	Kiribati	Korea*	Kuwait	Kyrgyz Republic
Laos	Latvia	Lebanon*	Lesotho	Liberia
Libya	Liechtenstein	Lithuania	Luxembourg*	Macau*

Table 9.A.1. (*cont.*)

Macedonia	Madagascar	Malawi	Malaysia*	Maldives
Mali	Malta*	Marshall Islands	Martinique	Mauritania
Mauritius*	Mexico	Micronesia	Moldova	Monaco
Mongolia	Montserrat	Morocco	Mozambique	Myanmar
Namibia	Nauru	Nepal	Netherlands*	Netherlands Antilles*
New Caledonia	New Zealand*	Nicaragua	Niger	Nigeria
North Korea	Norway*	Oman	Pakistan*	Palau
Panama*	Papua New Guinea	Paraguay	Peru	Philippines*
Poland*	Portugal*	Puerto Rico	Qatar	Réunion
Romania*	Russian Federation*	Rwanda	St Helena	St Kitts and Nevis
St Lucia	St Pierre & Miquelon	St Vincent & Gren.	Samoa	San Marino
São Tomé and Príncipe	Saudi Arabia	Senegal	Serbia and Montenegro	Seychelles
Sierra Leone	Singapore*	Slovak Republic*	Slovenia	Solomon Islands
Somalia	South Africa*	Spain*	Sri Lanka	Sudan
Suriname	Swaziland	Sweden*	Switzerland*	Syrian Arab Republic
Taiwan	Tajikistan	Tanzania	Thailand*	Togo
Tonga	Trinidad and Tobago	Tunisia	Turkey*	Turks & Caicos Islands
Turkmenistan	Tuvalu	Uganda	Ukraine*	United Arab Emirates
United Kingdom*	United States*	Uruguay*	Uzbekistan	Vanuatu*
Venezuela*	Vietnam	Virgin Islands	Yemen	Zambia
Zimbabwe				

Note: Source countries also marked with an asterisk.

Table 9.A.2. *Descriptive statistics*

	Obs.	Mean	Std. Dev.	Min	Max
Log Assets	9,396	−3.33	6.62	−9.21	13.20
Log Trade	11,031	2.41	3.53	−6.40	12.85
# Environmental Treaties, Joint	14,960	38.47	32.53	0	232
# Environmental Treaties, Host	13,403	78.08	50.09	1	278
# Environmental Treaties, Source	13,420	125.4	60.75	1	278
Log Distance	14,960	7.91	0.75	3.18	9.27
Log Host Real GDP	10,242	17.37	2.09	12.85	23.03
Log Source Real GDP	11,710	18.90	1.72	13.27	23.03
Log Host Population	11,862	8.56	2.08	3.00	14.06
Log Source Population	12,200	9.19	1.97	4.15	12.57
Regional Trade Agreement	14,960	0.106	0.31	0	1
Currency Union	14,960	0.014	0.12	0	1
Common Language	14,960	0.19	0.39	0	1
Log Host Area	14,960	10.63	3.20	0.69	16.65
Log Source Area	14,960	11.11	3.20	3.04	16.65
Common Land Border	14,960	0.01	0.12	0	1
Host Landlocked	14,960	0.17	0.37	0	1
Source Landlocked	14,960	0.08	0.28	0	1
Host Island Nation	14,960	0.21	0.41	0	1
Source Island Nation	14,960	.20	0.40	0	1
Common Colonizer	14,960	0.07	0.26	0	1

Note: Data averaged over 2001–03.

10 Diplomatic relations and trade reorientation in transition countries

E. R. Afman and M. Maurel

1 Introduction

After the fall of the Berlin Wall on November 9th, 1989 and the dissolution of the Soviet Bloc, western countries and firms entered eastern markets; inversely western markets are nowadays more open for eastern goods – trade no longer being organized by the Council of Mutual Economic Assistance (CMEA). Trade reorientation is one of Nauro Campos and Fabrizio Coricelli's (2002) "magnificent seven stylized facts of ten years of transition." Simultaneously with this economical reorientation, we witnessed the births of new diplomatic relationships, while older ties were renewed.

But there exists some variance: some countries invested more than others in new diplomatic relations. France and the Netherlands are for instance very active on the diplomatic front. These countries both created no fewer than ten new embassies in Eastern Europe and the Former Soviet Union within a time span of less than ten years. Some other countries were less active: they opened smaller consulates, or – for the moment – opted to stay out. Arguably, the decision to open an embassy is foremost a political one, but there is an economic meaning as well.

This chapter goes in search of the economic rationale behind permanent representations, the so-called "foreign mission." More specifically, we ask the empirical question whether diplomatic relationships could be associated with different trade intensities. Does a country with intensive missions abroad (like France or the Netherlands) export more than other countries if we control for other determinants of trade? Do transition countries that are more active on the diplomatic front export more?

Both theoretically and in practice these are important questions. Export promotion is often made explicit as one of the objectives of a foreign diplomatic mission. For example France explicitly sees the (future) role for embassies differing according to the level of development of the bilateral partner, where, especially in the case of emerging economies, "il faut faire fructifier les relations."[1] Hereto, embassies often have an export desk, which is in charge of helping companies on new markets with market analysis. As such it may reduce search costs for a branch of companies that subsequently trade with each other. In this sense, our focus on embassies and economic diplomacy may very well be of influence on the "intangible barriers to trade," as studied by Rauch (1999) and Möhlmann *et al.* in Chapter 8 of this volume.

Tinbergen (1962) was actually the first to connect politics and diplomacy with international trade, by including colonial ties in a gravity-type model. Van Bergeijk (1994) investigated diplomatic barriers to trade focusing on the diplomatic climate, separating positive actions and hostility. Rose (2007) considered the number of bilateral consulates and found a small, but positive significant effect of more foreign permanent representations on unilateral exports. He used a cross-section of 22 big exporting countries with some 200 import destinations. We employ basically the same strategy as Rose. We consider only trade *between* OECD countries on the one hand and transition economies on the other; and we exclude trade *within* these groups of countries. There are two reasons for this choice. First, the big Vinerian trade reorientation that took place in the last decade of the twentieth century could shed important light on the evidence of the effects of foreign missions on trade (given the high variance and momentum in these). Second, the transformation of planned socialist systems to market economies offers a new world of opportunities for exporters: from a policy point of view it is interesting to see whether countries which "stayed out" diplomatically have profited less from the new export opportunities. Also, from a methodological point of view, our research contrasts with that of Rose. First, we estimate the equation of Rose on a panel of countries using a dataset that measures bilateral diplomatic relations (the "Correlates of War" project) over time. The panel structure of the dataset allows for including pair-wise fixed effects and controlling for *country-pair* heterogeneity in the bilateral relationship, or for time-invariant typical characteristics between different pairs of countries. This overcomes the problem of biased estimates due to omitted variables, as argued by Cheng and Wall (2004). As in Afman (2006), we include foreign missions of the importing country in the exporting country as a variable of interest, since these representations also may be of help in reducing search costs. Second, we estimate the effect of diplomacy using an alternative framework proposed by Anderson and van Wincoop (2003), which allows us to compute the ad valorem tariff reduction equivalent to opening an embassy.

[1] www.diplomatie.gouv.fr/fr/ministere_817/ambassades-consulats_814/index.html#so_2.

In sum, our empirical contribution to the issue of foreign missions and exports is twofold. First, we add the group of transition economies to the evidence reported by Rose.[2] Second, we use panel data and correct for the heterogeneity and simultaneity bias by including country-pair specific fixed effects. The remainder of this paper is organized as follows. Section 2 introduces the trade transition that has been made in the economies coming from a socialist system. Section 3 discusses the methodology and data of the analysis. Section 4 presents the results and Section 5 concludes.

2   The trade transition

This section briefly discusses some basic facts of the trade reorientation, which accompanied the transformation of the economies that were originally under a socialist planning system. The main goal of this section is to construct the intuition behind the econometric tests.

Trade within the socialist bloc used to be organized by the CMEA with strict directives. Firms had to obey quantitative production targets and were initially not allowed to trade with each other. There was officially no international trade with market economies. Also in the East Asian socialist countries China, Mongolia, and Vietnam it was the government who decided what was produced where and to whom it was delivered. In the CMEA countries as well as in these socialist countries, there was no invisible hand: growth and development were hindered by a lack of efficiency. When market-based trade was allowed efficiency gains could be made. In the CMEA economies, however, there still were large inefficiencies with respect to the payment system with only barter, "buy-backs," and switches as payment instruments. In 1963 the CMEA created the transferable ruble, which was only a unit of account, but it permitted clearing-operations. In practice however, this led to cumulating debt for many countries since exports originating in the USSR were dominant and other countries were not capable of repaying the commercial credit.

The system of central planning changed in the final quarter of the twentieth century. In China, for example, land reforms were undertaken in 1978, which created an incentive scheme that made agriculture more efficient by stimulating local entrepreneurship. Later China implemented dual-track liberalization where firms were allowed to trade with each other, but under the condition that the targets set by the official plan were met.

[2] Rose included only Russia as an exporting country and included several transition economies as importing countries.

Some Eastern European countries developed outward-looking strategies for development (as for example the Gierek strategy). Hungary was one of the first socialist countries to officially liberalize trade. First it was internally and only on a small scale internationally (around 1980 some enterprises were allowed by the government to trade internationally) but later on a larger scale: around 1988 almost all firms had the authorization to trade internationally. Comparing within CMEA trade and international trade allowed economists to calculate the efficiency of their exports and imports, based in turn on bilateral exchange rates of the florint with the transferable ruble (which was the official unit of account at the time), and on the exchange rate of the florint with US dollars. This gave rise to an increased knowledge of the inefficiencies of the planning system.[3] Simultaneously, Gorbachev tried to reform the functioning of the CMEA, but bilateral accords were undermining his efforts. The Berlin Wall fell, and de facto the CMEA died in 1990. In 1991 the CMEA auto-dissolution was announced officially. In the following years markets were quickly liberalized. The rapid reorientation with western economies was accompanied by big Vinerian trade creation (see Maurel 1998a and 1998b; and Maurel and Cheikbossian 1998 for more on that issue).

In this chapter, we use a sample which consists of two groups of countries: one group, let us refer to it as "east," contains all transition economies (South/North Eastern Europe, Central Asia, China, Vietnam), and a second group, "west," contains the old EU-15 countries and other OECD countries, but without the transition economies Poland, Hungary, Slovakia, and the Czech Republic, which only recently joined the OECD. Figure 10.1 plots the evolution of trade reorientation between these two groups of countries over the period of time under consideration. This figure reflects that while OECD and European partners are important for our "east" group, the reverse is not true. Indeed, in 2000 the "east" countries received only 6 per cent of total exports from "west"; in 2006 this share has almost doubled to 11 per cent. Over the period 1995–2000, the share of exports from transition countries going to "west" countries has grown from 52 per cent to 61 per cent. Ever since, it has remained stable while decreasing slightly in the most recent years. Figure 10.2 focuses on exports from transition countries to the EU-15. Not surprisingly, the EU turns out to be a major partner for the New Member Countries, while it is less important for countries in Central Asia. Many factors can explain this pattern, such as the geographical

---

[3] In Hungary for instance international trade aimed at maximizing US dollar reserves. The exchange rate between the transferable ruble and the US dollar derived from the effective deals revealed that the official exchange rate was over its market value.

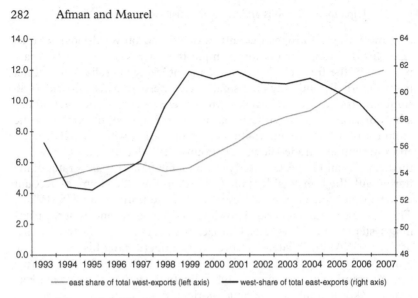

Figure 10.1. Trade reorientation (per cent share of total exports to "west" and to "east").
Source: authors' calculations on IMF DOTS.

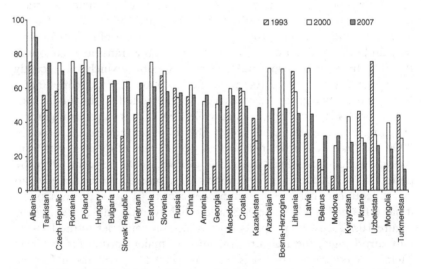

Figure 10.2. Exports from transition countries to the European Union (EU-15) (per cent share in total exports).
Source: authors' calculations on IMF DOTS.

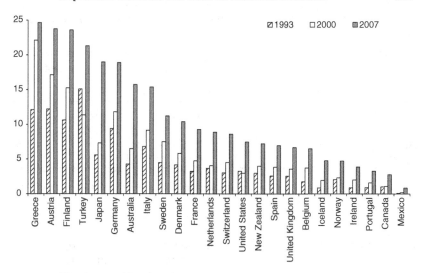

Figure 10.3. Exports from OECD economies to transition countries (per cent share in total exports).
Source: authors' calculations on IMF DOTS.

proximity to nations like Russia, India, and China, or the fact of being landlocked.[4]

Figure 10.3 concentrates on the other direction of trade, from OECD countries to transition economies. The sharp increase is striking in the export share going to the latter, which is particularly steep in the period 2000–05.

3   Data and methodology

How do exports and diplomacy correlate with each other? What is the influence of diplomacy on export performance for each country pair of the two groups?

For measuring economic diplomacy, we use the Diplomatic Exchange Data from the Correlates of War project (Bayer 2006). This dataset quantifies the intensity of diplomatic representation by counting the number of chargés d'affaires, ministers, and ambassadors for the period 1817–2005. We only use the data for 1995, 2000, and 2005. The resulting variable is labeled FM^t (index t indicates that this dataset has a time dimension). As compared to the fixed number of consulates used in Rose, our proxy has

[4] For more on this issue, see Raballand (2005).

Table 10.1. *Diplomatic relations: number of permanent foreign missions over time*

	Total			West–East			East–West		
	1995	2000	2005	1995	2000	2005	1995	2000	2005
None	835	730	635	410	338	292	425	392	343
Chargé d'affaires	66	55	32	46	41	23	20	14	9
Ambassador	640	764	892	314	398	464	326	366	428
Other	19	11	1	10	3	1	9	8	0

Source: authors' calculations on Diplomatic Exchange Data set, v2006.1, Correlates of War project.

a longitudinal perspective and includes information about changes in the diplomatic relationship over time and across country pairs. Table 10.1 below summarizes our variables of interest, where both directions of trade are distinguished.

Table 10.1 shows that diplomatic ties are increasing over time: the number of ambassadors increased from 640 in 1995 to 892 in 2005, while the absence of any diplomatic relations declined over time (from 835 countries having no export-promoting foreign mission in 1995 to 635 in 2005). The decreasing number of chargés d'affaires echoes the increasing number of ambassadors. The latter is a more prestigious position and as such is considered as a substitute for the position of chargé d'affaires. If we distinguish the two groups of countries, we see that the growth in the number of ambassadors of western countries in transition economies has been higher over this time-frame. In relative terms the growth in the number of ambassadors is impressive as well, from 41 per cent of all country pairs in 1995 to 57 per cent in 2005.

Countries which opened an embassy after 1995 experienced on average a nominal increase in exports of US$156 million (albeit with a large standard deviation). Relative to 1995 exports, the median increase of 2005 exports is 243 per cent. Figure 10.4 shows how average exports correlate with each type of foreign mission in the three most recent years covered by the CoW data. Exports to countries with strong diplomatic ties are high and growing.

We relate the previous created variable foreign missions (FM^t) to bilateral trade, controlling for other determinants using the workhorse of empirical trade analysis: the gravity model, which can be specified in different ways. Our first step relies upon Rose's (2007) specification (equation 10.1 below). Rose asks exactly the same question of the

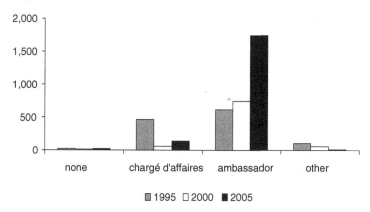

Figure 10.4. Average nominal exports by type of foreign mission and year (US$m).

economic importance of foreign missions, but he uses a larger sample. This strategy allows for a direct comparison.

$$\ln X_{ij}^t = \gamma_1 \cdot fm_{ij}^t + \gamma_2 \cdot fm_{ji}^t + \beta_1 \ln d_{ij} + \beta_2 \ln Y_i^t + \beta_3 \ln Y_j^t$$
$$+ \beta_4 \ln pop_i^t + \beta_5 \ln pop_j^t + \beta_6 \ln area_i + \beta_7 \ln area_j$$
$$+ \beta_8 EEA_{ij} + \beta_9 border_{ij} + \beta_{10} landl_{ij} + \beta_{12} dindu$$
$$+ \alpha_0 + \alpha_t + \alpha_{ij} + \varepsilon_{ij}^t \qquad (10.1)$$

Where:

- $\ln X_{ij}^t$ is the log of exports from country i to country j at time t.
- $fm_{ij}^t (fm_{ji}^t)$ is set equal to 1 when country i (j) has a representation in country j (i).
- d_{ij} is measured as the distance in kilometers between capital cities (CEPII database).
- Y_i^t is the GDP of country i on t (World Bank, WDI).
- pop_i^t gives the population (in million) of country i on t (World Bank, WDI).
- $area_i$ is the area of country i.
- EEA_{ij} is a dummy which values 1 if both countries are members of the European Economic Area.
- b_{ij} is a dummy that values 1 if country i and country j share a border.
- $landl_{ij}$ is 1 if at least one country is landlocked (CEPII).
- $dindu$ is a dummy variable indicating the direction of trade (values 1 if the exporter is an industrialized economy).

- α_0 is the intercept.
- α_t is a year-specific intercept (to account for "globalization," or increase in world trade integration over the last few years).
- α_{ij} is the fixed effect whose specification is open to debate, as discussed below.
- Finally ε_{ij}^t is the residual.

In a second step, we estimate the Anderson and van Wincoop (2003) gravity equation (equation 10.2 below), grounded on firm theoretical foundations, and introducing indexes of multilateral resistance. The latter are extremely useful for understanding some international trade puzzles, for example the McCallum border effect implying a regional trade much larger than its international counterpart. We mimic the formalization of trade cost factor proposed by Anderson and van Wincoop (2003) as follows:

$$t_{ij} = FM_{ij}FM_{ji}d_{ij}^{\rho}$$

where ρ is the elasticity of the distance.

Let us assume that $FM_{ij} = FM^{fm_{ij}}$, and symmetrically, $FM_{ji} = FM^{fm_{ji}}$. fm_{ij} (respectively fm_{ji}) is set equal to 1 when country i (j) has a foreign mission in country j (i); it is zero otherwise. $1 - FM$ represents the tariff reduction implied by opening an embassy. A key variable is σ, which stands for the elasticity of substitution between all goods and is assumed to be constant.

All this means that investing in a foreign mission in the partner country is a way for both the exporter and the importer of reducing the information costs, design costs, and various legal and regulatory costs as well as transport costs.[5] Deriving the following gravity equation is straightforward:[6]

$$\ln(X_{ij}^t/(Y_i^t * Y_j^t)) = (1 - \sigma) \cdot \ln(FM_{ij}) + (1 - \sigma) \cdot \ln(FM_{ji})$$
$$+ (1 - \sigma)\rho \ln d_{ij} - (1 - \sigma)P_i - (1 - \sigma)P_j$$
$$\Rightarrow \ln(X_{ij}^t/(Y_i^t * Y_j^t)) = (1 - \sigma) \cdot \ln(FM)fm_{ij}$$
$$+ (1 - \sigma) \cdot \ln(FM)fm_{ji} + (1 - \sigma)\rho \ln d_{ij}$$
$$- (1 - \sigma)\alpha_i - (1 - \sigma)\alpha_j + \varepsilon_{ij} \qquad (10.2)$$

---

[5] The new empirical literature on the export behavior of firms (Roberts and Tybout 1995; Bernard and Wagner 1997) emphasizes the large costs facing exporters.
[6] For the complete derivation of the gravity equation, see the Appendix at the end of this chapter.

If *coef* is the estimated coefficient for the mission observation at different levels of representation, the implied tariff reduction can be derived using the following formula: $1 - FM = 1 - exp(coef/(1 - \sigma))$.

3.1   Discussion of data

Our trade data come from the IMF Direction of Trade Statistics. We cover trade in two directions between a group of twenty-six OECD economies, and a group of thirty transition countries over three years. This gives a maximum of $2 * 30 * 26 * 3 = 4{,}680$ individual observations. We have however 255 missing values for the bilateral trade flows, while the coverage of explanatory variables is complete. To limit the impact of year-to-year fluctuations we calculate the trade average over three years, and all other time-variant variables are also averaged. This procedure reduces the number of missing values to 160. We have also 251 zeroes in our dataset. Taking logarithms leaves us with $4{,}680 - (160+251) = 4{,}269$ observations.

Missing values may correspond to either zero trade or very little trade which falls below the threshold required for the trade to be registered. Estimating only the strictly positive observations may lead to a selection bias, that results from the fact that the selection of a country as a trade partner may depend on variables that also influence the trade value. There is no perfect solution to this problem in the absence of variables that would explain the selection of a country but not the trade value that is exported. The most frequent approach is to assume that the selection bias is of second order, which is the approach we adopt here.

There is another issue, which is that of reversed causality and/or simultaneity. Export promotion is within the tasks of the government's diplomatic corps, whose resources are limited. Hence when the government optimizes its diplomatic structure, it decides where it opens a consulate or embassy, and where not; one of the factors behind this decision might be the "export potential/economic attractiveness." Trade is promoted by the existence of a consulate but potential trade might stimulate the demand for opening the very same consulate.[7] Another problem is that of simultaneity. For instance oil induces a higher demand for trade and at the same time the presence of oil attracts foreign missions. In both cases we have a two-way causal relationship, and in the latter case some of the foreign mission variables pick up the oil effect.

---

[7] Although (anecdotal) practical experience does not always support this view: diplomatic positions are often the result of political decisions, being made in isolation of economic cost-benefit rationale, thereby not implying simultaneity.

One way of dealing with the resulting bias is to specify the gravity equation with all possible specific omitted variables using country pair-specific fixed effects. This strategy is an alternative to that proposed by Rose (2007), who instruments the foreign mission variable with variables correlating with the number of foreign missions but not directly with exports. Rose uses a number of instruments (oil and gas reserves, and others to which he refers as "fun" instruments), and confirms his results.

4   Results

Estimates of equation 10.1 are reported in Table 10.2. Column (1) is based on the constraint that the intercept is the same for each country and for each year. Column (2) relaxes this constraint on time and allows for time-varying intercepts: this could be important if the model omitted important time-varying variables. Some countries may trade more than others, everything else being kept constant; there is no reason to pose the restriction that the intercept for each country should be one and the same within the current regression framework. Columns (3) and (4) allow for country-varying intercepts with and without time dummies. Columns (5) and (6) allow for each pair varying intercepts with and without time dummies. These final specifications are recommended by Cheng and Wall (2004).

This table brings interesting results. We see that the model "works": the estimated equation explains between 33 per cent and 85 per cent of the variance in exports. The coefficients of the controlling variables fit the expected pattern: distance and being landlocked reduce trade, while shared borders and EEA membership increase it. Our proxies of economic mass (GDP) have the expected sign and magnitude. The coefficients of population are unstable, reflecting maybe the weakness of their theoretical status in the gravity equation. According to Linneman (1966), the coefficient of population must be negative, referring to dominant home markets. Bergstrand (1985) argues that importer (exporter) population is used as a proxy for the characteristics of the commodity which is imported (luxury or ordinary) and exported (capital intensive versus labor intensive). In the gravity equation derived from the New Economic Geography (Anderson and van Wincoop 2003), population is replaced by GDP. The industrialized exporter dummy is only significant in the third and fourth columns.

Let us now concentrate on foreign missions: we find an important association between the number of foreign missions of the exporting country located in the importing country and exports. In five out of six estimations, the fact of having an embassy abroad comes out as having a

Table 10.2. *Gravity equations – specification Rose (equation 10.1)*

	(1)	(2)	(3)	(4)	(5)	(6)
Foreign missions i in j	0.11	0.07	0.32***	0.32***		
(Chargé d'Affaires)	(0.13)	(0.13)	(0.11)	(0.11)		
Foreign missions i in j	0.51***	0.50***	0.42***	0.40***	0.23*	0.20*
(Ambassador)	(0.07)	(0.07)	(0.06)	(0.06)	(0.12)	(0.12)
Foreign missions i in j	0.23	0.16	0.34	0.35*		
(Other)	(0.27)	(0.26)	(0.22)	(0.22)		
Foreign missions j in i	0.17	0.12	0.48***	0.48***		
(Chargé d'Affaires)	(0.13)	(0.13)	(0.11)	(0.11)		
Foreign missions j in i	0.51***	0.50***	0.49***	0.48***	0.15	0.11
(Ambassador)	(0.07)	(0.07)	(0.06)	(0.06)	(0.10)	(0.10)
Foreign missions j in i	0.01	−0.07	−0.01	0.00		
(Other)	(0.26)	(0.26)	(0.21)	(0.21)		
Distance	−1.16***	−1.13***	−1.28***	−1.28***		
	(0.03)	(0.03)	(0.04)	(0.04)		
GDP i	0.89***	0.94***	0.74***	0.78***	0.79***	0.79***
	(0.03)	(0.03)	(0.08)	(0.11)	(0.10)	(0.13)
GDP j	0.61***	0.66***	0.82***	0.86***	0.20***	0.80***
	(0.03)	(0.03)	(0.08)	(0.11)	(0.21)	(0.30)
Population i	0.14***	0.10***	−2.26	−2.59***	−1.57	−1.51
	(0.03)	(0.03)	(0.61)	(0.61)	(0.65)	(0.65)
Population j	0.27***	0.23***	0.68	−1.20	6.34***	1.98
	(0.03)	(0.03)	(0.66)	(0.68)	(1.49)	(1.92)
Area i	−0.02*	−0.02				
	(0.02)	(0.02)				
Area j	−0.03*	−0.04*				
	(0.02)	(0.02)				
EEA	0.57***	0.72***	0.05	0.05	0.24**	0.21
	(0.10)	(0.10)	(0.08)	(0.09)	(0.12)	(0.12)
Border	0.82***	0.85***	0.70***	0.70***		
	(0.16)	(0.16)	(0.13)	(0.13)		
Landlocked	−0.03**	−0.02	−14.14	−1.03***		
	(0.04)	(0.04)	(3.26)	(0.38)		
Industrialized	−0.15	−0.15	−10.58***	−20.0***		
	(0.11)	(0.11)	(3.38)	(5.14)		
Year00		0.08		0.17***		0.25***
		(0.05)		(0.05)		(0.07)
Year05		−0.28		(0.05)		0.05
		(0.06)***		(0.12)		(0.17)
Fixed effects	No	No	Yes: α_i and α_j	Yes: α_i and α_j	Yes: α_{ij}	Yes: α_{ij}
N	4,269	4,269	4,269	4,269	4,269	4,269
R^2	0.77	0.77	0.86	0.86	0.33	0.34
Hausman test					119	170
F	$F_{(17, 4251)}$	$F_{(19, 4249)}$	$F_{(122, 4146)}$	$F_{(124, 4144)}$		
	814	737	201	199		

Notes: *, **, *** denote significance at the 10%, 5%, and 1% level, respectively.

positive and significant correlation with bilateral exports. Our estimates are importantly higher than the ones reported by Rose (2007, table 1, page 30), which vary over the range [0.06–0.11]. In our sample, concentrating on the results where we found a significant outcome, more export-promoting foreign missions in the importing country are associated with between $e^{0.20} - 1 = 22\%$ and $e^{0.51} - 1 = 67\%$ more exports.[8] We believe the 26 per cent ($e^{0.23} - 1$) estimate from column (5) with bilateral fixed effects is the more reliable, and allows the argument that good bilateral diplomatic ties matter.

We turn now to the model of Anderson and van Wincoop. Our results are presented in Table 10.3; they allow computing the ad valorem tariff equivalent reduction implied by a Foreign Mission (rather than the associated extra trade). For this calculus, we need to make an assumption about σ, the elasticity of substitution between goods. We follow Anderson and van Wincoop (2003) in assuming that it can cover a wide range up to when goods are close to perfect substitutes. Assuming therefore that it is 5, 10, and 20, the Chargé d'Affaires estimate of 0.30 in 1995 corresponding to country i opening a foreign mission with a Chargé d'Affaires in the importing country i implies a tariff reduction equivalent of 7.2 per cent. Similarly, installing an ambassador is associated with a tariff-reduction of 2.5 per cent ($\sigma = 20$) to 11.5% ($\sigma = 5$).

5   Conclusions

This chapter is about the role of permanent foreign representations in post-transition trade patterns. Transition implied a big reorientation of trade flows and was considered as one of the main political events of the last century. On the one hand, Gros and Steinherr (2004, p. 71) indicate that Poland, Hungary, and Czechoslovakia achieved a huge trade transition between 1989 and 1992: the share of exports to industrialized countries rose in these three countries from around 25 per cent to more than 50 per cent over no more than three years. On the other hand western economies were fast to recognize independent newly created countries. Opening up a permanent diplomatic representation in those newly created countries was a political act, which created goodwill and irreversibility. We consider those two successful and speedy aspects of the transformation process. The question we ask is whether and how they relate to each other.

---

[8] A similar association is found for the representations of the importing country in the exporting country.

Table 10.3. *Gravity equations – specification Anderson and van Wincoop (equation 10.2)*

Dependent variable: $\ln(X_{ij}^t/(Y_i^t * Y_j^t))$	(1) year 1995	(2) year 2000	(3): year 2005
Foreign missions i in j (Chargé d'Affaires)	0.30*	0.38**	0.19
	(0.17)	(0.17)	(0.23)
Foreign missions i in j (Ambassador)	0.49***	0.41***	0.29***
	(0.10)	(0.10)	(0.10)
Foreign missions i in j (Other)	0.33	0.36	0.51
	(0.27)	(0.35)	(1.19)
Foreign missions j in i (Chargé d'Affaires)	0.27*	0.59***	0.78***
	(0.17)	(0.17)	(0.23)
Foreign missions j in i (Ambassador)	0.45***	0.47***	0.52***
	(0.10)	(0.10)	(0.10)
Foreign missions j in i (Other)	0.001	−0.13	0.82
	(0.27)	(0.35)	(1.19)
Distance	−1.30***	−1.44***	−1.36***
	(0.07)	(0.06)	(0.07)
Ad valorem tariff reduction equivalent of opening an embassy			
$\sigma = 5$			
Chargé d'affaire i in j	0.072	0.090	
Ambassador i in j	0.115	0.097	0.069
Chargé d'affaire j in i	0.065	0.137	0.177
Ambassador j in i	0.106	0.111	0.122
$\sigma = 10$			
Chargé d'affaire i in j	0.032	0.041	
Ambassador j in i	0.052	0.044	0.031
Chargé d'affaire j in i	0.030	0.063	0.083
Ambassador j in i	0.049	0.051	0.056
$\sigma = 20$			
Chargé d'affaire i in j	0.015	0.019	
Ambassador j in i	0.025	0.021	0.015
Chargé d'affaire j in i	0.014	0.031	0.040
Ambassador j in i	0.023	0.024	0.027
Country-specific fixed effects	Yes: α_i^t and α_j^t	Yes: α_i^t and α_j^t	Yes: α_i^t and α_j^t
N	1,310	1,432	1,485
R^2	0.74	0.72	0.71
F	$F(113, 1196)$ 30	$F(116, 1315)$ 29	$F(116,1368)$ 29

Notes: *, **, *** denote significance at the 10% 5%, and 1% level, respectively.

In order to investigate this question, we consider two groups of countries: transition countries, called "east," and industrialized economies "west." We use the foreign permanent representations for each pair observation. We estimate gravity models, using data on three recent years, 1995, 2000, and 2005. We run OLS, and include country fixed effects and pair-wise fixed effects by applying the procedure set out in Cheng and Wall (2004) to control for the heterogeneity bias.

From the first gravity estimation we found positive significant effects for both foreign missions of exporter i in importer j as from importer j in exporter i. These were more or less similar in size. Our preferred estimation implies an extra trade of about 25 per cent, which is close to Rose's (2007) finding. Our second gravity approach relies upon the Anderson and van Wincoop model. It tells us that opening an embassy is equivalent to an ad valorem tariff reduction varying from 2 per cent to 12 per cent. Taking all results together, a broader picture emerges: if we consider the post-transition trade reorientation of the last decade, diplomacy seems to be important. In most regressions, we find a large and positive significant association between the number of foreign missions and trade. These results suggest that investing in good bilateral relations has an economic rationale: a large network of foreign representations seems to have an important positive payoff to home economies in terms of exports, at least where the post-initial trade reorientation with transition countries is concerned.

REFERENCES

Afman, E. R. (2006). "Permanent Foreign Missions and Trade: The Case of (Post-) Transition Countries," University of Paris 1: Panthéon Sorbonne. Unpublished Master Thesis (M2R, DEA).

Anderson, J. E. and E. van Wincoop (2003). "Gravity with Gravitas: A Solution to the Border Puzzle," *The American Economic Review* **93**(1): 170–92.

Bayer, R. (2006). "Diplomatic Exchange Data set, v2006.1," online: http://correlatesofwar.org.

Bergeijk, P. A. G. van (1994). *Economic Diplomacy, Trade and Commercial Policy – Positive and Negative Sanctions in a New World Order.* Cornwall: Edward Elgar.

Bergstrand, J. H. (1985). "The Gravity Equation in International Trade: Some Microeconomic Foundations and Empirical Evidence," *The Review of Economics and Statistics* **67**(3): 474–81.

Bernard, A. B. and J. Wagner (1997). "Exports and Success in German Manufacturing," *Weltwirtschaftliches Archiv* **133**: 134–57.

Campos, N. and F. Coricelli (2002). "Growth in Transition: What We Know, What We Don't, and What We Should," *Journal of Economic Literature* **40**(3): 793–836.

Cheng, I.-H. and H. J. Wall (2004). "Controlling for Heterogeneity in Gravity Models of Trade and Integration," The Federal Reserve Bank of

St. Louis working paper series no. 1999–010E, http://research.stlouisfed.org/wp/1999/1999–010.pdf, version revised July 2004.
Feenstra, R. C. (2004). *Advanced International Trade*, Princeton University Press.
Gros, D. and A. Steinherr (2004). *Economic Transition in Central and Eastern Europe: Planting the Seeds*, Cambridge University Press.
Linneman, H. (1966). *An Econometric Study of International Trade Flows*, Amsterdam: North-Holland.
Maurel, M. (1998a). *Régionalisme et désintégration en Europe centrale et orientale: Une approche gravitationnelle*, Editions du CNRS.
(1998b). "Le régionalisme : les enseignements pour l'est européen", *Economie Internationale* **74**: 43–65.
Maurel, M. and G. Cheikbossian (1998). "The New Geography of Eastern European Trade," *Kyklos* **51**(1): 45–71.
Raballand, G. (2005). *L'Asie centrale ou la fatalité de l'enclavement?*, eds. L'Harmattan.
Rauch, J. E. (1999). "Networks versus Markets in International Trade," *Journal of International Economics* **48**: 7–35.
Roberts, M. J. and J. R. Tybout (1995). "An Empirical Model of Sunk Costs and the Decision to Export," World Bank Policy Research working paper series no. 1436, Washington DC.
Rose, A. K. (2007). "The Foreign Service and Foreign Trade: Embassies as Export Promotion," *The World Economy* **30**(1): 22–38.
Tinbergen, J. (1962). *Shaping the World Economy – Suggestions for an International Economic Policy*. New York: Twentieth Century Fund.

APPENDIX: DERIVATION OF EQUATION 10.2

This appendix replicates the exposition of Anderson and van Wincoop (2003), by starting from a CES-Utility function. Exports from country i to country j are identical to consumption in country j of goods originating in i. We let c_{ij} define total consumption of good i in country j. Utility in country j then equals:

$$U^j = \left(\sum_{i=1}^{C} \beta_i^{\frac{\sigma}{\sigma-1}} c_{ij}^{\frac{\sigma-1}{\sigma}} \right)^{\frac{\sigma}{\sigma-1}} \tag{10.A.1}$$

where σ is the elasticity of substitution.

p_{ij} is the cost-insurance-freight (cif) price in country j for goods originating in country i. This price depends on the trade costs t_{ij} between i and j as $p_{ij} = p_i * t_{ij}$, where p_i is the free on board (fob) price locally at the exporter. Trade costs can in fact be seen as iceberg transport costs: t_{ij} units must be shipped if one unit of a product is to arrive.

The nominal demand for region i goods by region j consumers satisfying maximization of utility subject to budget constraint $Y_i = \sum_j x_{ij}$ is given by:

$$x_{ij} = \left(\frac{\beta_i p_i t_{ij}}{P_j} \right)^{(1-\sigma)} y_j \tag{10.A.2}$$

Where P_j is the consumer price of j, given by:

$$P_j = \left[\sum_i (\beta_i p_i t_{ij})^{1-\sigma} \right]^{\frac{1}{1-\sigma}} \qquad (10.A.3)$$

Market clearance implies:

$$y_i = (\beta_i p_i)^{1-\sigma} \sum \left(\frac{t_{ij}}{P_j} \right)^{1-\sigma} y_j, \quad \forall i \qquad (10.A.4)$$

Defining world nominal income by $y^W = \sum_j y_j$ and income share by $\theta_j = \frac{y_j}{y^W}$, we get:

$$x_{ij} = \frac{y_i y_j}{y^w} \left(\frac{t_{ij}}{\Pi_i P_j} \right)^{1-\sigma} \qquad (10.A.5)$$

$$\text{Where } \Pi_i = \left(\sum_j \left(\frac{t_{ij}}{P_j} \right)^{1-\sigma} \theta_j \right)^{\frac{1}{1-\sigma}} \qquad (10.A.6)$$

One can show that:

$$P_j = \left(\sum_i \left(\frac{t_{ij}}{\Pi_i} \right)^{1-\sigma} \theta_i \right)^{\frac{1}{(1-\sigma)}} \qquad (10.A.7)$$

Assuming that trade barriers are symmetric, that is: $t_{ij} = t_{ji}$, it is easy to verify that one solution is $\Pi_i = P_i$

$$\text{And: } P_j^{1-\sigma} = \sum P_i^{1-\sigma} \theta_i t_{ij}^{1-\sigma} \quad \forall j \qquad (10.A.8)$$

The gravity equation then becomes:

$$x_{ij} = \frac{y_i y_j}{y^W} \left(\frac{t_{ij}}{P_i P_j} \right)^{1-\sigma} \qquad (10.A.9)$$

The final step is to model the unobservable trade factor cost t_{ij}:

$$t_{ij} = b_{ij} d_{ij}^\rho \qquad (10.A.10)$$

Where $b_{ij} = 1$ if regions i and j are located in the same country. Otherwise b_{ij} is equal to one plus the tariff equivalent of the border barrier between the countries in which the regions are located.

$b_{ij} = b^{1-\delta_{ij}}$, where $b - 1$ represents the tariff-equivalent border barrier and δ_{ij} is set equal to one if i and j are in the same country and zero otherwise.

By analogy, we assume:

$b_{ij} = FM_{ij} = FM^{fm_{ij}}$, where $1 - FM$ represents the tariff-reduction equivalent of opening a foreign mission and $fm_{ij}(fm_{ji})$ it is set equal to one when country i (j) has one foreign mission in country j (i).

11 Economic and financial integration and the rise of cross-border M&As

S. Brakman, G. Garita, H. Garretsen, and C. van Marrewijk

1 Introduction

Two waves stand out in the history of globalization. The first wave took place in between 1850–1913, and the second wave started after World War Two and continues until this day (see Bordo *et al.* 2003); moreover, Baldwin (2006) characterizes globalization in terms of two great unbundlings. In his view, during the first wave and much of the second, the fall in transportation costs and the removal of trade barriers spatially unbundled production from consumption, which enabled international specialization.[1] With the second unbundling, the start of which Baldwin (2006) dates at around 1980–90, production itself is increasingly geographically separated; that is, it is no longer the case that production takes place under a single roof. In this light, new technologies enable firms to relocate certain stages of the production process to other countries.

As Figure 11.1 shows, throughout the past fifteen years the growth rate of FDI has surpassed those of both world GDP and world trade. This increased importance of FDI has led to an enthralling and relatively new research agenda that tries to explain the existence of multinational enterprises or MNEs (see for example Markusen 2002; Barba Navaretti and Venables 2004; Helpman 2006; and Brakman and Garretsen 2008). A key feature of these models is the role of trade barriers or, in general, economic distance in determining FDI, since distance-related variables are crucial for understanding FDI patterns. For example, if FDI is mainly market-seeking, then larger trade costs will stimulate it. If, on the other

A first version of this paper was presented at the conference on "The Gravity Equation – Or: Why the World is not Flat," October 2007 at the University of Groningen, the Netherlands. We thank the conference participants, the New York 2008 NARSC international conference participants, Jens Südekum, and both anonymous referees for their useful comments and suggestions.

[1] This is the standard or textbook view of globalization.

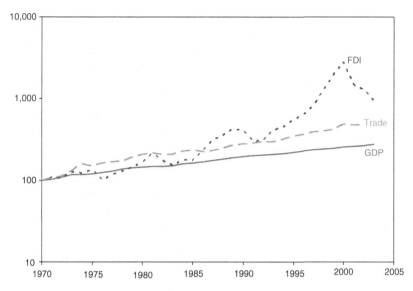

Figure 11.1. Development of GDP, FDI, and trade.
Source: van Marrewijk (2007, p. 325). Constant 2000 $; index, 1970 = 100; logarithmic scale.

hand, FDI is factor cost-seeking, then higher trade barriers will reduce it, since it would be more expensive to reimport intermediate products. Given that most FDI continues to take place between developed economies, the dominant motive for it seems to be market-seeking.[2] This last observation presents us with a puzzle, since the fall in trade barriers during the last two decades (e.g. EU integration) should have led to a *reduction* of market-seeking FDI. But, as Figure 11.1 illustrates, the opposite seems true (i.e. FDI has become more important).

However, FDI does not only take place because of factor cost-seeking or market-seeking motives. Other and sometimes related motives have also been brought to the fore. Cross-border M&As can arise because of managerial hubris (managers seeking personal prestige and remuneration), (stock market) profits that can be made because target firms are under-valued, or strategic motives with respect to competition in the markets in which the acquiring firm operates (see Chapman 2003 for an overview). Furthermore, the market-seeking motive can be more

[2] The share of FDI to developing countries is increasing; see Barba Navaretti and Venables (2004).

298 Brakman *et al.*

complicated in the sense that firms also might have an export-hub motive and seek entry into a highly integrated market (so decreasing trade costs within the integrated market can be consistent with an increase in FDI). There is evidence that these "third country" effects or spatial linkages are important (Garretsen and Peeters 2008), but also evidence that they are not (Blonigen *et al.* 2007).

Most importantly, however, is that the stylized dichotomy of FDI into market-seeking FDI or factor cost-seeking FDI might be too stylized, and that the relation between trade costs and FDI is more complicated. Most FDI is in the form of cross-border M&As. Recent developments analyzing cross-border M&As show that the market-seeking motive is not the only one that can explain FDI, and especially cross-border M&As. In oligopolistic settings, for instance, high trade costs also shield domestic firms from competition raising profits and thus the acquisition costs of the domestic firms. Trade integration therefore makes an M&A more instead of less likely (Horn and Persson 2001). Similar results can be derived in different contexts. With respect to privatization (selling of domestic firms) of state-owned firms to foreign ones, high (trade) barriers can make an acquisition too expensive for foreign firms (Norbäck and Persson 2004). Also the high domestic profits – in shielded markets – might induce lobby activities against foreign takeovers (Südekum 2008) or stimulate protectionist actions (Norbäck and Persson 2005). In all these cases economic integration stimulates (horizontal) FDI. In this literature, however, countries differ from each other by introducing trade costs. Recently Neary (2007, 2008) introduced comparative advantage besides trade costs in order to differentiate countries from each other. Also in this setting economic integration stimulates cross-border M&As. A reduction in trade barriers increases the profitability of an exporting firm in the foreign market and this makes a takeover more likely. It also increases competition in both markets, which further increases the likelihood of a cross-border M&A (as takeover costs become smaller). On the other hand, competition reduces profits of the acquirer, and this makes a takeover less likely. The balance is such that more economic integration leads to more M&As (Neary 2007 and 2008). Finally, Nocke and Yeaple (2007) show, in the context of heterogeneous firms, that the nexus between increased economic integration and market-seeking FDI is not as simple as the market-seeking motive presupposes, as it depends on the balance between different modes of entry. Allowing firm heterogeneity, Breinlich (2006, p. 26) finds for trade between the USA and Canada, that "there does not seem to be a robust link between cross-border M&As and trade liberalization. . ."

The literature thus seems ambiguous as to the effects of trade liber-alization and FDI, especially cross-border M&As. On the one hand the simple dichotomy between horizontal and vertical FDI suggests that eco-nomic integration should go hand-in-hand with less (horizontal) FDI. On the other hand more complex oligopolistic models comparing different modes of entry and/or firm heterogeneity show that the relation between trade costs and, especially, M&As is more complex. In this chapter, using a "new" gravity model approach, we will analyze the relation between distance and other determinants (notably financial integration), and the value of cross-border M&As.[3] Based on the Thomson dataset for M&As, we use an extensive dataset with firm-specific M&A data for 211 coun-tries during the period 1986–2005. Although this analysis does not test the relevance for a specific theory, the findings do allow us to investigate whether FDI is in line with the horizontal FDI model or by the more recent abovementioned alternatives.

The goal of the research herein is twofold: first, we want to establish whether our gravity approach can help unlock the value of cross-border M&As. To date, and despite its quantitative importance (see Section 2), gravity studies have mainly focused on trade or on FDI in general, and have largely ignored cross-border M&As (for exceptions, see Evenett 2004, and di Giovanni 2005). Second, and related to the abovemen-tioned observations, by focusing on the distance variable and on financial openness, we seek to find out if our gravity model can help us improve our understanding of the relationship between economic (and financial) integration on the one hand and the value of cross-border M&As on the other. Our main results are that market size is important for the value of M&As. Furthermore, the results are consistent with the predictions that economic integration stimulates M&As, insofar as the distance variable reflects integration. Concerning financial openness, the results are more ambiguous for countries that are already active in M&A activity; however, for the "passive" group (i.e. countries that do not engage in M&A activ-ity), financial openness seems to be a prerequisite to attract cross-border M&As.

The paper evolves as follows. In Section 2 we present several stylized facts on FDI, and in particular on cross-border M&As; furthermore, we outline how the recent rise of FDI, dominated by cross-border M&As, can be reconciled with the ostensible increase of economic and financial integration. Section 3 discusses our estimation strategy and introduces

---

[3] A companion paper (Garita and van Marrewijk 2008) analyzes the number of deals.

our gravity model by focusing on the "zero-gravity" problem. Section 4 presents our estimation results, and Section 5 concludes.

2   Cross-border M&As

Looking at FDI as a broad category obscures the fact that most FDI is in the form of cross-border M&As. Figure 11.2 shows a decomposition of FDI and it is clear that M&As constitute the bulk of it, whereas greenfield FDI is considerably less important than M&As. The main difference between these two forms of investments is that in an M&A "control of assets and operations is transferred from a local to a foreign company, the former becoming an affiliate of the latter" (UNCTAD 2000). However, it has not been until recently that models in international economics have started to emerge, which enable us to understand M&As. Neary (2007) is special in this literature as he explicitly introduces comparative advantage. Two motives are mentioned to explain M&As: *a strategic motive* (reduce competition, select a specific mode of entry, etc.) and *an efficiency motive* (cost reductions).

An explanation of *cross-border* M&As, however, also has to explain the cross-border part of the deals. This aspect is often reflected by trade (transport) costs. Trade theory suggests, however, that comparative advantage could be included in a full or general equilibrium explanation

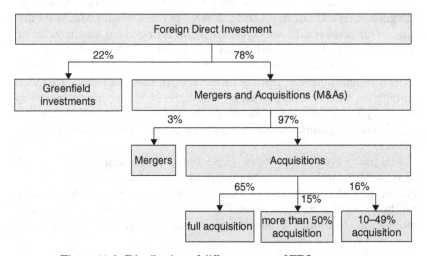

Figure 11.2. Distribution of different types of FDI.
Source: Brakman *et al.* (2007); data: UNCTAD (2000); 78–22 per cent split in value terms, other per cent in no. of deals

Table 11.1. *Overview of cross-border M&As*

	No. of deals	per cent
Cross-border M&As, 1986–2005	27,541	
Effective M&As	27,461	99.7
Average per cent of shares acquired		75.5
Average per cent of shares owned after deal		80.1
No. of horizontal M&As (two-digit level)	13,605	49.4

of M&As. Only recently, and in line with its empirical relevance illustrated in Figure 11.2, has the analysis of cross-border M&As become an important topic for research.

Our overview of the structure of cross-border M&As is based on Thomson's *Global Mergers and Acquisitions Database*, which provides the best and most extensive data source for M&As to date. Its main sources of information are financial newspapers and specialized agencies like Bloomberg and Reuters. Our Thomson dataset begins in 1979 and ends in August 2006. Initially, the focus in the Thomson dataset was on American M&As; nevertheless, systematic M&A data for almost all countries is available from the mid 1980s onwards. Therefore, in presenting the data we will focus on the period 1986–2005.

We collected information on all completed/unconditional *cross-border* M&As with a deal value of at least $10 million, which means that for the period 1986–2005 we have 27,541 cross-border M&As. As Table 11.1 shows, most M&As result in effective ownership; furthermore, about 50 per cent take place within the same sector (i.e. horizontal M&As). We can only speculate as to why this might be the case; however, as previously mentioned,[4] a likely explanation is that most cross-border M&A are market-seeking. That is, taking a competitor out of the market to reduce competition and raise profits. Furthermore, buying a firm outside one's own sector might be motivated by an efficiency motive, since it can be profitable to control a larger part of the value chain. Nonetheless, and regardless of the strategy, both motives increase profits after the takeover.

Figure 11.3 illustrates that the share of horizontal M&As is very stable over time when measured by the *number* of deals; fluctuating around the average of 49 per cent (ranging from a low of 45.1 per cent in 1986 to a high of 51.5 per cent in 1996). Horizontal M&As are substantially more

[4] Of course, strategic motives may (also) be at work here.

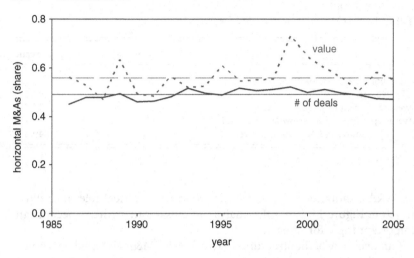

Figure 11.3. Horizontal (two-digit) cross-border M&As; share of total, no. of deals and value.
Note: Horizontal lines indicate averages for the period 1986–2005.

volatile when measured using the *value* of the deals; fluctuating around the average of 56 per cent, ranging from a low of 46.7 per cent in 1988 to a high of 73.0 per cent in 1999.

Those who would argue that the value of horizontal M&As has declined since 1999, are obviously obscuring the fact that the 1999 peak is not representative over a longer time horizon. Moreover, the 2005 value of horizontal M&As of 55.2 per cent is very close to the long-run average of 56 per cent. Using either measure we find little support for the argument that the share of horizontal M&As is declining. From an international economics perspective, the question arises whether existing theories of FDI can explain the dominance of horizontal FDI. On the face of it, this is not the case; assuming that during our sample period (1985–2005) trade costs (broadly defined) have decreased, the standard FDI model predicts that horizontal FDI should have become less important. In terms of the *proximity-concentration* tradeoff, a drop in trade costs shifts the tradeoff in favor of exporting. That is, with falling trade costs foreign markets are better served by exporting instead of (horizontal) FDI. However, recent extensions in the literature show that falling trade costs might nonetheless explain the rise of horizontal FDI, and thus the bulk of cross-border M&As (see the seminal contribution of Horn and Persson 2001). The puzzle put forward in this paper depends on whether or not trade integration indeed has taken place. Although the exact measurements

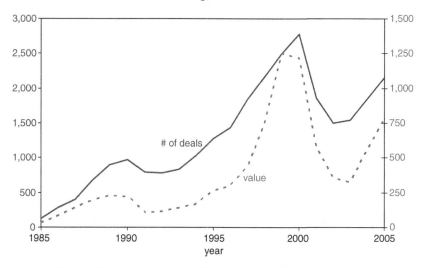

Figure 11.4. Cross-border M&As, 1985–2005; no. of deals and value.
Note: No. of deals (left-hand scale); value in 2005 $ billion (right-hand scale)

of trade costs are difficult (see Anderson and van Wincoop 2004 for a discussion), the consensus is that transportation costs, or more general barriers to trade, in the period under consideration have declined in general (Hummels 2007).

A historical perspective reveals another remarkable characteristic of (cross-border) M&As. Figure 11.4 depicts the evolution of all cross-border M&As over time for our sample period, both measured as the number of deals and the value of deals (in constant 2005 dollar billion, using the US GDP deflator). Clearly, even when looking at this relatively short period, there is substantial variation over time, with periods of rapid increase followed by periods of rapid decline. This corroborates the more general finding that M&As come in waves. To date, five merger waves have been identified throughout the twentieth century, three of which took place after World War Two (Andrade *et al.* 2001). The third wave took place in the late 1960s-early 1970s. The fourth wave ran from (about) the mid 1980s until 1990. The fifth wave started around 1995 and ended in 2000 with the collapse of the "new economy." Figure 11.4 also shows that a subsequent sixth merger wave started in the twenty-first century around 2003 (to end with the financial crisis of 2008).[5]

---

[5] Note that the data used in this paper covers the fourth and fifth waves.

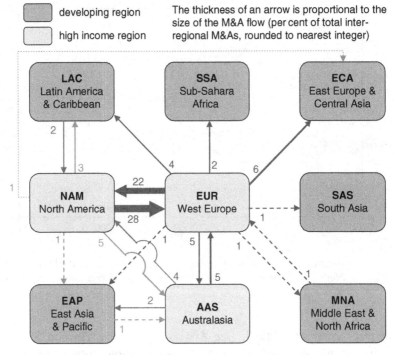

Figure 11.5. Inter-regional cross-border M&As; per cent of total (value), 2001–05.
Notes: All intra-regional M&As are excluded from the figure. The total value of inter-regional M&As is 100 per cent; only flows above 0.5 per cent are shown (this excludes fifty-three of seventy-two possible arrows).

In rounding up our stylized facts discussion regarding cross-border M&As, we focus on *inter*-regional M&As in our sample (see also Appendix A). This gives us an indication of the extent to which different global regions interact with one another by delivering more valuable cross-border M&As. Figure 11.5 depicts the inter-regional cross-border connections for the period 2001–05, rounded to the nearest integer. Since there are nine global regions there are seventy-two different inter-regional connections.[6] First, we note that by far the largest and most valuable inter-regional M&A flows are from North America to Western Europe (28

[6] Only nineteen of these flows appear in Figure 11.5, since the remaining fifty-three flows are rounded to 0 per cent. This already indicates that "zero" observations are important in the sample, and are important for the estimates (see Section 3).

per cent of the total), and vice versa (22 per cent of the total). Together these two flows account for 50 per cent of the value of all inter-regional M&As and clearly dwarf all other inter-regional connections. Second, Western Europe is buying substantial amounts of firms in Eastern Europe (6 per cent). Third, the other high-income region connections (between EUR and AAS and between NAM and AAS) are considerable (about 5 per cent each). Fourth, M&A flows toward East Asia and the Pacific are still rather small, certainly compared to the attention this receives in the popular media. Fifth, and finally, Western Europe is the M&A center of gravity *vis-à-vis* creating more value; in other words, it is the only global region with connections to all other regions.[7]

3   Methodology and estimation strategy

A standard tool now for dealing with distance-related cross-border economic interactions like bilateral trade or FDI flows is the gravity model first developed by Tinbergen (1962). After a period in which it fell out of fashion for its lack of theoretical underpinnings (despite its empirical success), the gravity model has seen a revival. It has become clear that it can be derived from (a wide range) of theoretical models with solid micro-foundations (see Anderson and van Wincoop 2003, for a trade survey and Bergstrand and Egger 2007, for an FDI foundation). Notwithstanding this revival, the number of models that produce a gravity-type specification is relatively large, thereby making the gravity model inapt as a tool to discriminate between different theoretical trade models (see Deardorff 1998; and Helpman *et al.* 2007). Our aim, however, is not to discriminate between theoretical trade models but merely to test the relevance of distance and other determinants for the value of bilateral M&A flows.

Econometrically, the estimations of the gravity model, be it for trade flows or FDI flows, are not without problems, given the "zero-gravity problem" (see Anderson and van Wincoop 2003; Feenstra 2004; Baldwin and Taglioni 2006; Bosker and Garretsen 2007; Bosker 2008). For our purposes this is an important issue, since the percentage of observations with "zero M&As," depending on the precise (sub) sample, is quite high (see the next section). The existence of zero M&A flows constitutes a problem because the often-preferred log-linearized gravity specification is undefined for observations with zero flows. A proper handling of these zero observations is therefore important (see Santos

---

[7] This is reminiscent of the role of Western Europe in inter-regional trade flows (van Marrewijk 2007).

Silva and Tenreyro 2006; Baldwin and Harrigan 2007; Helpman *et al.* 2007; Garita and van Marrewijk 2008). Furthermore, OLS estimates of the log-linearized model may be both biased and inefficient in the presence of heteroskedasticity.

A common method of handling the "zero-gravity" problem thus far has been to simply discard the zeroes by truncating the sample and using OLS, or simply to add a constant factor to each observation on the dependent variable and then estimate the gravity model through a Tobit estimation. These approaches are correct as long as the zero values are randomly distributed; however, if they are not random, as is often the case, then it introduces selection bias (see Bosker 2008). Until recently, this problem has been ignored in gravity studies, but it can be handled by means of sample selection correction. In this light, Helpman *et al.* (2007) propose a theoretical model rationalizing the zero trade flows and propose estimating the gravity equation with a correction for the probability of countries to trade. In order to estimate their model, they apply a two-step estimation technique (similar to sample selection models commonly used in labor economics). To implement the new estimator, one needs to find an appropriate exclusion restriction for identification of the second-stage equation, which can be quite difficult.[8]

The above suggestion to distinguish between *two groups* of observations to adequately deal with the zero-flow problem can be done in an empirically flexible way by using Lambert's (1992) zero-inflated approach (alternative names are "with zeroes," "zero altered," and "hurdle" models). This approach is similar to the Heckman Selection model but does not rely on the associated normality assumptions, and is therefore less restrictive (Heckman 1974; see Razin and Sadka 2007 for an application on FDI).[9] The zero-inflated model assumes that there are two latent groups of observations; an observation in the (always 0) *Passive Group* has an outcome of 0 with a probability of 1; an observation in the (potentially) *Active Group* might have a zero outcome, but there is a positive

---

[8] One could argue that the two-step estimation procedure used by Helpman *et al.* (2007) is not introduced for econometric purposes (i.e. to deal with the "zero-gravity" problem), but follows directly from their preferred trade-theoretical model (in the tradition of Melitz 2003). In the latter model, it is crucial to distinguish between the probability of trade and the volume of trade (or in their terminology, between the extensive and intensive margins of trade), which is exactly what their two-step-estimation procedure does. As to the use of the exclusion restriction (a variable that in the first (probit) step is included to influence the probability of trade but is not part of the second step as it is meant not to influence the volume of trade), Helpman *et al.* (2007) use religion (see also Bosker and Garretsen 2008).

[9] This avoids the difficulty of trying to find an appropriate exclusion restriction (Helpman *et al.* 2007).

probability that there is a non-zero outcome. This process is developed in two stages:

(i) model membership into the latent groups (Active or Passive) using a logit model and observed characteristics (so-called "inflation" variables because they "inflate" the number of zeroes).
(ii) model the value of cross-border M&As for observations in the Active Group via a Poisson or negative binomial regression.

The Poisson model imposes the restriction that the conditional mean of the dependent variable is equal to its variance. The negative binomial regression model generalizes the Poisson model by introducing an individual unobserved effect into the conditional mean which allows for overdispersion in the data (see Blonigen 1997; Wooldridge 2002). The approach can also use it for our non-integer data (the value of M&As; see Santos Silva and Tenreyro 2006, for trade flows). The Vuong (1989) test can be used for selection of non-nested models; repeated application provides overwhelming support in favor of the zero-inflated negative binomial (ZINB) model, such that we restrict attention below to reporting the ZINB results.

4   Estimation results

4.1   Baseline estimations

To test the model outlined above from the acquirer's perspective, we analyze the value of cross-border M&As undertaken by firms in a specific country for the period 1986–2005, giving us a total of almost 1 million observations. For both the acquiring and target country, and in line with the gravity approach, we include GDP and $GDP per capita$ as explanatory variables. As with bilateral trade, we expect GDP (per capita) to have a positive effect on cross-border M&As for both the acquiring (exporting) and target (importing) country. The bilateral (geodesic) distance ($Dist_{ij}$) between countries i and j is also included. As previously mentioned, cross-border M&As come in waves. Therefore, in order to deal with this feature we construct two variables $Wave_1$ and $Wave_2$, where the former (latter) denotes the number of cross-border M&As in the year (two years) prior to time t.

The variables *common language*, *colony*, and *common border* capture the transaction or information costs associated with cross border M&As; they are taken from the CEPII database. We also include *de jure* financial openness in our baseline specification, since cross-border M&As are an example of international capital flows. This variable (measured by the Chinn-Ito index) is thought to have a positive effect on M&As, in particular where it concerns the financial openness of the target country.[10] As we explained in Section 2, set against the recent FDI models, the rise of FDI (*in casu*, cross-border M&As) is not easy to reconcile with ongoing economic integration (falling trade or transport costs). Apart from economic integration, and different from gravity models of international trade, we expect that cross border M&As are also (or even mainly) driven by the degree of financial integration and/or other financial variables. When changing our baseline specification we will include various financial variables. In addition, we incorporate regional fixed effects (for the regions introduced in Figure 11.5). Note that these region fixed effects are different from the country-based distance effects.

Table 11.2 presents the estimation results for our baseline "gravity" model. The columns related to the active group give estimates for the group for which the observations are not necessarily zero; the columns with respect to the passive group give estimates for the always-zero group of observations. With the exception of the wave variables, we use the same characteristics for both groups. The signs for these variables are often opposite, which makes intuitive sense. Note that we have indeed a very large number of zero observations. The estimation results for the Active Group in Table 11.2 show that typical gravity variables help to explain the value of cross-border M&As between countries. A larger market size as measured by GDP leads to a higher value of M&As both from an acquirer and target perspective. GDP per capita only has a positive effect on the value of M&As from the target perspective, indicating that market size is not the only income effect determining the value of M&As, but also that the distribution of income is important. Regarding financial openness, we find that it is a *prerequisite* for M&As to take place (the variables are strongly significant in the column for the Passive Group), but that it is relatively unimportant in determining the value of M&As. Capital mobility seems to act as a cut-off or hurdle variable; without capital mobility M&As are unlikely to occur at all.

What is the relation between economic integration (here approximated by the distance variable D_{ij}) and M&As? If distance proxies increased economic integration, then we find evidence in favor of this strand of literature. That is, increased economic integration raises competition in the home market, which lowers profits of the target (and acquirer) and makes a takeover more likely. The negative sign of the *distance* variable

---

[10] See Chinn and Ito (2002, 2005) for more details on this index.

Table 11.2. *Baseline ZINB estimates*

	Active Group Negative Binomial		Passive Group Logit
	coefficient	inc. rate ratio	coefficient
Ln(GDP)			
acquirer	0.347***	100	−0.680***
target	0.372***	110	−0.708***
Ln(GDP per capita)			
acquirer	0.139		−1.354***
target	0.342***	49	−0.601***
Ln(Dist$_{ij}$)	−0.285***	−22	0.787***
Financial Openness			
acquirer	0.055***	9	−0.161***
target	0.028		−0.072***
Wave$_1$	0.00010**	7	
Wave$_2$	0.00022***	31	
Common Language[a]	0.400***	49	−1.143***
Colony[a]	0.454***	58	−1.022***
Common Border[a]	−0.136*	−13	−0.441***
McFadden adj. R^2	0.241	Region fixed effects	yes
Observations	255,468	Non-zero obs.	5,290

Notes: Zero Inflated Negative Binomial regression. Dependent variable is value of bilateral cross-border M&As. *, **, and *** indicate significance at 10%, 5%, and 1% level. For at least 10% significant variables: the coefficients can be interpreted as elasticities; the incidence rate ratio is calculated as: $100 \times [\exp(\beta) \times \text{std.dev.} - 1]$. Incidence ratios indicate the (percentage) change in the value of M&A if a variable changes by a standard deviation. [a] inc. rate ratio is calculated as: $100 \times [\exp(\beta) - 1]$ for a discrete change from 0 to 1.

is consistent with this line of reasoning, that is, the lower the distance, the higher the value of M&As. In addition, the wave variables indicate that initial M&As stimulate further M&As, and confirm one of the stylized facts related to M&As. These effects of economic integration are enlarged by the results for *common language* and *colony*; if integration takes place in already culturally integrated areas (e.g. areas that share the same jurisprudence), then this further stimulates M&As. In contrast to the standard effect for trade flows, the effect of a *common border* on M&A activity is negative. This is in line with expectations: given that an M&A takes place, the negative border effect indicates that firms want to create some distance. For nearby economies, alternative modes of entry are available. For example, at close range, exporting might be more profitable than setting up shop in foreign markets.

4.2   Baseline estimation sensitivity analysis

We also investigated the robustness of our results, by augmenting our baseline model with several "pull" and "push" factors that are considered important determinants of cross-border M&As (see Appendix B for estimation results). That is, while "push" factors may help explain the timing and magnitude of new capital inflows, "pull" factors may be necessary to explain the regional distribution of new capital flows (Montiel and Reinhart 1999).

4.2.1   US interest rates An important "push" factor is the level of interest rates in the home country, which we will proxy by the 10-year US bond yield. In the literature, there is a consensus that high real interest rates hamper FDI, other things being equal. Albuquerque *et al.* (2005) find a significant and negative relation between the US T-Bill yield and FDI inflows; moreover, Calvo *et al.* (2001) show that FDI inflows to emerging markets are lower during US monetary tightening. Our results are in line with the literature as far as the Active Group is concerned, since the *US yield* coefficient is negative and a one standard deviation increase in the US interest rate decreases the value of M&A activity by over 10 per cent.

4.2.2   Market structure Unlike the surge in capital inflows to developing countries in the 1970s and early 1980s, which were almost exclusively driven by commercial bank lending, capital inflows in the 1990s were associated with a stern rise in bond and equity portfolio inflows; much of these inflows have gravitated towards larger equity emerging markets, bypassing many countries (Montiel and Reinhart 1999). An often-given explanation is that markets must overcome a threshold set of requirements (market size, accounting standards, disclosure requirements, transparency, etc.) in order to attract capital flows. Accordingly, we augment our model by including the lagged stock market capitalization as proxy for the size of the domestic capital market (an indirect proxy for the size of the banking sector; see Montiel and Reinhart 1999); we lag this variable to take care of any endogeneity issues. The results are mixed. For the Active Group only the acquirer seems to benefit from a more developed stock market. For the Passive Group, the odds of remaining in this group decrease for the acquirer if the capitalization of the stock market increases; however, the odds of remaining inactive in M&As increase for the target as the stock market capitalization increases. We also add the Transparency International corruption index[11] (labeled

---

[11] The Transparency International corruption index ranges from 0 = highly corrupt, to 10 = highly clean.

Transparency) to proxy for the business environment in the local economy. The results are in line with expectations, where a less uncertain business environment will increase the value of M&As for the target country in the Active Group by 28 per cent.[12] For the Passive Group, making the business environment more transparent reduces the odds of remaining in this group for both acquirer and target by about 10 per cent.

4.2.3   Macro-economic distortions We use the black market premium as a measure of expected depreciation of the local currency and an index of distortions. Expected depreciation affects investment through several channels: (1) it is more attractive to hold foreign assets; (2) economic uncertainty is higher; (3) foreign capital goods are cheaper to import at the official rate. The first two points suggest a negative relationship between the black market premium and foreign investment while the third point implies the opposite. As an indicator of distortions the black market premium should be negatively correlated with the value of M&As. This is in line with our findings as a one standard deviation increase in the black market premium reduces the value of cross-border M&As for the Active Group by 30 per cent and increases the odds of remaining in the Passive Group by 44 per cent. Regarding the link between FDI and exchange rate uncertainty[13] the literature is mixed, as volatility can both discourage FDI (Cushman 1988) and produce an incentive to hedge against exchange rate shocks through foreign location (Aizenman 1991). In our comprehensive study we find that these two forces balance as exchange rate volatility does not influence the value of cross-border M&As (in contrast to Blonigen 1997, and Froot and Stein 1991).

4.3   Market potential

Following Blonigen *et al.* (2007), we introduce the market potential of the target country in our model among the set of regressors to analyze the economic platform motive for M&As. This variable is the distance-weighted GDP of countries surrounding the target country, where distance is measured in proportion to the distance between Brussels and Amsterdam (173 km, in accordance with Blonigen *et al.* 2007).[14] We find a *negative* effect for the market potential variable; this implies that a different market is more attractive as a target destination than as an attractive export platform. We conclude that the export platform FDI motive is not sustained

---

[12] The coefficient for the acquirer is not significant.
[13] As measured by the coefficient of variation of the bilateral exchange rate.
[14] Distances below 173 km are set equal to the normalization. Note that GDP of the target country itself is *not* included in the outside measure as it is already included separately.

Table 11.3. *Outside market potential ZINB estimates*

	Active Group Negative Binomial	Passive Group Logit
Ln(GDP)		
acquirer	0.269***	−0.650***
target	0.160***	−0.668***
Ln(GDP per capita)		
acquirer	0.252**	−1.497***
target	0.410***	−0.690***
Ln(outside market potential$_{tar}$)	−0.284***	0.784***
Ln(Dist$_{ij}$)	−0.260***	0.915***
Financial Openness		
acquirer	0.050**	−0.122***
target	0.009	−0.058***
Wave$_1$ (coef × 100)	0.008	
Wave$_2$ (coef × 100)	0.024***	
Common Language	0.411***	−0.831***
Colony	0.618***	−1.135***
Common Border	−0.094	−0.289***
Observations 184,702	Region. fixed effects	yes
Non-zero obs. 3,012	McFadden adj R^2	

Notes: Zero Inflated Negative Binomial regression. Dependent variable is value of bilateral cross-border M&As. *, **, and *** indicate significance at 10%, 5%, and 1% level.

by our data (see Table 11.3), in line with Blonigen *et al.* (2007). The other variables are consistent with our earlier findings; thereby indicating that GDP of the target is the dominant variable.

4.4   The baseline model over time

We are not only interested in the impact of distance (or economic integration) and financial openness on the value of cross-border M&As as such, but also or even predominantly on changes in this relationship over time. We thus estimated our baseline model in four five-year periods (1986–90, 1991–95, 1996–2000, and 2001–05). As previously mentioned, our working assumption is that both economic and financial integration have increased in our sample period;[15] therefore, we expect the effect of distance to change over time.[16] Table 11.4 shows that the

---

[15] Granted that, as is standard in gravity studies, distance not only reflects actual transport costs, but also other forms of trade barriers.

[16] See Appendix A; economic integration is bound to have a positive impact on cross-border M&As.

Table 11.4. *Baseline ZINB estimates, separate periods*

	1986–90	1991–95	1996–2000	2001–05
Active Group; Negative Binomial coefficients				
Ln(GDP)				
acquirer	0.354***	0.287***	0.365***	0.368***
target	0.423***	0.333***	0.417***	0.302***
Ln(GDP per capita)				
acquirer	0.039	0.078	0.257*	−0.066
target	−0.354**	0.300***	0.400***	0.338***
Ln(Dist$_{ij}$)	−0.256***	−0.269***	−0.361***	−0.279***
Financial Openness				
acquirer	0.084	0.064	0.225***	−0.023
target	0.112*	0.128***	0.024	0.000
Wave$_1$	0.0003	0.0003*	0.0001	0.0002
Wave$_2$		0.0005*	0.0003***	0.0005**
Common Language[a]	0.170	0.223*	0.587***	0.457***
Colony[a]	0.748***	0.341**	0.574***	0.390**
Common Border[a]	−0.213	−0.252*	−0.165	0.112
Passive Group; Logit coefficients				
Ln(GDP)				
acquirer	−0.595***	−0.649***	−0.691***	−0.727***
target	−0.671***	−0.662***	−0.718***	−0.765***
Ln(GDP per capita)				
acquirer	−1.378***	−1.032***	−1.365***	−1.534***
target	−1.167***	−0.703***	−0.497***	−0.566***
Ln(Dist$_{ij}$)	0.564***	0.772***	0.793***	0.910***
Financial Openness				
acquirer	−0.327***	−0.263***	−0.116***	−0.074***
target	−0.196***	−0.124***	−0.024	0.006
Common Language[a]	−0.716***	−1.246***	−1.094***	−1.244***
Colony[a]	−1.145***	−1.041***	−1.018***	−1.038***
Common Border[a]	0.269	−0.500***	−0.399***	−0.438**
McFadden adj. R^2	0.272	0.254	0.232	0.235
Observations	68,209	67,514	88,972	57,683
Non-zero obs.	667	1,235	2,242	1,288
Region. fixed effects	yes	yes	yes	Yes

Notes: Zero Inflated Negative Binomial regression. Dependent variable is value of bilateral cross-border M&As. *, **, and *** indicate significance at 10%, 5%, and 1% level.

results do not differ markedly from those for the total sample period regarding the impact of GDP (per capita), waves, common border, and common colony.

The distance coefficients for both the Active and Passive Groups have not fallen or even increased in absolute value terms (these results are similar to Disdier and Head 2008), implying that distance has not become less important over time.[17] This finding holds in particular for the Passive Group coefficients where the distance effect gets stronger over time. Two observations are important. First, why has the measured impact effect of distance increased over time? To understand this, one must realize that the estimated coefficients are reduced form estimates of equilibrium M&A decisions under changing circumstances. Economic integration is a *local* phenomenon (EU integration focuses on neighboring European countries, and similarly for NAFTA, ASEAN, etc.) which increases the attractiveness of nearby M&As, to which firms respond by engaging more in local M&A activity. This, in turn, is reflected in the increased impact of distance on M&As, particularly for the Passive Group. Second, what do the changed coefficients imply? In a nutshell, the higher impact of distance on M&As indicates that economic integration (reduction of distance, broadly measured) is becoming more important over time.

The effects of common language follow a similar pattern as the distance coefficients; that is, the coefficients increase over time (in absolute value) for both the Active and Passive Groups. This implies that as countries have moved to reduce transaction (business) costs between them, the value of cross-border M&As has increased accordingly. The effect of *colony* on the value of M&As decreases over time for the Active Group, whereas it remains relatively stable over time for the Passive Group. Regarding the common border effect, we find that it is relatively stable over time, but only affects the Passive Group. In other words, as economic integration increases, and countries start to "share" a common border, the odds of remaining in the Passive Group decrease considerably (approximately by 40 per cent).

5   Conclusions

Most FDI is between similar (developed) countries, predominantly in the form of M&As. This suggests that the market-seeking motive of FDI dominates the data. At present, this seems to be the consensus in the literature (Barba Navaretti and Venables 2004). This presents us with an empirical puzzle: we observe an increase of cross-border M&As together with increased economic integration. If the market-seeking motive indeed dominates, the increased integration should result in fewer M&As as markets can more easily be served through exports instead of FDI. The recent literature suggests two solutions to the puzzle: the export platform motive for FDI, and recently developed oligopolistic models that endogenize the costs of acquiring the target firms (more competition lowers the profits of the target firm and, ceteris paribus, stimulates M&As). In the former case,

---

[17] The only exception is the drop in value for the most recent period for the Active Group.

FDI in a specific country gives access to surrounding markets, whereas in the latter case M&As take place through a subtle balancing act between higher profits and higher takeover costs. Using a zero-inflated negative binomial model, we find evidence:

- against the export platform motive; target GDP is more important than distance-weighted GDP of surrounding countries (with a negative impact);
- in favor of the strand of literature that indicates a subtle balancing act between higher profits of the acquirer and lower takeover costs in a world characterized by increased economic integration;
- in support of financial openness as a necessary condition for M&As to take place; once a threshold level is reached, financial openness has little impact on the value of M&As;
- confirming the impact of ongoing economic integration on M&As, which like trade flows are becoming more local (impact of distance increases over time).

REFERENCES

Aizenman, J. (1991). "Foreign Direct Investment, Productivity Capacity and Exchange Rate Regimes," NBER working paper no. 3767.

Albuquerque, R., N. Loayza and L. Serven (2005). "World Market Integration Through the Lens of Foreign Direct Investors," *Journal of International Economics* **66**(2): 267–95.

Anderson, J. E. and E. van Wincoop (2003). "Gravity with Gravitas: A Solution to the Border Puzzle," *American Economic Review* **93**: 170–92.

(2004). "Trade Costs," *Journal of Economic Literature* **42**(3): 691–751.

Andrade, G., M. L. Mitchell and E. Stafford (2001), "New Evidence and Perspectives on Mergers," Harvard Business School working paper no. 01-070.

Baldwin, R. (2006). "Globalization: The Great Unbundling(s), Prime Minister's Office," Economic Council of Finland, September 2006.

Baldwin, R. and J. Harrigan (2007). "Zeros, Quality and Space: Trade Theory and Trade Evidence," NBER working paper no. 13214, Cambridge, MA.

Baldwin, R. and D. Taglioni (2006). "Gravity for Dummies and Dummies for Gravity," NBER working paper no. 12516, Cambridge, MA.

Barba Navaretti, G. and A. Venables (2004). *Multinational Firms in the World Economy*. Princeton University Press.

Bergstrand, J. H. and P. Egger (2007). "A Knowledge-and-Physical-Capital Model of International Trade Flows, Foreign Direct Investment, and Multinational Enterprises," *Journal of International Economics* **73**: 278–308.

Blonigen, B. A. (1997). "Firm-Specific Assets and the Link Between Exchange Rates and Foreign Direct Investment," *American Economic Review* **87**(3): 447–65.

Bloningen, B. A., R. B. Davies, G. R. Waddell and H. T. Naughton (2007). "FDI in Space: Spatial Autoregressive Relationships in Foreign Direct Investment," *European Economic Review* **51**: 1303–25.

316   Brakman *et al.*

Bordo, M. D., A. M. Taylor and J. G. Williamson (2003). *Globalization in Historical Perspective*, University of Chicago Press.
Bosker, M. (2008). *The Empirical Relevance of Geographical Economics*, Ph.D. thesis, Utrecht University.
Bosker, M., and H. Garretsen (2007). "Trade Costs, Market Access and Economic Geography: Why the Empirical Specification of Trade Costs Matters," CESifo working paper no. 2071, see also this volume.
(2008). "Economic Geography and Economic Development in Sub-Saharan Africa: On the Relevance of Trade and Market Access," CESifo working paper no. 2490.
Brakman, S. and H. Garretsen, eds. (2008). *Foreign Direct Investment and the Multinational Enterprise*, Cambridge, MA: MIT Press.
Brakman, S., H. Garretsen and C. van Marrewijk (2007). "Cross-border Mergers and Acquisitions: The Facts as a Guide for International Economics," in G. Gregoriou and L. Renneboog (eds.), *International Mergers and Acquisitions Activity since 1990: Recent Research and Quantitative Analysis*, MA: Academic Press / Elsevier, Chapter 2: pp. 23–49.
Breinlich, H. (2006). *Trade Liberalization and Industrial Restructuring Through Mergers and Acquisitions*, University of Essex discussion paper no. 619.
Calvo, G., E. Fernadez-Arias, C. Reinhart and E. Calvi (2001). "The Growth-interest Rate Cycle in the United States and its Consequences for Emerging Markets," Inter-American Development Bank working paper no. 458.
Chapman, K. (2003). "Critical Review Essay: Cross-border Mergers/Acquisitions: A Review and Research Agenda," *Journal of Economic Geography* 3: 309–34.
Chinn, M. and H. Ito (2002). "Capital Account Liberalization, Institutions and Financial Development: Cross-country Evidence," NBER working paper no. 8967.
(2005). "What Matters for Financial Development? Capital Controls, Institutions, and Interactions," NBER working paper no. 11370.
Cushman, D. O. (1988). "Exchange Rate Uncertainty and Foreign Direct Investment in the United States," *Weltwirtschaftliches Archiv* 124: 322–36.
Deardorff, A. (1998). "Determinants of Bilateral Trade: Does Gravity Work in a Neoclassical World?" in J. Frankel (ed.), *The Regionalization of the World Economy*, University of Chicago Press.
Di Giovanni, J. (2005). "What Drives Capital Flows? The Case of Cross-border Mergers and Acquisitions Activity and Financial Deepening," *Journal of International Economics* 65: 127–49.
Disdier, A.-C. and Head, K. (2008). "The Puzzling Persistence of the Distance Effect on Bilateral Trade," *Review of Economics and Statistics* 90(1): 37–41.
Evenett, S. (2004). "The Cross Border Merger and Acquisitions Wave of the Late 1990s," in R. Baldwin and L. Winters (eds), *Challenges to Globalization*, University of Chicago Press.
Feenstra, R. C. (2004). *Advanced International Trade*, Princeton University Press.
Froot, K. A. and J. C. Stein (1991). "Exchange Rates and Foreign Direct Investment: An Imperfect Markets Approach," *Quarterly Journal of Economics* 106(4): 1191–1217.
Garita, G. and C. van Marrewijk (2008). "Countries of a Feather Flock Together in M&A Activity," mimeo, Erasmus University Rotterdam and Tinbergen Institute.

Garretsen, H. and J. Peeters (2008). "FDI and the Relevance of Spatial Linkages, Do Third Country Effects Matter for Dutch FDI?" CESifo working paper no. 2191, January, forthcoming in *Review of World Economics*.

Heckman, J. J. (1974). "Sample Selection Bias as a Specification Error," *Econometrica* 42: 153–68.

Helpman, E. (2006). "Trade, FDI and the Organization of Firms," NBER working paper no. 12091.

Helpman, E., M. Melitz and Y. Rubenstein (2007). "Estimating Trade Flows: Trading Partners and Trading Volumes," mimeo.

Horn, H. and L. Persson (2001). "The Equilibrium Ownership of an International Oligopoly," *Journal of International Economics* 53: 307–33.

Hummels, D. (2007). "Transportation Costs and International Trade in the Second Era of Globalization," *Journal of Economic Perspectives* 21: 131–54.

Lambert, D. (1992). "Zero-inflated Poisson Regression, with an Application to Detect in Manufacturing," *Technometrics* 34: 1–14.

Markusen, J. R. (2002). *Multinational Firms and the Theory of International Trade*, Cambridge, MA: MIT Press.

Marrewijk, C. van (2007). *International Economics: Theory, Application, and Policy*, Oxford University Press.

Melitz, M. (2003). "The Impact of Trade on Intra-industry Reallocations and Aggregate Industry Productivity," *Econometrica* 71: 1695–725.

Montiel, P. and C. Reinhart (1999). "Do Capital Controls and Macroeconomic Policies Influence the Volume and Composition of Capital Flows? Evidence from the 1990s," *Journal of International Money and Finance* 18(4): 619–35.

Neary, J. P. (2007). "Cross-border Mergers as Instruments of Comparative Advantage," *Review of Economic Studies* 74: 1229–57.

Neary, P. (2008). "Trade Cost and Foreign Direct Investment," in S. Brakman and H. Garretsen (eds.), *Foreign Direct Investment and the Multinational Enterprise*, Cambridge, MA: MIT Press, pp. 13–39.

Nocke, V. and S. Yeaple (2007). "Cross-border Mergers and Acquisitions vs. Greenfield Foreign Direct Investment: The Role of Firm Heterogeneity," *Journal of International Economics* 72(2): 336–65.

Norbäck, P.-J. and L. Persson (2004). "Privatization and Foreign Competition," *Journal of International Economics* 62: 409–16.

(2005). "Privatization Policy in an International Oligopoly," *Economica* 72: 635–53.

Razin, A. and E. Sadka (2007). *Foreign Direct Investment*, Princeton University Press.

Santos Silva, J. and Tenreyro, S. (2006). "The Log of Gravity," *The Review of Economics and Statistics* 88(4): 641–58.

Südekum, J. (2008). "National Champions versus Foreign Takeovers," mimeo, University of Duisburg-Essen.

Tinbergen, J. (1962). *Shaping the World Economy: Suggestions for an International Economic Policy*, New York: Twentieth Century Fund.

UNCTAD (2000). *World Investment Report*.

Vuong, Q. H. (1989). "Likelihood Ratio Tests for Model Selection and Non-nested Hypotheses," *Econometrica* 57(2): 307–33.

Wooldridge, J. (2002). *Econometric Analysis of Cross Section and Panel Data*. Cambridge, MA: MIT Press.

APPENDIX A: REGIONAL DISTRIBUTION OF CROSS-BORDER M&AS

Table 11.A.1. *Regional distribution of cross-border M&As, 2000–05*

a. Number of deals (% of total); shaded cells: higher than 0.5%

from	AAS	EAP	ECA	EUR	LAC	MNA	NAM	SAS	SSA	sum
AAS	5.7	2.7	0.1	1.8	0.1	0.0	2.2	0.4	0.1	13.1
EAP	0.7	1.0	0.0	0.2	0.1	0.0	0.2	0.0	0.0	2.2
ECA	0.0	0.0	1.1	0.2	0.0	0.0	0.1	0.0	0.0	1.4
EUR	2.5	1.3	3.4	26.5	2.6	0.4	9.7	0.8	0.6	47.8
LAC	0.0	0.0	0.0	0.1	1.6	0.0	0.4	0.0	0.0	2.1
MNA	0.0	0.0	0.0	0.1	0.0	0.1	0.0	0.0	0.0	0.1
NAM	3.1	1.2	0.8	11.2	2.1	0.1	12.1	0.4	0.3	31.2
SAS	0.1	0.0	0.0	0.2	0.0	0.0	0.2	0.2	0.0	0.9
SSA	0.2	0.1	0.0	0.3	0.0	0.0	0.1	0.1	0.3	1.2
sum	12.2	6.3	5.5	40.6	6.6	0.6	25.0	2.0	1.3	100

b. Value of deals (constant 2005 $, per cent of total); shaded cells: higher than 0.5 per cent

from	AAS	EAP	ECA	EUR	LAC	MNA	NAM	SAS	SSA	sum
AAS	3.0	1.5	0.0	1.9	0.1	0.0	2.1	0.1	0.0	8.7
EAP	0.3	0.4	0.0	0.2	0.0	0.0	0.1	0.0	0.0	1.0
ECA	0.0	0.0	0.9	0.1	0.0	0.0	0.0	0.0	0.0	1.0
EUR	2.0	0.5	2.2	38.1	2.7	0.3	15.8	0.2	0.6	62.4
LAC	0.0	0.0	0.0	0.0	1.0	0.0	0.6	0.0	0.0	1.5
MNA	0.0	0.0	0.0	0.3	0.0	0.0	0.0	0.0	0.0	0.4
NAM	1.8	0.4	0.4	10.5	1.2	0.0	9.9	0.1	0.1	24.3
SAS	0.0	0.0	0.0	0.0	0.0	0.0	0.0	0.1	0.0	0.2
SSA	0.0	0.0	0.0	0.1	0.0	0.0	0.1	0.0	0.1	0.4
sum	7.1	2.9	3.5	51.3	5.0	0.4	28.6	0.4	0.9	100

c. Ratio of value of deals (per cent of total) to number of deals (per cent of total) shaded cells: higher than 1

from	AAS	EAP	ECA	EUR	LAC	MNA	NAM	SAS	SSA	sum
AAS	0.5	0.6	0.5	1.0	0.5	0.1	1.0	0.2	0.2	0.7
EAP	0.4	0.4	0.2	0.9	0.3	5.3	0.4	0.1	0.1	0.4
ECA	0.7	na	0.8	0.6	na	0.2	0.4	na	1.3	0.7
EUR	0.8	0.4	0.6	1.4	1.0	0.8	1.6	0.2	1.1	1.3
LAC	na	0.2	0.1	0.1	0.6	0.2	1.6	na	na	0.7

Table 11.A.1. *(cont.)*

c. Ratio of value of deals (per cent of total) to number of deals (per cent of total)
shaded cells: higher than 1

from	AAS	EAP	ECA	EUR	LAC	MNA	NAM	SAS	SSA	sum
MNA	3.7	na	na	6.3	na	0.4	na	0.2	0.1	2.6
NAM	0.6	0.4	0.5	0.9	0.6	0.3	0.8	0.2	0.3	0.8
SAS	0.2	0.1	1.8	0.2	0.1	0.1	0.1	0.2	0.9	0.3
SSA	0.2	0.2	0.1	0.5	0.7	0.0	0.6	0.2	0.4	0.4
sum	0.6	0.5	0.6	1.3	0.8	0.7	1.1	0.2	0.7	1

APPENDIX B: BASELINE ESTIMATIONS WITH DIFFERENT FINANCIAL MARKET VARIABLES

Table 11.B.1. *Exchange rate variability ZINB estimates*

	Active Group Negative Binomial		Passive Group Logit
	coefficient	inc. rate ratio	coefficient
Ln(GDP)			
acquirer	0.309***	85	−0.672***
target	0.351***	101	−0.711***
Ln(GDP per capita)			
acquirer	0.213**	28	−1.383***
target	0.339***	49	−0.600***
Ln($Dist_{ij}$)	−0.271***	−21	0.837***
Financial Openness			
acquirer	0.024		−0.173***
target	0.045**	7	−0.097***
$Wave_1$	0.00015***	10	
$Wave_2$	0.00019***	27	
Exchange rate var.	0.036		0.055
Common Language[a]	0.610***	84	−1.050***
Colony[a]	0.387***	47	−1.092***
Common Border[a]	−0.225**	−20	−0.311***
McFadden adj. R^2	0.249	Region. fixed effects	yes
Observations	211,256	Non-zero obs.	3,921

Notes: Zero Inflated Negative Binomial regression. Dependent variable is value of bilateral cross-border M&As. *, **, and *** indicate significance at 10%, 5%, and 1% level. For at least 10% significant variables the incidence rate ratio is calculated as: $100 \times [\exp(\beta) \times \text{std.dev.-1}]$.
[a] inc. rate ratio is calculated as: $100 \times [\exp(\beta) - 1]$ for a discrete change from 0 to 1.

Table 11.B.2. *US yield ZINB estimates*

	Active Group Negative Binomial		Passive Group Logit
	coefficient	inc. rate ratio	coefficient
Ln(GDP)			
acquirer	0.343***	99	−0.671***
target	0.383***	115	−0.710***
Ln(GDP per capita)			
acquirer	0.399***	59	−1.333***
target	0.341***	49	−0.587***
Ln(Dist$_{ij}$)	−0.290***	−22	0.765***
Financial Openness			
acquirer	0.078***	13	−0.178***
target	0.039**	6	−0.089***
US yield	−11.975***	−13	11.858***
Common Language[a]	0.421***	52	−1.131***
Colony[a]	0.493***	64	−1.011***
Common Border[a]	−0.114		−0.366***
McFadden adj. R^2	0.241	Region. fixed effects	yes
Observations	282,378	Non-zero obs.	5,432

Notes: Zero Inflated Negative Binomial regression. Dependent variable is value of bilateral cross-border M&As. *, **, and *** indicate significance at 10%, 5%, and 1% level. For at least 10% significant variables the incidence rate ratio is calculated as: $100 \times [\exp(\beta) \times \text{std.dev.} - 1]$.
[a] inc. rate ratio is calculated as: $100 \times [\exp(\beta) - 1]$ for a discrete change from 0 to 1.

Table 11.B.3. *Black market premium ZINB estimates*

	Active Group Negative Binomial		Passive Group Logit
	coefficient	inc. rate ratio	coefficient
Ln(GDP)			
acquirer	0.330***	85	−0.638***
target	0.379***	103	−0.643***
Ln(GDP per capita)			
acquirer	0.424***	64	−1.386***
target	0.256***	35	−0.579***
Ln(Dist$_{ij}$)	−0.289***	−23	0.611***
Ln(Black market prem)			
acquirer	−0.160***	−26	0.194***
target	0.003		0.202***
Wave$_1$	0.00054***	42	
Wave$_2$	−0.00037***	−26	
Common Language[a]	0.332***	39	−0.898***

Table 11.B.3. *(cont.)*

	Active Group Negative Binomial		Passive Group Logit
	coefficient	inc. rate ratio	coefficient
Colony[a]	0.556***	74	−1.046***
Common Border[a]	−0.248**	−22	−0.185
McFadden adj. R^2	0.226	Region. fixed effects	yes
Observations	94,182	Non-zero obs.	2,595

Notes: Zero Inflated Negative Binomial regression. Dependent variable is value of bilateral cross-border M&As. *, **, and *** indicate significance at 10%, 5%, and 1% level. For at least 10% significant variables the incidence rate ratio is calculated as: $100 \times [\exp(\beta) \times \text{std.dev.} - 1]$.
[a] inc. rate ratio is calculated as: $100 \times [\exp(\beta) - 1]$ for a discrete change from 0 to 1.

Table 11.B.4. *Transparency ZINB estimates*

	Active Group Negative Binomial		Passive Group Logit
	coefficient	inc. rate ratio	coefficient
Ln(GDP)			
acquirer	0.338***	98	−0.677***
target	0.410***	129	−0.694***
Ln(GDP per capita)			
acquirer	0.204*	27	−0.963***
target	0.103*	13	−0.426***
Ln(Dist$_{ij}$)	−0.295***	−22	0.763***
Financial Openness			
acquirer	0.107***	19	−0.248***
target	0.042*	7	−0.104***
Transparency			
acquirer	−0.008		−0.070***
target	0.083***	28	−0.062***
Wave$_1$	0.00002		
Wave$_2$	0.00023***	31	
Common Language[a]	0.408***	50	−1.095***
Colony[a]	0.452***	57	−0.981***
Common Border[a]	−0.199**	−18	−0.492***
McFadden adj. R^2	0.246	Region. fixed effects	yes
Observations	197,785	Non-zero obs.	4,002

Notes: Zero Inflated Negative Binomial regression. Dependent variable is value of bilateral cross-border M&As. *, **, and *** indicate significance at 10%, 5%, and 1% level. For at least 10% significant variables the incidence rate ratio is calculated as: $100 \times [\exp(\beta) \times \text{std.dev.} - 1]$.
[a] inc. rate ratio is calculated as: $100 \times [\exp(\beta) - 1]$ for a discrete change from 0 to 1.

Table 11.B.5. *Lagged stock market value ZINB estimates*

	Active Group Negative Binomial		Passive Group Logit
	coefficient	inc. rate ratio	coefficient
Ln(GDP)			
acquirer	0.356***	106	−0.654***
target	0.342***	101	−0.739***
Ln(GDP per capita)			
acquirer	−0.144		−0.931***
target	0.343***	49	−0.632***
Ln(Dist$_{ij}$)	−0.286***	−22	0.769***
Financial Openness			
acquirer	0.064**	11	−0.203***
target	0.030		−0.116***
Lag Stock Market Val.			
acquirer	0.005***	22	−0.008***
target	0.001		0.003***
Common Language[a]	0.252***	29	−0.972***
Colony[a]	0.571***	77	−0.972***
Common Border[a]	−0.279***	−24	−0.442***
McFadden adj. R^2	0.252	Region. fixed effects	yes
Observations	203,960	Non-zero obs.	3,608

Notes: Zero Inflated Negative Binomial regression. Dependent variable is value of bilateral cross-border M&As. *, **, and *** indicate significance at 10%, 5%, and 1% level. For at least 10% significant variables the incidence rate ratio is calculated as: $100 \times [\exp(\beta) \times \text{std.dev.} - 1]$.
[a] inc. rate ratio is calculated as: $100 \times [\exp(\beta) - 1]$ for a discrete change from 0 to 1.

12 The impact of economic geography on GDP per capita in OECD countries

H. Boulhol and A. de Serres

1 Introduction and main findings

Over the past several years, the OECD has quantified the impact of structural policies on employment, productivity, and GDP per capita (e.g. OECD 2003, 2006). The results from these studies, which have built on a vast academic literature, have contributed to a better understanding of the main channels linking policies to labor and product market outcomes in OECD countries. In doing so, they have also underscored the limits to the understanding of economic growth: only a limited part of the cross-country dispersion in GDP levels and growth rates can be explained by quantifiable policy levers, at least on the basis of standard macro-growth regression analysis.

This paper examines how much of the cross-country dispersion in economic performance can be accounted for by economic geography factors. To do so, an augmented Solow model is used as a benchmark. The choice is motivated by the fact that this model has served as the basic framework in previous work on the determinants of growth, thereby ensuring some continuity. It has long been recognized, however, that while providing a useful benchmark to assess the contributions of factor accumulation as a source of differences in GDP per capita, the basic Solow growth model ignores potentially important determinants. For instance, it leaves a large portion of growth to be explained by the level of technology, which is assumed to grow at a rate set exogenously.

This is a shortened version of Boulhol, de Serres and Molnar (2009). The authors would like to thank numerous OECD colleagues, in particular Sven Blöndal, Jørgen Elmeskov, Christian Gianella, David Haugh, Peter Hoeller, Nick Johnstone, Vincent Koen, Dirk Pilat, Jean-Luc Schneider, and Andreas Woergoetter, for their valuable comments as well as Philippe Briard and Martine Levasseur for technical assistance and Caroline Abettan for editorial support. The paper has also benefited from comments by members of the working party no. 1 of the OECD Economic Policy Committee, as well as the participants to the "The Gravity Model" conference, Groningen, October 2007.

In order to bridge some of the gaps, extensions of the model in the literature have generally taken four types of (partly related) directions: (i) R&D and innovation; (ii) goods market integration and openness to international trade; (iii) quality of institutions; and (iv) economic geography. The focus of this paper is on economic geography, although this is not totally independent from the other factors, in particular international trade. More specifically, for the purpose of this study, the concept of economic geography is examined through the proximity to areas of dense economic activity.

The key point of this aspect of geography is the recognition that proximity may have a favorable impact on productivity, through various channels operating via product and labor markets. In the case of product markets, one of the key channels is that proximity induces stronger competition between producers, thus encouraging efficient use of resources and innovation activity. Another is that an easy access to a large market for consumers and suppliers of intermediate goods allows for the exploitation of increasing returns to scale. Furthermore, the presence of large markets allows for these scale effects to be realised without adversely affecting competition. The scope for exploiting higher returns to scale is hampered by distance to major markets, both within and across countries, due to transportation costs. They also reduce the scope for specialization according to comparative advantage, another important driver of gains from trade along with the ability to reap scale economies.

The empirical strategy pursued in this chapter is as follows. In Section 2, the augmented Solow model, which is used as the basic framework, is first briefly described and estimated both in level and in error-correction forms, over a sample of twenty-one OECD countries over the period 1970–2004. The influence of proximity to major markets on GDP per capita is investigated in Section 3, introducing in the benchmark model various indicators of distance to markets, such as measures of market potential, market and supplier access, as well as the sum of distances to world markets and population density. Of these, market and supplier access measures are derived from the estimation of gravity equations. The various measures of distance to markets are all found to have a statistically significant effect on GDP per capita, with the exception of population density. The estimated economic impact varies somewhat across specifications, but it is far from negligible. For instance, the lower access to markets relative to the OECD average could contribute negatively to GDP per capita by as much as 11 per cent in Australia and New Zealand. Conversely, the benefit from a favorable location could be as high as 6–7 per cent of GDP in the case of Belgium and the Netherlands. In Section 4, the impact of distance is alternatively examined via the more specific channel of transportation and telecommunication costs. Based on broad indicators of weight-based shipping costs covering maritime, air, and road freights, transportation costs are found to have a negative and significant effect on GDP per capita through their effect on international trade, although the effects are quantitatively smaller than those found on the basis of measures of market access derived from gravity equations. The latter finding is consistent with transportation costs being only one aspect of costs related to distance. Conclusions follow in Section 5, which also discusses tentative policy implications.

2   General empirical framework

The empirical framework used to assess the influence of economic geography determinants is the Solow (1956) model augmented with human capital (Mankiw *et al.* 1992). Despite being derived from a specific framework, the empirical version of that model is sufficiently general to be consistent with some endogenous growth models (Arnold *et al.* 2007). It can be estimated either directly in its level form, or through a specification that explicitly takes into account the dynamic adjustment to the steady state. Estimates of the long-run relationship in static form have been used in the literature (e.g. Mankiw *et al.* 1992; Hall and Jones 1999; Bernanke and Gürkaynak 2001), in particular in studies focusing on income level differentials across countries. However, since the model has often been used in the empirical growth literature to examine issues of convergence, some form of dynamic specification has been more common.

A major drawback with the most common techniques based on dynamic fixed-effect estimators is that only the intercepts are allowed to vary across countries, implying that all countries converge to their steady-state at the same speed, an assumption unlikely to hold even among developed countries. To address the latter issue, previous studies have relied on the Pooled Mean Group (PMG) estimator, which allows for short-run coefficients and the speed of adjustment to vary across countries, while imposing homogeneity on long-run coefficients (Pesaran *et al.* 1999). However, even though the PMG estimation technique is intuitively appealing and perhaps the most suitable under some conditions, it is not without limitations. For instance, due to the large number of parameters and the non-linear constraints, the maximum likelihood estimation technique is prone to problems of convergence on local optima, which sometimes generates unstable or implausible estimated parameters.

For the purpose of this study, the model is first re-estimated with only the basic determinants included in the specification, i.e. proxies for investment in physical and human capital, population growth, and technical progress. Then, a number of determinants are added to the benchmark specification throughout the rest of the paper, but the set of additional variables is limited to those related to economic geography factors. One exception is the measure of exposure to international trade which is used to assess the impact of transportation costs on GDP per capita (Section 4).

The empirical version of the augmented Solow model is re-estimated over a panel dataset comprising twenty-one countries and thirty-five years of observations (1970–2004). In what will serve as the reference model for the rest of the paper, the level of GDP per working-age person in country i and year t (y_{it}) is regressed on the rate of investment in the total economy ($s_{K,it}$), the average number of years of schooling of the population aged 25–64, which is used as a proxy for the stock of human capital – average number of years of schooling – (hc_{it}), and the growth rate of population (n_{it}) augmented by a constant factor introduced as a proxy for the sum of the trend growth rate of technology and the rate of capital depreciation ($g + d$), with all variables expressed in logs.[1] Technological progress is captured alternatively by a linear time trend or time dummies.

The results presented in this paper are based on both a level specification, using a least-square estimator (that corrects for heteroskedasticity and contemporaneous correlations), and an error correction specification, using the PMG estimator. Due to persistence in the series, control for first-order serial correlation is systematically made when the level specification is estimated. The functional forms of the equations estimated in level and error-correction forms are respectively specified as follows (see Bassanini and Scarpetta 2001 for details):

Level specification (AR1)

$$Logy_{it} = \alpha \cdot Log\, s_{K,it} + \beta \cdot Log\, hc_{it} + \varphi \cdot \Delta Log\, hc_{it}$$
$$+ \gamma \cdot Log(n_{it} + g + d) + \varsigma_i t + e_i + e_t + u_{it}$$
$$u_{it} = \rho \cdot u_{it-1} + \varepsilon_{it}, \varepsilon_{it} i.i.d. \tag{12.1}$$

Error-correction specification (Pooled Mean Group)

$$\Delta Log\, y_{it} = -\lambda_i \cdot \lfloor Logy_{it-1} - (\alpha \cdot Logs_{K,it} + \beta \cdot Loghc_{it}$$
$$+ \gamma \cdot Log(n_{it} + g + d) \rfloor + a_{0i} \cdot \Delta Logs_{K,it}$$
$$+ a_{1i} \cdot \Delta Loghc_{it} + a_{2i} \cdot \Delta Log(n_{it} + g + d)$$
$$+ e_i + \varsigma_i \cdot t + \varepsilon_{it} \tag{12.2}$$

---

[1] Following a standard approach in the literature, this constant factor ($g + d$) is set at 0.05 for all countries (Mankiw *et al.* 1992).

Table 12.1. *Basic framework: regression results*

Augmented Solow model[a]

Dependent variable GDP per capita	level AR (1) (1)	level AR (1) (2)	level AR (1) (3)	Error correction PMG (4)	Error correction PMG (5)
Common parameters					
Physical capital	0.184***	0.156***	0.199***	0.292***	0.572***
	(0.019)	(0.024)	(0.017)	(0.030)	(0.059)
Human capital	0.334***	0.792***	−0.063	0.861***	−0.006
	(0.127)	(0.053)	(0.156)	(0.199)	(0.189)
Population growth[b]	−0.006	−0.016	−0.003	−0.392***	−0.661***
	(0.018)	(0.028)	(0.018)	(0.067)	(0.101)
Time trend					0.015***
					(0.002)
Rho[c]	0.884	0.911	0.775		
Country-specific parameters					
Lambda[d]				−0.190***	−0.086***
				(0.025)	(0.017)
Time trend	no	no	yes	yes	no
Fixed effects					
Country	yes	no	yes	yes	yes
Year	yes	yes	yes	no	no
Sample size					
Total number of observations	696	696	696	695	695
Number of countries	21	21	21	21	21

Notes: Standard errors are in brackets. *: significant at 10% level; ** at 5% level; *** at 1% level.

[a] The functional forms corresponding to the "level" and "error-correction" specifications are reported in Section 2.2. In the level specification, standard errors are robust to heteroskedasticity and to contemporaneous correlation across panels. In the error-correction specification, only long-term parameters are reported.

[b] The population growth variable is augmented by a constant factor $(g + d)$ designed to capture trend growth in technology and capital depreciation. This constant factor is set at 0.05 for all countries.

[c] rho is the first-order auto-correlation parameter.

[d] The parameter *lambda* is the average of the country-specific speed adjustment parameter.

where e_i and e_t are country and year fixed effects, respectively, and t is a linear time trend. The parameters α, β, γ and ς are the long-run parameters on the three basic determinants and the time trend. The parameter ρ is the first-order autocorrelation coefficient used in the level specification.[2] The other parameters capture short-run dynamics and will not be reported in the table of results. Finally, u_{it} and ε_{it} are the residuals.

The results from re-estimating the empirical version of the augmented Solow model are presented in Table 12.1. The first three columns refer to the level specification and the last two are based on the error-correction specification. Focusing on the level specification, the coefficient on human capital is quite sensitive to the control for fixed effects and or time trends. In particular, it comes out significantly higher when country fixed effects are excluded (column [2]), suggesting that an important part of the information contained in the average number of years of schooling is related to differences in average levels across countries. Moreover, it completely drops out when country-specific time trends are included in the regression in addition to country- and year-fixed effects (column [3]).

Turning to the error-correction specification, the results shown in the fourth column are similar to those obtained in the earlier OECD analysis based on an almost identical specification (with country fixed effects and country-specific parameters on the time trend) and the same estimation method (PMG). The speed of adjustment parameter suggests rapid convergence to the steady-state, a result which is influenced by the introduction of country-specific time trend parameters. Also, the parameter estimate on human capital suggests a strong effect, with one extra year of schooling leading to an increase in GDP per capita by around 8 per cent in the long run for the average OECD country. However, here again, the significance of the human capital coefficient depends on whether or not the trend is assumed to be common or country specific (column [5]). The rest of the paper investigates whether distance to markets can contribute to explaining GDP per capita differences across countries on top of the usual determinants of the augmented Solow model.

3   Economic distance

In this section, different measures of proximity to markets or centrality are introduced and tested in the empirical analysis as potential determinants of GDP per capita. Some of them are simple measures based on GDP, country size, population, and distances *vis-à-vis* other countries. The others are model-based measures derived from bilateral trade flows.

---

[2] Doing so makes it close to a growth rate or error correction model specification, with constraints imposed on the short-term dynamics (see Beck and Katz 2004, for further details). In that sense, 1 minus the first-order correlation parameter can be compared with the annual speed of convergence.

3.1   Why proximity matters

The role of geographic distance and the influence of neighboring countries have largely been neglected in traditional growth theory which
relies essentially on national characteristics, e.g. factor endowments and
technological progress. Yet, the clustering of economic activities is a well-
known phenomenon that raises questions about the extent to which the
proximity to high-income neighbors matters for a country's own income.
The development process might indeed be hindered in countries that are
distant from centers of economic activities.

Distance can affect productivity and income levels through various
channels, including trade, foreign investment and technology diffusion. There is ample evidence showing the importance of distance for
trade and FDI flows (e.g. Nicoletti *et al.* 2003), as well as for technology spillovers (Keller 2002; Ertur and Koch 2007). Furthermore,
trade and FDI are obvious channels of knowledge spillovers (Eaton and
Kortum 1994 and 1996), which reinforces the impact of distance on
productivity.

Focusing on the trade channel, distance directly raises transport and
other trade costs and is an obstacle to both domestic and foreign trade.
There are a number of inter-related ways through which this channel
affects productivity. Greater proximity to world markets increases the
opportunity to concentrate resources in activities of comparative advantage. It also encourages specialization of firms that can attain efficient
scale and more generally exploit increasing returns in specific fields of
production. Moreover, stronger competition pressures force companies
to use available inputs efficiently and encourage them to innovate and
maintain a competitive advantage.

In addition to influencing GDP per capita via its impact on technical
efficiency, distance can also affect external terms of trade. A relatively
remote and sparsely populated country has to internalize transport costs
into producer prices of tradeable goods in order to remain competitive
in world markets or otherwise suffer lower sales. Because, by definition,
the factor prices of mobile factors tend to be equalized across locations,
the costs of remoteness are born by the immobile factors, i.e. mostly
labor in an international perspective. Indeed, even if technologies are the
same everywhere, firms in more remote countries can only afford to pay
relatively lower wages (Redding and Venables 2004).

In addition to its direct impact on incomes, geography might have
an influence through other factors such as physical or human capital.
Returns to physical and human capital might be higher in countries having
a better access to large markets (Redding and Scott 2003). In turn, a high

return to skills increases the incentive to invest. As regards human capital, Redding and Scott provide some evidence that the world's most peripheral countries have relatively low levels of education, a feature found also in the case of European regions (Breinlich 2006).

3.2   The distance of OECD countries to world markets

In this section, four measures of proximity to markets or centrality are constructed and compared. The first one is population density. The second one depends solely on distances between countries. The third one is a simple measure based on distances *vis-à-vis* other countries and the size of their GDPs, and the last one is a model-based measure derived from bilateral trade flows. Section 4 is specifically dedicated to the effects of economic distance measured by transport costs.

3.2.1   Population density, sum of distances, and market potential Population density, defined as the ratio of population to surface area, is an indicator of proximity to the domestic market. The higher the density the lower the aggregated domestic transport costs. However, the critical shortcoming of this measure is its failure to take into account the effective access to foreign markets.

A simple measure of distance to markets that does so is one based on bilateral distances.[3] From the perspective of empirical analysis, this measure is attractive because it is based on exogenous characteristics of geography. Although the sum of the distances of each country to Tokyo, Brussels, and New York has been commonly used in the empirical literature, the choice of these three locations is arbitrary and creates issues of endogeneity.

Hence, a better alternative is to sum the distances to all countries (Head and Mayer 2006):

$$Distsum_i = \sum_j d_{ij} \tag{12.3}$$

In order to compute *Distsum*, the world was divided in thirty-two areas: Africa, Australia, Austria, Belgium, Brazil, Canada, China, CIS countries, Denmark, Eastern Europe, Finland, France, Germany, Greece,

[3] The geography variables are taken from the CEPII (*Centre d'études prospectives et d'informations internationales*) database. For details, see the notes at www.cepii.fr/distance/noticedist_en.pdf.

Ireland, Italy, Japan, Korea, Latin America (other than Brazil and Mexico), Mexico, the Middle East, the Netherlands, New Zealand, Norway, Portugal, Spain, Sweden, Switzerland, Turkey, the United Kingdom, the United States, and Asia (other than the countries already included). Pure distance measures, however, fail to take into account the size of markets. Moreover, this measure depends on how geographic areas are constructed. For example, a different picture would be obtained if the European Union was considered as one entity or, alternatively, North America was disaggregated into states/provinces.

Therefore, a more refined measure of proximity to markets is market potential, which is defined as the sum of all countries' GDP weighted by the inverse of the bilateral distance (Harris 1954):

$$Market\ Potential_i = \sum_j \frac{GDP_j}{d_{ij}} \qquad (12.4)$$

The market potential measure must take into account, for a given country, the domestic market and include its own GDP weighted by the inverse of internal distance. Because the internal distance is generally smaller than external distances, it is associated with a greater weight and is therefore a sensitive parameter for measures of centrality. The most commonly used distance indicators combine geodesic capital-to-capital distances between countries and internal distances based on surface areas.[4] It follows that market potential is likely to be positively correlated with population density due to the domestic component.

3.2.2   Market and supplier access Although it is an intuitive indicator of centrality, market potential is an ad-hoc way of capturing the influence of distance to markets. In particular, the weighting of foreign markets in the market potential computation is based solely on distances, regardless of the true accessibility of these markets. In that respect, market *potential* is a very crude measure of market *access*. Indeed, accessibility depends, in addition to distance, on trade policy and cultural relationships, among other determinants. A better approach consists in looking not only at the *potential*, but rather at the *actual* accessibility to countries' markets.

---

[4] The underlying assumption behind the internal distance $d_{ii} = 2/3\sqrt{area_i/\pi}$ is that a country is a disk where all suppliers are located in the center and consumers are located uniformly over the area. An alternative measure consists in using the largest cities in each country both for external and internal distances. This entails some differences depending on the size of the countries. However, the results in this paper proved to be robust to the choice of the distance definition.

Box 12.1 Construction of market access and supplier access measures

Market and supplier access measures are derived from the estimation of a gravity-like relationship. As is common in the literature, trade costs in the bilateral trade specification are assumed to depend on three variables: bilateral distance, common border, and common language. Noting $X_{i \to j}$ as the export from country i to country j and d_{ij} the bilateral distance, the following equation is estimated for each year t:

$$Log\ X_{i \to j,t} = s_{it} + a_t.Log\ d_{ij} + b_t.Border + c_t.Language$$
$$+ m_{jt} + v_{ijt}$$

where the so-called freeness of trade (ϕ), which is inversely related to trade costs, is given by $Log\ \phi_{ijt} = a_t.Log\ d_{ij} + b_t.Border + c_t.Language$ (about the importance of the specification of trade costs for the estimation of gravity equation, see Bosker and Garretsen in this volume). The estimates of "intra-country" freeness of trade, ϕ_{iit}, are computed based on the same formula applied to internal distance, common border, and common language. s_{it} and m_{jt} are unobserved exporter and importer characteristics, respectively. For each year, they are proxied by country fixed effects. According to the model (see Boulhol and de Serres 2010, for details), these effects capture some characteristics of the countries related to the number of varieties, expenditures on manufactures, price indices, etc. Market and supplier access, respectively MA and SA, are then constructed from the estimated parameters of the bilateral equation according to:

$$MA_{it} = \sum_k m_{kt} \cdot \phi_{ikt}; \quad SA_{it} = \sum_k s_{kt} \cdot \phi_{ikt}$$

For all the countries, market access (supplier access respectively) is computed as a weighted sum of unobserved importer characteristics m_j (exporter characteristics s_i respectively) of all countries. Only the weights put on each partner change across countries, with these weights being a function of estimated trade costs. If a given country k has a large market capacity m_k, countries having low trade costs with country k, i.e. a high freeness of trade, put a high weight on m_k and tend to have a high market access. A similar argument applies to supplier access for countries having low trade costs with partners having a large export capacity. Note that this is the same principle as that applied to market potential, whose computation boils down to weighting all countries' GDP by the inverse of the bilateral distances.

A measure based on such an approach has been proposed in the new economic geography literature, which has revived the concept of proximity to markets and formalized the role of economic geography in determining income. Using the methodology proposed by Redding and Venables (2004) and described in Box 12.1, measures of market and supplier access have been derived from bilateral trade equations estimated over the period 1970 and 2005 for the thirty-two countries/areas covering 98.5 per cent of world trade flows in goods (see Boulhol and de Serres 2010 for details).

3.2.3   Comparison of the different measures The various measures of centrality discussed in the previous sub-section have been computed for most OECD countries and Table 12.2 reports the computed values for 2005, plus the average of the country ranking over the different measures. To facilitate the comparison, each of these measures is scaled such that the average across countries is a hundred for each year. The cross-country pattern is reasonably close across indicators. Linear correlation is especially high, at around 95 per cent, between market potential, market access, and supplier access (and the average ranking). Ranking the countries enables us to distinguish five groups:

• The remote and sparsely populated countries: Australia and New Zealand;
• Low-income peripheral countries;
• High-income peripheral countries, Korea and North America;
• Continental Europe, the United Kingdom, and Japan;
• The centrally located and dense economies of Belgium and the Netherlands.

As expected, access measures are negatively correlated to the sum of distances and positively correlated to population density, suggesting that market and supplier access encompasses these different geographical dimensions. Besides, population density is an important factor explaining the position of Japan and Korea at or above what could be expected from the pure sum-of-distances measure.

Given the size of its own market, the relative position of the United States in terms of market potential or market access might look surprising. As shown by the first column in Table 12.2, which gives the simplest measure of proximity, one reason is that the United States is much further from markets than European countries. Another reason is that the size of the domestic market is not in itself an adequate indicator of market potential or access to markets. To see this more closely, Table 12.3 breaks down market potential and market access into their domestic and foreign components, respectively. Looking for example at market potential, it is

Table 12.2. *Measures of proximity/distance to markets, 2005*

Average across countries = 100 for each indicator   Average ranking[a]

	Sum of distances (Distsum)	Market potential	Market access	Supplier access	Population density	
Australia	214	21	25	23	2	1.4
Austria	69	124	116	123	78	16.2
Belgium	69	194	236	222	113	21.8
Canada	113	111	126	86	3	10.6
Denmark	68	136	119	130	97	18.0
Finland	72	79	66	74	12	8.0
France	70	153	145	137	84	18.2
Germany	68	152	154	172	197	21.6
Greece	76	70	61	55	63	7.2
Ireland	73	107	100	101	46	11.8
Italy	72	116	115	110	150	15.2
Japan	139	127	111	163	266	15.6
Korea	131	85	104	154	406	14.2
Mexico	149	44	44	33	43	4.0
Netherlands	69	183	221	199	308	22.8
New Zealand	234	20	26	25	14	2.2
Norway	70	93	76	80	11	9.8
Portugal	81	76	73	59	90	8.4
Spain	77	89	96	73	67	10.0
Sweden	70	91	75	84	15	10.6
Switzerland	70	144	136	147	143	18.8
Turkey	78	60	52	52	75	6.6
United Kingdom	70	169	158	136	189	19.4
United States	119	82	92	64	27	7.6
Linear correlation coefficient						
Sum of distances		−0.69	−0.57	−0.52	−0.17	−0.62
Market potential			0.96	0.92	0.50	0.97
Market access				0.93	0.53	0.92
Supplier access					0.71	0.95
Density						0.62

[a] All the countries are ranked based on each of the five indicators, 1 standing for the most remote country and 24 for the most central one. The average ranking is the average of these five rankings.

true that the domestic component represents two-thirds of the total for the United States whereas that share is only 22 per cent for the Netherlands and 4.5 per cent for Canada. Still, the domestic market potential for the United States is only 30 per cent greater than that for the Netherlands,

Table 12.3. *Domestic and foreign components of market potential and market access, 2005*

Base: "World" = 100

	Market potential			Market access			Internal distance[a]
	Total	Domestic	Foreign	Total	Domestic	Foreign	Km
Australia	21	4	17	25	9	17	1,043
Austria	124	14	110	116	13	103	109
Belgium	194	27	166	236	69	167	68
Canada	111	5	106	126	7	120	1,188
Denmark	136	17	120	119	16	103	78
Finland	79	4	75	66	6	60	218
France	153	39	114	145	32	113	278
Germany	152	63	89	154	73	81	225
Greece	70	8	62	61	9	52	136
Ireland	107	10	97	100	12	88	100
Italy	116	43	73	115	54	61	206
Japan	127	99	28	111	83	28	231
Korea	85	34	52	104	61	43	119
Mexico	44	7	37	44	10	34	528
Netherlands	183	41	142	221	96	126	77
New Zealand	20	3	17	26	9	18	195
Norway	93	7	86	76	6	70	214
Portugal	76	8	68	73	12	62	114
Spain	89	21	68	96	40	55	268
Sweden	91	7	84	75	8	68	252
Switzerland	144	24	120	136	19	117	76
Turkey	60	6	54	52	6	46	332
United Kingdom	169	60	109	158	65	93	186
United States	82	54	28	92	64	28	1,161

[a] The underlying assumption behind the internal distance $d_{ii} = 2/3\sqrt{area_i/\pi}$ is that a country is a disk where all suppliers are located in the center and consumers are located uniformly over the area.

even though its GDP is twenty times bigger. This is because the internal distance of the United States is fifteen times bigger. What matters is not the size of the total domestic market, captured here by the GDP, but that size relative to internal distance.[5] In any case, these considerations have

[5] In that context, the higher calculated total market potential for Canada than for the United States reflects the specific capital-to-capital measure of distance. Whereas the internal distance for the United States is 1,161 km, the capital-to-capital distance between the two countries is 737 km. Hence, this measure of distance gives the US GDP a greater weight for Canada than for the United States itself. This feature disappears when the

very limited consequences for the econometric analysis that follows, since they refer essentially to the levels of the proximity measures and most of the regressions include country fixed effects.

3.3   Empirical analysis: augmented Solow model and proximity

The impact of access to markets on GDP per capita has been tested in different contexts and all these studies find that proximity has an important impact on GDP per capita.[6] However, none of them has focused on developed countries despite their widely varying access to markets. In a broad sample covering both least and most developed countries, Australia and New Zealand generally appear to have overcome the "tyranny of distance" (Dolman et al. 2007). However, this inference might be misleading if the data do not enable important country specificities to be accounted for. Focusing on a more homogenous group over a large period using panel techniques should therefore lead to a more reliable estimate.

This sub-section assesses the impact of the different measures of proximity/distance on GDP per capita when added to the usual explanatory variables in the augmented Solow framework.[7] Table 12.4 presents a first set of results obtained from the GDP per capita level specification. In order to identify the sum of distances and population density measures, country fixed effects have to be removed and, therefore, the first two columns include country effects, whereas the last two do not.[8] This first set of results indicates that the effect of proximity is robust to the various measures. Market potential, the weighted sum of market and supplier access, and the sum of distances are all highly significant with the expected sign, with only population density not having any strong link

distance measure takes into account not only the capital but also the biggest cities in each country (see Boulhol and de Serres 2010). As shown in the chapter by Head and Mayer in this volume, distances can suffer from serious mismeasurements. However, the results presented in the empirical part herein are robust to the different distance measures in the CEPII database. This is because, although the levels of distance to markets vary across measures, the variations through time are almost insensitive to the choice of a particular measure. In the empirical analysis, the latter matters as country fixed effects are included.

[6] Redding and Venables apply their framework to a cross-section of 101 countries, while Breinlich (2006), highlighting that regional income levels in the European Union display a strong core-periphery gradient, tests the impact of market access using a panel of European regions over 1975–97. Head and Mayer (2006) conduct a similar exercise based on European sectoral data over a shorter period. Concurrently, Hanson (2005) develops a model assuming labor mobility and tests it using data covering US counties. Combes and Overman (2004) present a survey of studies replicating Hanson's approach for various European countries.

[7] Based on a cross-section of 148 countries, an earlier study showed that proximity (market potential) explains a significant fraction of the income pattern even after controlling for the usual determinants in Solow-type regressions (Hummels 1995).

[8] As in Section 2 (Table 12.1), the human capital parameter is very sensitive to whether country fixed effects are included.

Table 12.4. *Basic framework with proximity variables*[a]

Dependent variable GDP per capita	level AR (1) (1)	level AR (1) (2)	level AR (1) (3)	level AR (1) (4)
Physical capital	0.178***	0.174***	0.178***	0.156***
	(0.020)	(0.019)	(0.020)	(0.024)
Human capital	0.313***	0.317***	0.928***	0.813***
	(0.115)	(0.122)	(0.070)	(0.051)
Population growth[b]	−0.003	−0.005	−0.006	−0.014
	(0.018)	(0.018)	(0.023)	(0.028)
Market potential	0.086***			
	(0.023)			
Weighted sum market and supplier access		0.056***		
		(0.015)		
Sum of distances			−0.210***	
			(0.023)	
Population density				0.008
				(0.005)
Rho[c]	0.863	0.882	0.946	0.913
Fixed effects				
Country	yes	yes	no	no
Year	yes	yes	yes	yes
Sample size				
Total number of observations	696	696	696	696
Number of countries	21	21	21	21

Notes: Standard errors are in brackets. *: significant at 10% level; ** at 5% level; *** at 1% level.
[a] The functional form corresponding to the "level" specification is reported in Section 2.2. Standard errors are robust to heteroskedasticity and to contemporaneous correlation across panels.
[b] The population growth variable is augmented by a constant factor $(g + d)$ designed to capture trend growth in technology and capital depreciation. This constant factor is set at 0.05 for all countries.
[c] rho is the first-order auto-correlation parameter.

to GDP per capita.[9,10] This confirms that, as expected from the previous section, population density is a much weaker indicator of proximity to markets than the other three. Based on the estimates related to the sum

[9] Due to the strong correlation between market and supplier access, the specific effect of each indicator cannot be identified. However, the explanatory variable in the model is a weighted sum of the two indicators, the weights being given by structural parameters; see Boulhol and de Serres (2010) for details.
[10] Because the right-hand side access variables are generated regressors, the standard errors might be underestimated. To check the extent of the standard error bias, bootstrap techniques are used to obtain appropriate standard errors for the specification in levels *without*

of distances (which do not control for country fixed effects), an increase of 10 per cent in the distances to all countries triggers a decrease of 2.1 per cent in GDP per capita.[11]

In order to test the robustness of the proximity effects across specifications, the following results focus on the indicator that rests more firmly on sound theoretical grounds, i.e. market and supplier access. The first three columns of Table 12.5 add the weighted sum of market and supplier access to the specifications shown in columns (1) to (3) of Table 12.1, respectively. Market and supplier access is always highly significant, being robust to the inclusion of country and year dummies, as well as country-specific time trends. Moreover, the estimate for the access variable is around 0.06 in all cases, while the parameters for human and physical capital are mostly unchanged compared with Table 12.1. This result suggests that the impact of centrality to markets acts on top of these usual determinants. Also, the fact that excluding the country effects does not alter the parameter significantly means that the access effect is identified by the variation through time as well as across countries.

The estimated effect of access is fairly robust to the treatment of physical capital, human capital, and the access variables as being potentially endogenous (column [4]).[12] Finally, in the last column, the error correction specification is tested using the pooled mean group estimator. Here again, the impact of centrality seems to be orthogonal to the other dimensions, although the level of the parameter is somewhat higher.

Figure 12.1 presents the contribution of market and supplier access to GDP per capita for the 2000–04 period, based on the estimates in

---

first-order correlation. Each bootstrap resamples the 36,000 bilateral trade observations to recalculate market and supplier access, the resampling being done within country-pair bins. The standard errors are based on 200 replications of the GDP per capita estimated equation. Based on this exercise, the non-bootstrapped standard errors are underestimated by around 10–20 per cent, which does not alter the significance level of the results.

[11] This would imply, for example, that the relatively large distance of Australia from world markets compared with the United States accounts for a GDP-per-capita gap of around 12 percentage points (given the values of the sum of distances measure reported in Table 12.3, $0.21.\ln(214/119) \approx 0.12$).

[12] In order to try to overcome the potential endogeneity bias, the sum of distances variable, *Distsum*, is an ideal instrument. Taking advantage of the panel dimension of the data, the effect of this time-invariant instrument is allowed to vary through time. In other words, a set of instruments, $Z_{it} = Distsum_i.h_t$, are used where the h_t are time dummies. In addition, the robustness of the estimates was also tested by using, as in Redding and Venables, the foreign component of market and supplier access only. That way, the domestic component, which is the most problematic, is taken out. The specification in column (1) gives a parameter of 0.033 (s.e. 0.016) for foreign access instead of 0.056 (s.e. 0.015) for total access. The other reported parameters are unaffected.

Table 12.5. Sensitivity of proximity effects across specifications[a]

Dependent variable GDP per capita	level AR (1) (1)	level AR (1) (2)	level AR (1) (3)	level AR (1) IV (4)	Error correction model PMG (5)
Common parameters					
Physical capital	0.174***	0.166***	0.188***	0.171***	0.307***
	(0.019)	(0.019)	(0.017)	(0.060)	(0.032)
Human capital	0.317***	0.750***	−0.069	0.855***	0.902***
	(0.122)	(0.075)	(0.149)	(0.208)	(0.186)
Population growth[b]	−0.005	−0.008	−0.002	0.005	−0.411***
	(0.018)	(0.022)	(0.018)	(0.019)	(0.067)
Weighted sum of market and supplier access	0.056***	0.066***	0.064***	0.091**	0.131**
	(0.015)	(0.009)	(0.016)	(0.044)	(0.054)
Rho[c]	0.882	0.952	0.820	0.868	
Country-specific parameters					
Lambda[d]					−0.176***
Time trend	no	no	yes	no	yes
Fixed effects					
Country	yes	no	yes	yes	yes
Year	yes	yes	yes	yes	no
Sample size					
Total number of observations	696	696	696	696	695
Number of countries	21	21	21	21	21
First stage regressions[e]					
Hausman test				$0001^A(4) = 12.4$ $(P = 0.015)$	
Hansen J-stat				$0001^A(29) = 5.87$ $(P\ value = 1.00)$	

Table 12.5. (cont.)

Dependent variable GDP per capita	level	level	level	level	Error correction model
	AR (1)	AR (1)	AR (1)	AR (1) IV	PMG
	(1)	(2)	(3)	(4)	(5)
Physical capital				Shea R² = 0.059 (P value = 0.238)	
Human capital				Shea R² = 0.182 (P value = 0.000)	
Weighted sum of market and supplier access				Shea R² = 0.092 (P value = 0.002)	

Notes: Standard errors are in brackets. *: significant at 10% level; ** at 5% level; *** at 1% level.

[a] The functional forms corresponding to the "level" and "error-correction" specifications are reported in Section 2.2. In the level specification, standard errors are robust to heteroskedasticity and to contemporaneous correlation across panels. In the error-correction specification, only long-term parameters are reported.

[b] The population growth variable is augmented by a constant factor $(g + d)$ designed to capture trend growth in technology and capital depreciation. This constant factor is set at 0.05 for all countries.

[c] *rho* is the first-order auto-correlation parameter.

[d] The parameter *lambda* is the average of the country-specific speed adjustment parameter.

[e] The instruments used in column (4) are $Z_{it} = D\text{istsum}_i \cdot h_t$ where the h_t are time dummies. The tests reported for the Instrumental Variables estimator read as following. The Hausman test is a joint test of exogeneity of physical capital, human capital, and market and supplier access. Exogeneity is rejected and this is due to human capital only (this is seen when including residuals from the first-stage regressions in the main equation). The overidentification test is the Hansen test. It is computed without the AR(1) process for the residuals. For first-stage regressions, Shea partial R² (i.e. based on the excluded instruments only) are reported for each potentially endogenous regressor, along with the P-value of the F-test. These statistics reveal that weak instruments could be an issue for physical capital only.

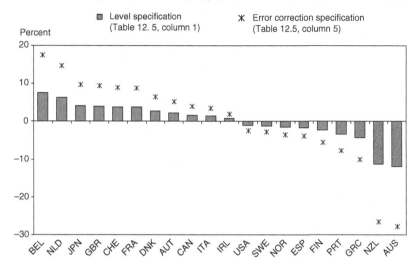

Figure 12.1. Estimated impact of market and supplier access on GDP
per capita: deviation from average OECD country in 2000–04
Notes: Contributions of market and supplier access to GDP per capita
are based on Table 12.5. They are computed as differences to the average country and on average over the period 2000–04. For example,
based on the estimate from the level specification, the favorable access
to world markets that Belgium benefits from compared with the average
country would contribute to as much as 6.7 per cent of its GDP. Because
of a break in the series due to the reunification, data for Germany were
used only for the period 1970–89. Therefore, Germany is not included
in the figure.

columns (1) and (5), which are representative of the level and error-
correction specifications respectively. Unsurprisingly, Australia and New
Zealand are the big losers from their geographic position. To a lesser
extent, Greece, Portugal, and Finland suffer compared to the average
country. The beneficiaries are core European countries, especially Belgium and the Netherlands. As noted above, the order of magnitude
of the geography effects varies substantially depending on the specifications. For example, market and supplier access is estimated to penalize
Australia and New Zealand by around 11 per cent of GDP in the level
specification. The effect would be almost three times as large based on
the error-correction specification, which is hardly plausible. Conversely,
Belgium and the Netherlands benefit by around 6–7 per cent compared
to the average country in the level framework and by 16–18 per cent in
the error correction one.

Table 12.6. *Size of country fixed effects and share of variance explained by fixed effects*[a]

	Average GDP per capita, 1970–2004 (deviation from the OECD average)	Fixed effects augmented Solow Table 12.1, column 1	Fixed effects augmented Solow + geography Table 12.5, column 1
Australia	7.9	1.9	13.3
Austria	8.5	5.2	2.8
Belgium	4.0	7.3	−0.5
Canada	12.2	7.2	5.4
Denmark	11.3	10.8	8.1
Finland	−3.5	−4.1	−2.0
France	7.6	9.5	5.3
Greece	−30.8	−26.0	−22.5
Ireland	−20.6	−13.0	−14.2
Italy	0.2	6.9	4.9
Japan	−4.2	−13.2	−16.2
Netherlands	6.5	7.0	0.7
New Zealand	−21.1	−24.6	−13.7
Norway	27.9	22.7	24.0
Portugal	−44.6	−36.3	−33.6
Spain	−21.1	−10.1	−9.0
Sweden	13.7	15.4	16.1
Switzerland	29.1	21.9	17.8
United Kingdom	−0.4	3.0	−2.0
United States	17.5	14.6	15.2
Standard deviation	0.191	0.161	0.147
Variance	0.036	0.026	0.022
Share of variance		0.716	0.599

[a] Because of a break in the series due to the reunification, data for Germany were used only for the period 1970–89. Therefore, Germany is not included in the table.

An alternative way to assess the explanatory power of the geography variables is to compare the standard deviation of the fixed effects before and after the inclusion of these variables. In the augmented Solow model, these country fixed effects account for 72 per cent of the cross-country variance in GDP per capita (Table 12.6).[13] When geography variables are included, the variance explained by the fixed effects is reduced from 72 per cent to 60 per cent.

[13] The dispersion across countries of the average (log of) real GDP per capita over the period is 0.191, whereas the standard deviation of the country fixed effects in the estimated steady-state (Table 12.1, column [1]) is 0.161 and $(0.161/0.191)^2 =$ 72 per cent.

The country fixed effects may in this regard be interpreted as the estimated difference in productivity levels relative to the average country and on average over the whole period of estimation. Based on the standard augmented Solow model (i.e. ignoring geography), the estimated country fixed effects put Australia slightly above the average country, while New Zealand lags by 25 per cent. Once geography is controlled for, Australia moves 13 per cent ahead, suggesting that it has managed to overcome the effect of its unfavorable location, whereas New Zealand remains behind the average country, but only by 14 per cent. Taking geography determinants into account does not change the relative position of the United States, which lies 15 per cent ahead of the average country. Also, the estimated favorable fixed effects for Belgium and the Netherlands in the augmented Solow framework appear to be almost entirely due to centrality.

4   Transport costs

In this section, the influence of proximity to large markets on GDP per capita is examined through the working of a direct channel: transportation costs. The cost of transporting goods is obviously closely linked to distance. However, shifts in modes of transport, technological improvements in long-distance shipping, and changes in fuel costs have influenced the relationship between geographic distance and economic distance. To some extent, the impact of transport costs was implicitly captured in the measures of market and supplier access derived in the previous section. Nevertheless, the development of indicators of transport costs allows for assessing directly their impact on trade and GDP per capita, separately from other factors affecting market access, such as variations in the degree of openness to trade across various foreign markets as well as over time.

Transport costs constitute only one source of total trade costs, albeit an important one. According to recent estimates, broadly defined trade costs of "representative" goods expressed in ad valorem tax-equivalent terms can be as high as 170 per cent in industrialised countries (Anderson and van Wincoop 2004) with transport costs amounting to 21 per cent, the rest being accounted for by border-related trade barriers (44 per cent) and retail and wholesale distribution costs (55 per cent).[14] Excluding distribution, transport costs would on the basis of these estimates account for about one-third of international trade costs. This covers the contribution

---

[14] The overall cost is computed as $1.21*1.44*1.55 - 1 = 1.7$. Border-related costs include policy barriers (tariffs and non-tariffs), information and enforcement costs, as well as costs due to the use of different currencies, rules, and legal frameworks.

of both direct (freight charges including insurance) and indirect (holding cost for transit, inventory costs, etc.) transport costs. The empirical analysis presented in this section is based on estimates of freight charges for air, maritime, and road transportation of merchandise that are directly taken from Golub and Tomasik (2008). Indirect costs, which are usually inferred from trade flow regressions rather than directly observed, are not covered by these measures. In addition, the cost of international telecommunications (also taken from the same source) is considered insofar as it affects trade in services and, to a lesser extent, trade in goods via its impact on back-office operation, financing, etc. The impact of transport costs on GDP per capita is then examined indirectly via its impact on exposure to cross-border trade.

4.1   Evolution of transport and telecommunications cost indices

The main findings from the computation of real transportation cost indices for OECD countries by Golub and Tomasik can be summarized as follows:

- Not surprisingly, transport costs are highest for Australia and New Zealand with a cost over $2\frac{1}{2}$ times that observed in North America. This is followed by Japan, but at a substantially lower level. The indicator suggests largely similar costs across European countries, below that observed for Japan. They are lowest in Canada and the United States, owing largely to a lower contribution from maritime freight charges.
- As regards the profile over time, the perception that the relative influence of costs related to distance is fast diminishing is not supported, at least not by recent trends in international shipping costs.[15] This apparent puzzle was already noted in earlier studies (in particular Hummels 2006). In the case of maritime transport, special factors such as rising fuel prices and port charges may have played a role in offsetting the gains from technological improvements. Moreover, studies based on micro-data (Blonigen and Wilson 2006) that compare prices for shipping similar goods and similar maritime routes but via different modes (i.e. using containers or not), suggest that the benefit from containerization may not be as large as presumed (all else being equal).
- One area where the presumed death of distance does not seem to be at all exaggerated is international telecommunications since costs in this

---

[15] Some evidence of a downward trend in the relative price of merchandise transportation appears in the case of air transport, but even then it depends on the choice of deflator between the GDP deflator and the narrower index of manufacturing goods prices.

area have fallen in all countries to the point where they are no longer significant anywhere. In fact, historical data indicate that the substantial cross-country variations that still prevailed in the early 1970s had largely disappeared by the late 1980s, and since then the downward trend has continued, bringing costs to basically zero during the early 2000s.

Evidently, firm conclusions in the area of international transport costs need to be qualified due to limitations of data availability and measurement. It is not clear how data on road transport, for instance, reflect the gains in quality terms such as those from the use of global positioning systems which allows for precise tracking of the material in transit. In a similar vein, measured price indices for ocean shipping may not adequately reflect improvement in the service provided, for instance time savings brought about by containerization. Also, the importance of time as a trade barrier has been stressed in earlier studies (Hummels 2001; Nordås 2006; Nordås et al. 2006).[16]

4.2   Impact of transport costs on openness to trade and GDP per capita

The impact of transport costs on GDP per capita is assessed indirectly via their effects on individual countries' exposure to international trade (Table 12.7).[17] This approach is based on the presumption that transportation costs matter for GDP per capita only insofar as they matter for openness and that trade contributes to GDP. In order to assess the contribution of international trade to GDP per capita, a measure of exposure to international trade (trade openness) is first added as a determinant in the augmented Solow model.[18]

The results appear in columns (1), (3), and (5) of Table 12.7, where the specifications vary only according to the combination of fixed effects and/or time trend included. The coefficient on trade openness is positive and significant in all three cases—albeit only at the 10 per cent level in

---

[16] Likewise, the indicator of international telecommunication from Golub and Tomasik only captures one type of telecommunications and therefore may exaggerate the extent of the decline in effective costs.

[17] The impact of transport costs on foreign direct investment is not examined here. However Brakman et al. in this volume use a gravity framework to examine the main factors or motives driving FDI flows in the context of integrating markets and falling trade costs.

[18] Trade openness is measured as the average of export and import intensities (i.e. as a ratio of GDP) and is adjusted for country size. The adjustment is made by regressing the raw trade openness variable on population size and by taking the estimated residual from that panel regression as the measure of trade exposure that is included as an additional determinant in the augmented Solow specification.

Table 12.7. *Basic framework with openness to trade*[a]

(Costs of transport and international communications used as an instrument for trade openness)

Dependent variable GDP per capita	level AR (1)	level AR (1) IV	level AR (1)	level AR (1) IV	level AR (1)	level AR (1) IV
	(1)	(2)	(3)	(4)	(5)	(6)
Physical capital	0.175***	0.171***	0.164***	0.218***	0.208***	0.196***
	(0.020)	(0.022)	(0.023)	(0.030)	(0.021)	(0.022)
Human capital	0.234*	−0.273	0.740***	0.724***	0.210*	0.221**
	(0.122)	(0.324)	(0.058)	(0.068)	(0.112)	(0.112)
Population growth[b]	−0.016	−0.018	−0.038	−0.033	−0.028	−0.044*
	(0.023)	(0.025)	(0.031)	(0.029)	(0.025)	(0.026)
Trade openness	0.035*	0.029	0.048***	0.107***	0.068***	0.106***
	(0.020)	(0.061)	(0.017)	(0.040)	(0.020)	(0.039)
Rho[c]	0.886	0.890	0.941	0.954	0.844	0.855
Time trend	no	no	no	no	yes	yes
Fixed effects						
Country	yes	yes	no	no	yes	yes
Year	yes	yes	yes	yes	no	no
Sample size						
Total number of observations	633	633	633	633	633	633
Number of countries	21	21	21	21	21	21

First-stage regressions for the trade openness variable[d]

Excluded instruments

Overall transport costs	-0.473**	-0.683***	-0.144**
	(0.233)	(0.065)	(0.062)
Costs of international communications	0.023	-0.148***	-0.009
	(0.024)	(0.030)	(0.027)
Sum of distances (average through time)	-0.018***	-0.004**	-0.027***
	(0.004)	(0.002)	(0.002)

Statistical tests

Hausman test	$0001^A(1) = 2.76$	$0001^A(1) = 3.57$	$0001^A(1) = 5.10$
	$(P = 0.096)$	$(P = 0.059)$	$(P = 0.024)$
Hansen J-stat	$0001^A(31) = 23.8$	$0001^A(31) = 10.3$	$0001^A(31) = 31.2$
	$(P\ value = 0.820)$	$(P\ value = 1.000)$	$(P\ value = 0.458)$
Partial R^2	Shea $R^2 = 0.062$	Shea $R^2 = 0.152$	Shea $R^2 = 0.190$
	$(P\ value = 0.917)$	$(P\ value = 0.000)$	$(P\ value = 0.000)$

Notes: Standard errors are in brackets. *: significant at 10% level; **: at 5% level; *** at 1% level.

[a] The functional form corresponding to the "level" specification is reported in Section 2.2. Standard errors are robust to heteroskedasticity and to contemporaneous correlation across panels.

[b] The population growth variable is augmented by a constant factor $(g + d)$ designed to capture trend growth in technology and capital depreciation. This constant factor is set at 0.05 for all countries.

[c] *rho* is the first-order auto-correlation parameter.

[d] The instruments used in column (2), (4) and (6) are overall transport costs, costs of international communications and $Z_{it} = Distsum_i.h_t$ where the h_t are time dummies. The tests reported for the Instrumental Variables estimator read as following. The Hausman test is a test of exogeneity of the trade variable. The overidentification test is the Hansen test. It is computed without the AR(1) process for the residuals. For first-stage regressions, Shea partial R^2 (i.e. based on the excluded instruments only) is reported for the potentially endogenous regressor, along with the P-value of the F-test.

the first case—and varies from 0.035 when both year and country fixed effects are included (column [1]) to twice that size when a time trend is included instead of year fixed effects (column [5]). The coefficients on the other variables do not vary much across specifications, except in the case of human capital, where the coefficient shows the same sensitivity to the treatment of fixed effects as reported in previous sections. A comparison of Table 12.7 with the first three columns of Table 12.1 also shows that adding the trade variable does not have much impact on the parameter values of physical and human capital.

Taken at face value, these results provide evidence that greater openness to trade leads to higher GDP per capita. However, it has long been recognized that given the uncertainties as regards the direction of causality, the introduction of trade as an additional determinant in the Solow model cannot be used as conclusive evidence of a positive influence on GDP per capita, regardless of the apparent size and statistical significance of the estimated parameter.

To address the endogeneity problem, an instrumental variable (IV) procedure is adopted, allowing for the indicator of overall transport costs and the cost of international telecommunications to be used as instruments for the measure of openness to international trade in the augmented Solow model. The sum of distance, defined in the previous section, is also used as an instrument. The procedure is similar to that used in Section 3 and the results are reported in columns (2), (4), and (6) of Table 12.7. The estimated effect of (instrumented) trade openness on GDP per capita (second stage reported in the top panel) is significant in two of the three specifications (columns [4] and [6]), and the estimated coefficient is in these cases higher than when actual trade openness is used (columns [3] and [5]). However, this result no longer holds if one controls for both country and year fixed effects, where the coefficient on trade openness is not significant (column [2]).[19] As for the results from the first-stage regression (bottom panel), they show that overall transport costs have a significant (negative) impact on trade openness in all three IV specifications, although with large variations in the parameter estimates.

Overall, these results indicate that transportation costs contribute to reduce the exposure to international trade and that in turn the latter appears to have a significant impact on GDP per capita. In contrast,

---

[19] The statistical tests reported at the bottom of Table 12.7 indicate that when both year and country fixed effects are included (column [2]). The instruments add little information and are therefore considered as weak.

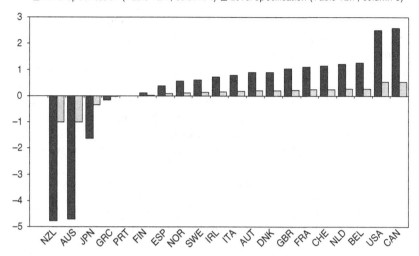

Figure 12.2. Estimated impact of transportation costs on GDP per capita: deviation from average OECD country in 2000–04
Notes: Contributions of transportation costs to GDP per capita are based on Table 12.7. They are computed as differences to the average country and on average over the period 2000–04. Because of a break in the series due to the reunification, data for Germany were used only for the period 1970–89. Therefore, Germany is not included in the figure.

the effect of international telecommunications on trade openness is significant only when country fixed effects are not included, and therefore the evidence is much weaker. The results from the IV procedure provide some evidence that trade openness may have a causal influence on GDP per capita, consistent with earlier findings (e.g. Frankel and Romer 1999).

Against this background, the contribution of transport costs to GDP per capita is reported in Figure 12.2. In order to provide a range of estimates, the contribution is calculated on the basis of coefficients obtained from two specifications based on Table 12.7 (columns [4] and [6], respectively). On this basis, high transport costs relative to the OECD average are found to reduce GDP per capita by between 1.0 per cent and 4.5 per cent in Australia and New Zealand, where the effect is largest. At the other end, the lower transport costs for Canada and the United States contribute to raise GDP per capita by between 0.5 per cent and 2.5 per cent.

5   Conclusion and policy implications

This paper examines how much of the dispersion in economic performance across OECD countries can be accounted for by economic geography factors. More specifically, the proximity to areas of dense economic activity has been examined through the estimation of gravity equations. Various indicators of distance to markets and transportation costs have then been added sequentially as determinants in an augmented Solow model, which is used as a benchmark. Three measures of distance to markets are found to have a statistically significant effect on GDP per capita: the sum of bilateral distances, market potential, and the weighted sum of market access and supplier access.

The estimated economic impact, which varies somewhat across specifications, is far from negligible. For instance, the lower access to markets relative to the OECD average could contribute negatively to GDP per capita by as much as 11 per cent in Australia and New Zealand. Conversely, the benefit from a favorable location could account for as much as 6–7 per cent of GDP in the case of Belgium and the Netherlands. The impact of transport costs on GDP per capita is also found to be statistically significant, albeit less so in economic terms. For instance, differences in transport costs relative to the OECD average contribute to reduce GDP per capita by between 1.0 per cent and 4.5 per cent in Australia and New Zealand. At the other end, the lower transport costs for Canada and the United States contribute to raise GDP per capita relative to the average OECD country, but only by a small margin varying between 0.5 per cent and 2.5 per cent. These quantitatively smaller effects are consistent with transportation costs being only one aspect of distance-related costs.

Considering the substantial estimated effect that distance/proximity to major markets has on GDP per capita, one issue is whether there is a role for public authorities to subsidize international transport, at least in the most remote countries, so as to partly compensate for negative distance-related externalities. Budgetary subsidies for urban passenger transportation are common in many OECD countries, but are rare for long-distance, notably cross-border, transportation of goods.

However, long-distance transportation already benefits from large implicit subsidies. Most importantly, many transportation activities result in environmental damage, and transportation companies and their clients are not charged for this degradation. This is notably the case for air pollution and greenhouse gas emissions in some modes of transportation where regulations on emissions are lax and fuel use is lightly taxed, air and maritime transportation being prime examples. In most countries, road transportation also benefits from not having to pay for the congestion it causes and free access to the road network. Any decisions to provide additional subsidies to transportation would also have to take into account the cost of raising funds for this purpose, and the risk of failure in managing such subsidies.

Less controversial public policies can also contribute to reduce the cost of transportation by strengthening competition in transport industries, which have in the past been heavily regulated. For example, port efficiency varies widely across countries and affects shipping costs significantly, in part due to regulatory restrictions hampering competition in port services (Clark et al. 2004). Considering that since the mid 1980s domestic regulation has been eased to some extent, at least in air and road transport, further gains in this area may come from reductions in regulatory barriers to cross-border freight transport, an area where less progress has been achieved. Competition pressures in international air routes often remain fairly weak due to restrictive bilateral air service agreements and limits to ownership of national carriers. Road transportation on many international routes is hampered by lack of "cabotage" rights, while international scheduled maritime freight services are still operated as price-setting cartels on many key routes, reflecting that this activity is exempted from national competition legislation in many OECD countries.

REFERENCES

Anderson, J. E. and E. van Wincoop (2004). "Trade Costs," *Journal of Economic Literature* **42**(3): 691–751.
Arnold, J., A. Bassanini and S. Scarpetta (2007). "Is it Solow or Lucas?" OECD Economics Department working paper no. 592.
Bassanini, A. and S. Scarpetta (2001). "Does Human Capital Matter for Growth in OECD Countries? Evidence from PMG Estimates," OECD Economics Department working paper no. 282.
Beck, N. and J. N. Katz (2004). "Time Series Cross Section Issues: Dynamics, 2004," paper presented at the 2004 Annual Meeting of the Society for Political Methodology, Stanford University.
Bernanke, B. S. and R. S. Gürkaynak (2001). "Is Growth Exogenous? Taking Mankiw, Romer and Weil Seriously," *NBER Macroeconomics Annual*.
Blonigen, B. and W. Wilson (2006). "New Measures of Port Efficiency Using International Trade Data," NBER working paper no. 12052.
Boulhol, H., A. de Serres and M. Molndr (2009). "The Contribution of Economic Geography on GDP Per Capita," *OECD Economic Studies*, 289–323.
Boulhol, H. and A. de Serres (2010). "Have Developed Countries Escaped the Curse of Distance?" *Journal of Economic Geography* **10**(1): 113–39.

Breinlich, H. (2006). "The Spatial Income Structure in the European Union—What Role for Economic Geography?" *Journal of Economic Geography* 6(5): 593–618.

Clark, X., D. Dollar and A. Micco (2004). "Port Efficiency, Maritime Transport Costs, and Bilateral Trade," *Journal of Development Economics* 75: 2.

Combes, P.-P. and H. G. Overman (2004). "The Spatial Distribution of Economic Activities in the European Union," in V. Henderson and J.-F. Thisse (eds.), *Handbook of Urban and Regional Economics vol. IV*, Amsterdam: Elsevier–North-Holland.

Dolman, B., D. Parham and S. Zheng (2007). "Can Australia Match US Productivity Performance?" Australia Government Productivity Commission, staff working paper, March.

Eaton, J. and S. Kortum (1994). "International Patenting and Technology Diffusion," NBER working paper no. 4931.

(1996). "Trade in Ideas: Patenting and Productivity in the OECD," *Journal of International Economics* 40: 3–4.

Ertur, C. and W. Koch (2007). "Growth, Technological Interdependence and Spatial Externalities: Theory and Evidence," *Journal of Applied Economics* 22: 1033–62.

Frankel, J. and D. Romer (1999), "Does Trade Cause Growth?" *American Economic Review* 84: 1.

Golub, S. S. and B. Tomasik (2008). "Measures of International Transport Cost for OECD Countries," OECD Economics Department working paper no. 609.

Hall, R. E. and C. I. Jones (1999). "Why Do Some Countries Produce so Much More Output per Worker than Others?" *Quarterly Journal of Economics* 114: 1.

Hanson, G. H. (2005). "Market Potential, Increasing Returns and Geographic Concentration," *Journal of International Economics* 67: 1.

Harris, C. (1954). "The Market as a Factor in the Localization of Industry in the United States," *Annals of the Association of National Geographers* 44: 4.

Head, K. and T. Mayer (2006). "Regional Wage and Employment Responses to Market Potential in the EU," *Regional Science and Urban Economics* 36: 5.

Hummels, D. (1995). "Global Income Patterns: Does Geography Play a Role?" Chapter II of Ph.D. Thesis, University of Michigan.

(2001). "Time as a Trade Barrier," unpublished paper, Purdue University.

(2006). "Transportation Costs and International Trade in the Second Era of Globalization," *Journal of Economic Perspectives* 21: 3.

Keller, W. (2002). "Geographic Localization of International Technology Diffusion," *American Economic Review* 92: 1.

Mankiw, G. N., D. Romer and D. Weil (1992). "A Contribution to the Empirics of Economic Growth," *Quarterly Journal of Economics* 107: 2.

Nicoletti, G., S. Golub, D. Hajkova, D. Mirza and K.-Y. Yoo (2003). "Policies and International Integration: Influences on Trade and Foreign Direct Investment," *OECD Economics Studies* 36.

Nordås, H. (2006). "Time as a Trade Barrier: Implications for Low-Income Countries," *OECD Economic Studies* 42.

Nordås, H., E. Pinali and M. G. Grosso (2006). "Logistic and Time as a Trade Barrier," OECD Trade Policy working paper no. 35.

OECD (2003). *The Sources of Economic Growth in OECD Countries*, Paris.

(2006). OECD *Employment Outlook*, Paris.

Pesaran, M. H., Y. Shin and R. Smith (1999). "Pooled Mean Group Estimation of Dynamic Heterogeneous Panels," *Journal of the American Statistical Association* **94**: 3.

Redding, S. and P. K. Scott (2003). "Distance, Skill Deepening and Development: Will Peripheral Countries Ever Get Rich?" *Journal of Development Economics* **72**: 2.

Redding, S. and A. J. Venables (2004). "Economic Geography and International Inequality," *Journal of International Economics* **62**: 1.

Solow, R. (1956). "A Contribution to the Theory of Economic Growth," *Quarterly Journal of Economics* **70**: 1.

Index